KU-473-499

The Most Creative, Escape the Ordinary, Excel at Public Speaking Book Ever

All the help you will ever need in giving a speech

Philip R. Theibert

Author of *How to Give a Damn Good Speech*

BUSINESS BOOKS

Winchester, UK
Washington, USA

First published by Business Books, 2012
Business Books is an imprint of John Hunt Publishing Ltd., Laurel House, Station Approach,
Alresford, Hants, SO24 9JH, UK
office1@jhpbooks.net
www.johnhuntpublishing.com

For distributor details and how to order please visit the 'Ordering' section on our website.

Text copyright: Philip R. Theibert 2012

ISBN: 978 1 78099 672 1

All rights reserved. Except for brief quotations in critical articles or reviews, no part of this
book may be reproduced in any manner without prior written permission from the publishers.

The rights of Philip R. Theibert as author have been asserted in accordance with the Copyright,
Designs and Patents Act 1988.

A CIP catalogue record for this book is available from the British Library.

Design: Stuart Davies

Printed and bound by CPI Group (UK) Ltd, Croydon, CR0 4YY

WREXHAM C.B.C LIBRARY LLYFRGELL B.S. WRECSAM	
C56 0000 0564 780	
Askews & Holts	25-Jul-2013
808.51	£14.99
ANF	WR

We operate a distinctive and ethical publishing philosophy in all
areas of our business, from our global network of authors to
production and worldwide distribution.

Warning: Contains material that may overstimulate your creative side and make you the most astonishing, cleaver, spellbinding speaker they ever heard!!!!

To Peggy - for always being there.

Introduction

Have to give a speech? Don't worry. You now have your own speechwriter, your own idea man, your own creative team to make your speech stand above the rest. This book makes you a speech giving genius and guarantees your next speech will zoom past intriguing, insightful, intelligent and interesting.

This book will make your next speech the most original speech your audience has ever heard.

Use these ideas and you will never be in danger of boring your audience. They won't need their chairs; they will only need the edge!

This is the ultimate speech idea book. It contains over 200 original, never seen in print before, ideas, tips, complete speeches, lists. Peruse over 300 pages packed with material designed to get those gears spinning, designed to give you that creative spark, designed to ensure that you stand out as a speaker with original ideas, a great sense of humor and a unique take on life.

Plus this original material will get you thinking, "Hey, if that specific list works as an opening, why don't I try a list of _____"

And every tip, every idea in this book comes with extensive directions on how to fit it into a speech.

Plus, this book contains over 200 quotes! Not to mention, numerous speeches that you can lift right out of this book and give without changing a word.

Here is just a peek at what this book can offer you. A complete list would be too long for this short introduction. But consider just some of the original material this book will provide for your next speech.

Lessons of baseball that can be applied to business (complete speech)
Key signs that you may be fired
Extensive (over 25) Communication Tips (complete speech)

Shakespeare's Business Advice (complete speech)
Strange terms
Business slogans
Driving humor
Personal relationship advice
Humorous landscaping tips
Reasons to smoke
Graduation speech (complete speech)
Volunteer speech (complete speech)
Coffee facts
True cost of hiring employees (complete speech)
Words that you never want to see in the same sentence
Over 50 things NOT to say
Career advice
Humorous job interview questions
Things you never want to hear
Making a good impression
The importance of details
Real rules
Tying education into the real world (complete speech)
Funny T-shirts
Safety tips with humor
Sales speech (complete speech)
Overcoming denial (complete speech)
Country song titles
Finding a sense of purpose (complete speech)
Ten steps to a great speech (complete speech)
15 tips for a great PowerPoint (complete speech)
Oddservations
The key to creativity (complete speech)
Braking news
Things you discover too late
The PowerPoint presentation from hell (complete speech)
What not to say to teachers

Creating your own opportunities (complete speech)
Scary phrases
Things that never turn out well
Things that should be banned
Things that never mix well
Halloween material
Valentine material
New rules for football (complete speech)
What coaches really think
Wedding speech material
Material for July 4th and other patriotic holidays
Check this out – checks to avoid
The Church can teach marketing (complete speech)
Great material for holidays – Thanksgiving, Christmas, New
    Year's – including complete short speeches
Humorous winter survival tips
Surviving a Road Trip
How to flunk any class (complete speech)
Great innovations in sports
Get some attitude (complete speech)
Nicknames
Fat facts
Complete analysis of several speeches – learn from the pros
Warning labels
Key signs of growing old
The changing face of America (complete speech)
List of insecurities
Going to work tired humor (complete speech)
Short speech on acceptance
100 annoying things
Things you never want your doctor to say
St. Patrick's Day material
Diet myths
Business headlines…

Imagine! That is less than one third of what this book offers as you plan your next speech! You would have to brainstorm with a professional speechwriter to create this many ideas for your speech.

How powerful is this book? Just spend five minutes flipping through the pages and you will see new ways of approaching a speech, new ways you never even thought of.

Plus, you will never give another boring speech in your life.

And yes, remember, while most speakers recycled the same old jokes and stories, you have in your hand original, creative material that will light up your brain cells and inspire you to create even more great material.

Go get them! Your audience is waiting!

1

Here is a list of what we can learn from playing a sport, in this case, baseball. But the lessons apply to many sports that kids play. This can be a complete speech that you can give to a youth group. Or you can choose specific lessons and apply them to almost any business speech. For example you could say, "I want to cover several important lessons we can learn from baseball. The first one is "Take chances: You can't steal second with a foot on first." Take a big lead every now and then. Nothing is guaranteed. You may get thrown out. But you may not. How does that apply to our business? Are we too set in our ways, are we not exploring new opportunities, new ways of doing things. Do we need to take more chances for this company to grow?"

Quote: A baseball game is simply a nervous breakdown divided into nine innings.
~Earl Wilson

Lessons of Baseball

- Attitude matters: Tuck in your shirt, run to your position. Don't goof off on the bench, don't throw your helmet. The person with a good attitude makes a good employee.
- Bounce Back: You will strike out, you will make an error and you will get thrown out stealing. Use these setbacks as a learning experience. Watch the ball into your glove, lay off high pitches, make yourself a better player. A bad player dwells on the mistakes and it affects his whole game. Too many people in life are so upset by the past that it ruins their future. Don't be one of them.
- Collect Yourself: A pick-off attempt is made. You dive back into first. Call time, brush yourself off, straighten your hat, then lead off again. Learn to take small moments in life to collect yourself.
- Don't be intimidated: It's the pitcher's job to intimidate you. He

will throw curve balls at your head. Who owns that plate – you or the pitcher? If the pitcher takes control, you lose. Same lesson in life. Who controls your life? You do. Don't get intimidated, stand close to the plate and get your swings in.

- Consequences: If you throw a helmet, you sit out two innings. You use a cuss word, you sit out a whole game. There are consequences for your actions. Again – it's the same thing in life, except the consequences can be a lot tougher.

- Find your strength: People have weaknesses and strengths. If you're not a power hitter, 'hit them where they ain't'. I had a player this year with cerebral palsy on the right side. He was the best left-handed pitcher I had. People who find their strengths in life usually succeed.

- Take chances: You can't steal second with a foot on first. Take a big lead every now and then. Nothing is guaranteed. You may get thrown out. But you may not.

- Pick your battles: Don't fight every bad call. You can fight one every now and then. But remember the umpire is always right. There is a lesson in fighting authority here. Learn it.

- Take responsibility: Don't blame your bat, your glove, the sun, your teammates. They did not make an error, they did not strikeout. You did. Take responsibility, blame no one else and move on. The person who can take responsibility and move on to the next task is the person people hire.

- Focus: When you're batting – focus. Ignore the fans, the other coaches, the dugout chatter, the catcher's mouthing off. Learn to focus. You will be in a busy office, a loud classroom, a busy airport – you will be surrounded by distractions in life. Focus on the task at hand.

- Perspective: People blow things out of proportion. Often it is the parents in the stands. It is a game. If you lose, the sun will come up tomorrow. There will be other situations in life when bosses, co-workers, in-laws, spouses, your teenagers will lose a sense of perspective. Keep yours.

- Laugh at yourself: You will do something stupid – trip over first base, get hit on the head with a fly ball, throw the ball into the dugout, run into another player. Every player eventually does something stupid. Laugh it off and do your best the next time.

- Be honest: If you're catching and the coach asks how the pitcher is throwing be honest; the coach must make a decision that will affect the whole team .You may want to protect the pitcher, but if his curve ball is hanging – tell the coach. People deserve honest feedback throughout life. Give it to them.

- Support your teammates: People make mistakes in baseball and life. Do not rub their faces in the mistakes they make. If you must say something, say something positive, encourage your teammates.

- Master the basics: Learn the basics. Know how to bunt. Every job in life has basic skills. The person that masters the basics is the one people have confidence in.

- Be confident: Always go to bat thinking you WILL get a hit. Be anxious to get into the batter box, so you can show them your stuff. When you give a speech later in life, remember, you will be a hit and this is the chance to 'strut your stuff'.

- Adjust: Adjust to the pitcher's off-speed pitches, adjust to the umpire's strike zone, shift your position in the field according to who is batting. Life and baseball are a series of small and big adjustments. If the umpire calls you out on a low strike, don't complain. You now know the umpire has a low strike zone. Use that knowledge next time you are up. If you get called out again on the same pitch, it is because you failed to adjust.

- Analyze the situation: There are ways out of a jam. Should you intentionally walk someone, throw the ball low for a double play, move in to make the play at home, guard the line to take away the extra base hit? Challenges have solutions – look for solutions on the baseball field and in life.

- Think small: Getting nine runs seems like a lot. But if you break that task down, that is only a run an inning. That can be accomplished by bunting, stealing, hit-and-run, sacrifice flies – think of all the ways to get the job done – one inning at a time.

- Practice: You want to hit a baseball. Hit lots of baseball. You want to be good in math – do lots of problems – whatever you choose – practice.

- Clean up after yourself: Your mother is not in the dugout. After the game throw away all the water bottles, gum wrappers, put away the helmets and the catcher's gear. Later, your spouse will like you more if you don't leave messes.

- Anticipate: Where will a left-handed batter hit the ball? Where will he hit it off a fast pitcher or slow pitcher? Anticipate where the ball is going! Those in life, who know where the ball is going, end up in the right place.

- Be alert: There will be long innings. But keep your head in the game. That's why catchers yell the outs, there's infield chatter, you throw the ball around the horn, you watch how the catcher is shifting for an outside or inside pitch, you keep saying, "What do I do if I get the ball?" Baseball trains you to be constantly vigilant – a useful skill in life.

- Learn the culture: When you get hit, don't rub. Never talk about a no-hitter. Don't step on the foul lines when running off the field. Are these things logical? No. But many cultural traditions are not logical, yet people expect you to behave in a certain way. Learn the culture you are dealing with.

- Pay attention to details. If you are on first base, check the pitcher's heel. A right-handed pitcher has to lift his back heel before he throws over. If you know that, there is no reason you should be picked off. What signs are you missing from competitors, management, peers?

- Be organized: If you are playing first base, when you come off the field, put a ball in your glove. That way, you won't waste time next inning looking for a ball.

- Be prepared: If you are a catcher and the odds are that the runner will take off, don't call for a curve. Call for a fastball on the outside corner. That works like a pitchout – you have a chance of getting a strike and gunning down the runner. Think ahead of your competition and be prepared for their next move.

- Teams win or lose together: If a teammate drops a ball and the winning run scores, don't blame him. A lot of factors go into winning and losing a ballgame, and you just can't blame one incident. People could have hit the ball better, make a few more double plays, eliminated walks, avoided pass balls. Remember, it is never one player's fault; failure is always a combination of factors. So is winning.

- Look for the unique edge: Pulling your pants legs down to your ankles may look cool, but what does it accomplish? Wear your socks high. When your socks show, it is harder for the umpire to call a low strike. The high socks give him a visual clue of where the strike zone really is. Plus, you have to admire the hitter who leans over the plate, wearing a baggy shirt. The baggy shirt has increased his chances of being hit by a ball and getting a free trip to first base. This gives you an edge. What do you need to do in business to gain and maintain an advantage?

- Have a game plan: If you are facing a pitcher who throws heat, don't swing at anything above the waist. Chances are you won't catch up with it. You can catch up with a fastball waist high or lower. What is your game plan when you are going to a meeting, seeing a client, your plan for that job interview?

- Be aggressive: Go up to bat thinking you will get a hit. When you're older, walk into an office thinking you will make a sale. If you think you will strikeout in baseball or life, you have dug yourself a hole.

- Recognize the spin: A curveball has a different spin than a fastball. It has a different speed. The pitcher may have a different release point for each pitch, a different arm motion for each pitch; perhaps you can see him adjusting the ball in his glove. But what is the pitcher throwing you? What spin does it have on it? People will throw you ideas your whole life. But watch for the 'spin' they deliver the ideas with.

- Know where the wall is: If you are playing outfield, as you get close to the wall, put your arm out. Know when you will crash into the wall and not be able to make a play. Same theory in life. We all have limits. Know where your wall is and don't crash through it. Take time off to relax.
- Enjoy: The baseball season, like life, is short. Enjoy the sun, spitting sunflower seeds, chewing gum, bending your hat brim, playing catch, the smell of glove oil, sliding into second, rounding third at full speed – learn to enjoy moments in life.

2

Here is a funny list about the key signs that you might be fired. In your opening, you can read selections from the list, then say, "But we all know that being fired is no laughing matter. We all have responsibilities we must pay for. But what is the best way to guaranteed that a year from now, we all have jobs. We must work together to ensure that this company and all of us succeed. Let me cover some ways we can all work together, work smarter and ensure a bright future for all of us."

Quote: Getting fired is nature's way of telling you that you had the wrong job in the first place.
~Hal Lancaster

Key Signs You May be Fired

If you think you may be fired, canned or even 'right-sized' it might be time to turn off those computer games, quit downloading those hard-metal websites, turn off the streaming video soap operas and look around. Here are 10 clues your job may be in peril:

- You're out of the loop: You drive to work and your parking space is occupied. By your desk.

- You never go to special training: They stopped sending you to sensitivity training, after you wore an "I hate everyone" T-shirt to a diversity meeting.
- You get the silent treatment: You can clear a room faster that the Asian flu. You walk in and all your co-workers leave for 'lunch'. Yet it is only 9 a.m. A mime talks to more people a day than you do.
- You receive a bad review: Your last review was so toxic, you had to wear gloves to pick it up. Being described as a "pathetic loser whose height of achievement is making coffee" can't be good. Your review sounds more like a police report and your IQ is compared to Shamu the Whale.
- You tend to make the same mistake over and over.
- You are perceived as the company clown: Sure it got a few laughs, but using the boss' toupee to dust your cubicle was not the brightest move.
- Your superior is leaving paper trails: You receive memos, written in toilet paper, confirming every time the boss chewed you out. The memos are also posted on the office bulletin board, right next to the copier photo of your butt and the police photo of you after that bar fight 'got out of hand'.
- You and your boss are not getting along: Performance is a 'subjective' judgment and managers get rid of people they don't like. In other words, dating the boss' daughter, driving her home when you were drunk, and vomiting on his doorstep was not a 'career-enhancing' move.
- You have trouble making lists and organizing data.
- Your mentor is gone: The executive who always championed your career was last seen boarding a plane for Bolivia with a suitcase full of cash.
- You publicly messed up: You showed the wrong PowerPoint. Instead of the sales chart, the video of the last 'trade show' gets shown and it is hard to explain how topless dancers 'wandered'

into your sales booth. Whoops, what happens here, doesn't always stay here.

- You are not good with numbers: You have trouble counting to 10.
- New blood takes over: When a new manager takes over, he has to take charge. The best way to do this is 'shake things up'. In other words, fire you and bring in his brother-in-law.
- You're assigned special projects: You've been relieved of your core duties so that you can work on 'special projects'. This would involve a bucket, a mop and the men's room.
- You receive outdated equipment: The whole office gets new computers. You get an abacus, a wooden pencil and a can with a string (for local calls only).
- Your bonus is reduced: Everyone in the office gets an all-expense paid trip to Hawaii. You get a free pizza and tokens at Chuck E. Cheese.
- You deny reality: So there are the top ten reasons that your job might be in jeopardy. You might want to turn off that rerun of *The Real World* you're watching on your computer and look around. Looks like your friend's job is in jeopardy. Couldn't be yours.

3

Following is an extensive list of communication tips. Communicating is an essential part of any business. Miscommunication, for instance the wrong specs for the product, can cost millions of dollars. Miscommunication with customers, as we all know, can also be costly. This is a great speech to give to employees, emphasizing, "What steps we should all take to ensure that we all communicate and don't screw up customer orders, products, future plans..."

You can also choose selected items from this list. For instance, you can start your speech with Item 11 on the list. Note how it is a ready-made opening for any speech on communication. Here it is:

"Communication makes your reputation. Beware of how you approach each communication opportunity. Every time we communicate, we are either improving or destroying our reputation as a person of integrity, manners and professionalism. Even a quick bit of gossip in the hallways sends a message to other people what you 'are about'. Every e-mail you send, again, however minor that e-mail is, gives everyone a chance to judge you. Because when you think about it, your professional reputation hangs upon two threads. The first one is what you do. People can and will judge you by your actions. The second thread is your communication skills. You judge someone by what they say, how they phrase it and the intent behind their words. So communication is not just a casual activity where you toss off an e-mail or a sound bite in the hallway to friends. Every word you say and write determines how people judge you now and how they will react to your ideas in the future. Never say anything, even a casual opinion, in the workplace, unless you have done the research to show that you know what you are talking about."

After that opening, you can say, "And because communication is so important to your reputation, and our reputation as a company, we must ask ourselves, are we sending our customers, vendors, shareholders the right messages? Is it time to sit back and analyze what we are doing wrong and right?"

Take your time, highlight the material you like in this list, and you will have plenty of material for any speech on communication.

Quote: The most important thing in communication is to hear what isn't being said.
~Peter Drucker

26 Essential Business Communication Tips

- **People judge you by the way you write:** Once, when I was finished interviewing a CEO for a speech, he walked to his desk and pulled out a file. Then he said, "I have over 5,000 employees and I can't keep track of all of them. But I can tell a person's thought process, by what they write and how they write it." He showed me a file filled with e-mails, letters and reports from employees The CEO said, "When I see a well-written document that reflects a good thought process and the ability to put ideas into action, I put that document in the folder and tell my managers to watch that person." The point is obvious. People judge our thought process by how we put words on paper, on how we logically develop our ideas, how we back up our ideas.

- **Tailor your communication:** One size does not fit all. You communicate with individuals and every individual is different, ranging from your boss to your spouse to your best friend. And there is no way that you talk to all three the same way. You tailor your communication to fit the listener's needs. This also applies when dealing with different cultures – you must tailor your communication to meet the cultural traditions and in addition to meet the listener's individual personality. And of course, you also must tailor the communication depending on the customer.

- **Always research your audience:** Ask questions, then ask more questions. What type of data is your audience expecting? Why are they expecting it? What are they going to do with it? How do they want it presented? Ask these key questions in advance, perhaps by an e-mail, followed by a phone call, and you have a good chance of hitting the target.

- **Sell a lifestyle:** We buy things because we want to create a script, for example the script of a loving family sitting around the fire. Or we buy a sports car because we want to create the myth of being young and free (which is why many middle-aged men buy sports cars). Think about any catalog, like the LL Bean catalog. They aren't selling clothes; the catalog is about creating a lifestyle, long walks in the woods, front porches, fireplaces that the customer wants as his or her lifestyle. This has nothing to do with logic, everything to do with emotion and selling your customer a lifestyle script they want to write themselves into. That is why I can buy a golf shirt for $8 at Wal-Mart, but will pay $50 for the same shirt with a Polo logo. On a certain level, I have thrown logic out the window, to sell myself a concept of being a 'Polo' type person. Think about the last product you bought. What lifestyle script were you buying into? What script were you writing for yourself? What scripts are you writing for your customers or audience?

- **Selling ideas:** Communication is the business of selling ideas. We sell ideas all day long, to our friends, to our boss, to our kids... Remember, you can only sell one idea at a time. So focus on the idea you want to sell, package it from your audience's perspective and don't try to sell multiple ideas. Sell one main idea at a time.

- **Have confidence:** It is a lot like the old joke, if you can't be sincere, at least fake it. Imagine a doctor who walks into your hospital room and she gives you no sense of confidence. The best way to develop confidence as a speaker is to KNOW your subject, know your audience and practice, practice, practice.

- **Audiences are kind:** Audiences tend to be sympathetic. They respect anyone who has the courage to face an audience. So if someone 'messes up' a word or a slide and has to correct themselves, this actually could be a plus. The audience roots for the underdog, sees you as a human, not as some smooth talking speaker, and actually may identify with you more and actually listen more closely. There is such a thing as being too 'slick'. A good speaker has to maintain that 'Aw Shucks' attitude too.

- **Handouts are crucial:** Handouts are the important part of the presentation. After you show a slide, it's gone. But people take the handouts back to their desk and this helps them remember your key points. A simple handout at the end, that lists your key points and what you would like your audience to do, what action steps you want them to take, is always a valuable tool in getting your ideas across.

- **Presentations get you in front of the right people:** Why don't you just e-mail the information to people? A presentation gets you face-to-face with the people who can make a difference, they can implement your ideas, and they can act upon your suggestions. So don't lecture to them, study their reactions, ask questions to see if you are all on the same page. When they walk out of a room, you should know their depth of understanding of your presentation. You should know what follow-up steps you need to take, so your audience completely understands what you were discussing, why it was important and what steps they are expected to take.

- **Be specific:** When asking or receiving information avoid vague words. Avoid saying I need it "soon". What is "soon"? An hour, a day, a week? Also avoid the word 'almost'. As in, "The report is almost completed". Is it 90% complete? 80% complete?

- **Communication makes your reputation:** Beware of how you approach each communication opportunity. Evert time we communicate, we are either improving or destroying our reputation as a person of integrity, manners and professionalism. Even a quick bit of gossip in the hallways sends a message to other people what you 'are about'. Every e-mail you send, again, however minor that e-mail is, gives everyone a chance to judge you. Because when you think about it, your professional reputation hangs upon two threads. The first one is what you do. People can and will judge you by your actions. The second thread is your communication skills. You judge someone by what they say, how they phrase it and the intent behind their words. So communication is not just a casual activity where you toss off an e-mail or a sound bite in the hallway to friends. Every word you say and write determines how people judge you now and how they will react to your ideas in the future. Never say anything, even a casual opinion, in the workplace, unless you have done the research to show that you know what you are talking about.

- **Get feedback:** How do you know that people are receiving the message you're sending? What steps can you take to double-check? Every person brings their own set of perceptions to every meeting, every phone call, e-mail, in short, any type of communication. A good communicator looks for feedback, verbal, body language, all types of feedback. You can only be sure your message 'got through' if you check the feedback. Was the project completed; was it completed the way you requested? Did you just give directions and not check to see if your message was received? Hmm, perhaps there is a reason the project was not completed the way you envisioned?

- **What does your audience need to know:** We are often tempted to tell everything we know about a subject. But every communicator must ask, "What does my audience already know and what do they need to know?" Remember you are not showing off your knowledge, you are trying to provide the audience with information they need and can use.

- **Be human:** You build a relationship by sharing confidential experiences with another person. And if they accept you and they share experiences with you, a friendship has been born. And isn't that what a good communicator does, reaches out, shows he or she is human, shares a painful experience with you?

- **Communicators ask critical questions:** Managers know the basics of finance and accounting and all that 'business stuff', but businesses which are successful year after year, have critical thinkers who ask hard questions such as, "Why do we do things that way?" "Where are our new markets and why?" "What new products must we develop?" If no one in the organization is a 'pain', always asking questions and doing research on the markets, the competition, the future... the company will not grow and prosper.

- **It's not about you:** In publishing, the first question you ask when you read a manuscript is, "Who will buy this book?" What readers' needs does it meet? Publishers are in business to market books to readers, otherwise there is no revenue. And too many manuscripts are writer-based and not reader-based, no specific audience is in mind and, even though it may be well-written, there is no perceived market, no target audience, or the book is aimed at a market the publisher does not serve, e.g. a mystery book is sent to a publisher who publishes how-to books, and the manuscript is rejected. In other words, sell ideas based on the client's needs, not yours.

- **Keep it Simple:** Too often, the speaker gets too clever with slides and special effects and the audience is dazzled and distracted by the slides, which don't back up the speaker's main points. PowerPoints need to be simple and direct 90% bullet points that highlight your main ideas. Don't put these long, long paragraphs on slides. The audience will read through the paragraph, ignore the main idea and the speaker.

- **Remember WIFM:** Every audience is tuned into Radio Station WIFM: What's In It For Me. Also remember every audience member has an invisible sign around their neck that reads: Make Me Feel Important.

- **Communication skills get you promoted:** Having lived in the corporate world a long time and having worked with CEOs, I quickly figured out that to them an accountant was an accountant, an engineer was an engineer, and so forth. But an accountant who could communicate ideas, he was always promoted to the next level. In other words, in many occupations everyone has the same job skills, so the criteria for the next promotion are leadership and communication, the so-called 'soft skills'.

- **A proposal markets your personal skills:** A proposal markets the skills of the author. Quite simply, the quality and content of the proposal indicates to the client the quality of work that you and your company can do. If important segments are left out, if key issues are ignored, if the proposal is packed with grammar and spelling errors, what does this say about the quality of work? It makes the client realize you don't pay attention to detail, so why should you win the project?

- **Keep a Journal:** Many people know what they want to say, but they have trouble getting the ideas from their heads onto the paper. And a journal does exactly that. It gives you practice in articulating your ideas, getting the ideas from your head onto paper, so that you and others can understand them better. Here is another way of looking at it. Let's say you want to hit a baseball. The only way to practice is to hit lots of baseballs, have hitting practice and more hitting practice. You become a good hitter by hitting. That is what a journal is – it is writing practice, so when you have that big game, that big report due, you are comfortable with putting your ideas on paper.

- **Read extensively:** A good way to learn to write is read. Imagine if you are a painter and you never look at any other paintings, you never see how other artists use color, shading, composition? The same analogy applies to writing. How does a writer learn, if he or she doesn't read, see how other writers use words, develop their ideas, support their ideas? In other words, a good writer should read something every day and analyze it, see how it is put together, what makes it flow, what makes it 'work' for the reader. Read an editorial in the newspaper, then go back and outline it, see what the writer used for an opening statement, see how he developed his argument, see what support he used. In short, good writing means you need to be a comprehensive reader and really focus and analyze on writers' techniques to win the audience over.

- **Be credible:** What is your main criteria for choosing a mechanic, a doctor, dentist, accountant? Yes, you know you can trust them. All good relationships start with trust. It is the same with a writer and a reader. Before a reader will trust you, you must convince them 'you know your stuff'. And this convincing depends on sound research, credible sources and good citations, so the reader can double-check if they want to.

- **Solve the right problem:** I met a friend the other day at a

Mexican restaurant and we were served by a waitress who kept swishing her ponytail over our food. I ordered a bourbon and water, she didn't know the difference between scotch and bourbon; our chip dish was never refilled, although we asked three times; the salsa was literally frozen. What does this have to do with communications? Let's say we give the restaurant a marketing proposal. We throw in ads and promote a Mexican ambience in the restaurant and urge they offer drink specials. We can give them a great proposal and it can be a fantastic marketing plan to drive people to the restaurant. But we are addressing the wrong problem. What is the problem? People don't return. Why don't people return? Now there is the gist of the proposal. You need to train management to oversee employees (I didn't see any manager walking around), you have to put employees through an extensive customer service program, you have set service goals, e.g. a chip dish never sits empty. So when you do a proposal: 1. Make sure you are addressing the correct problem; 2. Include follow-up measures to ensure the steps proposed are actually implemented. For example, propose that all employees go through extensive customer service training. Then put a measurement in place, a customer service test they have to pass, before they can start serving customers.

- **Learn sales techniques:** People tend to deny reality. For instance, how many people still smoke despite the high risk of cancer, how many people are way overweight, despite the risks of heart disease? How do you overcome this 'denial' mechanism people have? Is it best to keep hitting them over the head with the bad consequences of their decisions, or is there a better way? What does this have to do with how people receive your communications? People tend to be protective of their habits, be they good or bad, and they will defend them and be closed to positive suggestions. You may trying to help, suggesting how a process at work may be changed, but remember, people don't like change, so don't be surprised at negative reactions and forge ahead. In fact, one of the biggest obstacles that salespeople face is this resistance to change. Study a good book on effective sales techniques and you are also learning how to overcome negative reactions from customers.

Let's say you are going for a job interview but your shirt or blouse is wrinkled and your shoes aren't shined, or there is a small coffee stain on your pants. What does this tell the interviewer? It tells him or her that you don't care about paying attention to details. You don't think that it is important to iron your shirt, polish your shoes, in short you don't care enough to look professional. Now extend that analogy to writing, even a simple e-mail. You don't care enough to put in a clearly defined subject so the reader knows what you're writing about. You use their instead of there, it's instead of its, your instead of you're. You use a period where there should be a question mark and your thoughts seem to go all over the place. Hmm – what does that say about your attention to details? Isn't it sending the same message as a coffee stain on your blouse, a wrinkled shirt...?

4

Business, as you know, is much more complicated than selling a product and making money. The good business person knows how to deal with customers, employees, stress, ups and downs.

And perhaps the best bits of business advice were written over 500 years ago by Shakespeare. Shakespeare was the Dale Carnegie of his time and he knew what made people tick. And has human nature changed that much over 500 years?

Of course, you may not want to stand up in front of an audience and read this entire list. I don't blame you, neither would I. But this list offers a wealth of ideas and quotes that you can use in any business speech. You can weave an entire speech around these tips. Pick just five and you have a good, concise, five

minute speech.

Here is a quick example. Using tip number 2, you can say, "Shakespeare once said, 'We know what we are, but know not what we many be.' Think of how that applies to our company. We know what we are, a good reliable company that makes a good product. But have we been too content? Is it time for change? What may we be? What steps do we need to expand our business and enhance job security for us all? Well I would like to share a few ideas with you..."

So remember take your time going through the list below and highlight five quotes and you will be amazed at how the speech writes itself. Note that next to each quote is a specific tip on how you can use that quote in a speech.

Quote: The remarkable thing about Shakespeare is that he really is very good, in spite of all the people who say he is very good. ~Robert Graves

Business Tips from Shakespeare

- **Every cloud engenders not a storm:** You need to know your business. Know how to forecast the future. Don't panic and make rash decisions. Read the "clouds" carefully

- **We know what we are, but know not what we may be:** What can your business grow to be? Always look to the future.

- **Hell is empty and all the devils are here:** It is business and your competition does not exist to be your friend. They will take away your customers in a heartbeat. What can you do to prevent that?

- **Nothing can come of nothing:** You have to have a solid foundation for the future. Know your strengths and your company's strengths and build upon them.

- **Sweet are the uses of adversity, Which, like the toad, ugly and venomous, wears yet a precious jewel:** Don't get discouraged. Adversity can be good; it can help you discard the habits that are hurting you and help you discard the employees and practices that are hurting your company.

- **Let every man be master of his time:** Always ask, "Is this the most profitable use of my time. How is it helping me or my company grow?"
- **'Tis an ill cook that cannot lick his own fingers:** Be proud of your product or service, if you aren't, why should a customer be?
- **There is nothing either good or bad, but thinking makes it so:** Attitude is everything and you set your attitude, no one else does. You can be positive or negative. Negative never wins customers.
- **Action is eloquence:** Action is the only way to get results.
- **Have more than thou showest, speak less than thou knowest:** Under promise and over deliver. You will keep your customers happy. You will surprise and delight your boss.
- **If you can look into the seeds of time and say, which grain will grow, and which will not, speak then to me:** Know the market and know which products or services (seeds) will most likely grow in the business climate you are facing.
- **Such as we are made of, such we be:** Quality in, quality out.
- **One man in his time plays many parts:** Remember as a manager you must wear many hats. You must be a wise money manager, a motivator, a seer, a philosopher...
- **Modest doubt is call'd the beacon of the wise:** If a deal sounds too good to be true, it probably is. Be skeptical; use your 'abilities of doubt' before committing yourself or your company's resources to anything.
- **The fault, dear Brutus, is not in our stars, but in ourselves, that we are underlings:** Don't complain if you don't like your job, if you can't make enough sales, if you don't get promoted. Find out what is holding you back and get more education, call on more clients – be in charge of your fate.
- **What's gone and what's past help should be past grief:** Don't waste time worrying about the past. That won't help you, your employees or your business. Learn from past mistakes and move on.

- **I must be cruel only to be kind:** Sometimes you have to be tough. Letting that employee go might benefit you both in the long run. He or she might find a better job they like and you might find a better employee.
- **Brevity is the soul of wit:** A good business communicator gets to the point and his client and audience appreciates that.
- **Let me embrace thee, sour adversity, for wise men say it is the wisest course:** Don't ignore bad news. Embrace it. Are sales down? Did you get rejected for that job? You can't ignore these facts. Instead find out what happened and correct it. Avoiding bad news never helps anyone.
- **He is well paid that is well satisfied:** Remember employees and you work for more than a paycheck. How can you make the workplace more pleasant and productive for everyone?
- **Our doubts are traitors, and make us lose the good we oft might win, by fearing to attempt:** You lose the sale you don't call on.
- **Make use of time, let not advantage slip:** Introduce that new product now. Call on that potential customer now. If you don't your competition will.
- **This, too, shall pass:** A good business person has a sense of perspective. Things will change – will you be ready for changes?
- **Wisely and slow. They stumble that run fast:** Don't just call on customers. Don't barge into their offices without an appointment. Plan your sales call.
- **Many strokes, though with a little axe, hew down and fell the hardest-timber'd oak:** People do not change their beliefs or attitudes or habits overnight. Every good public relations person knows that you must keep 'getting the word' out in gentle effective ways. Do not beat people over the head.
- **Self-love, my liege, is not so vile a sin as self-neglecting:** Take care of yourself, balance your life. A tired, stressed-out, burned-out employee is no good to anyone.
- **The course of true love never did run smooth:** Just like love, business has ups and downs. Don't panic, adjust.

- **There's small choice in rotten apples:** Offer your clients good services and good products!
- **He hath eaten me out of house and home:** Watch your overhead. Every dime you spend on rent, utilities, employees, office supplies, travel is a dime taken away from profits. Don't let overhead 'eat you out of house and home'.
- **The fool doth think he is wise, but the wise man knows he be a fool:** You do not know everything. Surround yourself with people who are wiser, have more experience and can give you good advice. These can be mentors in your personal life.
- **There is a tide in the affairs of men which, taken at the flood, leads on to fortune:** Timing is everything. What moves should you be making now?
- **I am wealthy in my friends:** The best way to get a job or customers is through networking. Wherever two or more are gathered, go make friends and network.
- **Some are born great, some achieve greatness, and some have greatness thrust upon 'em:** Chances are that you will have to achieve greatness. What is your game plan to do so?
- **How use doth breed a habit in a man!:** It is easier to keep customers, than to find customers. It is easier to keep existing business than to find new business. Make sure your products or services become a "habit" with your customers and they will keep coming back.
- **Though this be madness, yet there is method in 't:** Check out every idea. Think outside the box. Sometimes the great idea that can make your money, sounds silly or "mad" at first.
- **What a piece of work is a man! How noble in reason! How infinite in faculty! In form and moving how express and admirable! In action how like an angel! In apprehension how like a god! The beauty of the world! The paragon of animals!:** The lesson is simple. Man has amazing capacities. Remember your employees are your company's best resource.
- **'Tis but a base, ignoble mind that mounts no higher than a bird**

can soar: Set high expectations for you and your employees. Set high expectations for yourself. Always challenge yourself and your employees. That is the only way you get better, improve your product, and improve your sales.

- **The man that hath no music in himself, nor is no moved with concord of sweet sounds, is fit for treasons, stratagems and spoils:** You must be a good judge of character. Watch out for those whose sole ambition is to get ahead; you may be their stepping stone.

- **But he that filches from me my good name robs me of that which not enriches him, and makes me poor indeed:** Remember that reputation is everything. You choose a doctor, lawyer, mechanic, insurance agent because you trust them.

- **The insolence of office:** Don't be impressed by your title, no one else is. Be human.

- **Give me that man that is not passion's slave:** Don't be shocked when the CEO is taken down by having an affair with the secretary. Passion is powerful and has taken down many a man and woman. Hire people based on character and ability.

- **There are more things in heaven and earth, Horatio, than are dreamt of in your philosophy:** Twenty years ago, could you dream that iPODS, cell phones, laptops would exist? What product can you produce that no one has thought of yet?

- **Uneasy lies the head that wears a crown:** If you wear a "crown", you should be uneasy. So what if you have the highest selling product in the market? Someone is always trying to overthrow the king. Who is trying to take your market, overthrow you and what must you do to stay "King"?

- **To climb steep hills requires slow pace at first:** Always start with a good product, a good service, and start with a few customers. Satisfy them and the "hill" your business must climb will be much easier.

- **How sharper than a serpent's tooth it is to have a thankless child:** Don't be a "thankless child". If a boss or customer or teacher does something nice for you, thank them.

5

Why would you share "terms from diners" with your audience? Well, audiences are attuned to strange words and phrases. People want to learn new things and unique phrases capture their attention. You can transition into your speech by saying, "And here are some terms from our industry I would like to share with you..." Or you can say, "Many of you were not familiar with the terms I just tossed out. And you might have been momentarily confused. Imagine now that you are a customer and we keep throwing strange terms at you? How would you feel?"

Note that in the second transition, I used a series of questions. For instance, "How would you feel?" Questions are a god way of keeping your audience involved and interested.

Now here are some strange terms from diners. Should I be bold enough to say a 'hash' of strange terms?

Quote: Food is an important part of a balanced diet.
~Fran Lebowitz

- Axle grease / cow paste – Butter
- Birdseed – Breakfast cereal
- Blonde with Sand – Coffee with cream and sugar
- Blowout patches – Pancakes
- Bowl o' red – Chili con carne
- Bow-wow / bun pup – A hot dog
- Bucket of mud – A bowl of chocolate ice cream
- Bullets – Baked beans
- Burn the Brits – Toasted English muffin
- Chickens on a raft – Eggs on toast
- Cow feed – Salad

- Cowboy – A western omelet
- Draw one in the dark – A cup of black coffee
- Fifty-five – A glass of root beer
- Fish eyes – Tapioca pudding
- Flop two – Two fried eggs over easy
- High and dry – A sandwich without butter or mayonnaise
- Hockey puck – A well-done hamburger
- Houseboat – A banana split
- In the alley / out back – Served as a side dish
- Java / Joe – Coffee
- Keep off the grass – No lettuce
- Life preservers – Doughnuts
- Mike and Ike – Salt and pepper shakers
- Murphy – Potatoes
- On the hoof – Any kind of rare meat
- On wheels – An order to go, a takeaway
- Paint it red – Put ketchup on an item
- Put out the lights and cry – Liver and onions
- Sand – Sugar
- Sea dust – Salt
- Sinkers and suds – Doughnuts and coffee
- Squeeze one – A glass of orange juice
- Two cows, make 'em cry – Two hamburgers with onions
- Vermont – Maple syrup
- Whiskey down – Toasted rye bread
- Wreck 'em – Scramble the eggs

6

Slogans are always fun to entertain an audience with. Plus it is a good chance for audience participation. You can engage your audience by saying, "I am going to give you some popular slogans. You can write down the answers on the tablet in front of you. Let's

see how well you do."

By the way, "Let's see how well you do" is an important phrase to use. It gives your audience a challenge and a reason to listen to you. And audiences will rise to a challenge.

After reading a few slogans, you can transition into your speech by talking about your company's slogan or saying, "Sure advertising is important, it gets the customer into the door. But once there we have to deliver a good product and customer service."

Quote: You can tell the ideals of a nation by its advertisements. ~Norman Douglas

- Where do you want to go today? – Microsoft
- Snap, Crackle, Pop – Rice Krispies
- The Real Thing – Coca-Cola
- Where's the beef? – Wendy's
- Plop, plop; fizz, fizz; oh, what a relief it is. – Alka Seltzer
- Sharp Minds, Sharp Products – Sharp
- Finger lickin' good. – Kentucky Fried Chicken
- He keeps going and going and going. – Energizer Batteries
- It's everywhere you want to be. – VISA
- We make money the old-fashioned way... We earn it. – Smith Barney
- The ultimate driving machine. – BMW
- Live in your world, play in ours. – Sony PlayStation and PlayStation 2 gaming consoles
- When it absolutely, positively has to be there overnight. – Federal Express
- Once you pop, you can't stop. – Pringles
- How do you spell relief? – Rolaids
- We're number two; we try harder. – Avis Rental Cars
- The World's Online Market Place – eBay
- Nothin' says lovin' like something from the oven. – Pillsbury

- Don't leave home without it – American Express
- Think Different – Apple
- We try harder – Avis
- Takes a licking and keeps on ticking. – Timex
- What happens here stays here. – Las Vegas
- You've come a long way, baby. – Virginia Slims Cigarettes
- Does she or doesn't she? – Clairol
- Tastes great, less filling – Miller Lite
- The mind is a terrible thing to waste. – United Negro College Fund
- Hey, Mikey… he likes it! – Life Cereal
- They're gr-r-r-r-eat! – Kellogg's Frosted Flakes
- A silly millimeter longer – Chesterfield Cigarettes

7

Everyone drives. And everyone has been frustrated when they are behind a senior citizen driver whose right turn blinker has been flashing for the last hour. This list is a good way to connect with your audience. Especially if they are baby boomers. As baby boomers, we can hear old age knocking on the door and can laugh at things that we are beginning to do, just like our parents. After reading some items from the list, you can say, "That list is humorous, but over 75 million baby boomers are approaching old age and many of them are our customers. What can we do to offer them better service?"

Quote: If you drink don't drive. Don't even putt.
~Dean Martin

Signs It's Time to Quit Driving

When should you retire your car keys? When are you too old to drive? A clue would be going the wrong way on a freeway ramp, parking on your neighbor's cat or confusing that darn brake with the other pedal, whatever they call it. But here are 30 signs it's time to get out of the driver's seat.

- Your turn signal blinks and blinks and blinks and blinks and ...
- Your Depends leak and form that silly puddle on the seat.
- You get lost a lot. You go to the grocery store and end up in a lake.
- A 30 looks like an 80 on your speedometer.
- Your daily schedule is one doctor appointment after another.
- If the cat was a bit quicker, you wouldn't have hit it.
- You come home and there are always strange dents and pieces of hair on your car.
- Reverse and Drive? Heck, anyone can confuse those two.
- Your neighbors no longer park their cars on the street.
- You keep searching for a radio station that plays Lawrence Welk.
- You remember when radios only had two buttons to twist.
- People keep waving at you with their middle finger.
- Henry Ford sat behind you in the third grade.
- You can't turn your neck to check the next lane.
- Driving at night is the impossible dream.
- You go from zero to 60 in an hour.
- Your GPS is a 20 year old atlas.
- You first stop at Circle K is the bathroom.
- Why are you in the car and WHERE are you going?
- Who needs depth perception?
- You remember when spare tires were real tires, not donuts.
- You look for the crank on the front of the car to start it up.
- You keep a bottle of Geritol in your cup holder.
- You lock yourself out of your car on a daily basis.
- Those fire engines really need louder sirens.
- You spend an hour thinking, "The wiper button is here somewhere."
- You pull the car over on the parkway, so you can take your daily

nap.
- You wonder why nobody plays the Beatles anymore.
- You can't find eight-track tapes anywhere.
- You think the Highway 40 sign means the speed limit.

8

A quick funny speech on dating. It is not easy to talk to school groups, youth groups or church groups. But here is a quick funny speech you can use to get some important points across about relationships.

Plus, you can use this as an opening and then transition into, "You will notice two themes running through that list. First people, like our customers, want to feel special. Second there are some people, after you do some investigation, are not people you want to be associated with. And I agree, we don't want to go after every customer because..."

Quote: I'm dating a woman now who, evidently, is unaware of it.
~Gary Shandling

Five Funny Dating Tips

It is a jungle out there and it is not easy meeting the right person. But it can be done if you follow these dating tips:

- **Use the phone first:** Before you go on a date with someone, chat with them over the phone. There are certain red flags you should look for. If a recording says the call is being monitored, this could mean your potential date is in prison and just getting out next week. If you hear three or four kids crying in the background, two or three dogs barking in the background, or someone hollering, "Bubba, shut your trap, I'm on the telephone," these might be good reasons to rethink the date. Of course, if you call and the number has been disconnected, hmmm, need we say more? Also watch how the person answers the phone. If they say, "Joe's morgue, you stab them, we slab them," this is an indicator that it could be a bad date punctuated by bad jokes. If the person answers the phone with a lisp, then says, "Wait a minute, let me get my teeth," you might want to think twice about a good night kiss on that first date. And watch out if directions to your date's house include, "When you leave the paved road…"

- **Pay attention to your date:** It is always a good idea to pay attention to your date, or as the old saying goes, if you can't be sincere, fake it. Even though he is reliving his high school football days when he was 100 pounds thinner, or she is telling you about how romantic her third wedding was, act like you care. If he keeps adjusting his toupee or she keeps readjusting her dentures, do not despair. Your blind date is human and just needs attention and love and you can make it work. Of course, having said that, if your date shows up wearing overalls, no shirt, and a tobacco-stained moustache, still pay attention. Pay close attention to where the nearest exit is and plan your escape route.

- **Go someplace special:** Where he or she meets you on the first date says a lot about your expectations in a relationship. Good places not to meet are:

McDonald's – who wants fries with their relationship?

A cheap bar – who wants a mate who likes cheap liquor and lots of it?

The Thrift Store – who wants a mate who has a collection of clothes from the 70s?

A Starbucks – who wants a date who thinks it is financially sound to spend five bucks on coffee?

His friend's house – where they sit around playing computer games.

Motel 6

Pre-school – where he has to pick up his three kids.

Adult bookstore.

Strip club.

Hell's Angels meeting .

- **What do you really know about him?** Before you go out with them, ask his friends some questions? Does he go to the library or strip bars? Does he go home and watch TV or stumble out of a different watering hole every night? Is every Friday reserved for his mother or his probation officer? Of course, you have to very careful about this. I don't recommend stalking him to find out the answers. For some reason this tends to upset people. So don't pop out of the bushes and scare him or her. Stay in the bushes until they go to bed, then sneak home.

- **Check out the family:** This is very important. Always ask to meet her or his parents on the first date. If his family includes a wife – not a good sign. In fact, it is good if you can double-date with the parents. You can see how his parents interact, how they get along, how they treat each other. Does the father drink five martinis in an hour, does the mother go to the ladies room depressed and come out looking very, very happy? Does his father keep saying, "Why is divorce so expense? Because it's worth it." Now most experts don't think that inviting his or her parents out on the first date is a good idea, but you do marry into the family. And it is always good to see just how crazy they can be, before you get any further involved with your potential mate.

9

It is always good to tie the speech into the time of year. Here is a good speech to give around springtime when many people are thinking of ways to improve their landscaping. You can give this speech to a local civic club or a gardening club. Or you can incorporate it into a regular speech by just using one or two of the tips and saying, "Now those were bad ideas for landscaping. But let me

share some good ideas with you about..."

Quote: Beauty is in the eye of the beholder and it may be necessary from time to time to give a stupid or misinformed beholder a black eye.
~Miss Piggy

Five Funny Landscaping Tips

It's spring. And that means it's time for some key landscaping tips. Let's look at the five key landscaping mistakes everyone should avoid.

- **Mistake Number One: Having a pet cemetery in your front yard:** One, it's very tough to mow around all those crosses. And once you start burying pets in your front yard, you have to make decisions. Do you bury every pet? Or do you just flush the goldfish down the toilet and put the hamster in a plastic bag and dump it in the garbage. The basic dilemma here is which pet is important enough to bury, which one is a throw-away? And of course, I think there may be a zoning ordinance against using your front yard for a pet burying ground.
- **Mistake Number Two: Hanging onto old campaign signs:** This falls under the 'get over it' syndrome. So Gore did not win. But let's face it, the Gore campaign sign is looking a bit ragged, it makes you look like a sore loser, so it is time to toss it.
- **Mistake Number Three: Old cars:** Sooner or later, you have to let go of things. And that old Pinto sedan you drove in high school may inspire memories of what a nerd you really were, but there is no need to have it still parked in the front yard. Move it around to the back and use it for a barbecue as Pintos do well with fire. The rule of thumb here, according to landscaping experts, is that it is acceptable to have only one car on blocks in your front yard, and it has to be a classic car, like a '57 Chevy. A rusted '57 Chevy still manages to look cool. A rusted Pinto, well,

just looks pathetic.

- **Mistake Number Four: Mowing your grass:** Many people buy into the theory that it is important to have a well-kept lawn. This means a lot of money as you have to buy a lawnmower, fertilizer, weed-killer, weed-eater, edger, hose, sprinkler and the sad truth is, your lawn will always look pathetic next to your neighbor's, who is retired and has nothing better to do but work all day on his lawn. You have better things to do. Attend your kids' baseball games, drink beer, attend your kids' softball games, drink beer – did I mention drinking beer? Oh, I digress. Anyway, do not fall into the trap of mowing your lawn. Go the 'environmental route'. Tell your neighbors you are worried about global warming and thus have thrown away your lawnmower. You have decided to go with a natural prairie look. This basically involves letting your grass grow and throwing in some wild flowers. Your front lawn will look like a prairie in bloom, long grass and wild flowers blowing in the wind. At least, this is the story you tell your wife and your neighbors.
- **Mistake Number Five:** Following Tip Number Four. What are you crazy? If you don't mow your grass and buy lots of stuff to keep it green, when the economy goes to hell, who can we blame? We can blame YOU for not going to your local hardware store and buying lots of grass related stuff! Flowers blowing in the wind? Are you kidding? You thought I was serious. Next thing you know, you will be burying pets in your front yard.

10

This can be used a short humorous speech for a youth group or it can be incorporated into a larger speech about the importance of asking the right questions. You might say, "Here are some key questions that a father wants his daughter to ask about any date." Then transition into your speech by saying, "And we need to ask

some important questions ourselves..."

Quote: A man can sleep around, no questions asked, but if a woman makes nineteen or twenty mistakes, she's a tramp.
~Joan Rivers

Dad's Rules for Dating
26 Questions You Need to Ask Your Date

- Does he have a job?
- Can he pay for the dates? Why are you paying for him?
- Does he show up on time? This is a sign of respect.
- Does he always want to go to bars for your dates? This is a sign of future drinking problems.
- Does he always want you to 'chill' with him and his friends? This is a way to avoid actually talking about important issues, like does he have a job.
- Does he say, "I will apply for the job tomorrow?" Why not today?
- Have you met his family? Why not?
- Have I met him? Why not?
- Does he have a skill? Is he going to trade school, college to get a skill? If he has no skill, you will support him and the kids. Is this worth it?
- Does he have a parole officer?
- Does he do 'recreational drugs'. There is nothing recreational about drugs.
- How does he treat his parents?
- Does he spend more money on his car than on you?
- Can you see him supporting a family? Check it out – does he have a job!
- Does he get a lot of calls from bill collectors?
- Does he get a lot of calls from other girls?
- Does he pay for everything with a credit card?
- Do his parents pay all his bills?

- Can he name the last five Presidents?
- Does he pay alimony or child support and he is only 20?
- How many speeding tickets does he have?
- What church does he attend?
- Does he have a dog or cat? How does he treat it?
- Is he always busy on Friday night? See number 16.
- Would I treat your mother the way he treats you?
- Why did I spend all that money on braces for you to ride on the back of a motorcycle?

11

It is best not to lecture to people. All that does is turn them off. And when you have to give a speech on a tired subject, like the dangers of smoking, there is little new you can say about the subject that your audience has not heard. So how do you get a new twist on an old subject? Make a list that tells them the benefits of smoking. This technique can be used in many situations. For example, why give them the same old speech on the danger of violating safety rules. You can use the below list as an example and make up your own list for "Benefits of Violating Safety Rules".

Quote: Smoking is one of the leading causes of statistics.
~Fletcher Knebel

30 Reasons to Smoke

- You don't have to worry about nursing home expenses.
- Playing Russian roulette with your lungs adds excitement to life.
- The kids can pay their own college tuition.
- Taste buds are overrated.
- Early wrinkles make you look more mature.
- Smoking in bed adds excitement to falling asleep.
- One less person for the social security system to worry about.

- Some woman like kissing an ashtray.
- Too many people have white teeth. You will stick out with yellow.
- Only real men can smoke outside when it is minus ten degrees.
- Cancer is big business; you keep a lot of people employed.
- By paying extra taxes on cigarettes, you help the economic stimulus program.
- Tobacco farmers have to work too.
- You support "Made in America". The US makes close to 500 billion cigarettes a year.
- Remember you are a victim. One day you can sue tobacco companies. Could be worth big money. And makes lawyers rich.
- You keep those people employed at Circle K. Cigarettes account for 34% of convenience store sales.
- We have too many role models already.
- Your dry cleaner is always happy to get the smoke out of your clothes.
- Money spent on cigarettes means no vacation with the spouse's relatives.
- You give non-smokers a reason to feel superior.
- You keep anti-smoking campaigns in business.
- Those coughing spells limit conversations with your mother-in-law.
- Gives you reasons to take extra breaks at work.
- Get a chance to see if those smoke alarms in airliner bathrooms really do work.
- No one smokes, then no one buys lighters. An entire industry is destroyed.
- It is always fun to see people panic when you light up by the gas tanks.
- Keeps you from doing sweaty things like jogging. Which doesn't look like that much fun anyway.
- Dead men don't have to pay alimony any more.
- Smoking is the gift that keeps giving undertakers business.

- It is fun keeping people standing in line while the clerk looks and looks for your brand of smokes.

12

Graduation Speeches are hard to give. What can you say that has not already been said? Here is a complete graduation speech that you can add to, put in some of your own personal stories. And this is a multi-use speech. As you read it, you will note that with a few subtle changes, it can also be used for a speech on volunteering, or it can be changed into an inspirational speech for a youth or church group.

Quote: With regards to volunteer organizations, 10 percent of the people do 90 percent of the work.
~Don Mashak

Quit Searching for the Meaning of Life

Do not ask, "What is the meaning of life?", rather give meaning to life.

I am over 50 and have been brought back from death two times – as a result of two terrible car crashes. I have been in comas and I have had 11 concussions, all plunging me into a darkness that I struggled to escape. (Put in your own story here.)

I mention all of this to show, that after being dead, and brought back to life, I have a simple request.

Please NEVER tell me you are searching for the meaning of life.

Finding the meaning of life is irrelevant. What is important, what is crucial is that you give meaning to your life and you give meaning to the lives around you.

Be a beacon. Be a role model. Help others. Okay, you can shoot me for saying three clichés in a role, but it is so true.

Don't waste your time, searching for the meaning of life. Instead give meaning to life. Volunteer. Help a child learn to read. Give blood, coach a children's team, build houses for the homeless.

You find a good man or woman, stick with them. You couldn't send a better message to those around you, a better message to your kids. By sticking with a good woman or man, you define the meaning of life and love for those around you.

Heck, I don't care what you do, but in the doing you define your values, you pass your values onto others, your spouse, your kids, the people you help. By volunteering you become a role model, you define the meaning of life and pass that onto generation after generation after generation.

The meaning of life cannot be found in shopping malls, the latest Hollywood scandal, ocean cruises or even football game after endless football game. These are merely distractions. But you can give meaning to life by volunteering, by helping those struggling through a bad time.

My favorite quote is from the old TV show *Taxi*. It is, "America, it's a tough town."

And America is a tough town. Single mothers are struggling to raise kids. People are scared to see a doctor as they have no health insurance. Many are a paycheck away from being homeless. In every children's hospital, in every state, in every city, there are thousands of kids fighting just to fight another day.

So volunteer. Prove that you do believe people are important. Put your values into action and give hope and meaning to your life and those around you. Finally, I don't mean to be brutal, but if you are searching for the meaning of life, stop. Quit, throw in the towel. Because life is not about looking for bliss, contentment and the meaning of life.

You are on earth to give, to define goodness for those around you. Remember everyone walks around with an invisible sign around their neck saying, "Make me feel important." So make someone feel important, add meaning to their existence by doing something good for them.

In short, find someone's life you can add value to. And in doing so, you start to define the meaning of life.

13

Everyone drinks coffee at meetings. And face it, for some strange reason, we all love trivia. So it is always interesting to share some interesting facts about coffee with your audience. After choosing some coffee facts from the list, you can transition into your speech by saying, "And now I would like to share some news that, like coffee, is designed to wake you up. I am pleased to announce, that beginning next month, we are going to offer some new services to our customers____."

> Quote: If this is coffee, please bring me some tea; but if this is tea, please bring me some coffee.
> ~Abraham Lincoln

- You must drink at least 80 cups of coffee in quick succession to die of caffeine.
- Coffee can affect your body in as little as 15 minutes.
- A goat herder discovered coffee around 850 AD in Egypt when he found his goats dancing around a shrub with red berries (coffee beans).
- Coffee can contain about 150 mg of caffeine.
- The diet pill Dexatrim contains 200 mg of caffeine.
- No-Doz contains 100 mg of caffeine.
- Americans consume 45 million pounds of caffeine a day.
- The average coffee drinker drinks 2.5 cups a day.
- Coffee does not make a drunken person sober.
- Coca Cola has 64 mg of caffeine. RC cola only has 34 mg.
- In the US, about 80% of adults drink coffee every day.
- Women metabolize caffeine about 25% faster than men.

- Caffeine was on the International Olympic Committee (IOC) list of prohibited substances for many years.
- Coffee uses the same channels that amphetamines, cocaine, and heroin use to stimulate the brain.
- It takes about 12 hours to completely get rid of the effects of caffeine in your system.
- Lab mice injected with caffeine were protected against developing Alzheimer's disease.

14

Sad, but true, many employees complain about being underpaid and overworked. It is always good to be open and honest with employees and share financial data with them. And employees must know that they cost your company more than a paycheck. You can weave the facts below into a good basic financial speech for employees so they know the 'true cost' of hiring a worker. If you place some of these facts and figures on a PowerPoint, you have a ready-made slide show that you can share with students, student achievement and other student economic groups.

Quote: Never confuse the size of your paycheck with the size of your talent. ~Marlon Brando

The True Cost of Hiring You: A Short Lesson in Labor Economics

A key concept in any economic discussion is labor. You are the labor when you work for someone. You may be deemed 'an employee', but in economic terms, you are 'the cost of labor'. And to understand the true cost of labor, you must look at what companies truly pay for an employee.

To be an effective economic thinker, you cannot think as an 'employee'. Escape that mindset and think like a CEO. To top management you are 'labor' and there are costs in hiring you that reach far beyond your hourly wage.

For example, when you get hired, the true cost of hiring you is your hourly rate plus additional costs. In other words, your employer pays you $10 an hour, but it costs him at least an extra five dollars to keep you employed and happy. Again, if you get paid an hourly rate $10, you cost your company at least $15.

And this additional cost increases every time your company faces health insurance increases and every time the federal government imposes new regulations and various employment taxes.

Let's look at an example. You are paid $10 an hour and you get paid $400 a week. But as a $400-a-week employee you really cost your company $626.20 a week.

These additional costs include:

Mandatory Costs (required by law)
- Federal Social Security Tax 7.65%
- Federal Unemployment Tax 0.80%
- State Unemployment Tax 2.9%
- Workers' Compensation 4.3%
- Total Mandatory Cost 15.65%

Hiring Costs (cost involved in putting an employee into the payroll system)
- Recruiting, hiring, training
- Bookkeeping, payroll 6.90%
- Severance Pay 0.10%
- Total Hiring Cost 7.00%

Discretionary Costs (which are not that discretionary if you want to recruit good employees)
- Vacation 4.90%
- Holidays 3.40%
- Sick Pay 1.30%

- Pension Plan 5.40%
- Profit Sharing 1.20%
- Health & Life Insurance 11.9%
- Bonuses & Incentives 0.40%
- Contribute to Thrift Plan 0.60%
- Non-Working Time 3.50%
- Miscellaneous Benefits 1.30%

Total Discretionary Costs 33.9%

TOTAL ADDITIONAL COSTS 56.55%

15

Here is a fun list of two words you never want to see together. You do not have to use the whole list; pick and choose the ones you like or invent your own. This can be used in several ways. It can be a fun exercise for a creativity seminar. Have the employees break into several groups and try to think of two words that don't go together in a sentence. This also makes a good opening for a speech. After reading some words from the list, you can say, "And two words in our business that we never want to see together are..."

Quote: Bad news isn't wine. It doesn't improve with age.
~Colin Powell

What two words do you never want to see in the same sentence? Here are some examples:

- Trailer and tornado
- Repair and transmission
- Wife and lawyer
- Lawnmower and toes
- Basement and flood

- Doctor and whoops
- Pilot and error
- Jet and black box
- Mother-in-law and visit
- Sever and finger
- Condom and leak
- Hair and lice
- Termites and house
- Foreclose and home
- Side effect and death
- Politician and taxes
- Drinking and driving
- Cannibal and hungry
- Piercing and infection
- Boyfriend and unemployed
- Boyfriend and probation
- IRS and audit
- Tuition and increase
- Job and merger
- Flu and swine
- Angry and spouse
- Great and depression
- Heart and attack
- Downsize and job
- Son and police
- Speeding and $500

16

People have fundamental insecurities. And every comedian knows that if you joke about people's insecurities, they tend to laugh, as you have hit a nerve. That is why jokes about sex work. They make people feel slightly uncomfortable, yet always produce a laugh.

Having said that, let me also warn you to never use any joke about sex in a business setting. But, besides sex, there are sensitive areas you can poke fun at and they tend to get a big laugh. For instance, who isn't sensitive about losing a job, their income and the lifestyle? The list below talks about "What NOT to say to someone when they lose a job." It is always best to precede a list like this by identifying yourself with the material. To demonstrate this, note the lead-in I have written before the list. You can transition into your speech by saying, "That is a funny list, but it also hits a nerve, as I don't think of us want to be unemployed. How do we prevent that? Quite simply, by working together as a team."

> Quote: I'm always described as 'cocksure' or 'with a swagger', and that bears no resemblance to who I feel like inside. I feel plagued by insecurity.
> ~Ben Affleck

(To protect myself from being called insensitive) I have been through numerous job layoffs and realize that there is one difference between a recession and a depression. When your friend loses a job, it is a recession. When you lose a job, it is a depression.

And I know how scary it is to lose a job, but in the spirit of 'chin-up', here are some tips on:

What Not to Say to a Friend Who has Lost a Job

- Does this mean I have to buy the beer?
- How is that stimulus package helping you?
- You know, my 22 year old son just got a job right out of college, with no experience, starting at $80,000 a year.
- Now you can concentrate on losing weight.
- Eat, drink and be merry. You got nothing to get up early for.
- You will have really LONNNG weekends.
- Hey, you were looking for a job when you found this one.
- Can't your five year old cut lawns?

- Can your wife work at Hooters?
- So the lay-off benefits were two cases of Prozac?
- Every day is Casual Friday.
- You should stay away from gun shows until you calm down.
- Hey you weren't paranoid – they really did can your butt.
- Well I guess it's 'home sweet home' for you.
- Anyone can find another job, if they have a medical degree.
- No job chances, no skills, no common-sense – heck run for elected office.
- You're NOT that old to start looking for another job.
- Have you thought about changing careers? I hear the Catholic Church is looking for priests.
- No money, no job? There goes that 25 year old girlfriend.
- Since you have days off, come by and visit me at work.
- If you dyed your hair, you'd look younger for job interviews.
- You're not too old to find a job; a lot of social security cards have roman numerals.
- You can always go Green. Plus you can put "I am biodegradable" on your resume.
- Boy! That drinking really caught up with you.
- So your boss didn't think those dirty jokes were funny?
- Wow – I heard tents are on sale at Wal-Mart.
- You have some great recommendations from your youth. Who else can put Jesus and Moses on their resume?
- Hey since you lost that expense account, looks like we're meeting at McDonald's for lunch.
- So they let you keep that life insurance policy that doesn't cover death?
- Hey, look on the bright side, you have to pay fewer taxes.
- Top Ramen is on sale this week.
- Wow – and you still have to pay alimony.
- Hey you can get hooked on soap operas.
- So now you really have to find that rich spouse.
- Don't wear that leisure suit to your next interview. I've heard

rumors they are out-of- date.
- I heard there are over 100 ways to cook SPAM.
- You couldn't even pass a urine test?
- They didn't think those 800 calls to Bambi and Kandi were research?
- You don't have to watch TV in the living room all day. Move it to the bedroom.
- Well you don't have to worry about 'all work and no play'.
- Look at all the money you will save on dry cleaning.
- You get to spend more time with your mother-in-law.
- My probation officer can give you a recommendation.
- Hey at least you won't work yourself to death.
- You have time to talk to those telemarketers. You know the ones with jobs...
- Now you won't have to wait eight hours to go home.
- Bummer, the only advantage of the flu was calling in sick.
- Isn't it ironic that the people working at the unemployment office are employed?
- You just eliminated your day-care expenses.
- Now you can save gas. Heck you have all day to walk to the bar.

17

Sooner or later, you will be asked to speak at a career fair or give young people advice about landing their first job or that 'good job' right out of college. Again, what advice can you offer that hasn't been given, ranging from double-check your resume, dress like a professional, do your homework on the company, prepare some good questions to ask, and make sure you send a follow-up thank-you.

You can avoid all the clichés and offer career advice which is actually amusing to your audience. The list below offers an offbeat and interesting approach to giving career advice. It also can serve triple-duty. Besides acting as an entire speech, you can choose some of the questions and form them into a short opening.

Then you can say, "Actually that is probably the worse advice I can give you, but today I don't want to give you advice on finding a job. There are many books, websites, counselors, mother-in-laws who can give you THAT advice. Rather I would like to share my own career path with you."

Share your own career path with the audience? Why would they want to hear that? Because people love stories. And if you can tell them about the struggles and challenges you faced as you forged a career, they will identify with you much more than if you give them the same old career advice they hear at every career fair.

Another way to use the list below? If you are lucky, or unlucky depending on how you view it, you may be asked to lead a seminar at the career fair. You can say, as you lead the seminar, "One thing employers look for in employees, besides a good GPA and a strong work ethic, is creativity. And I thought it would be fun to do a quick creativity exercise."

Then you can break the team into groups and they have to come up with funny questions not to ask at an interview. This will give you an insight into how creative the people in your group are, and if one person stands out, is head and tails above the others in creativity, he might be the one you should think about hiring.

And finally, one more way to use the following list. Feel free to add your own questions to it, and if you have a booth at the career fair, it is a fun handout and a way to have people pick up the handout and remember your company's name.

You can even have a contest and have people write their own stupid interview question and place it into a box on your table. The winner gets a small prize and you get a free mailing list, as well as a list of some people it might be good to hire down the road.

The contest also leaves people with a good impression of your company and makes them think that you might be a great company

to work with.

Who knew there were so many ways to use a simple list? Having said all of that, here is the list.

Quote: I've missed more than 9000 shots in my career. I've lost almost 300 games. 26 times, I've been trusted to take the game winning shot and missed. I've failed over and over and over again in my life. And that is why I succeed.

~ Michael Jordon

26 Questions NOT to Ask at a Job Interview

In today's tough economy, it is important to look your best in a job interview. So here are 26 questions you should NOT ask at your next job interview. Trust me on this. They have never worked for me.

- Does my probation officer count as a reference?
- Does my tongue piercing look infected?
- How many porn sites can we cruise a day?
- How strict is that 8 o'clock starting time?
- Do you think this rash is contagious?
- Is there a bikini day for the little ladies?
- I have a slight housing problem. Is it okay if I sleep in my office?
- Do you have showers here?
- Just how tight is security at night?
- Do you double-check the websites we go to?
- Do you think mayonnaise looks like pus? I always have.
- Just what body parts aren't we allowed to touch at work?
- How many tattoos am I allowed to get on my face?
- Do I get a company jet?
- You look uptight. Are you always this anal?
- Do you have colored people working here?
- Are we allowed to smoke in our cubicles? I mean – you know – pot?
- My theory of customer relations is, "Screw them if they can't take

a joke." Does that match your mission statement?
- Is a thong okay to wear on casual Fridays?
- Resume? Free spirits don't believe in resumes.
- Skills? I can burb my ABCs.
- Does the CEO get pissed if I use his parking space?
- Only TWO weeks of vacation?
- Do you have cable TV?
- Eight hours... a day????
- If I were a Siamese Twin would I get one or two cubicles? One or two parking places?

18

We all don't like certain things. For instance, no one likes a tone-deaf singer who says, "I want to sing one more song." Here is a list of what you don't want to hear people say. Again, pick and choose what you want to use or use the entire list as an opening. And after using some bits from the list, you could say, "And there are things that our customers don't want us to say. Plus customers don't want to hear excuses. They want to see results. So how can we guarantee that we provide customers with results not excuses? Well I have a few ideas I would like to share with you..."

Quote: A child of four would understand this. Send someone to fetch a child of four.
~Groucho Marx

Things You Never Want to Hear
- Doctor operating on you: I am a little confused here.
- Airline Pilot: Hmm even the black box isn't working.
- Lawyer: So how do you feel about jail?
- Flight Attendant: Whoops watch your step – that toilet is overflowing again.

- Car Dealer: What warranty?
- Teacher: Stupid parents, stupid kids.
- College Registrar: Whoops, none of these courses transfer.
- Real Estate Agent: Think double-wide.
- Family Doctor: So how long did you want to live anyway?
- Sales Clerk: I don't think we have anything that big.
- Lover: It stings when I pee.
- Lover: It is just a small rash. It should go away.
- Weight Watchers: Our scales don't go that high.
- Eye Doctor: Hmm, Seeing Eye dogs make nice pets.
- Dentist: Now I can pay that college tuition!
- Vet: Which one of you am I seeing?
- Mother-in-law: I left your father-in-law and I need a place to stay.
- X-ray Technician: Whoops – left that machine on too long.
- Coach: Good news, bad news. You didn't make the team, but we do need a team mascot.
- Mother: Well, I am not sure who your REAL father is, but…
- IRS: Thanks for the laugh.
- Career Advisor: Practice saying, "Do you want fries with that?"
- Accountant: So I was a few zeros off?
- Stockbroker: What is the worst case scenario?
- Zookeeper: Do you want to be let back in your cage? Here's a banana.
- Student: Dad, my teacher teaches sex in a new way…
- Car Dealer: GM will be around for years.
- Cub Fan: What could happen?
- Mechanic: Your engine is like a hemophiliac bleeding oil
- Husband: I am running away with my friend Bob.
- Gynecologist: Can you say Octo?
- Michael Jackson: Need a babysitter?
- Neighbor: Actually meth labs are pretty safe.
- Airline passenger: You mind if my baby sits here?
- Boss: I can give you a good reference.

19

We have all heard about the importance of making a good first impression. At least one time or another, everyone has heard that saying, "It is important to make a good first impression". This list of "Things Men Don't Want To Hear on the First Date" ties into the importance of making a good first impression. This list always works because it hits the audience on another level. We have all been on bad first dates and I think, deep down inside, we all firmly believe the number one rule of a relationship, "Never sleep with anyone crazier than you".

This list always makes an audience laugh. And this list provides a very easy transition into your speech. All you have to say, "So saying those things will ensure that you make a bad first impression. But now let's talk about how we can make a good first impression with our _____."

Quote: A man can be happy with any woman, as long as he does not love her.
~Oscar Wilde

Things Men Do Not Want to Hear on the First Date

- What is that cologne you are wearing, *Eau de Homeless*?
- They never did find my ex-husband's body.
- Three kids over 21; you think one of them would have a job.
- I am planning to move out of the halfway house soon.
- I carry a gun because some days I feel like shooting someone's pecker off.
- I love expensive wines. Have you ever tried that Boones Farm?
- I like men when they are smoking. That's why I set my last husband on fire.
- I always sleep with my pit bulls.
- With Depends, I can sleep through the night.
- I know you shouldn't talk about sexual diseases on the first date

but...

- Cocaine is SO expensive these days.
- Anger management problems my ass!!!!
- I told my psychologist I would take up a new hobby. Stalking takes up SO much time.
- How do you think crack compares to meth?
- I am pretty sure it is just a fever blister...
- I bet you were cute when you were younger...
- So you don't exercise much, do you ?
- I Tasered the last guy that tried to kiss me.
- You kinda look like Woody Allen.
- Is it okay if I leave my front teeth at home?
- Did you know I was still married?
- Why don't you meet me at my house? But I get off house arrest in a few weeks.
- Actually it was easier getting on welfare than I thought.
- You mind if I smoke this cigar?
- So much stress, so much medication.
- Thank God for credit cards.
- My ex-husband is doing better controlling his jealous rages.
- I didn't mean to hit my ex THAT hard with the baseball bat.
- So, we're a couple? Going steady? What, you afraid to make a commitment?
- Kitchen knives can do more than carve steak.
- I hate it when I get my Prozac and bladder control medicine mixed up.
- You mind if I call my parrot?
- So after I smashed the TV, I said, "Now do you want me or football?"
- I just am saying that Danielle Steele can write circles around that Shakespeare guy.
- I really need to get that AIDs test soon.
- At your age, you're just lucky to have hair.
- If this is such a fine Italian restaurant, why don't they serve

SpaghettiOs?
* I have only seen gay men drive this type of car.
* Have you thought about weight watchers?

20

Many people think baseball is boring. But the things that are boring are the things you do not take the time to understand. Examining the details of anything, for instance a piece of art, seeing how the artist used shading, composition, light, different colors to get his ideas across, can make what you thought was a boring painting come alive.

How can you use this opening to transition into a speech? You can choose several items from the list, then say, "Obviously I am talking about more than baseball. I am talking about the importance of paying attention to details. And here are some details about our business that I hope will give you a better understanding of our company..."

Quote: It's the little details that are vital. Little things make big things happen.
~John Wooden

How to Watch a Baseball Game: The Importance of Paying Attention to Details

Hey – here are some fun things to watch for in a baseball game. By no means is this a complete list, but it will give you a better feeling for the game and might help you appreciate the strategy in baseball!

* You have a man on first base and a right-hand pitcher. To throw over to first base, the pitcher has to pick up his back heel. It is fun to focus on his back heel and predict if he is throwing over to first base.

- Watch the catcher. He will always position his glove on the inside or outside part of the plate. The pitcher wants to hit that glove every time. If he misses the corners and the ball ends up over the middle of the plate, it's home run city. Is the pitcher hitting the catcher's target most of the time? If he is not, then he is getting tired, or else he is just a poor pitcher.
- How many pitches are up in the strike zone? Two or three in a row? This means the pitcher may be getting too tired to follow through and it is time to take him out.
- Watch the ad on the wall behind home plate. There is a new ad there every inning. How do they do that? It is computer animated.
- Watch how close the batter stands to the plate. If the pitcher is throwing a lot of outside pitches, the batter will try to crowd the plate, so he can reach the outside pitch easier. It is the pitcher's job to throw a hard inside pitch every now and then to keep the batter honest, to keep the batter from crowding the plate. Is the pitcher claiming control of the plate or is the batter?
- Are they playing good baseball? One way to tell: is the outfielder hitting the cut-off man? A good throw from the outfield should hit the cut-off man in the chest. If the outfielder overthrows the cut-off man or throws it to the side, that means the cut-off man cannot fire it to home and get the runner out. Little things mean a lot.
- Are they playing good baseball? A fly ball is hit over the second basemen's head. The second basemen and right fielder both chase the ball. If possible, the right fielder should catch the ball. Why? The second baseman is facing away from the infield. If he catches the ball, he needs to turn and throw the ball. The fielder is coming towards the ball, facing the infield. He can catch the ball and his momentum is carrying him towards the infield, which makes for a more accurate throw. Plus he has the whole infield in front of him, so he can see where the runners are and where he should throw the ball.

- How aggressive is the other team at breaking up the double play? Are they sliding into second with their legs high, trying to take out the second baseman and ruin the double play, or are they merely sliding in, making no attempt to break up the double play. How smart is the pitcher? When the count is 0 and 2, never throw a good pitch. Throw it in the dirt, throw it outside, see if the batter will chase it. If the batter doesn't fall for it, you still have three balls left to play with.
- How are the infielders positioning themselves? If the pitcher throws slowly, chances are the batter will turn on the ball quickly and hit it down the baseline. Is the third baseman playing close to the line? If the pitcher throws fast, it will be harder to turn on the ball and the batter will be late hitting the ball. Is the third baseman cheating towards short?

21

Are you talking to a parenting group? A church group? This is a great list to start any parenting speech with. Every parent in the audience will enjoy it. This is also a good opening for a business speech. Again, there will be parents in the audience and they will appreciate the humor. After reading a few of the "real rules" of parenthood, you can then say, "In short, the 'real rules' I have just covered reflect the reality of being a parent. And I would like to talk about the realities facing our company during the next quarter. The real rules of business we must deal with."

Quote: Reality is a crutch for people who can't handle drugs.
~Lily Tomlin

The Real Rules of Parenthood
- The kid will like the box better than the toy.
- Even the most expensive clothes for a young child will be worn

inside out and backwards.

- Sugar is the fifth major food group.
- The kid that is not tired will be asleep in five minutes when put in bed.
- Kids don't need naps – parents just need time out.
- The teenage daughter whom you have protected, who you made ride in a car seat until she was five, will date a boy with a motorcycle.
- For no apparent reason, kids, especially young boys, think it is cool to swallow coins.
- You want your kid to read all summer; he wants to learn to burb his ABCs.
- Your star student will become a teenager and date a girl dressed in black with piercings and who is known as the rehab queen.
- You think of it as your kid's bedroom floor. She thinks of it as a big shelf.
- Just when you have money saved up to buy that new gas grill, your kid will fall off his bike, destroy his front teeth and you WILL NEVER see a new gas grill.
- Their mother does not think it is funny when you use that old joke, "I have problems with the school bus. It keeps bringing my kids back."
- All the kids in the back seat of the car will only have to use the bathroom 20 minutes after you leave the truck stop and you are in the middle of NOWHERE!
- Their mother finds no humor in it when you call the kids' Catholic school, "Our Lady of Perpetual Payments."
- The same kid, who is flunking remedial math, can figure out the most complex video game in less than half an hour.
- You do not want to hear, "It's okay, Dad, when I wear long sleeves they can't see the tattoo."
- Your son will think dropping out of high school to become a rock star is a great idea.
- Never buy your kids a new car. Buy them junkers, which they

will wreck anyway.

- Kids think that laptops will not be stepped on if they leave them on the floor.
- The kid that has trouble writing an essay can text 50 messages to her friends in an hour.
- The same six year old kid that crashed her bike into the bushes will one day drive your car.
- Your teenager thinks there is a gas fairy that fills up the car when it is empty.
- Always check your gas gauge after your teenager has driven the car. Unlike teenagers, you cannot drive the car on gas fumes alone.
- Your kid thinks MTV news is real news.
- There is no such thing as fun for the entire family.
- Despite what your son thinks, chasing after girls and drinking beer is not the point of college.
- Remind your kids that cats do not like baths in the toilet.
- The same kid who jogs all day to get in shape for soccer cannot mow a lawn.
- Memorize this phrase: "What were you thinking." Example: When you are in the emergency room, ask your son, "What were you thinking when you jumped off the roof with an umbrella?"
- After five tickets, your son will realize that stop signs do mean STOP!
- You will always wonder how the cell phone got flushed down the toilet.
- Sometimes you don't care if your kids go to a bad or good college. Just so they go.
- Don't rent out your kids' rooms. Even if they are 30. They will be BACK!
- Your daughter thinks it is okay if her 22 year boyfriend does not have a job.

22

Many students get turned off by education, because they see no connection between what they are learning in the classroom and real life. If you have to speak to a school group, a good speech will make that connection for them, will show how a school assignment is not just busy work, but prepares them for real life. Here is a complete speech for a school group, telling them how essays translate to real life:

> Quote: Develop a passion for learning. If you do, you will never cease to grow.
> ~Anthony D'Angelo

I know that you all often sit in the classroom asking, "How is any of this going to help me in real life?"

Well, a lot of things you learn in school are actually geared to helping you in real life. Let me give you one example. Think about writing essays. I know that is one of your least favorite things to do.

Why do you write essays? Why do they put you through the torture of writing in school?

First let me offer my voice of experience. I have a friend who has been a speechwriter for over 20 years. And he told me this story about the importance of writing. He said, "I know that executives often judge you by your writing. Once, when I finished interviewing a CEO for a speech, he pulled out a file. Then he said, "I have over 5,000 employees and there is no way I can keep track of all of them. But I can tell a lot about a person's thought process, by what they write and how they write it."

He showed me the file and it was full of e-mails and letters and reports from employees.

The CEO said, "I do see a lot of writing. And when I see a well-written document that reflects a good thought process and the ability to put ideas into action, I put that document in the folder and tell my managers to watch that person."

The point, I know, is obvious. People, even CEOs, judge us and our thought process by how we put words on paper, on how we logically develop our ideas, how we back up our ideas.

That takes us back to the importance of writing essays. Here is a secret that they never tell you. It is not about writing essays; it is about developing a thought process that shows you are an educated human being. When you graduate from high school or college, the least an employer expects is that you can clearly articulate your opinions and communicate ideas to fellow workers, customers and your bosses.

Remember that thesis statement they kept pounding in your head. A thesis statement merely tells what your paper will cover. For instance, you are arguing for the drinking age to be lowered to 18. Your thesis statement will say: "The drinking age should be lowered to 18 because the current law is giving too many kids a criminal record, does not take into account the maturity of 18 year olds, and wastes law enforcement resources which could be better allocated somewhere else."

And then the rest of your paper will back up these arguments.

Yeah, yeah, yeah. So what? You have heard that nonsense about a thesis statement before.

Okay, think about this. You want a raise. You are not just going to storm into your boss' office and demand a raise. Well, you could but that wouldn't do much except get you thrown out on your butt. You need to go in and have logical arguments prepared and be ready to back up each argument.

Whoops – that sounds a lot like an essay. And a thesis statement.

So before you go into your boss' office you have a thesis statement prepared. "I deserve a raise because I have increased sales by 20%, improved the company's efficiency by 10% and…"

Well, you get the idea. And remember what else essays teach you. Be prepared to back up each statement you make in the thesis statement. So when you offer your boss reasons for giving you a raise – guess what. He expects you to back them up.

Two more quick examples of how a thesis statement can help you in the real world. Applying for a job? Write a thesis statement explaining why you are the best person for the job and have examples to back it up. Selling a product? Write a thesis statement explaining the benefits of your product and, again, be able to back the benefits up.

Yes, a thesis statement teaches you to think logically.

Okay, but why does your teacher keep saying, "Where are your sources, where are your sources…?" Obviously just to annoy you.

Hmm, maybe not?

Think about this. What are your main criteria for choosing a mechanic, a doctor, dentist, and accountant? You can trust them. All good relationships start with trust. It is the same with a writer and a reader. Before a reader will trust you, you must convince them 'you know your stuff'. And this convincing depends on sound research, credible sources and good citations, so the reader can double-check if they want to.

APA or MLA is not about leaning a system. Heck, you may never use APA again. APA does force you to carefully document your sources and to leave a 'paper trail' that your readers can follow. That is a valuable skill that every manager must have. Sad to say, try firing an employee without careful documentation. Another example, what happens if you develop a new product and someone gets injured by it? You better have exact documentation that shows the product was safety tested and retested.

We live in a very litigious society, and as a manger to protect yourself and your company, you better learn the importance of credible sources and documenting them correctly.

Hey – that is the skill APA and MLA style teaches!

Another example, if a CEO gives a speech (and as a speechwriter, I have seen this happen) and he makes as statement, tosses out a few statistics, he better be able to confirm that stat is right and he can confirm the sources.

To show how important accuracy is, President Obama once claimed that if you took America's Muslim population it would make "one of the largest Muslim countries in the world."

Ow! The next day the press was all over that stat and pointed out that, "The most generous estimates put America's Muslim population at about 8 million, which would barely place the US in the top 42 Muslim countries."

Some final thoughts. Your teacher gets upset when your essay is late, because you must learn to write under pressure and to deliver the product on time. If your boss wants the weekly report on her desk every Wednesday, but you toss it on her desk two days late, guess what? That is a good way to get fired.

And remember that life is about selling ideas. We are always selling ideas, to our spouses, our kids, our family, our bosses. And the best way to sell any idea is to develop a thesis statement that clearly explains the key points of your ideas and then back up the key points.

A simple example. You are trying to convince your wife that you need a new boat. Good luck on that one.

Seriously, you can line up your arguments by saying, "A boat will provide quality family time for us and the kids, it will offer us a cheap vacation every weekend and you can use it to take potential clients on a nice cruise around the lake."

Hey, that sounds like a thesis statement!

Hmm, maybe there is something to all this essay writing.

23

Here is a list of some possible T-shirts for parents. You can choose some T-shirt slogans and then you can say, "I am sure that anyone who is a parent can identify with those sayings, because, let's face it, raising kids is a tough and demanding task. Today, I would like to talk about some other tough and demanding tasks facing our

business _____.″

Quote: Few things are more satisfying than seeing your children have teenagers of their own.

~Doug Larson

We need some T-shirts for parents...

Here are Some Ideas You Can Print on Your T-shirt:

- Duct Tape: The perfect babysitter.
- My Kid is an Over-Achieverrr like I were.
- You make Daddy's hair fall out.
- Giving a kid sugar is like putting amphetamines in your coffee.
- My kid can't even spell Potential.
- Only you can prevent mommy's nervous breakdown.
- Does parenting have a fast forward button?
- You were the result of a mistake. I married your father.
- Whiskey: The natural sleep aid.
- Don't even think about thinking about it.
- If it were a snake it would have bit you.
- If you had a brain, you'd take it out and play with it.
- Time-out is for parents.
- We are not playing banker. No handouts!
- Parents for Year-Round School.
- Guitar Hero? How About Homework Hero?
- Bedtime. Brush your teeth, wash your face, untie your sister.
- If God wanted you to text all day, He would have given you ten thumbs.
- Cell phones, remote controls and hamsters do not like water. Got it?
- Beer is Prozac for dads.
- You were dreaming about Daddy and the babysitter.
- You did what?
- Your best survival skill is to shut up and go to your room NOW!

- No! Your little brother does not need a tattoo.
- Allowance? I'm allowing you to stay alive.
- You're just a little person who does not pay rent.
- What did you think would happen?
- Use your head. Buy a hat.
- Definitely his mother's side of the family.
- We will not trade your sister for a puppy.
- Your economic stimulus? Get a job.
- My kid is a spelling chimp.
- Don't talk to strangers. And your dad gets stranger every day.
- Kids are natural drunks.
- Yes alcohol kills brain cells. Look at your father.
- Abuse a parent, go to your room.
- I'm only letting you live so you can pay my social security.
- Take the cat out of the washer.
- Yes we're having pizza again.
- Visit your grandparents.
- No, twelve is not too young to join the army.
- POS: Parent Over Shoulder.
- If you have to ask, the answer is NO.
- Prozac? That's Mommy's niceness medicine.
- Don't all the kids stay all day at Sunday School?
- Why does the school bus keep bringing you back?

24

Here is an example of how you can take standard safety tips and by adlibbing add some humor to what, otherwise, would be a dull speech. Note the adlibs in the parentheses. This is a good speech to give to schools, Toastmasters and civic clubs around the Fourth of July.

Quote: You may be a redneck if your lifetime goal is to own a fireworks stand.

~Jeff Foxworthy

How to Be Safe on July Fourth

The Consumer Product Safety Commission reports that about 10,000 people were treated in hospital emergency rooms for firework injuries. Children 10 to 14 years old had the highest injury rate among all age groups. Hmm, why do I find that easy to believe?

The CPSC urges that you follow these guidelines for a safe Fourth of July:

- Do not allow young children to play with fireworks under any circumstances. Sparklers, considered by many the ideal 'safe' firework for the young, burn at very high temperatures and can easily ignite clothing. Children cannot understand the danger involved and cannot act appropriately in case of emergency. (This also applies to Uncle Waldo who, after four beers, tends not to understand anything and will merely run around in circles screaming like a little girl if his clothes catch on fire.)
- Older children should only be permitted to use fireworks under close adult supervision. Do not allow any running or horseplay. (The key word here is adult supervision. That does not mean your 18 year old neighbor with the tattoos and body piercings.)
- Light fireworks outdoors in a clear area away from houses, dry leaves or grass and flammable materials. (Or you can light the fireworks on your front porch. The firemen were just sitting around anyway and needed something, like a good house fire, to liven up their evening.)
- Keep a bucket of water nearby for emergencies and for pouring on fireworks that don't go off. (And when the evening is over, you can also dump the water on your husband and sober him up.)
- Do not try to relight or handle malfunctioning fireworks. Douse

and soak them with water and throw them away. (Love this tip. Gosh, if the firecracker doesn't light once, give it to Bubba to hold, and try to relight it.)

- Be sure other people are out of range before lighting fireworks. (Yes, this includes your mother-in-law.)
- Never ignite fireworks in a container, especially a glass or metal container. (It's called making a bomb and police, for some odd reason, frown on metal or glass fragments flying everywhere. I bet your neighbors might be a bit annoyed too.)
- Keep unused fireworks away from firing areas. (Kinda like not smoking around the gas tanks. Never a good idea.)
- Store fireworks in a dry, cool place. Check instructions for special storage directions. (This makes sense. Soggy, wet fireworks just aren't any fun.)
- Observe local laws. (Like if fireworks are outlawed in your town, don't be setting them off – at least not in front of the police or fire station.)
- Never have any portion of your body directly over a firework while lighting. (Never would have thought of this. That's the last time I will hold that firework between my legs before setting it and myself on fire.)
- Don't experiment with homemade fireworks. (Check the first tip about Uncle Waldo. If Uncle Waldo thinks making homemade fireworks is a good idea, remember the source. This is Uncle Waldo and his last good idea was driving a police car home.)

25

I have written many speeches for CEOs. Here is a complete speech that you can give to a sales force. Or as always, steal stuff you like from it and weave into your speech.

Quote: Sales are contingent upon the attitude of the salesman –
not the attitude of the prospect.
~W. Clement Stone

Sample Sales Staff Speech

Today, I wanted to offer some advice about things we can all work
on.

Then, I remembered what a fourth grader once said about
advice. He was doing a paper on Socrates and he wrote, "Socrates
went around giving people advice and they poisoned him."

So I will stay away from the advice and discuss some of the
driving forces behind our success as a company and your success as
a salesperson.

We know it takes hard work to be successful. And we have
worked hard to be successful in one very key area – we have worked
very hard to develop relationships with the operators, the end users
of the product. We must ensure they can depend on the consistent,
high-quality products we provide to them each and every day.

We must remind ourselves that value, not just price has to be a
driving force behind our success.

We must avoid what many call the "Yugo Trap". In the 1980s, a
new automobile reached North America from behind the Iron
Curtain. It was called the Yugo, and its main attraction was price.
About $3,000 each.

But the only way they caught on was as the butt of jokes.

Remember the guy who told his mechanic, "I want a gas cap for
my Yugo." "OK," the mechanic replied, "that sounds like a fair
trade."

Yugo was offering a lousy value proposition. The cars literally
fell apart before your eyes.

And the lesson was simple: price is just one component of value.
No matter how good the price, the most cost-sensitive consumer
won't buy a bad product.

That is why value is such an important part of our equation for our end users.

And value must be driven by our commitment to quality.

Let me be very clear about this.

When we talk about quality, we are talking about far more than the quality of our products and service.

We are also talking about the quality of our relationships and the quality of our communications and the quality of our promises to each other and our end users.

In short, we must think about quality in terms of truth and integrity.

Let me repeat that, we must think beyond the quality of our products. We must also think about quality in terms of truth and integrity.

The glue that holds all relationships together, including the crucial relationship between you and our end users, is trust. And trust is based on integrity.

It's critical that we live by the integrity upon which this company was built. We have all read recent newspaper articles are about some of our competitors who been tarnished for doing things that are not according to policy. It would be a shame for any of us to get ourselves into that position. We are very well-respected in the industry, not only by our consumers but also by our customers.

We want to be truthful and honest each and every time we deal with our customers.

Remember no company is just given integrity. A company earns integrity and trust from the relentless pursuit of honesty at all times

And let me make this very simple. We don't need PhDs in ethics to do what is right. What is right can be determined by three basic questions.

Would I want to read about it on the front page of the newspaper?

What would mom say?

What would my children think?

Let me move on here and share a few more thoughts.

I think it is very important to emphasize that we expect a lot out of you, but you should and will receive a lot out of us.

We are committed to providing you with the resources and guidance to help cultivate and enhance your skills and competencies.

For instance let's talk about paperwork.

Have you've seen a flock of birds like ducks or geese or pelicans in the sky – and you find that they always fly in a 'V'.

Did you ever notice that one side is always longer than the other? Know why?

There are more birds on that side.

Okay, it doesn't take a genius to figure that out. It also doesn't take a rocket scientist to realize more time on paperwork means less time serving customers.

That's why we continue to develop better resources and tools to eliminate the unnecessary paperwork you have to deal with.

We are also working on new training programs to develop new skills as people move through their careers at our company. We are actively working, through the HR department, on ways to enhance employees' everyday lives to incorporate ways to address the demands put upon each employee every day.

But despite the support we can offer you, our company cannot give you one thing. We cannot give you the passion to achieve goals and grow professionally. It's got to come from within.

But we, as leaders, do have a responsibility to supply you with the tools that build success and an environment that allows your passion to flourish. And we are committed to do just that.

We invest heavily in training and new technology because they are significant. We constantly develop new products for segmented markets to ensure that you have a full arsenal, a great mix of exciting new products and highly respected brand names to offer our customers.

But we cannot just develop products and throw them out there. We know that.

There are already too many products on the market.

Your everyday supermarket now carries roughly 40,000 items, twice as many as a decade ago.

For example, more than 16 varieties just of Colgate toothpaste, 75 types of Pantene hair care treatments, 110 varieties of Hallmark greeting cards, and untold numbers of other products.

I mention this because that ties back into our commitment to quality. We are not going to throw products at our customers, just because 'it is the thing to do'. We will continue to carefully analyze each segment of our business, see where the opportunities for growth are and then supply you with the best products to develop and grow those markets.

I firmly believe that the best vision is insight. And we develop new products, improve existing products, and launch new campaigns based on insights on what the customer needs, not what we think they need.

To paraphrase George Bush, let's chat further about "that vision thing".

The famed Supreme Court Justice Oliver Wendell Holmes once boarded a train in Washington, then later realized he had lost his ticket. The conductor recognized him and said, "Don't worry about it, sir. I'm sure when you find it, you'll send it in."

Justice Holmes replied, "Young man, the question is not 'Where is my ticket?', but rather, 'Where am I supposed to be going?'"

And to pare it down to its simplest level, isn't that what vision is about? On a corporate level and a personal level, we must all ask ourselves, "Where are we going?"

We all need a vision of "where we are going" and how we want to grow this company.

Once we agree on that vision, that goal, we must focus on how to reach our goals.

That means we must focus on priorities.

The best way to manage your time is to list the twenty important things that you have to do.

By the way, if you have more than twenty important things to do, you need a different type of professional advice that I can't offer.

Take the twenty most important things that you have to do and rank order them from one (the highest priority) to twenty (the lowest priority).

Think about this – WHY spend your entire life working on 13s, 14s, 17s, 19s?

FOCUS ON THE FIRST FIVE!

The first five will help you achieve your goals. Number 20 will not.

Now, let's talk a little more about attitude.

We must accept our current sales environment. We can't wish for the 'good old days'. We must look for new ways to operate instead of letting the challenges worry us.

To be a winner you must:

Be positive – believe in yourself.

Learn from others' ideas.

Don't give up.

Remember, you determine your own attitude.

Let me touch upon an important fact of our sales philosophy: We let you take charge of your career. You are empowered to move forward.

Whenever I say empowered, I am reminded of a cartoon that I came across in a business journal some time ago.

Imagine, if you will, a meek subordinate cowering before the large impressive desk of his superior. His boss glares over the rims of his spectacles and says, "Jones, we're going to give you more responsibility. We're going to make you accountable for everything that goes wrong around here."

Thankfully that is not the way empowerment works here.

It may be both comforting and unnerving to note that 'the company' does not determine your future. It's the decisions and the choices you make that will inevitably determine your destiny. You own your career – you manage its progress. So I encourage you to take charge!

And when you take charge, good things happen.

Let me now switch to another important topic.

Above all, I want to challenge you to seek out new ways to address and solve problems, and seize opportunities. Find new ways of looking at things.

Yet, what do I mean by "new ways of looking at things" and "seizing opportunities"?

Perhaps this creative thinking is best exemplified by how Safeway in the UK has been reinventing retailing, especially by leveraging customer information.

Like a lot of grocers, Safeway has been collecting product data for a long time. But collecting data and using it is two different things. And Safeway USED the data!

They pinpointed their most profitable customers. They found that only 8 of the 28 orange juices they carried were profitable. So, they reduced their orange juices, and increased their profitability.

They discovered they were carrying 200 different cheeses. So, let's reduce the number of cheeses. Wrong. The data said the most profitable customers were buying the least profitable cheeses. So it was important for Safeway to carry these unprofitable cheeses.

Safeway knows a typical customer buys the same 125 products. So they developed customized shopping lists for customers and customers could scan their Safeway cards and get a personalized shopping list, along with up-to-date product promotions. Safeway wrote the shopping list in the same way that items were laid out in the store.

Safeway found that what shoppers hate most is waiting at on line to check-out. So, Safeway gave customers PDAs to scan products as they shopped. Customers placed foods in their bag, got an itemized receipt as they left the store. No more checkouts.

Why did I mention all of this?

We are not Safeway, but the thought process they are employing is what we all must do.

Like Safeway, we must all look for better ways to serve our

customers, creative ways to solve problems and creative ways to make life better and more productive for our customers.

Let me leave you with some thoughts from Henry Ford.

He once said, "You can do anything if you have enthusiasm... Enthusiasm is the spark in your eye, the swing in the gait, the grip of your hand, the irresistible surge of your will and your energy to execute your ideas... Enthusiasm is at the bottom of all progress! With it, there is accomplishment. Without it there are only alibis."

26

Here is a good speech to give to a civic club during lunch or to a sales force. This speech talks about the difficulty of changing people's minds and how the key to any successful sales pitch is credibility. This can also be used as a speech on how to get people to adopt your ideas. In short, this is a complete speech that can be used to motivate a sales force, tell how to communicate a new idea, or to talk about the difficulty of communication.

And as always, you do not need to use the entire speech. Just go through it, highlight the material you like, and then weave it into your own speech. Like the other material in this book, this speech is geared towards helping you get those creative gears working and offers ways to help your speech rise above the ordinary.

Quote: Denial ain't just a river in Egypt.
~Mark Twain

How Do You Overcome Denial: The Difficulty of Communication and Sales

Let's talk about the difficulty of communication. First, people tend to deny reality. The company has been losing money for months, and yet people are shocked when they are laid off. They say. "I didn't see it coming."

The truth is they saw it coming, but denied it. And to protect themselves, they could have started taking classes to get a new skill, they could have taken a second job working at the local liquor store at night, they could have started a part-time business on the side.

But they didn't. They ignored the truth, which was so obvious, that their company was going down the drain and they took no actions to protect themselves.

But I am not blaming these people. As they say denial runs deep. I found out the power of denial when my friend's wife left him. The warning signs were so blatant. Someone told my friend she saw his wife checking into a hotel. Then his wife went on trips to Las Vegas without him.

My friend would walk in and she would quickly hang up the phone; she would come home and instead of hugging him, she would rush and take a shower.

And he never suspected anything. Then one day he came home, there was a note on the table, her closet was cleaned out and she had moved in with another man. This lesson taught my friend the power of denial and how hard it is to get a new idea across to anyone.

My theory on how tough it is to change people's habits, how tough it is to even get them to listen is reinforced by two recent studies.

An Ohio State study showed:

A new study provides some of the strongest evidence to date that Americans prefer to read political articles that agree with the opinions they already hold. Researchers found that people spent 36% more time reading articles that agreed with their point of view than they did reading text that challenged their opinions.

A recent University of Illinois study showed:

The researchers found that people are about twice as likely to select information that supports their own point of view (67%) as to consider an opposing idea (33%). Certain individuals, those with close-minded personalities, are even more reluctant to expose themselves to differing perspectives. They will opt for the information that corresponds to their views nearly 75% of the time. The researchers also found, not surprisingly, that people are more resistant to new points of view when their own ideas are associated with political, religious or ethical values."

The point is people tend to deny reality, hence my example at the beginning of people who deny they may lose their job.

Quite frankly, it takes a lot for people to change. How many people still smoke despite the high risk of cancer? How many people are way overweight, despite the risks of heart disease?

This leads us to a very basic question in communications.

How do you overcome this 'denial' mechanism people have?

Is it best to keep hitting them over the head with the bad consequences of their decisions, or is there a better way?

People tend to be protective of their habits, be they good or bad, and they will defend them and may be closed to positive suggestions. You may be trying to be helpful, suggesting how a process at work may be changed, but remember, people don't like change, so expect negative reactions and forge ahead anyway. In fact, one of the biggest obstacles that salespeople face is this resistance to change

So how can we get people to listen to our new ideas and convince them to change?

The one step, that I heard which made sense, was said by a VP of Communications for a major company. She said that the secret to communications was "subtle pressure consistently applied."

Think about that.

"Subtle pressure consistently applied."

Closely applied with that philosophy was another statement she made. "Whenever two or more are gathered, preach the gospel."

Moving on, I think that the best public relations book that

anyone can buy is *How To Win Friends and Influence People* by Dale Carnegie.

I also know that any attempt to change anyone's habits, at work or at home, must start with credibility, what the Greeks called ethos.

Why do you choose a doctor, a dentist, a mechanic, a financial planner? You trust them. They have established their credibility with you.

Look, I know I haven't given anyone the ultimate answer on how to sell your ideas and concepts to people. I do know that it is never easy, any good communicator must know that denial runs deep and that any attempt to introduce change must begin with the communicator's credibility.

27

It is always fun to make up country song titles. These country songs are geared towards surviving the recession. Well, some people call it a recession. As the old quote goes, "A recession is when your neighbor is out of a job. A depression is when you are out of a job."

These country songs make for a great introduction; then you can say, "Well, as they say, if you play a country song backwards, you get your wife, dog and job back. Thank God, we don't have to write a country song about our company, as we are doing well and let me share some highlights with you…"

Quote: I don't like country music, but I don't mean to denigrate those who do. And for the people who like country music, denigrate means 'put down'.
~Bob Newhart

Country Songs for the Recession
• I Want a Woman that Bounces Like My Checks

- She Used to Be the Only Stimulus I Needed
- I Don't Mind the Overtime
- She's Asking for Toast in the Breadline
- Honey, Pour Me Another Bottle of Whine
- Our Accounts are Sinking, so I am Drinking
- I'm Collecting Bills While She Collected my Bill
- She Gave Me a Line in the Unemployment Line
- My Stocks Done Got Slaughtered in the Wall Street Stockyard
- Jesus is the Only Savings Account I Have
- My Interest in You Ain't Compounding
- I Want a Beer as Cold as a Banker's Heart
- My Hand's Out for a Handout
- That No Account Stole My Bank Account
- My Baby Done Left Me – One Less Mouth to Feed
- My Dog Died – We're Having Stew Tonight
- Next Time You Cheat, Honey – Pick a Rich Man
- All My Exes Moved Back In
- I Have those Foreclosure Blues
- Bubba Shot the Banker
- Don't Believe My Wallet Can Stand Another Bailout
- I Thought Only Jail Birds Got Bailed Out
- All My Taxes Go to Texas
- Guess My Credits Cards were Bigger than Your Wallet
- My Double-Wide has Doubled Back to the Bank
- I am Going to Live Forever, I Can't Afford to Die
- I Love You, Honey, But Your Sister's Richer
- The Pool Table and Me Have Empty Pockets
- If You Can't Be Good, Get an MBA
- My Heart Ain't the Only Thing that's Broke
- If You Got the Money Honey, I've Got the Time (by Hank Williams)
- I'm Here to Get My Banker Out of Jail
- Jesus Don't Look, I Ain't Turning the Other Cheek
- Welcome to Dumpsville, Population Me

- Another good song for bankers: Is It Cold in Here, or Is it Just You?
- This Depression is Depressing Me
- Madoff Got the Gold Mine, I Got the Shaft
- I Still Miss My Banker but My Aim is Getting Better
- Take This Job and Shove It – That Was a Joke, I Am So Sorry!!!
- My Pension Plan Is As Gone as You
- My Job and Wife Told Me Good By – I Will Miss My Job
- She's as Faithful as My Stockbroker
- The GM Song: Buying Toyotas Toyed With Me
- I'm Living Off Bones, My Boss is Living Off Bonuses
- Goodbye Small Town USA
- God is Great, Beer is Good, the Economy is Crazy
- I Am Feeling Lower than the Stock Market
- The Only Real Estate I Got is Reality

28

Many programs that companies start, fail. Why is that? After the big lunch launching the program, after the reward system you set up for employees, the program still flops, arrives at the customer service center DOA. So the question becomes, "How do I get my employees to back my programs, how do I get their commitment?" The answer is simple. To sell a program, you must sell a sense of purpose, something that is on a higher level, than just making money.

The speech below explains how important the concept of purpose is. It is a complete speech you can give managers on the importance of installing a sense of purpose in employees. And again, feel free to go through the speech and steal material for your other speeches. Interestingly enough the speech can also double as a "How-To Write a Mission Statement" speech.

Quote: The purpose of life is a life of purpose.

~Robert Byrne

Why Your Employees Need a Sense of Purpose

Think about this: If there is no sense of obligation to a larger entity, be it a company, or a state, or a nation, why shouldn't every man be in it for himself?

The classic example was the buffalo herds. There was no one 'in charge' of the buffalo herds and every man shot as many buffalo as he could. After all, the more buffalo I shoot, the more money I make selling hides. There was no sense of obligation to preserve the buffalo, there was no greater purpose, the only objective was to make money.

Whoops, we almost bypassed an important word – **Purpose**. Buffalo hunting was merely about making money, with no sense of a higher purpose.

That brings us to the gist of this speech. If you want your company to succeed, you must establish a sense of loyalty and purpose in your employees. They must have a purpose they are working for. And that will lead us to mission statements, eventually.

But let's talk about purpose. Let's say you are a tree chopper and the first day your boss tells you to go chop ten trees. You do that and the boss is so pleased that the next day he asks you to chop 12 trees. You take your handy little ax, stroll out to the forest and chop down 12 trees. Well this continues, and at the end of the month, the boss has you chopping down 20 trees a day.

But you are dissatisfied, as you realize this could go on forever. The boss can keep raising the number of trees you chop down, until one day you lay down exhausted and just can't chop down any more trees. Heck, then he will replace you and get someone younger and stronger to chop down trees.

The boss has given you no purpose for chopping down trees. He didn't inspire you by saying how the trees you chopped down help make homes for people or a wooden deck where friends and family could gather. That would at least give you a sense of purpose, a reason to keep cutting down trees.

And while the boss had you chop down trees, you were feeling used. When you became worn out, why wouldn't he cast you aside? He didn't show his loyalty by offering vacations, benefits, bonuses.

And the boss had violated a basic tenet of bossdom. Whenever two or more employees are gathered, tell them, and keep telling them the purpose of their work. Stress the higher goal you, as a team, are all working for.

This all can be quickly encapsulated by the classic story of brick layers.

A gentleman saw three men laying bricks. He approached the first and asked, *"What are you doing?"*

Annoyed, the first man answered, *"What does it look like I'm doing? I'm laying bricks!"*

He walked over to the second who replied, *"Oh, I'm making a living."*

He asked the third bricklayer the same question, *"What are you doing?"*

The third looked up, smiled and said, *"I'm building a cathedral."*

The third man had a sense of purpose.

Okay, I apologize for that old story. But it does lead us to the importance of mission statements. Do not think of them as mission statements. They are really purpose statements and are designed to let employees and customers know why your company exists. Of course the obvious answer is "to make money", but as we saw with our tree-chopping story, that answer will rarely inspire employees or give them a 'sense of purpose', a higher calling if you will.

So I repeat, your mission statement is really your purpose statement.

Consider this rather lengthy mission statement from Starbucks: **To inspire and nurture the human spirit – one person, one cup, and one neighborhood at a time. Here are the principles of how we live that every day:**

Our Coffee

It has always been, and will always be, about quality. We're passionate about ethically sourcing the finest coffee beans, roasting them with great care, and improving the lives of people who grow them. We care deeply about all of this; our work is never done.

Our Partners

We're called partners, because it's not just a job, it's our passion. Together, we embrace diversity to create a place where each of us can be ourselves. We always treat each other with respect and dignity. And we hold each other to that standard.

Our Customers

When we are fully engaged, we connect with, laugh with, and uplift the lives of our customers – even if just for a few moments. Sure, it starts with the promise of a perfectly made beverage, but our work goes far beyond that. It's really about human connection.

Our Stores

When our customers feel this sense of belonging, our stores become a haven, a break from the worries outside, a place where you can meet with friends. It's about enjoyment at the speed of life – sometimes slow and savored, sometimes faster. Always full of humanity.

Our Neighborhood

Every store is part of a community, and we take our responsibility to be good neighbors seriously. We want to be invited in wherever we do business. We can be a force for positive action – bringing together our partners, customers, and the community to contribute every day. Now we see that our responsibility – and our potential for good – is even larger. The world is looking to Starbucks to set the new standard, yet again. We will lead.

Our Shareholders

We know that as we deliver in each of these areas, we enjoy the kind of success that rewards our shareholders. We are fully accountable to get each of these elements right so that Starbucks – and everyone it touches – can endure and thrive.

Onward

Okay, some of that may sound like nonsense to you. But you have to admire what Starbucks is trying to accomplish with that mission statement. Above all, they are trying to tell their employees, customers and communities why they exist. The PURPOSE behind Starbucks. And if employees buy into that purpose, they won't see Starbucks as a commons, where they grab what they want and leave. Employees will see themselves as part of a community effort, striving towards some basic, worthwhile goals.

Let's take a quick gander at McDonald's mission statement:

"McDonald's vision is to be the world's best quick service restaurant experience. Being the best means providing outstanding quality, service, cleanliness, and value, so that we make every customer in every restaurant smile."

Okay – again note the sense of purpose embedded in that mission statement. "To make every customer smile."

Finally State Farm sells insurance. And I have been meaning to talk to my agent about my high premiums. But for employees, State Farm makes it clear that they exist for a purpose higher than selling insurance. Again note the sense of purpose embedded in the mission statement:

State Farm: "To educate and build relationships with our current and future customers. To establish and preserve our neighborhoods and schools, and to demonstrate the good neighbor philosophy through our education and safety programs, volunteer efforts and our alliances with many diverse communities."

Okay, let's wrap this up.

You always want to avoid "The Problems of the Commons" in

your company, where every employee, much like a buffalo hunter, is in it for themselves. To imbue a sense of belonging and teamwork in employees, you must take their work out of the mundane world of hourly labor and imbue it with a sense of purpose. And you must communicate that sense of purpose to employees "when and wherever two or more are gathered."

That sense of purpose must be crystallized in a mission statement. View a mission statement more as a 'purpose statement' stating the higher reasons your company exists.

29

You might belong to a civic club or a group like Junior Achievement. And you have to give a speech about business. Here is a complete speech you can use to teach students or even employees how to make a good speech. Plus this makes a great handout you can pass onto employees who want to improve their speaking skills. Think of the following as a 'five minute' course in how to give a speech.

Quote: The very best impromptu speeches are the ones written well in advance.
~Ruth Gordon

Ten Key Steps to a Great Speech

No matter where you end up in business, you will have to give speeches to employees, shareholders, customers. So here are some key rules for giving a speech.

- All speeches follow a basic pattern, "Tell them what you are going to say, say it, tell them what you said."
- You do not need to open with a joke, despite what everyone tells you. Chances are the audience has heard the joke before and will

laugh politely – and they are really thinking is, "What a lame joke." Plus why waste time looking for jokes to open your speech, when you should be focusing on what message you want your audience to walk away with?

- The best opening is to compliment your audience. This creates an instance rapport with your audience. For instance, "I am very flattered to be asked to speak to you tonight. I recognize that you are all outstanding professionals and am honored to share some thoughts with you tonight about _____."

- Know the organization you are speaking to. For instance if you are addressing the Society of Professional Engineers, do some research and find out how long the organization has been in existence, some milestones it has accomplished, some famous members and perhaps its future goals. You can add these to your opening, showing that you care about the organization that they belong to.

- Know your audience. Why did they invite you? What are their main concerns? What do they want to learn from your speech? You cannot guess at what they want. Talk to someone who scheduled the speech and find out what THEY want you to discuss. Not what YOU want to discuss.

- Don't get fancy. Simply say, "I am here tonight to talk about _____." For instance, you might say, "I am here to talk about the importance of sales training to an organization."

- Next – don't cover too much in a speech. Cover three key points. After you introduce your topic, break it into three key points. For example, "There are three important reasons that you should have a comprehensive training program for your salespeople. First, a comprehensive training session will help them to use their time wisely. Two, it will help them identify leads they might miss. And third, it will teach them the importance of follow-up and closing the sales."

- The three key points are the outline of the speech. Let's look at our example of why organizations need a comprehensive sales training program. You will cover:

a. Using time wisely.

b. Identifying and finding leads.

c. Follow up and closing a sales.

Bingo, there are the three main parts of your speech.

- Back up each section with specific examples, stats and a good war story. For instance, look at the first point you want to make, Using Time Wisely. Tell the audience how people who go through professional sales training are 50% more efficient. Tell the audience the key ways that salespeople waste time. Then tell a story. Audiences love stories. Tell a specific story about someone who went through sales training and how he or she increased the use of their time, how they became more efficient.

- The ending. Tell them what you said. Simply repeat the three key points you covered, emphasize why they are important. Then thank the audience for letting you speak and once again tell them how great they are and how honored you were to speak with them. Politeness goes a long way!

That's all folks. Remember there are three key parts to every speech. In the opening, you told them, 'What you were going to say'. You clearly laid out your main topic and the three key issues you would cover. Then 'You say it'. You covered your three key points and brought them home to the audience with stats, examples and a great story. Then you wrapped up the speech 'Telling them what you said'. You emphasized your key points and reminded them why the points were important.

See giving a speech is not that hard. Just stick to your main topic, reinforce your three key points and you will be a hit. Don't worry about being a comic or entertaining the audience. They want you to be professional and share important information with them.

And, of course, make sure that your fly is not at half mast or your blouse is unbuttoned.

30

Again if you have to talk to a group of students, here is a great speech on PowerPoint. This can also be used to help employees improve their communication skills. And it can be copied as a handout to pass out to employees to improve their communication skills.

> Quote: There are many true statements about complex topics that are too long to fit on a PowerPoint slide.
> ~Edward Tufte

15 Key Steps for a Good PowerPoint

Please don't torture your audience with a bad PowerPoint. Please consider these tips.

- Do you really need to use a PowerPoint? With a PowerPoint it is tough to connect with your audience, to make contact with them. Many times with a PowerPoint, people dim the lights. This gives your audience an opportunity to sleep.
- If you deem that a PowerPoint is necessary, remember the audience is thinking about other things too. Picking up the dry cleaning, why is Jonny flunking math, did I pay the electric bill? Always give them a handout after the speech which they can use to remember the key points.
- Offer to e-mail the presentation to anyone who wants a copy. Then, they can print it out and share it with their fellow workers.
- Your first slide should clearly state what your topic will cover. For example: Five Key Ways to Increase Sales.
- Never put a mission statement on a PowerPoint. They are boring, no one pays attention to them and it shows unoriginality.
- Never use paragraphs on a PowerPoint. People will be so busy reading the paragraph that they won't hear you.
- If you make the mistake of putting a paragraph on a slide, don't

torture your audience by reading it aloud to them. They have all gone to school and can read for themselves. Spare all of us the pain. Instead, simply say, "Please take a moment and read this paragraph."

- Use bullet points and limit each slide to three bullet points at the most. If your slide has ten bullet points on it, you have overwhelmed your audience and destroyed the very reason you use bullet points.
- Think of bullet points as talking points.
- Use very simple graphs. Bar graphs and pie charts are nice. A graph with a bunch of lines looks like one of those machines you hook up to a heart patient.
- This is in black and white. See how easy it is to read. My point? Keep it simple. You are not Walt Disney. You are not there to entertain, but rather to get your point across. Black and white can accomplish that easily and quickly.
- Your type should at least be 28 points. Bigger if possible. That way the people in back can see it.
- Don't get fancy. Don't use all the crap when the slide spins onto the screen or SLOWLY appears on the screen. It is very clever, sure, but your audience has seen clever graphics thousands of time and just wants you to get to the point.
- Don't put in clever sound effects. Please!
- Remember you are there to communicate information. Do it as clearly and concisely as possible. Don't say we lost $135,723 dollars this quarter. Just say we lost about $136,000 this quarter.

31

Oddservations are just funny observations you can start a speech with. You can choose some oddservations from the list below and say: "Have you ever wondered why _____?" Then you can say, "One thing we shouldn't wonder is _____." Everyone has

strange thoughts during the day that can be used as 'Oddservations'. Write down some of your Oddservations and work them into your speech.

Quote: You know an odd feeling? Sitting on the toilet eating a chocolate candy bar.

~George Carlin

Some Oddservations

- Never go drinking with a clown. How can you tell if he's drunk? His nose is already red and he falls down for laughs.
- I think that parking meters should have roll-over minutes. You get back to your car and if you have 50 cents on the meter, you push a button and you get your money back, at least 50 minutes worth.
- Why can your wife go out with her girlfriends, but people laugh when you go out with your boyfriends?
- If you have red hair, you are a redhead. So if you have black hair are you a blackhead? If you have blond hair are you a whitehead?
- Do homeless kids have homework?
- You buttered your bread, now lie in it.
- Down South, you might could've gone to your mamma's, if you hadn't been fixing to get knee crawling drunk.
- What a chore for Sally to sell cell phones by the sea shore but for the chore how many cell phones can Sally sell by the sea shore?
- Don't cats always look like they are posing for pictures?
- Doesn't the beat in every country music song always sound like someone is riding a horse in the background? You have the canter, the trot, the gallop...
- Would you rather have a man or woman boss?
- I would hate to fill a clown's shoes.
- Death is a tough act to follow.
- One day we will all look back on this and plow into a parked car.
- If I buy two Ford Focus autos, do I have Foci?

• How come you never see a baby squirrel?

I hate team building exercises, but here are some that might be tolerable: Get drunk for lunch. Give the boss a wedgie. How many body parts can you Xerox? The customer is an idiot. Write a Mission Statement over three Beers, two whiskeys and three martinis. Explain this phrase, "Nobody would get into anything if they knew what they were getting into."

32

Many companies hire 'creativity consultants'. Many companies host seminars on creativity. Actually creativity is not that complicated. Try to think outside the box. Isn't it amazing how a cliché can really explain creativity?

Here is a short speech on creativity you can deliver to students, your sales force, a local civic group. Also you do not have to use the whole speech. You can simply use some of the stories in it. Or you can add stories of your own; good stories to add include stories about how your employees have been creative and helped the company. This accomplishes two purposes. It recognizes employees and shares a story that is close to home, a story about someone your audience may know.

Quote: A hunch is creativity trying to tell you something.
~Frank Capra

The Key to Creativity

Creativity takes a new way of looking at the obvious. Let me offer some examples.

When I was a child, it was complicated to make a heavy bat. To make a heavy bat, filled with lead that on-deck hitters could warm up with, you would drill a hole in the bat, melt the lead, pour the lead into the bat and let it cool. Bingo, a heavy, lead-filled bat.

That is the way that coaches, for years, made on-deck bats.

Then Elston Howard, a Yankee catcher and the first black player on the Yankees, who probably in his later years spent too much time in the bullpen, had an idea. He asked, "Why do we drill a hole and fill the bat with lead. Why don't we make a lead donut and just drop it over the bat?"

Bingo! And it worked. Plus the hitter could drop the lead over his own bat. Warm up with it. Take the lead donut off and use the bat to hit with.

The point is, Elston looked at things in a different way which is the epitome of creativity.

Next, let's discuss how an outsider can bring a fresh perspective, a new way of looking at the obvious. In every school for years, the high school football field was right next to the soccer field. Right next to it! And soccer players kick a football ALL day long. They were kicking specialists. But NO ONE noticed. Not one coach figured out that, "Hey, we can kick soccer style."

So, for years, no one figured out that the best way to kick a football was from the side, not straight on.

It took a kid from Hungary to show them. And even that was by accident, because his high school did not have a soccer team.

Pete Gogolak was the first kicker who kicked sideways. He emigrated from Hungary in 1956 and joined the NY Giants in 1965. He explains that when he kicked soccer style at a mass kicking tryout at Ogdensburg High School, he confused everyone. No one had seen anything like it. Gogolak stood at a 45-degree angle, confusing his holder.

"I'll never forget the expression on my holder's face. He said, 'Hey, Gogolak, in this country you line up straight. If you line up that way, you'll either hit it into the stands or hit me in the butt.'" Gogolak said.

The first football season was in 1869. It took almost 100 years for football to figure out that you kicked a ball sideways. The point, it took an outsider to show the establishment a new way of looking at things.

Before the can opener, cans were opened with a hammer and chisel. For 48 years they opened cans with a hammer and chisel or used a knife to jab around the can. What the hell, it worked.

Then along came American Ezra Warnet, who invented the can opener. But wait ! Here is an example of how strong tradition is. It took people ten more years to throw away the hammer and chisel. The can opener only became popular when it was given away for free with canned beef.

But what was Ezra's insight? People were used to opening cans with a stabbing, jabbing motion, much like the field goal kickers who were used to kicking the ball straight.

Ezra said, "Hey, why not use a circular motion. A can is round. Let's use a round motion."

He threw out tradition. That is SO important. He THREW out tradition.

Okay, the lead donut, soccer-style field goal kicking, and the can opener. Each one was invented YEARS after football, baseball and the can were introduced. What took so long?

People had accepted, "This is the way it is done." And closed their minds to new ideas, new concepts.

Make sure you don't make the same mistake.

33

Here is an extensive list of things you hate to see. You can always add you own ideas to the list. It makes a great speech opening. You can say: "Here are some things I hate to see_____." Then you can segue into your speech with: "And some of the things I hate to see in our industry include _____."

Quote: Even a paranoid can have enemies.

~Henry Kissinger

50 Things You Hate to See

- Flashing blue lights in your rear view mirror and empty beer cans on the floor
- Flashing blue lights in your garage in the morning and wondering how they got there
- An IRS envelope in your mailbox
- No tire iron in your trunk
- A flat spare tire
- That little red oil light
- Any gas price sign
- Red spots on your private parts
- Letter announcing upcoming teacher conferences
- The blue screen of death on your computer
- Any new improved Windows program
- Any politician who says he has an alcohol problem and that he is why he had an affair
- The Red Sox win – Anything
- Big women in spandex
- Flabby men in muscle shirts
- Your 33 year old kid on your doorstep with a suitcase and a note pinned on him from his ex-wife
- Religious fanatics knocking on your door
- One more righteous politician talking about global warming
- An empty bourbon bottle
- A cab driver with two empty bourbon bottles next to him
- A secretary called Bambi
- A doctor called Bubba
- Your summer electric bill
- Your winter heating bill
- Credit card statements AFTER Christmas
- An unbuckled child

- Your pilot drinking next to you in the airport lounge
- Your priest next to you at the topless bar
- A politician with his hand in your pocket
- Your neighbor buying a pit bull
- A vengeful woman
- Your kid's cell phone bill
- Your kid walks five batters in a row
- An ambulance driver who always gets lost
- A police car AFTER you go through the stop sign
- A long red light
- A short green light
- A surgeon called Shaky
- A neglected child
- A struggling single mother
- A tractor ball pitcher – he keeps plowing the ground with the ball because he throws his pitches in the dirt
- A computer virus
- A new government regulation
- Your ex's number on caller-ID
- A doctor reach for his rubber gloves
- Cold French fries
- Warm beer
- A flag-covered coffin
- Bed sores on nursing home patients
- Another list like this

34

Here is a funny list you can pick and choose from. It is called "30 Ways to Tell if Your Brakes are Bad". You can start your speech by saying, "I would like to share some ways you can tell your brakes are bad." Then segue into, "And here are the signs we need to look for to see if our customer service is…"

Quote: I couldn't repair your brakes, so I made your horn louder. ~Anon

30 Ways to Tell If Your Brakes Are Bad

I have seen some articles that ask, "How Do You Know When You Need a Brake Job."

I am not an expert, but this should be easy to answer, in fact here 30 ways to tell if your brakes are shot. Remember you have precious cargo riding in your car. You have that 24 pack of beer in your trunk. Oh yeah and your family. So the safest thing to do is give the car away to someone you hate, leave it parked on the street with the keys in it, or actually break down and go to a repair shop and get the brakes fixed.

Key warning signs it's time to get new brakes:

- You can only stop by pulling on the emergency brake.
- Your breaks squeal louder than a crooked politician.
- Your brakes have more miles on them than Cloris Leachman.
- Other drivers get angry when you rear-end them just to stop.
- You start coasting up to stop signs when you are a mile away.
- You hear a screeching sound and your mother-in-law is not in the car.
- You WANT your ex-wife to drive your car. Fast!
- Your last brake job was when you bought the Ford Fairlane.
- You have a 50-50 chance of stopping at red lights.
- You stop by running into the back of the garage.
- All the neighborhood kids jump out of the way when they see you driving.
- That annoying brake light NEVER goes off.
- You pour ten gallons of brake fluid into the reservoir every month.
- You have to pump the brakes 50 times to even slow the car down.
- You envy Fred Flintstone and the way he and Barney stopped their car.

- There's that funny smoke coming from the back tires.
- Everyone refuses to ride with you. Even your dog.
- You always stop the car by slamming the gears into Park.
- You always slow down by shifting to first.
- When you stop, the car pulls more to the right than a conservative politician.
- You wave happily at cops as you coast through stop signs.
- Driving. It's not a job. It's an adventure.
- There is always a stream of brake fluid running down your driveway.
- Convenience store clerks hide under the counter when they see you pull into the parking lot.
- You go downhill REALLY fast.
- Your brakes grind more than your coffee maker.
- You drive 25 miles an hour on the freeway. Just in case.
- Insurance agents cry when you walk into their office.
- Your chances of stopping are as high as Palin being our next President.
- Stop on a dime? Hell, you couldn't stop on a runway at LaGuardia.

Okay it's time we put a stop to this. Sorry – couldn't resist.

35

Here is a list of "Things You Discover Too Late". You can pick and choose items from this list. You can say, "Let me share some humorous things that many of us learn too late," then segue into, "Let me share with you some things we don't want to learn too late at _____."

Quote: Experience is a good school. But the fees are high.
~Heinrich Heine

Things You Discover Too Late

- The cop with the radar gun.
- No toilet paper in the stall.
- The fish WAS too raw to eat.
- The hole in the mosquito netting.
- It really was poison ivy.
- No brake fluid.
- The toilet seat was up AFTER you sat down.
- She did LIKE your best friend.
- Don't blame everything on MOOD SWINGS. It might be you.
- Don't brush your teeth in the dark. Preparation H and toothpaste both come in tubes.
- You do need to be best friends first.
- Your parents were right – pretty much about everything.
- You do learn the hard way.
- The electric company is serious about shutting off your power.
- Check the transmission fluid.
- The IRS has no sense of humor.
- After the second drink, cheap bourbon and expensive bourbon taste the same. Now that would have saved some money.
- She WAS the best thing in your life.
- Protected sex is cheaper than a baby.
- Love is blind. It can also be deaf and dumb.
- Life's tough, it's tougher if you don't learn from your mistakes.
- A sense of humor in a mate goes a long way.
- It would have been cheaper to call a cab.
- Little things add up. Five bucks a day on Starbucks is $150 a month.
- The only normal people are the ones you don't know well.
- Your kids do pick your nursing home.
- It is important to check out your spouse's parents. The seed doesn't fall far from the tree.
- You did need to check your cell phone charge.
- There are no bathrooms after that truck stop you just passed.

- Boats are expensive.
- Buying a summer cabin gives you two houses to take care of.
- He is married.
- There is a reason bars are dark. She looked so much younger.
- Never propose when you are drunk.
- Never play cards with a man called Doc, never eat at a place called Mom's and never sleep with a woman crazier than you.
- For my son: The importance of having a job and income when you start dating.
- Always check the expiration date on the milk.
- Never accept a drink from an urologist.
- It takes a village to raise an idiot. It takes parents to raise a child.
- Shut up and listen.
- When in a hole, quit digging.
- You determine your mood.
- You can't be THAT stupid, but you are.
- You succeed through failure.
- "You can get more with a kind word and a gun than you can with a kind word alone." – Al Capone.
- Life is too short. Ask her out! You will never see her again if you don't.
- Don't race trains to the crossing.
- When dating don't ask, "Can I change him." Ask, "Is this the worse he is going to get?"
- When coaching a kid's team, never say, "What could happen?"
- The keys locked inside the car.
- Tattoos are forever.
- Pit bulls don't like to be teased.
- Neither do their owners.
- You left the coffee pot on.
- You left the water running.
- Your Triple A membership ran out last week.
- Barking dogs do bite.
- Your wife doesn't like you having a girlfriend.

- Your kid lied about having car insurance.
- He wasn't the only fish in the sea.
- You're allergic to shellfish.
- That was a rattlesnake.
- Your friend is NOT an expert on wild mushrooms.
- Tongue piercings do get infected.
- He's never really planned to leave his wife.
- The movie did deserve only one star.
- The restaurant employees didn't wash their hands.
- You're over your credit limit. AFTER you ate that fancy dinner.
- Your gas gauge isn't working.
- The flashlight has no batteries.
- You should have paid attention when they evacuated for the hurricane.
- Your husband lied when he said he was a long distance truck driver.
- Don't feed the bears.
- There were reasons her other husbands left.
- That tracing device your wife's private investigator left on the car.
- You didn't know everything at 18.
- You ain't going to live forever.
- You did have high blood pressure.

36

Here is a humorous speech you can give to students or employees on "How NOT to use PowerPoint".

Or you can open your speech by saying, "We have all seen PowerPoints from Hell. Here are some tips on how to make a bad PowerPoint." Then share some of the points and say, "You will be relieved that I will not follow any of those tips. In fact we spent a lot of time and effort building the PowerPoint you will see, because we think the subject is crucial to our success."

You can also use the below tips as a humorous handout before the meeting and people can read it before you speak. Then you can say, "Much as I would like to follow the tips I passed out, you will be glad to hear that I have too much respect for you as an audience to make you suffer through a bad PowerPoint. And I think the subject we are going to discuss requires your full attention because..."

Quote: It's not how strongly you feel about your topic, it's how strongly they feel about your topic after you speak.
~Tim Salladay

Here are Some Tips on How to Create "The PowerPoint Presentation from Hell"

- Be sure to find the longest mission statement and put it on one slide. Audiences love nothing better than a long block of copy, in small type, all jammed onto one slide. And, of course, make sure you read the mission statement as slowly as you can, because the audience cannot read. And ignore the snoring from the back. It couldn't be because you took five very painful minutes to read a mission statement that no one cared about.
- Make the audience guess what your presentation is about. Heck, everyone loves a good mystery. Do not have a title slide that at least gives the audience a hint about your topic. Audiences love to sit until halfway through the presentation. They love to wait until that light bulb comes on and they say to themselves, "OH! That is what he is speaking about."
- Find a font that no one can read. Like Algerian, Bauhaus, Bernard, Blackadder, Bradley Hand, Brush Script. Yes, be sure to use what we call an 'eye-strain' font.
- Use lots of clever transitions in your PowerPoint. Be sure the slides take forever to appear on the screen, because they fade, spin, do jumping jacks and go out for a cup of coffee. Everybody loves waiting ten minutes for each slide to appear.

- Use bullet points. They make your ideas stand out. In fact bullet points are so good, use lots and lots of them. Try to set a record for jamming as many as possible on one slide. I think the record of bullet points is held by a scientist in England. He was able to jam twenty on one slide. But come on, go for the gold. You can beat that record.

- Charts and graphs are good. But don't make them simple. Make them as complicated as the Los Angeles freeway system, where they stack one freeway over another and another and another. Put as many numbers and lines as you can in the graph. That way no one will have any idea what the graph represents and your expertise will never be questioned.

- Throw in some bad grammar. And some spelling missteaks. That should show your lack of prrof reading and It will keep the audience amused and enhance their respect ofr you. o rmaybe not.

- Forget about contrast. It is way overrated. Put white words on a yellow background. And if you combine that background with an 'eye-strain' font, you can put anything you please on the slide, as no one can read it anyway.

- Test the equipment? Why should you do that? Go into the room and fumble with the computer for a good ten minutes then give the audience a dazed look and say something stupid like, "Gosh it worked yesterday" or "Gee we seem to be having technical difficulties" or the audience's favorite: " Can anyone come up here and fix this?" When you can't run the equipment the audience thinks the only technical difficulty in the room is your brain. And messing up the equipment is a sure way to help management lose confidence in your abilities.

- Make sure that your graphics have nothing to do whatever with your material. Be talking about how to keep your dog safe during a storm and show a picture of a clown. Be talking about how to refinance your mortgage and show a race car going around the track. This will keep your audience terribly confused, but they will be fascinated by the dead cat photo you show while discussing buying a new car.

- Of course we have saved the best for last. The people in the back of the room don't need to see your slides. Heck, if they were that interested, they could sit up front. So make the type on the slides as small as possible. I would go with 8 point type. In a script no one can read, with yellow on a white background. Is that the perfect presentation or what? Of course assume that everyone wants a copy of this masterpiece so jam up everyone's e-mail by sending them multiple copies. You just can't have too much of a good thing.

37

And here is a fun list you can use in early fall when school is beginning. Again you can pick and choose from the list or add your own. You can say, "With school beginning, I thought I would share some things you should not say on the first day of school. Then you can segue into, "And there are some things we should not say to our customers..."

Quote: If there were no schools to take the children away from home part of the time, the insane asylums would be filled with mothers.
~Edgar W. Howe

The Top 30 Things Not To Say to Your Child on the First Day of School

- Kiss a pretty girl for me.
- Don't worry. We are renting out your room and you can sleep in the gym.
- Sure, you can take your pet snake for show and tell.
- Food fights are fun.

- Be good and you will be lonely.
- See if a hundred dollars will buy you an A.
- I am not packing your lunch. Steal that Johnson kid's lunch money.
- Was your teacher hot?
- Those that can, do. Those who can't, teach.
- Do you know that the bottom quarter of every entering college class goes into teaching.
- Heck, she's had all summer off. Make her earn her money.
- Is your gun loaded?
- Sleep late, nothing happens on the first day anyway.
- There are ways of getting around that security screening.
- Is your flask full?
- Boy, did your teacher sleep around in college.
- You can't take both, you have to choose. Either the handgun or the whiskey.
- Tell your teacher that your dad didn't mean to embarrass her at the strip club. Everyone needs a summer job.
- Don't hide the principal's toupee this year.
- Remember "No child left behind". They gotta pass you.
- Don't run a tattoo parlor out of your locker. That really pissed off the principal last year. Use the janitor's closet. It might be better.
- It's a free country. Tell the teacher you'll damn well smoke where you please.
- I put a beer in your lunchbox. We were out of milk.
- Algebra is for sissies. You will never need it.
- When you write about "What I Did This Summer", leave out the part about the sheriff and the meth lab – okay?
- Screw them if they can't take a joke.
- Sure you can do anything you want on the Internet at school.
- Last time I checked, we lived in AMERICA!
- If you mix the right chemicals at the lab, we're talking you can close down the school for at least a month.
- Ask the teacher out for a drink after school, she had a tough day.

• Don't let that priest behind you.

38

Many people trap themselves in a box and think they have to work for somebody. But there are plenty of job opportunities where you can be your own boss and create your own business. Just look around your neighborhood at all the small businesses ranging from the accountant working out of his house, to the local insurance agent, to the immigrant who opens a restaurant, to the man who started his own lawn service, to your neighbor who took a chance and opened his own coffee shop. Here is a free motivational speech you can use to urge people to create their own opportunities. This can be a speech for Junior Achievement, for a civic club, for students, for a career fair. Feel free to replace the stories in the speech with stories of your own.

> Quote: The critical ingredient is getting off your butt and doing something. It's as simple as that. A lot of people have ideas, but there are few who decide to do something about them now. Not tomorrow. Not next week. But today. The true entrepreneur is a doer, not a dreamer.
> ~Nolan Bushnell, founder of Atari and Chuck E. Cheese's

Do You Have a Serf Mentality: Create Your Own Opportunities
What bothers me about people in America is that we have developed a serf mentality. We feel like we have to work for somebody and when the economy gets bad, we sit at our desks, worrying about being laid off. We worry about who will pay our health insurance, who will take care of us.

Here's a news flash. Get rid of the serf mentality. The fear that you have to work for somebody. That you need a corporation or business to provide for you. Create your own opportunities.

Chances are you will get laid off sooner or later. That is the way America works now. So start preparing now.

I have a friend who was an example of the serf mentality. She used to work in corporate communications and guess what is the first area they cut? That's right – corporate communications. Even worse, she was an executive speechwriter. And guess who the CEO cuts first in corporate communications to show he is 'sharing the pain'. That's right – his speechwriter. Whoops, that would be my friend.

I used to sit at my corporate desk and hear every one rage against the corporation. How it wasn't taking care of them. If they got laid off, who would give them a job, who would give benefits, who would take care of them?

Notice the wrong mentality. It is the serf mentality. *Who* is going to take care of me? If the king kicks me off his land, *who* will take care of me? What other king can I work for?

My friend realized, she sat at her desk, that everyone was worried about the corporation not taking care of them. That she was surrounded by people who had the wrong thought process. The right thought process was expressed by another friend of mine, who ran a small ad agency.

He said, "After a while people have to grow up and learn to create their own opportunities."

And that is a valid question you must ask yourself. Are you still hanging onto the serf mentality, wanting the corporation to take care of you, or are you creating your own opportunities?

Two stories that illustrate my point. I had another friend who knew that sooner or later 'Big Brother' was not going to take care of him. He had to escape the serf mentality and create opportunities for himself. So he completed his Masters in English and that gave him the opportunity to teach for on-line universities out of his house. Plus he created his own website and began selling his writing services. Plus he wrote several books.

In short, my friend was no longer worrying about losing a job. He no longer felt he had to work for someone. He went out and created his own opportunities.

One more story. I knew a man who was laid off by a corporation. And he would sit and fret and send out resumes and try to find another corporation to work for.

Then there was a man called Mario. He was an immigrant and he had no formal education. He went up and down every block, knocking on every door, recruiting clients for his landscaping business. He would cut your grass, plant a tree, trim a hedge...

And Mario was a great businessman.

And a year later, Mario had a big new truck, new mowers and two of his brothers working for him. Mario was busy creating his own opportunities, and my neighbor next door was still sending out resumes.

Are you creating your own opportunities? Or are you still mired in the serf mindset?

39

None of us likes to hear bad news. Here is a list of scary phrases you can work into your speech. You can say, "Here are some humorous scary phrases _____." Then segue into, "And here are some phrases I don't want to hear at our company..."

Quote: He who laughs has not heard the bad news.
~Anon

Phrases You Don't Want to Hear
- You need a root canal.
- You have the right to remain silent...
- Sir, do you know how fast you were going?
- He wasn't wearing a seat belt.
- Another increase in gas prices today.

- And Congress is back in session today.
- Honey, we need to talk.
- I'm sorry, sir, your credit card was declined.
- We have lost a wheel. This might be a rough landing.
- It builds character.
- I know you have been with the company for 15 years, but...
- Thank you for your recent application. We had many candidates for the job and we regret to...
- Well, it is the transmission and...
- Happy 30th birthday.
- Life begins after 40.
- We have reviewed your tax returns and...
- Jones, can you see me in my office?
- I am sorry, sir, the warranty ran out.
- Look on the bright side...
- Your monthly payments have been increased to...
- We're from the government and we're here to help you.
- We're going to have to quarantine you for a few days.
- It's interesting that you should say that...
- Did you back up your data?
- Well, she is taking you back to court, as it seems...
- Wow, that bald spot is growing.
- Whoops, there was a slight mix-up in the lab and...
- Your proctologist called.
- There might be a slight chance of erectile dysfunction.
- We have tickets for the play, Mr. Lincoln.
- "Attila the Who" is outside?
- Today, car executives came back to Washington, seeking another...
- OPEC got together today and decided to...
- We should have New Orleans cleaned up and back to normal by...
- We should have IRAQ stabilized by...
- And we can do it without tax increases.

- You can always put off retirement until…
- Politicians admit that the recovery is taking longer than expected.
- The President is certain that if he can get the Middle East warring factions together at the conference table…
- Today, the biggest federal budget in history was approved by…
- The government will now run health care…
- Look this won't hurt…
- I can't understand. It was a simple operation…
- Don't worry, Mrs. Jones, they have made major advancements in adult diapers…
- Well, it appears that his life insurance policy expired two days before…
- Well I hope you have a sense of humor because…
- What could happen?
- Relax, honey, I know all about electricity.
- Honestly, honey, why waste money on a plumber?
- Hmm, what happens if I pull this wire?
- We regret to inform you…
- Bernie Madoff was handling your portfolio and…
- Today the Dow Jones set a new record, plunging to…
- Honey, do you know where the shut-off valve is?
- It's only a small leak, we should be able to make it back to port.
- Mr. Jones, many men can function without…
- A few more troops on the ground and we…
- Oh, that can't be good.
- You mean it was the other tooth?
- Your tests came back positive.
- Well here's an analogy. We can either rotor rooter your veins or use Liquid Drano.
- The good news is that you are eligible for unemployment.
- It seems that they increased your deductible, so…
- Well at the time it seemed like a good idea, but…
- If I had known at the beginning…

- Well, it wasn't exactly clear but I went ahead and…
- I am sober enough to drive.
- What did you say?
- Hey, it's not exactly perfect, but…
- Well, not exactly a profit…
- We have some questions about these deductions.
- I think we can make it a month or two without health insurance.
- I am positive the gun is not loaded.
- Can you say octuplets?
- You might want to sit down…
- Do you take this man as your…?
- Well you've had a good run with the company, but…
- It seems like our pension fund made some bad investments…
- College tuition will raise another ten percent.
- Dad, I know what I'm doing.
- Honey, who is Bambi?
- Hmm, it seems there is a small problem…
- Normally I am not that far off in my calculations.
- Remember, that was just an estimate.
- Well when we got into the engine, we found…
- I have an idea…
- It happens to a lot of people your age.
- Of course, you have to remember, you're not as young as you were.
- Have you thought about giving up drinking?
- Dear, Jerry Springer is on the phone.
- It's not rocket science, honey, a two year old can figure it.
- Now which terminal is positive, which one is negative?
- Now that's an interesting development.
- What was I thinking?
- Who knew a few zeros could make such a big difference?
- Didn't see that coming.
- I wish it could have worked out differently.
- I love you, but…

- Okay, let's try Plan B.
- Well, we can be just friends.
- What was that?
- How many times have I told you...?
- Well, Mr. Jones, not every kid is college material.
- Hmm, whoops, took a bit too much off the top, Mrs. Jones. But I think we can fix it by...
- Well, your hair didn't come out exactly blonde...
- Everyone gains a few pounds at your age.
- How was I supposed to know?
- Dad, where is the fire extinguisher?
- The Democrats have an overwhelming majority in Congress.
- But this time is different...
- First, we know it's not your fault, but...
- You better call your lawyer.
- With good behavior, you should get out in...

40

Here is a list of things that don't "turn out well". You could say, "I think we will all recognize these things that don't turn out well. They include _____." Then you can segue into the speech by saying, "But let's look at some things that may turn out well for us if _____."

Quote: Good decisions come from experience, and experience comes from bad decisions.
~Anon

Things That Never Turn Out Well
- Relax, the game warden is never around.
- Watch how fast this car can go.
- Oh yes! The Cubs are in the playoffs this year.

- Those weather guys always exaggerate, we can ride out this hurricane.
- Go ahead and have some soup. I am sure the restaurant didn't keep it out all day.
- Just one more drink and I'm going home...
- We never have a pop quiz on Tuesday...
- I really think I can dye my hair at home...
- This outlet isn't working. Let me just unscrew it...
- We have enough gas to make it to the next exit...
- Who needs an annual checkup?
- We'll just cut back by not paying the car insurance.
- Expired license tags? I'll send a check in next week.
- This check won't clear for at least three days.
- All you have to do is go to Dave's and pick up a package. It's an easy $100.
- Hmm, if I just up these deductions, the IRS will never notice.
- The tire doesn't look that flat.
- Relax, your wife will never find out.
- Honey, I bought a motorcycle.
- You can always sell a kidney. You have two of them and the black market...
- Did I leave the iron on?
- He won't turn out like his father.
- I'll check the oil level next week.
- My parents are gone. Why don't you guys come over for a few beers?
- Honey, I don't need directions.
- Layoffs? Naw, I've been with the company 20 years. They need me.
- If we put one trillion into an economic stimulus...
- The brakes feel a bit squishy...
- I am sure that thumping noise is nothing.
- And you can make easy monthly payments...
- Although I am out of town, son, I want you home by twelve.
- It's just a minor throbbing. This toothache should go away.

- Your check's in the mail.
- Have I ever misled you?
- I know I can change him.
- He just needs a good woman in his life.
- I'm pretty sure you can hike there. It doesn't look like poison oak.
- I tell you. You worry too much.
- We will just stay one night at the Bates Motel.
- Don't worry, he can't get out.
- I don't need to wear protection.
- Don't worry about the expiration date, go ahead and drink it.
- Well, I won't get hooked on smoking, I'll...
- We don't need to get to the sale early.
- The house will appreciate in value.
- Look what I ordered off late night TV.
- Just hold this firecracker for a moment.
- The kids know gun safety.
- Sure you can mix beer and vodka.
- I can skip my Prozac for a few days.

41

Another great opening. After you read some items from the list, you can say, "But what I have to say is good news and should not scare you. I am pleased to announce that _____."

Quote: You're born, you die. And in between you make a lot of mistakes.
~Anon

When Anyone Says Any of the Phrases Below — Watch Out!
- I can text and drive.
- This won't hurt.
- Ignore that towing sign. They never tow anyone.

- She'll think it's funny.
- I'll pick up my birth control pills next week.
- How bad can he get?
- You worry too much about what your parents think.
- Sure our career college credits transfer, well not exactly everywhere.
- He'll get over his anger management issues.
- I can study tomorrow.
- I can give you a ball-park estimate.
- Oh, he never bites.
- Sure, you can go ten miles over the speed limit. It's like an unwritten law.
- I can handle my liquor.
- Sure I can live in the same town with my ex.
- Relax, there won't be a line.
- The boss will never catch us, we sneak out we play golf...
- Your dad won't even know the car is gone.
- Don't worry, my husband never comes home early.
- I can drop out of school and start making some real money.
- Heck, she's only been married three times.
- But my restaurant will succeed in this location. Those other guys had bad restaurants.
- I can handle spicy foods.
- He hasn't missed a field goal all year. He is Mr. Reliable.
- Gosh, that sounds like a great deal.
- Heck, an idiot could do it.
- I can cut my own hair.
- Anyone can ride a bull.
- Who needs to wear a helmet?
- What happens if I push thus button?
- The security cameras don't work. They're fake.
- I can double my paycheck at the casino.
- There's never a test on the summer reading list.
- Sure run the red light, there are no cops around.

- The undercurrent is not that bad.
- Who needs a safety harness?
- Who needs sunscreen?
- I'll just disconnect the airbag.
- Relax, our Guard unit will never be deployed.
- There are no sharks in these waters.
- We can win the war in a year.
- Sure I'm the governor, but they will never find out. I ran on a platform of family values.
- So what's two extra sleeping pills?
- It's a private lake, but the fish are public.
- Small town cops are stupid.
- To be honest with you…
- I'll put the check in the mail tomorrow.
- He has not given a home run up all year with the bases loaded.

And there you have it. Phrases that never work out well. Yet, there is always the hope that they will. Isn't that what makes us humans? Our faith in our fellow man.

42

A funny list of things you should never say to a Hell's Angel. After reading some items from the list, you could say, "And here are some things we should not say to our customers…"

Quote: There are no mistakes in life, only lessons.
~Anon

In the interest of self-preservation, here are –

Things You Should Never Say to a Hell's Angel
- Harley Davidson. Is that your boyfriend?

- Who hit you with the ugly stick?
- Get on your little bike and pedal home.
- When are you taking her back to the zoo?
- So do you like Harley between your legs?
- Is that Smell Angels?
- What? You majored in Dumb at Reform School.
- When are you going to take the training wheels off?
- Hey, Tinker Bell.
- Tell your old lady the new line of 2013 brooms is in.
- I wouldn't wear a helmet either. A brain injury might make you smarter.
- Isn't it time for your yearly bath?
- Are you gay?
- So how long have you been walking on two feet?
- So how much Avon do you sell a year?
- So did you buy that vest at the lingerie party?
- So where does she graze at night?
- Is that your breath or is your mouth farting?
- Nice tooth.
- Why don't you waddle over here?
- Stand here. I want to sit in the shade.
- So how big do you have to buy your panties?
- Well, aren't you a cutie.
- What's your nickname? Candy, 'cause you're easy to lick.
- So when you get dressed up, how tight are your skirts?
- I like that color of lipstick on you.
- Hmm, I must have made a mistake. I thought this was a pool hall, not the ladies room.
- Can I order you a Shirley Temple?
- So besides being a good argument for birth control, do you have any other functions in life?
- I bet you were the Warden's girlfriend.
- Hey, Pinhead.
- So where do you keep your teddy bear on this tricycle.

- Thank God it only has two wheels, anymore you'd have trouble counting them.
- I have a new slogan for you. Born to be dumb.
- Saddlebag? I thought that was your purse.
- So do you store your tampons in there?
- So how was that bikini wax?
- How cute. My little girl has a tattoo just like that. Does it wash off with soap?
- Hey, Mary.
- Bambi. What a cute name for a bike.
- The only line you walk is cocaine.
- So where did you find the crack whore?
- Is that a black eye or did you mess up your eyeliner again?
- Hey, Shirley.
- Hell's Angels. So you must be Sister Angelica?
- So where do you keep your doll collection?
- So what are you smoking? Virginia Slims?
- So what does this thing do? Forty going down hill with a good tailwind?
- So do you have a twin sister?

43

And another list of what not to say to Hell's Angels.

Quote: When you are in a hole, quit digging.
~Number one rule of public relations

25 More Things Not to Say to Hell's Angels
- Are your Depends too tight?
- So I hear that you are the Viagra poster boy.
- Don't leave the cycle by the curb. They're collecting trash tomorrow.

- What is the official drink of Hell's Angels? Geritol?
- So you must save a lot of money on toothpaste.
- Go to Wal-Mart, they're having a sale on teeth. Look for the Geezer aisle.
- So I bet you have two or three prostate exams a year. It feels so good.
- I bet road rash isn't the only rash you worry about.
- Hey, Barbie.
- Wolf whistle – a REALLY bad idea.
- Where's the crank to start that tricycle.
- Is it tough to ride a bike in high heels?
- So, do you need a crane to hoist your old lady onto the back of your bike?
- She looks old. What's her bra size? 34 long?
- Hey this parking space is for real bikes. Why don't you park that scooter on the sidewalk?
- So Smells-R-Us is your favorite store?
- I bet a tube of toothpaste lasts you for three years.
- Toys"R"Us called, they want their scooter back.
- So do you take the training wheels off before you enter Sturgis?
- Is that paper bag for your old lady's head?
- Hell, I'd be drinking too, if I had to ride that piece of crap.
- Why don't you ride by the nursing home and pick up another girlfriend.
- So Hell's Angels is 60 years old? So you must have started riding with them when you were 29?
- My name? You'll have to beat it out of me.
- Does the bike mess up your pantyhose?

44

And here is a list of things that should be banned. After reading from these list you can say, "And here are some things that should

be banned in our industry _____." Or you can be positive and say,
"Well those are some things that should be banned. Let's look at
some things that should be encouraged..."

Quote: If I could believe the Quakers banned music because
church music is so damn bad, I should view them with approval.
~Ezra Pound

60 Things That Should Be Banned

- Viagra commercials
- Victoria Secret commercials when you are watching baseball
  with your eight year old son.
- Jerry Springer
- Diet root beer
- $2 cup of coffee
- Underage drinking laws. We are turning a whole generation of
  18 year olds into criminals.
- Elvis Impersonators
- *Sex in the City* movie sequels
- Cage fighting
- Laws forbidding smoking in pubs
- Strict marijuana penalties
- Spandex
- Disco revivals
- Long red lights
- Short green lights
- Jogging
- 50% of all government regulations
- Career politicians
- Pop Warner football
- Fox News
- Ties
- Electric razors
- The terms Afro-American, Italian-American, Irish-American,

French-American (last time I checked we were a melting pot and we were all Americans)

- Canada
- Instant diets
- Aerobics. Any kind!
- The play *CATS*
- The first three quarters of pro basketball games
- That annoying "You Got Mail"
- Muscle shirts
- Ponytails on men
- Comb-overs
- Donald Trump
- Cheery morning disc jockeys
- Righteous people
- People who don't turn off cell phones in movies
- Colorizing black and white films.
- Tom Cruise
- Broccoli
- Eggplant
- Cauliflower
- Celebrity memoirs
- Mayonnaise
- Boston Red Sox fans
- Bankers
- Stimulus plans
- Skinny women
- Fishing licenses
- Hnagovers, HNgove, I mean GHanm hangovers
- The MF word
- The phrase: Like, you know
- Press conferences by repentant politicians
- Reruns of *MASH* – come on – who hasn't seen EVERY episode
- Public television fund raisers
- College football coaches who make over one million a year

- The Federal Reserve Board
- Elected judges
- Plastic water bottles
- Government ownership of car companies, banks, health care, liquor stores, electric companies...
- Mixing Coke with bourbon

45

Here is a fun list of things that do not mix. After reading some items from the list, you can say, "But in our company, there are some things that do mix, very well."

Quote: Two things are infinite: the universe and human stupidity, and I'm not sure about the universe.
~Einstein

50 Things That Do Not Mix

- Drinking and chainsaws
- Juggling and chainsaws
- Halloween and chainsaws
- Jogging and quicksand
- Texting and driving
- Teasing and snakes
- Cola and wine
- Beans and Ex-lax
- Politics and affairs
- Fire and Bambi
- Budget and Congress
- 40 Plus and skateboards
- Deer and cars
- Chicken and crossing road
- Road rage and traffic jams

- Water and grease fire
- Auburn and football
- Teenager and reality
- Viagra and Pinocchio
- ADHD and air traffic controllers
- Tickling and bears
- Head and windshield
- Matches and propane tank
- Disco and revival
- Fashion and spandex
- Wives and mistresses
- Dating and secretaries
- Beer and Vodka and Gin and Bourbon and Scotch and...
- Clowns and loaded weapons
- Bullets and your body
- Chicago Cubs and World Series
- Women and the Catholic Church
- Hangovers and airline pilots
- Mimes and debates
- Motorcycles and black ice
- Minnesota Twins and leads
- Hotel parties and cops
- Ice fishing and skinny dipping
- Tight bike shorts and old men
- Advice and teenagers
- Smoking and lungs
- Goldfish and cats
- Pythons and hamsters
- Business retreats and the boss' wife
- Dark alleys and safety
- Humor and airport security
- Forgiveness and child molester
- Women's Lib and Afghanistan
- Doctors and timeliness

- Diet and easy

46

Here is a list of original Halloween costumes. This is a list you can read from around Thanksgiving. Then you can say. "And moving on from those original costumes, I would like to share some original ideas with you..."

Quote: Eat, drink and be scary.
~Anon

Halloween Costumes That Make a Statement

- Banker – Dark suit and mask. Walk around all evening with your hand out.
- Lawyer – Wear a T-shirt that says on front, "Lawyer". Put a shark fin on the back of the T-shirt.
- Savings Account – Carry an umbrella with big holes in it. Your T-shirt says, "My Rainy Day Fund".
- Environment – Dress like a globe. Attach a heat pack to your globe. You are global warming.
- IRS Agent – Dark suit and a really big bag with a dollar sign on it and an obvious hole in the bottom.
- NFL player – A striped prison suit, a helmet, and handcuffs.
- Banking Executive – Hawaiian Shirt, a lea around your neck, shorts, sandals and a sign around your neck that says, "Bank Exec – thanks for the retreat".
- Major League Baseball Player – Wear a Yankee jersey and carry a baseball bat that is wrapped up to resemble a big pill bottle. Have a big STEROIDS written on the bat.
- Economic Stimulus Recipient – Wear a hobo outfit and a sign around your neck saying, "Economic Stimulus Recipient".
- GM Executive – Wear a black suit, a hard hat that says General

Motors and have a sign around your neck that says "Will Work for Bailout Money".

- Homeless – Get a big box, cut holes in it for your hands and feet. Write on it, "Home Sweet Home". And then underneath that write, "At least I can afford the mortgage".
- Congress – Wear at lampshade on your head, a tie, and a martini in your hand and a T-shirt that says, "Do not disturb – Congressman at work".
- Bitter Ex – This works if you are recently divorced. Buy a big rat trap, tape a picture of your ex to it and wear it around your neck.
- CPA – Mess up your hair. Get a pair of nerdy glasses with white tape in the middle. Wear your pants too high and a pair of white socks with sandals. Your T-shirt says – "Accountants Gone Wild".
- Justice – Wear some dark sunglasses, carry a white cane and wear a T-shirt that says "Justice".
- Economist – Wear some dark sunglasses, carry a white cane and wear a T-shirt that says "Economist".
- David Letterman – Wear a T-shirt with letters and envelopes taped all over it.
- Taxpayer – Wear a T-shirt with Sugar Daddy candy wrappers all over it. And a sign around your neck that says, "How The Gov Sees You".
- Economist – Dress like a fortune teller (a gypsy look) and carry a crystal ball that is all cloudy. On the bandana round your head write Economist.
- Taxpayer – This is a costume for a couple. One has a T-shirt with a picture of a screwdriver on it. Under the picture it says IRS. The other person has a T-shirt with a big screw on it. It says "Taxpayer".
- Health care reform – Wear a T-shirt. On front it says, "Health Care Reform". Then put a big fake bandage on your bottom. The back of your T-shirt says, "Pain In the Butt".
- Financial Planner – Make a big spinner. When you spin the arrow it lands on squares that say: "Didn't see that coming." "Your

guess is as good as mine." "The market will go up and down." "It sounded like a good investment." "Trust Madoff." Attach the spinner to a T-shirt that says "Financial Planner at Work".

- Inflation – Cut the valves off beach balls and sticks them all over your shirt, then attach fake $1,000 bills. Then a bill from Starbucks that says: "One coffee – $999"
- Dopey – Wear a T-shirt with small rocks attached. You're stoned.
- Congressional Planner – Paint a target on a T-shirt. Attach a toy arrow that has missed the target by a lot. Your T-shirt says, "Congressional Planner".

47

Another fun list you can use around Halloween. After choosing some of the following safety tips, you can say, "But let's discuss some real rules we should all follow when _____."

Quote: On Halloween, the parents sent their kids out looking like me.
~Rodney Dangerfield

Top 30 Rules for a Safe Happy Halloween

- Do not use a chainsaw for a pumpkin carving tool.
- After your children carve the pumpkin, do not drop the pumpkin and say, "Look, I made squash."
- Do not hang your daughter's Barbie doll from a noose on the front porch.
- Do not go trick or treating with the Hell's Angels.
- Do not tell the cop you like his costume but he would like better in tighter pants.
- Do not drink and ride the broomstick home. Your mother-in-law needs it back by the morning.
- Do not pass out beers to kids when you run out of candy.

- Do not drink and use a carving knife on the pumpkin. This never works out well.
- Do not throw eggs at the police car.
- Take the keys away from anyone that has been drinking and hide his car around the block. Encourage him to call the cops and report that his car was stolen.
- Do not use a firecracker to light your pumpkin.
- Do not go to work as a clown and say you are the CEO.
- Do not go to the Animal Shelter Society Halloween party dressed as Michael Vick.
- Do not wear a gorilla costume to the zoo and say, "I've escaped. I've escaped!"
- Do not dress up as the Grim Reaper, go to your ex's house and say, "I've come for you."
- Stay away from Elm Street.
- When you run out of gas, lock your doors and have your wife knock on the door of that 'deserted house'.
- Do not drink and use a staple gun to hand up decorations.
- Never open the door to an adult wearing a hockey mask.
- Do not hang outdoor lights when it is raining or there is lightning. Let your kids do it.
- Do not pass out candy with a bloody pitchfork.
- Know what activities your kids are attending and what time they will get home so you can be back from the bar in time.
- Do not let your kids trick or treat at the house made out of ginger-bread.
- Be sensitive: Do not dress as a hunchback and say you play football for Notre Dame.
- Do not use your neighbors' pumpkins to kick field goals over the fence.
- Never leave a drunk unattended in a room with a lit candle
- If your wife dresses as a witch, don't tell her to go away for a 'spell'.
- Do not call your wife's hair spray 'scare spray'.

- Do not call the blood bank and ask for a withdrawal.
- Do not tell the kid dressed like a ghost, "Looks like you have a mouthful of sheet."

48

You can use this opening by saying, "Let me share with you the top ten rejected Valentine's Day Cards." Then read all or some of the list. Then you can say, "But I would like to share some good ideas that we have created to improve our market share. I am sure that our customers will embrace, not reject these ideas."

Quote: If love is blind, why is lingerie so popular?
~Anon

The Top Ten Rejected Valentine's Day Cards
- You are the cream that holds my dentures in.
- You are like new elastic in my underwear.
- You are the road kill in my stew of love.
- You are the clippers for the hangnails of life.
- You are as close to me as lint in my belly button.
- Without you, I am a clown without big shoes.
- You are the rehab for my love addiction.
- You cure the jock itch of my love.
- You are Tums to the heartburn of my love.
- You warm the cockroaches of my heart.

49

Here are some fun ideas you can use around football season. What new rules might you add for football? Pick and choose from some of the rules below and then you can say, "Unfortunately in day-to-

day life we cannot change the rules. So here are some rules and regulations we must remember _____."

Quote: Sure, luck means a lot in football. Not having a good quarterback is bad luck.

~Don Shula

Proposed New Rules for Football

Nobody has asked me, in fact people rarely do, but I am not easily discouraged. Therefore, I think it is time to change the rules in football. Here are the new rules:

- If you are kicking a team's butt and are ahead by 21 points at halftime, you can only have nine men on the field in the second half. The other team can have 12.
- Penalties should be like hockey. If someone has, say, a holding penalty, they have to sit out for four downs and the other team gets a man advantage.
- If the kick goes over your head and goes into the end zone, why should you get an automatic 20 yards? That's nonsense. The ball should be on the ten yard line, not the 20.
- I hate field goals. Two teams pound each other for four quarters (which makes a dollar) and then the field goal kicker comes on and decides the game. They need a new rule that a field goal can never win a game. This means a sliding point system. If your team is ahead by two points, a field goal by the other team can only be worth one point. If the game is tied, no field goals are allowed. You have to score a touchdown to win.
- No more extra point kicks. How boring. They make them every time. You have to run or pass the ball to get that extra point.
- If the other team tackles your quarterback in the end zone and gets a safety, they do not get the ball. You have to start on the one yard line and they can get as many safeties as they want, or else you can dig yourself out of the jam. Kinda like real life, when

your back is up against the wall, you gotta dig yourself out.

- There should be errors in football. Just like in baseball. If you make an error in baseball, the other team gets on base. So if a receiver drops an easy pass, his team should be punished and backed up five yards.

- Why are penalties always even numbers? Five, ten yards? There should be a sliding scale. If it is holding, but not blatant, instead of ten yards, only penalize the other team 7.5 yards.

- In hockey if you are losing by one goal, you can pull your goalie and add an extra offensive player. If there is one minute left in the football game and you are losing, you can add one extra player.

- No more fair catches. If you are scared of getting hit, don't catch the ball. Let it bounce. What is all this hand waving? Catch the damn ball and run. Why should you be rewarded for not running?

- Bring back leather helmets. I have no idea why, but the concept amuses me.

- Half the game is intimidation. The quarterback should be scared of getting hit. Heck it is FOOTBALL! So eliminate all these fancy flak jackets the QB wears to protect himself. Those flak jackets take away the intimidation factor.

- Bring back tear-away jerseys. If you can't make a decent tackle, the guy deserves to get away.

- Add time on to the clock. I took this idea from soccer. As if I even understand soccer. Millions of years of evolution and we have opposable thumbs which set us apart from primates and they invent a game where you can't use your hands? Please! But no more yardage penalties. If you get a penalty, the other team gets an extra offensive play at the end of the game. If you have ten penalties, the other team gets ten extra plays. Let's say you have ten penalties called against you and the other team has eight called against them, which means they get two extra plays.

- Every player has the same number. Again, I have no idea, but the concept amuses me.

- The quarterback cannot stand behind the center. He must stand to either one side or the other. This will make snapping the football exciting, not automatic.
- You can have as many men on the line or in the backfield as you want. This is America, it is a free country. You want ten men in the backfield, you take the consequences.
- Bring back the flying wedge. I know, I know, you have heard this before. I have no idea, but it amuses me.
- You commit a foul in basketball, you get a free throw. If you commit a penalty in football, the player you fouled gets a try at a field goal. If he makes it, it is one point.
- Put the goalpost in the first row of the stands. This will make field goals harder to make and create fan excitement.
- Three players on both teams have to be 'iron men' and play offense and defense all game.
- The team with the cutest cheerleaders gets seven extra points. Hey, this is a very sexist rule, but I am all for it. And the cheerleaders showing the most skin when they are playing in Green Bay in December gets extra points for either bravery or stupidity. Or frostbite.
- The team with the most celebrities in the stands that that the TV cameras can pan on, gets an extra seven points.
- If a team goes an entire month without one player being arrested, they get to move up one rank in the standings. Thus a fifth-rate team automatically advances to fourth place.
- Any football player that can actually name the commissioner of football earns a chance of a real job when they blow out their knees and the league casts them out to actually fend for themselves.
- If any obnoxious football player dumps Gatorade on the poor coach when the temperature is below 40 degrees, the entire team is punished and must begin the next game with a seven point deficit. In other words, the score board automatically reads minus

seven.

- The last chance gasp. If your team is in last place, you get to play one game against the winner of your division. If you beat the top dog, you make the playoffs.

50

At the beginning of the football season, coaches have to talk to the press and often times stretch the truth. Here is a funny list of what they really think. You can pick and choose what you like, then you can say, "And let me tell you all what I really think of you. I think we have the best employees..."

Quote: Football incorporates the two worse elements of American society: violence punctuated by committee meetings. ~George Wills

What College Football Coaches Really Think: Inside the Mind of a Football Coach

- Team leader? Heck, he could mess up a two car parade.
- The only pass he can complete is at a pretty girl.
- Dumb? We had to draw him a map to his own locker.
- He needs to go to Wal-Mart when they have a sale on hands.
- Dumb? We had to write, "FRONT", on his jock strap
- He's majoring in 'You Knows'.
- The offense is simple, hand the ball off to anyone left standing in the backfield.
- The only thing he can catch is a cold.
- Academically ineligible? The kid is as dumb as a rock and that's insulting the rock. He had to show up for remedial coloring, the only two requirements are color within the lines and put the crayons back in the box when you are done.
- Dumb? He needs to come to practice early as it takes him an hour

to figure out tying his shoes.

- A few minor infractions. Heck, this kid should have applied to state prisons, not colleges. He is a criminal justice major. He's got the criminal part down to a fine science.
- He's a wonder receiver. We wonder when he will catch a pass.
- It's all about desire. And by the end of the first quarter, after watching this team play, I have a strong desire to shoot myself or get drunk.
- He thought SAT meant sit down and he waited for the command to stand. He was still sitting two hours after the test was over.
- We have a rebuilding year. The smart seniors have left and we have freshmen who are greener than Kermit the Frog. It took a whole practice just to show them how to put their helmets on. They need a GPS system to find the goal lines. They were up all night studying for their urine tests.
- Defense? Unless we arm these kids with bazookas, the other team will establish a campground in the end zones. We will wear them down, because they will be scoring so much. There are more holes in our defensive line than a screen door. We are going to have to buy an extra scoreboard to keep track of their points.
- We have a good kicking game. We are going to get our butts kicked all over the field.
- How many games will we win? Well if the rest of the teams get wiped out by swine flu and they replace then with the cheerleading squad, we have a good chance of winning, maybe, one or two games.
- We believe in field goals. In fact our goal is to get off the field before we get beaten to a pulp.
- We expect to have a good running game. In fact, I should be run out of town by the second or third game.
- We all deserve a second chance. In other words, he broke a few team rules. Like forgetting to go to class, showing up drunk at practice, accepting money from a booster, bribing his teachers to pass him. But hey, the kid is a starter and we all make mistakes.

- We expect to have a tough defense. It's going to be tough for them to defend anything.
- We have a good kick return game. The other team will be able to return kicks all night long.
- We're small but quick. Yep, we can give up more touchdowns quicker than anyone else in this league.
- This team is based on character. If it was based on talent, we wouldn't be in last place.
- We have a lot of junior college transfers. Because no one else wanted them, which is why they went to junior college in the first place.
- It might take some time for the young players to develop. I didn't say develop into football players, you note.
- I have confidence in this team. Yeah, I am confident that they will have me looking for a job next year.
- We had a good recruiting year. We finally recruited someone to dress up in that stupid mascot suit. I hope they didn't think I was talking about players.
- This team will surprise some people. At how bad it really is.
- Running pass routes are all about timing. Talking about timing, I have seen better hands on a clock.
- We will put some fear into some people. Mainly the fans. By midseason they will fear coming to games.
- We will depend upon the pass. We hope that this season passes as soon as possible.
- We have a good line. In fact I have been handing you a great line about how we might actually win a game this year.
- This game is funny. The ball bounces funny and anything can happen. Like we might actually win a game.
- We think we will be in the Bowl picture. Yep, we will all be at the bowling alley after this season is over.
- This team has great prospects. For losing the most games in university history.
- This team will be tough. Tough to support, tough to believe in,

tough to win a game.

- We haven't decided on a starting quarterback this year as one has the brains of a seagull, one has the hands of a statue, and the other will flunk out by Tuesday.
- We had some great opportunities to win the game. But the other team's bus didn't break down and they actually showed up.
- You can't win games if you keep making mistakes. Like the mistakes we made in recruiting these sorry players.
- We have some gifted athletes on this team. Unfortunately, they are gifted in science and math, not football.
- We're just going to take it one game at a time. Otherwise I would break down and cry.
- We have a good game plan. We plan to leave town as soon as possible after the game.
- They have a lot of talent but nothing can be taken for granted. Except they will beat us by a gazillion points.
- This team does not have a drug problem. Even though they thought the white chalk lines were cocaine.
- You just have to make first downs. And by the first quarter I am REALLY down.
- Penalties killed us. Yeah right, our lack of talent killed us.
- We have a lot of returning players next year. Unfortunately.
- I am pleased to hear that although we had a disappointing season the university still supports me. Thank God I have those photos of the college president and that bimbo.

51

If you have to give an informative speech at Toastmasters or at a local civic club, here is a quick little speech you can give. It also makes a great opening you can pick and choose some stats from, because it talks about something most of us get involve in, sooner or later – marriage.

But what is interesting, when you hear these stats, you will notice they reflect our changing morals and values. In fact, after you read off some of these stats, you can say, "I bet you noticed that these stats show how Americans' moral and values change over time. But I would like to make one important point. When you look at our company, we have not changed the basic philosophy that has served us well all these years. And that is _____."

By the way, also notice the one-liners that are woven into the speech. If you just read a bunch of stats, your audience will have the MEGO factor. My Eyes Glaze Over. But by ending some of the stats with a one-liner you accomplish two things. People are not good at remembering facts, especially from a speech. But if you can tie a one-liner into that fact, it acts as a mnemonic device, helping the audience remember the fact. And by tying into a one-liner, you are giving the audience time to digest what you are saying. Remember a speech is like a good meal, it needs to be digested one bite at a time.

Quote: I love being married. It's so great to find that one special person you want to annoy for the rest of your life.
~Rita Rudner

What Americans Really Think About Marriage and Other Changing Values

The Gallup surveys, bless their little souls, exist just to amuse me. They don't know this, but they do. One of their latest surveys revolves around marriage and how Americans feel about it.

The lead off question is a doozy. How do you feel about sex between an unmarried man and woman? Fifty-seven percent of Americans thought it was morally acceptable, while 40% thought it was wrong.

The next question cuts to the chase. How do you feel about married men and woman having an affair? Six percent thought it was morally acceptable. 92% thought it was morally wrong. The percentage favoring affairs would have been higher, but no politicians were interviewed.

How about divorce? Well, 62% of Americans think it is morally acceptable, only 30% think it is morally wrong. Unfortunately none of the 30% were my ex-wives.

How about having a baby outside of marriage? This was called the John Edwards question. The answers will surprise you. Fifty-one percent of Americans think it is morally wrong, but 45% are okay with it.

I found the next question amusing. But then again, that is why they take these surveys – to amuse me. How do Americans feel about polygamy? I would have said I never took that math class in high school, and boy would I have been wrong. Polygamy means having more than one wife at the same time. Why would anyone do that to themselves? It would be like stereo hell. Most Americans think it is morally wrong, in fact, 91% do. Only 7% agree with polygamy, but their wives were telling them to say that.

How about gay marriage? Except the Gallup poll is classier than that. They call them "marriages between same-sex couples." This was interesting. In 1991 only 27% of Americans thought they should be valid. That number is now up to 40%! And 49% would oppose a constitutional amendment banning gay marriages and 48% would favor it.

And here is the stat that shows how much our world has changed. In 1958, only 4% approved of marriages between whites and non-whites. Now 79% of America approves.

Well there you have it. Americans' attitudes towards marriage. My attitude, in case you care, reflects Lewis Grizzard's immortal line, "I don't think I will get married again. I will just find a woman I hate and buy her a house." And of course a tip of the hat to James Thurber who said, "The most dangerous food is wedding cake."

52

Need some material for a wedding speech? Don't panic. Here it is!

Quote: Never get married in the morning, because you never know who you'll meet that night.
~Paul Hornung

Top 20 Rules of Marriage for Men

- Shut up and listen.
- She could be right.
- There is a difference between teasing and being mean. Don't cross the line.
- Never disrespect her.
- It is okay to go to bed angry with each other. It beats staying up all night and fighting.
- Be polite to her family. Even if they drive you crazy. This goes along with respecting her.
- She comes first, the kids come second, the dog comes third, football games come fourth. Hmm, except maybe the Super Bowl.
- Be honest.
- If she loses her job, get a second job and quit complaining about the lost income.
- Work as a team at home. The housework should be 50/50. This means more than taking out the garbage. Wash dishes, clean toilets. Do something to help.
- It is not her job to pick up after you or do your laundry. You are a big boy. Act like it,
- The kids will treat their future wives the way you treat yours. Think about that.
- Go on a picnic.
- Take walks.
- Invite her fishing.

- A blender is not an anniversary gift.
- Neither is a power tool.
- You may dread anniversaries. She doesn't. Suck it up and do something romantic.
- Be reliable.
- Be kind, be kind, be kind.

53

The Constitution was signed in Philadelphia on September 17, 1787. Thus September 17 is honored as Constituent Day. And here is a quiz you can use to encourage audience participation if you ever have to give a speech about the Constitution. And yes, this material is also good for July 4th: Here are 25 great facts you can fit into a speech on the constitution.

Quote: The US Constitution doesn't guarantee happiness, only the pursuit of it. You have to catch up with it yourself.
~Benjamin Franklin

- **Which State did not send deputies to the Constitutional Convention?**
  Rhode Island and Providence Plantations.
- **Where did the deputies to the Constitutional Convention assemble?**
  In Philadelphia, in the State House where the Declaration of Independence was signed.
- **When did they assemble?**
  The meeting was May 14, 1787, but a quorum was not present until May 25.
- **How large was the population of Philadelphia?**
  28,000; including suburbs, about 42,000.
- **What was the average age of the Constitutional Convention**

deputies?

About 44.

- **Who was the oldest member of the Constitutional Convention?**
Benjamin Franklin, 81.
- **How many lawyers were members of the Constitutional Convention?**
34 out of 55.
- **Who was the "Sage of the Constitutional Convention"?**
Benjamin Franklin.
- **Who was the "Father of the Constitution"?**
James Madison, of Virginia.
- **Was Thomas Jefferson a member of the Constitutional Convention?**
No. he was in France as the American Minister to France.
- **How did Thomas Jefferson help write the Constitution?**
Although absent from the Constitutional Convention and during its ratification, Jefferson insisted that the Bill of Rights, the first ten amendments, be adopted.
- **How long did it take to frame the Constitution?**
Less than one hundred working days.
- **How much was paid for the journal kept by Madison during the Constitutional Convention?**
Congress authorized $30,000 to buy Madison's journal and other papers.
- **What was the Connecticut Compromise?**
Each State should have two senators, and the number of Representatives was to be based upon population, protecting the rights of the small States, while the majority of the population was fairly represented.
- **Who engrossed (wrote) the text of the Constitution for signing?**
Jacob Shallus, an assistant clerk of the Pennsylvania State Assembly. He got paid 30 dollars. And his name never appears on the document.
- **Did all of the deputies to the Constitutional Convention sign**

the Constitution?

Only 39 signed. Fourteen deputies had departed for home, and three – Randolph and Mason, of Virginia, and Gerry, of Massachusetts, refused to sign.

- **Did George Washington sign the Declaration of Independence?**
No. He was with the army in New York City.
- **What are the measurements of the original Declaration of Independence?**
The Declaration of Independence: 29 7/8 inches by 24 7/16 inches.
- **The measurements of the original Constitution?**
The Constitution: four sheets, approximately 28 3/4 inches by 23 5/8 inches each.
- **How many words are there in the Constitution?**
4,543 words, including the signatures.
- **How many words in the Declaration of Independence?**
1,458 words.
- **How many States needed to ratify the Constitution?**
Nine.
- **In what order did the States ratify the Constitution?**
Delaware, Pennsylvania, New Jersey, Georgia, Connecticut, Massachusetts, Maryland, South Carolina, New Hampshire, Virginia, and New York. After Washington had been inaugurated, North Carolina and Rhode Island ratified.
- **How did they decide to address the President of the United States?**
The Senate wanted "His Highness the President of the United States of America and Protector of their Liberties". The House wanted "the President of the United States". The Senate agreed.
- **How many States does it take to block an amendment?**
Thirteen.

54

Here is a list of personal checks to avoid. If you are giving a talk on any money topic, this is a fun list to start off with. Then you can say, "But at _____, we take financial responsibility seriously..."

Quote: Money is better than poverty, if only for financial reasons. ~Woody Allen

30 Cute Personal Checks to Avoid

I have never liked those cute personal checks. They are just too cute. And money should be serious. Checks should be serious. Can you imagine if the government started printing cute money with cartoon characters on it? Please!

But I am convinced there are some cute personal checks you should avoid. Here is a list of the top 30.

- Three Stooges: You're the fourth stooge if you think this won't come back and stick you in the eye.
- I love Lucy: Ricky, I bounced another check!
- Tigger: They keep bouncing.
- Balloon checks: Full of hot air.
- Halloween: Want scary – try cashing this.
- Scooby-Doo: It's a mystery why you even accepted this check.
- Snoopy: This dog won't hunt and this check won't cash.
- Unicorn: A mythical creature and a mythical check.
- Firefighters: Don't get burned by this one.
- Dental Checks: Painful to try and cash.
- Stocks and Bonds: Now that gives me a real sense of security!
- Las Vegas: Take a chance on these.
- Real Estate: The value of this check drops faster than the housing market.
- Country Music: Your wife leaves, your dog dies and your bank account is wiped out.

- Baseball: Strike Three.
- Hockey: Hockey check? You gotta love the pun. No teeth in this check.
- Fishing: The ones that got away. With your bank account.
- Playing Cards: Accepted by Jokers everywhere.
- Big Lips: Kiss it goodbye.
- Ozzy Osbourne: Now there is a financial endorsement.
- Bugs Bunny: What's up, doc? Not this check.
- Mickey Mouse: A Mickey Mouse idea that this will cash.
- Carousel Horses: This check goes around and around.
- Chevy Checks: Right into bankruptcy.
- Spiderman Checks: You got snared by this one.
- Charlie Brown: A real loser of a check.
- Marilyn Monroe: A bombshell of a check.
- Bowling: No spare change left.
- Golf: More holes in the bank account than a golf course.
- Pin-ups: It's a fantasy that there is any money in the account.

55

Here is a good quiz you can work into any speech you have to give on any patriotic holiday.

Quote: A Bill of Rights is what the people are entitled to against every government, and what no just government should refuse, or rest on inference.
~Thomas Jefferson

The Bill of Rights Quiz
Do You Know Your Ten Amendments?

Quiz
- This amendment states that the punishment for crimes or bail

shall not be excessive nor cruel and unusual.

Amendment VIII

- This amendment provides for speedy public trials by jury for those indicted in criminal cases.

Amendment VI

- The states or the people retain the powers not specifically granted to the federal government in the Constitution.

Amendment X

- Citizens were angry that the British quartered soldiers in the colonists' homes. This provision addressed that concern.

Amendment III

- This Amendment protects individual religious freedom, free speech, a free press, and the freedom to petition the government by written word, marching, and picketing.

Amendment I

- Provides protections in law such as double jeopardy where a person cannot be tried twice for the same offense.

Amendment V

- Provides for jury trials in civil cases.

Amendment VII

- This is a catch-all clause that retains for the people other rights not specifically mentioned in the Constitution.

Amendment IX

- Individuals have the right to own firearms and maintain a militia for their mutual protection?

Amendment II

- Guarantees that citizens be safe from unreasonable searches or arrests without a warrant.

Amendment IV

56

Here are some rules to speed up baseball. Again you can read

some off, and then say, "But we don't make the rules. We must follow them. Especially when it comes to safety_____." This is a good opening to use during baseball season.

But you can also use it during the winter. If you do, you can introduce the speech by saying, "I know you all must be tired of winter. I know I am, and my thoughts have been turning to spring training. Because once they start spring training, I know that spring is right around the corner. But let's be fair, although I am a baseball fan, I think we need some rules to speed up the game. Come on, when the third baseman comes in after one inning with cobwebs hanging from his ears, you know it is taking too long to play the game. So here are some ways to improve the game."

Then you can say, "It is always easy to suggest ways for other people and businesses to improve, but we must take a hard look at ourselves and ask ourselves – what do we need to do to improve?"

Quote: The biggest room in the world is the room for improvement.
~Anon

Changing the Rules of Baseball

I have played and watched baseball for years and have some ideas to make the game move faster. To speed it up, the new rules include:

- The batter should get three balls and two strikes. Which reminds me of one of my favorite jokes, "What do you do with an elephant with three balls. Walk him and pitch to the giraffe."
- You can only have two outfielders. Makes it much more interesting and gives the outfielders more exercise.
- No batter is allowed to wear any protective equipment except a helmet. This reestablishes the inside pitch.
- If you steal second, you get to go to third for free. But third base is changed to 100 feet, not 90 feet from home plate.
- The umpire has to stand behind the pitcher. I really believe that is

a better angle to see the ball go over the plate and where it hits the catcher's glove. This eliminates the catcher framing bad pitches.

- The pitcher needs to wear a helmet. The ball is coming off the bat so quickly that a pitcher will get killed one day. It took a death before they made base coaches wear helmets.
- If a foul ball is hit so hard that it goes over the fence, that is a heck of a hit. The batter should be rewarded. Therefore any foul ball hit over the fence is not counted as a strike.
- Any double play can be counted as three outs and the inning is over. This will speed up the game.
- Bring back the spitball. I have no idea why, but it will amuse me and the fans.
- One inning each game, the team must bring in a female softball pitcher. And they get to pitch from the same distance as they did in college. This will give some really great pitchers an opportunity to play. And it would be a fascinating inning. But the female pitcher must also bat once every game.
- Each inning, every player, except the pitcher, must play a different position.

57

Have to give a speech on marketing? You can use this entire speech or just steal some ideas. This speech can be presented before a host of marketing groups as well as to college students, your local chamber of commerce, Toastmasters or Junior Achievement. And of course you can take some examples from the speech and weave them into another speech on marketing.

Quote: Many a small thing has been made large by the right kind of advertising.
~Mark Twain

Churches Teach Key Marketing Techniques: What Selling Religion Can Teach You

If you want to learn key lessons about marketing, if you want to learn about selling an intangible product, a product that your customers cannot touch or feel, look to your local church. And remember the cardinal rule of public relations – "Perception becomes reality". Now this is not a diatribe for or against God. This is not to say that God does or does not exist. But God is intangible and how do you make the intangible real? How do you make people believe in something they cannot see or trust?

In short, the church can teach you valuable marketing techniques.

First, you build a monument. That sounds funny, but if I want you to believe in something intangible, I am going to build a monument. A big soaring monument. That is why the church built those cathedrals in the Middle Ages. If you had any doubt that God existed, you would double-check your doubts. You would say, "Heck, he has to exist. Why would they build this majestic cathedral if he didn't?" Even to this day, churches are some of the most spectacular structures around.

But note that the towering church helps make you believe. This same concept works in business. Think about banks. They deal in an intangible called trust. They need your money so they can survive. And you are not going to put your faith in some flimsy shack. But if you see a solid brick building, with a big safe in it – wow you can trust that bank. And all the bankers will be out in the open, or have big glass windows on their offices so you can see them at work. This proves that the bank has nothing to hide.

In short, banks and churches have the same problem. They have to make people believe in them, trust what they are saying. And one approach is through visual symbols that overwhelm your reason, that make you believe in them.

This concept of using visual symbols to earn your trust is also used by lawyers and other professionals. Why does a lawyer always have his picture taken with a stack of law books on his desk or a shelf full of law books behind him or her? Again, the law books are the symbols that help instill trust.

The church also instills a need in people through fear. If you don't believe in God, you will go to hell. Fear is a powerful concept to make people believe in your product. Remember the famous Fram oil filter commercial. You could invest in a Fram oil filter or your engine would explode down the road someday. The classic line was, "Pay me now or pay me later." Not unlike religion. "Believe in me now or pay later."

Again, I am not being cynical about religion, but am merely pointing out that the many techniques that religion uses to earn your trust and belief are also used by the business world.

The church was one of the first institutions to use a powerful symbol: The cross. You see a cross; you know it is a church and that Jesus died for you. Not unlike the McDonald's Golden Arches. You see the Golden Arches, you know that it is a McDonald's and it is cheap, good, clean food. The cross represents everything the church stands for and the Golden Arches represent everything that McDonald's stands for. A good symbol or icon can be powerful for any business.

Testimonials are also important to any business. If you show me a before and after picture of someone who lost weight, I will believe. Getting back to Fram, if you show me a car in a junkyard, because they didn't use your oil filter, I believe. The church was one of the first institutions to recognize the importance of testimonials to show how powerful their product, God, was. Think about this, the Bible is full of testimonials.

Another good marketing tip from the church. Build a community. Give people reasons to come to church. Have choirs, prayer meetings, bible studies, counseling services, volunteer activities. A lot of people feel isolated, separated from society and the church offers a social life and a sense of community to them. Barnes and Noble does this well as does Starbucks. Barnes and Noble is not about just selling books, neither is Starbucks. In fact no one goes to

Starbucks for the coffee, coffee is coffee; they go for the fireplaces, the small tables, the sense of belonging to a really neat place. Same thing with Barnes and Nobles. They don't sell books. They sell a community with reading groups and coffee shops and big comfortable chairs to sit in.

Know where your future customers are coming from. The church knows that this generation of kids will be their customers for life, if they can get them hooked now. That is why the church has youth activities, Sunday schools, Bible camps and that is why confirmation at the age of 13 is a big deal. It gets kids involved. Again Barnes and Noble knows that the future is kids. That is why the children's section is always one of the biggest sections in the store. Get them believing in God, they will keep coming back. Get them hooked on books, they will keep coming back.

A final point. It is hard to communicate. The public is bombarded with thousands of messages a day. Have one clear consistent message. The church's message has not changed in thousands of years. Believe in God, lead a good life, go to heaven. In business, have one clear, consistent message that reassures people. Like the church, Allstate has one of the best slogans of all times, "You're in Good Hands".

Remember that you can learn a lot of sales techniques, even selling a product that your customers cannot feel or touch, by looking at the way that churches sell God. Have an impressive building, use the concept of fear, have an icon that everyone recognizes, use testimonials, create a community, hook them when they are young and have a consistent clear message. These are only a few of the sales and marketing techniques that the Church can teach you.

58

It is Thanksgiving and you have to give a Thanksgiving speech at Toastmasters or your local civic club. Here is a quiz that will

encourage audience participation.

Quote: We're having something a little different this year for Thanksgiving. Instead of a turkey, we're having a swan. You get more stuffing.

~George Carlin

The Thanksgiving Quiz: Beware – At Least Ten False Answers

- There were 250 million turkeys raised in the United States during 2009.
- California has passed a law requiring that citizens can only eat organically raised turkeys. **False**
- The biggest turkey producing state is Minnesota which produces 45.5 million turkeys a year.
- The United States produces 709 million pounds of cranberries a year.
- The health effect of cranberries is doubled when mixed with vodka. **False**
- The typical American consumes 13.8 pounds of turkey a year.
- Farmers make 3.8 billions dollars a year selling turkeys.
- There are three places in America named after the Turkey: Turkey, Texas; Turkey Creek, Louisiana and Turkey, North Carolina.
- There are five places in America named after the Cranberry.
- The ACLU has petitioned the Supreme Court to ban Thanksgiving. They charge the original Thanksgiving holiday was religious in nature and violates the separation of church and state. **False**
- There are 28 places in America named after Plymouth Rock.
- Because of a turkey shortage, the government will urge families to use meatloaf instead of turkey this year. **False**
- The average cost of a turkey is $1.33 a pound.
- There are 1.1 billion pounds of pumpkins produced in the US every year.

- The first Thanksgiving was held in 1621 and lasted three days.
- The average American waistline expands by two pant sizes during Thanksgiving week. **False**
- Thanksgiving is always held on the fourth Thursday of November.
- Turkey is the Indian word for politician. **False**
- The average weight of turkeys purchased for Thanksgiving is 15 pounds.
- For over 50 years, the National Turkey Federation has presented the President of the US with a live turkey and two dressed turkeys in celebration of Thanksgiving. Harry Truman was the first president to receive this honor in 1947. Each year, the live turkey is 'pardoned' by the President and most recently has been flown to Disney World to serve as the grand marshal of the Disney World Thanksgiving Day Parade.
- The top five popular ways to serve leftover Thanksgiving turkey are: sandwiches, soups or stews, salads, casseroles and stir-fry.
- Because families are together and drinking, Thanksgiving is the top day for murder in the US. **False**
- About 45 million turkeys are eaten at Thanksgiving, 22 million at Christmas, and 19 million at Easter.
- The 'snood' is a long, red, fleshy growth from the base of the beak that hangs down over the beard.
- You are less likely to gain weight during Thanksgiving if you drink a beer with your turkey; the beer supplies bacteria to better digest the turkey. **False**
- A baby turkey is called a poult and is tan and brown.
- A group of turkeys is called a Congress of Turkeys. **False**
- The 'carbuncle' on a turkey is the red-pink fleshy growth on the head and upper neck.
- The 'wattle' is the bright red appendage at the neck.
- Pilgrims invented football so future generations could enjoy the holiday. **False**
- Only Tom turkeys gobble. Hen turkeys make a clicking noise.

- Turkeys have approximately 3,500 feathers at maturity.
- Plan to buy at least one pound of uncooked turkey per person.
- Turkeys are becoming popular household pets and a leash to walk your turkey has been developed by the Humane Society. **False**
- If the temperature is 180° F in the thigh and 170° F in the breast, the turkey is safe to eat.
- Broad-breasted white is the most common turkey raised in the United States.
- President Andrew Jackson ranked turkey hash #1 among his favorite foods.
- Congress passed an official proclamation in 1941 declaring that Thanksgiving will be a legal holiday.
- The Indians at the first Thanksgiving were from the Wampanoag tribe.
- Thanksgiving Day is a more heavily traveled day than Wednesday.
- The average Thanksgiving long distance trip length is 214 miles, compared with 275 miles over the Christmas/New Year's holiday.

59

Here is a funny short informative speech you can give to any Civic Club or Toastmasters meeting. Feel free to add your own adlibs.

Quote: What we're really talking about is a wonderful day set aside on the fourth Thursday of November when no one diets. I mean, why else would they call it Thanksgiving?
~Erma Bombeck

How the Turkey Gets to Your Thanksgiving Table: The Short, but Happy Life of Turkeys

Let's talk turkey.

Sure you have that nice plump turkey at your dining room table, but we don't need to talk about your mother-in-law. Let's talk about the other turkey, the one you have cooked for your guests.

What journey did that turkey take to end up dead on your table? What did he do wrong? Actually nothing, although being born a turkey is not exactly winning the birth lottery. If you believe in reincarnation, being reincarnated as a turkey ensures you a lifespan of less than a year and a retirement plan that includes being roasted then torn apart and eaten by humans.

But let's look at the journey the turkey takes to be your guest at Thanksgiving.

The turkey you are eating this Thanksgiving started as an egg back in May. To meet the demand for Turkey during Thanksgiving and Christmas, during May, millions of turkey eggs are placed in incubators. After four weeks of incubation, a baby turkey (a poult) applies to preschool.

Whoops – wrong information there. After four weeks of hanging around the incubator, a baby turkey is hatched and is moved from the hatchery to a barn that is climate controlled and protects the turkey from predators, disease, talk show hosts and rap music.

For the next four to five months, the turkeys take up smoking and drinking, figuring, "What the hell, my life is short anyway, might as well enjoy it. And hey, what are my chances of getting cancer?"

No, sorry, that was wrong. That information came from the part of my brain that has been heavily damaged by years of walking into parked cars. For the next four to five months, the turkeys roam freely around the barn, eating their way through many pounds of feed, which consists of corn and soybean meal along with some vitamins and minerals.

What about the manure turkeys produce? Well, 100 turkeys which are about 16 weeks old will eat 93 to 115 pounds of feed a day. And they are quite productive. These same 100 turkeys will produce 108 to 115 pounds of manure a day. And, this fact is totally random: turkey manure is 75% water.

Anyway what is the turkey's reward for eating and sleeping all day for five months, just hanging around and getting fat? Yep, a free trip to the slaughterhouse. And after that it goes downhill for the bird.

According to the USDA, "Turkeys continue through the processing either as whole birds or in parts. They are frequently washed and kept chilled throughout the entire process to prevent the growth of harmful bacteria. Whole birds are chilled in ice, water, or in a mixture of ice and water. Turkeys to be sold fresh are quick-chilled to 40° F or lower, but must not go below a temperature of 26° F. Fresh turkeys should be refrigerated and used within 1 to 2 days from purchase, or they can be frozen for safekeeping. Those to be sold frozen are rapidly frozen in blast freezers. The commercial blast freezer quickly takes the turkey to a freezing temperature, ensuring optimum safety and quality. They are then stored in freezers at 0° F or below. Both fresh and frozen turkeys are transported in refrigerated trucks to their destination."

Well, there you have it. How the turkey makes it to your Thanksgiving Table. No need to thank me. Just enjoy your turkey and the football games. And no – there are no commercial blast freezers for mother-in-laws.

60

Another short fun informative speech you can give to any club or Toastmasters during the Holiday Season.

It is packed with facts about Christmas trees which you can weave into an opening, then you could say, "But the problem with the Christmas tree business, and I know I am saying the obvious here, is that it is seasonal. That is not good for a business if you have bills that you have to pay every month. That is why it is important to diversify, so you have a product that you sell all year. A classic example of diversification is the guy who cuts grass in the summer and uses his truck to snow plow in the winter. But that leads me to the essence of my speech. What are we doing at our company to ensure that we have business all year? Let me _____."

Quote: Never worry about the size of your Christmas tree. In the eyes of children, they are all 30 feet tall.
~Anon

Growing Christmas Trees: Christmas Tree Farms are Big Business

Pull the covers over your head. Do not get out of bed until January 2 for your wallet's safe being. It has happened again. The Holidays have snuck up behind and smacked you alongside your head, taken out your wallet, spent all the money in it and maxed out your credit cards while you checked your bank balance everyday to see if you can buy that one last gift for that special person who will sell it at a garage sale next year. The gift will still be in its original wrapper.

And while you are stressed out over spending way too much money, you get blessed with an extra sense of guilt when you pass that Santa ringing his bell and you don't take all the change out of your pocket and throw it into his pot. You just put your head down, pretend you don't see the homeless man dressed as Santa and plow your way into the crowd merrily coughing and sneezing on each other, happily spreading germs, as you all get ready for the Holidays.

But there is no bigger joy than putting your family in the car and happily speeding off to buy a dead tree, which you will put in your house, because there is nothing like a fire hazard sitting right in the middle of your living room. A fire hazard which sucks up over a quart of water a day, just so brown needles don't fall all over the presents.

But Christmas trees are BIG business. And isn't that what Christmas is ALL about. Making money off selling dead trees? There are over 21 million trees cut around the country each year for Christmas. There are over 22,000 Christmas tree farms in the US and they take up over 447,000 acres of land, which is about equivalent to the inside of the Mall of America. Or maybe not.

And the state of Oregon is happily filled with little animals escaping the sound of chainsaws. Oregon is the nation's top producer of rainy weather and Christmas trees. Oregonians happily chop down over 6.5 million trees each Holiday season. Clackamas County alone cuts down about 3 million Christmas trees a year.

A historical note, in case you care, Clackamas County is named after Mr. Clackamas, who left the East to escape to the West, because everyone kept making fun of his name. That of course is totally false; it is named after the Clackamas Indians. And Clackamas County's claim to fame is Mt. Hood which is 11,235 feet high. Yes, you are allowed to say you live in the Hood.

But back to Christmas trees. Farmers make over 500 million a year selling Christmas trees, the Christmas tree industry hires over 100,000 people and 98% of all Christmas trees are grown on farms.

And the most Christmas tree farms are not in Oregon, but Pennsylvania which has 2,164. And besides Oregon and Pennsylvania, other states that produce over one million Christmas trees a year include Michigan, North Carolina, Washington and Wisconsin. And, I found this somewhat odd, Christmas trees are grown in all 50 states including Hawaii and Alaska.

Talking about Christmas tree farms, more than 2,000 trees are usually planted per acre. On an average, 1,000–1,500 of these trees will survive. In the North, maybe, 750 trees will remain. Almost all trees require shearing to attain the Christmas tree shape. At six to seven feet, trees are ready for harvest. It takes six to ten years of fighting heavy rain, wind, hail and drought to get a mature tree.

But wait, there is even more to know about Christmas trees. And you were worried there wasn't more? The bestselling trees are Scotch pine, Douglas fir, Noble fir, Fraser fir, Virginia pine, Balsam fir and white pine.

155

61

Have to give a speech around the holidays – here is a fun Christmas Tree quiz with questions you can ask your audience.

Quote: One of the most glorious messes in the world is the mess created in the living room on Christmas day. Don't clean it up too quickly. ~Andy Rooney

The Christmas Tree Quiz

Do you know your Christmas Tree Facts? Take this quiz and find out. Do well and you get a hug from Santa. Do badly and you are cleaning up the reindeer stall. Just answer True or False. If you cannot determine the false answers, lay off the eggnog.

- Oregon is the leading producer of Christmas trees – 6.5 million in 2002.
- To protect the environment, Oregon no longer uses chainsaws to cut down Christmas trees, but rather uses squads of roaming beavers. **False**
- The bestselling tree is Scotch pine.
- Scotch Pines also produce the Scotch for your Christmas Toddy. **False**
- More than 2,000 trees are usually planted per acre.
- In the United States, there are around a half billion real Christmas Trees growing on US farms.
- In the United States, there are more than 12,000 cut-your-own farms.
- Cut-your-own farms are the leading reason people go to the emergency room during the Holiday season. **False**
- In 1979, the National Christmas Tree was not lighted except for the top ornament. This was done in honor of the American hostages in Iran.
- In 1979, the National Christmas Tree was not lighted except for

the top ornament because Congress was late in paying the electric bill. **False**

- The tradition of an official Chicago Christmas tree was initiated in 1913 when one was first lit by Mayor Carter H. Harrison in Grant Park.
- Mayor Carter H. Harrison was lit when he announced the idea of putting a Christmas tree in a park. **False**
- The first decorated Christmas tree was in Riga, Latvia in 1510.
- The first Christmas tree retail lot in the United States was started in 1851 in New York by Mark Carr.
- The first Christmas tree retail lot in the United States was started in 1849 by the Catholic Church to supplement their bingo earnings. **False**
- Christmas trees take an average of 7–10 years to mature.
- Men take an average of 40 years to mature.
- Christmas trees are grown in all 50 states including Hawaii and Alaska.
- 100,000 people are employed in the Christmas tree industry.
- 98% of all Christmas trees are grown on farms.
- In 1856 Franklin Pierce, the 14th President of the United States, was the first President to place a Christmas tree in the White House.
- Putting a tree in the house led to Franklin Pierce's divorce. **False**
- About 21% of United States households have a real tree, 48% have an artificial tree and 32% have no tree.
- 73 million new Christmas trees will be planted this year.
- You should not burn your Christmas tree in the fireplace; it can contribute to creosote buildup.
- Cherry and hawthorns were used as Christmas trees in the past.
- Thomas Edison's assistant, Edward Johnson, came up with the idea of electric lights for Christmas trees in 1882.
- Christmas tree lights were first mass produced in 1890.
- In the first week, a tree in your home consumes a quart of water per day.

- During the Christmas season, daddy consumes as much as a quart of bourbon a day. **False**
- Michigan grows a larger variety (13) of Christmas trees than any other state.
- Because they never win the Rose Bowl, people in Michigan have turned their attention to growing different varieties of trees. **False**
- The government once banned tinsel because it contained lead. Now it's made of plastic.
- Real Christmas trees are involved in less than one-tenth of 1% of residential fires and only when ignited by some external ignition sources.
- Uncle Frank while smoking and drunk often falls asleep under the Christmas tree and has the record for burning down the most houses. **Could be true.**
- In 2007 the retail market value of the 31.3 million trees purchased at the mean average purchase price of $41.50 was $1.3 billion.
- If you understand the phrase 'mean average purchase price' you are better at math than 80% of Congress. **False**
- Helicopters help to lift harvested Christmas trees from farms.
- An acre of Christmas trees provides for the daily oxygen requirements of 18 people.
- 93% of real Christmas tree consumers recycle their tree in community recycling programs, their garden or backyard.

62

Christmas Safety Speech – here is a speech you can give or steal some tidbits from to add to your own speech about Christmas safety.

Quote: I once bought my kids a set of batteries for Christmas with a note on it saying, "toys not included."
~Anon

Protect Your Family with Common Sense

Let's start off with one important fact. When you bring a live Christmas tree into your home, you are putting a fire hazard right in the middle of your living room. According to the United States Fire Administration (USFA), "Christmas trees account for 200 fires annually, resulting in 6 deaths, 25 injuries and more than $6 million in property damage."

What is the best way to prevent a Christmas tree fire? Keep the tree wet.

As the USFA points out, "Well-watered trees are not a problem. Dry and neglected trees can be."

How hard is it to set a wet tree on fire?

According to the USFA, "For comparative purposes, the NIST fire safety engineers selected a green Scotch pine, had it cut in their presence, had an additional two inches cut from the trunk's bottom, and placed the tree in a stand with at least a 7.6 liter water capacity. The researchers maintained the Scotch pine's water on a daily basis. A single match could not ignite the tree. A second attempt in which an electric current ignited an entire matchbook failed to fire the tree. Finally they applied an open flame to the tree using a propane torch. The branches ignited briefly, but self-extinguished when the researchers removed the torch from the branches."

In other words, setting a wet Christmas tree on fire is as hard as getting a straight answer from a politician.

The USFA also offers these tips to keep your home safe from a Christmas fire.

- Needles should be green and hard to pull back from the branches, and the needles should not break. The trunk should be sticky to the touch. Bounce the tree trunk on the ground. If many needles fall off, the tree has dried out and is a fire hazard.
- Do not place your tree close to a heat source, including a fireplace or heat vent. The heat will dry out the tree. Do not flick cigarette ashes near a tree. Do not leave your tree up for longer

than two weeks. Keep the tree stand filled with water at all times.

- When disposing of your tree, never put tree branches or needles in a fireplace or wood-burning stove. Take the tree to a recycling center or have it hauled away by a community pickup service.
- Inspect holiday lights for frayed wires, bare spots, gaps in the insulation, broken or cracked sockets, and excessive kinking or wear.
- Do not overload your electrical sockets. Do not link more than three light strands, unless the directions indicate it is safe. Connect strings of lights to an extension cord before plugging the cord into the outlet. Periodically check the wires; they should not be warm to the touch.
- All decorations should be nonflammable or flame retardant and placed away from heat vents.
- Never put wrapping paper in a fireplace. It can result in a large fire, throwing off parks and embers and may cause a chimney fire.
- If you use candles, place them in holders where they cannot be easily knocked down. Never leave the house with candles burning.
- Never put lit candles on a Christmas tree. Do not go near a Christmas tree with an open flame – candles, lighters or matches.

63

It is winter and everyone has struggled through ice and snow to hear your speech. In your introduction, offer your audience some funny winter survival tips. As always, you can add your own. Then you can say, "I would also like to share some helpful tips with you on how our company can survive and prosper in this economy..."

Quote: The problem with winter sports is that – follow me closely here – they generally take place in winter.
~Dave Berry

Winter Survival Tips

- Do not get out of bed. Get a stack of good books and stay under the covers and read them all winter. When you see the first robin at your window, you can venture outside. Of course if you do not go to work all winter, you may lose your job. But hey you were looking for a job when you found that one.
- Encourage your elderly neighbors to spend the winter in Arizona. Tell them you do not want them slipping on the ice. When they move to Arizona for the winter, move into their house and jack up the heat. Hey, you don't want the house to look empty.
- People say get a remote control starter for your car. I found it is a lot cheaper to buy your wife a good pair of boots and have her start the cars.
- Screw the air quality. Buy a big snow blower and who cares about the exhaust. It beats shoveling one thousand feet of snow.
- If you cannot buy a snow blower, buy your teenage son a shovel and tell him that snow shoveling will be an Olympic event at the next Winter Olympics.
- Have NetFlix deliver videos and Dominos deliver pizza. There is no need to go outside for food or entertainment.
- Have Triple A on speed dial. Sell your kids if you need money for a membership. When it is minus 20 out, it is so nice to stand by the fireplace, look out the window and watch Triple A change the flat tire for you.
- Do not keep guns around the house. Winter will strip away your sanity day by day.
- Have a big calendar and count off the days until baseball spring training. That is the only way to maintain any hope.
- Resist any urge to cross-country ski. The people who cross-country ski also think marathons are fun. Think about it!
- When the Super Bowl is over and you are staring at three more months of winter, remind yourself it is a good thing you got rid of the guns.

- Move to Arizona.
- Move to California.
- Move anywhere WARM!
- Have *The New York Times* delivered on Sunday. Who cares how many trees they chop down for that one edition? It is worth every damn tree for great reading and your sanity.

64

Here is another great opening you can use during the Holidays. And after reading this humorous list, you can say, "And I would like to give you a more serious list, the list of what we must accomplished over _____."

Or you can say, "Well there are the top ten Holiday fears, but I think we nothing to fear about the future. I firmly believe that in large part, due to your sales efforts this year, we are in a strong position to face the future. But then again, as you know we have competitors out there who would love to steal our market share. So even though we hold a strong market position now, we can only continue to be a leader through your efforts. And of course, we must do our part too. We must continue to supply you with great products to sell and we must keep introducing new products that will meet our customers' needs. Towards that end, let me share with you some of the new products (or services) that we will launch in the coming year..."

Quote: Marry an orphan: you'll never have to spend boring holidays with the in-laws.
~George Carlin

Top Ten Holiday Fears

The Institute of Holiday Studies has released the top ten fears that people face during the Holidays.

- **Parkaphobia:** The fear that you will circle and circle the parking lot for ever, never actually making it into the mall. You will run out of gas on the 100th time you circle and you will slowly starve to death in your car.

- **Planeaphobia:** The fear that someone in your family will actually expect you to pick them up at the airport, when you even offer to pay for their taxi, no matter how much it costs. Similar to parkaphobia, you will be doomed to circling the airport for ever, while their plane is an hour late, they stop for a latte on the way to the baggage counter, then spend two hours looking for their lost bag, which will come in tomorrow, meaning you get to make another trip to the airport.

- **Giftaphobia:** You and your new boyfriend are exchanging gifts for the first time on Christmas. You both promised to keep it simple. But what does 'simple' mean to your boyfriend. Will he give you a diamond and all you give him is a CD of his favorite band. Or will he give you a blender, severing the relationship for ever and forcing you to find a new date for New Year's.

- **Treeaphobia:** You constantly check the needles on the tree hoping they're not too dry, knowing that your family is doomed and will die in a blazing inferno when the tree catches on fire. A characteristic of treeaphobics is they buy the tree the day before Christmas and dispose of it on Christmas afternoon.

- **Turkeyaphobia:** Every year you have to check the Internet to see how many minutes per pound you cook the turkey. Lurking in the back of your mind is that the turkey will be undercooked and that you and your guests will all be writhing on the floor dying of salmonella poisoning. You always make the dog taste the turkey first.

- **Bargainaphobia:** You search the ads, circle the best buys, show up at the store five hours before it opens, but in the back of your mind is the fear that your sister-in-law has out bargained you again and when you proudly show the computer you got for $400, she will announce that she got the same computer off the

Internet for $250. A common characteristic of bargainophobia is resisting the urge to strangle your sister-in-law.

- **Elfaphobia:** The fear that your fiancé will turn into an elf after you marry him and you will be forced to live with him forever because of that darn 'death till you part' bit that the minister snuck into your wedding vows.

- **Cancel phobia:** The fear that all the football players catch swine flu at the same time and all the Holiday Bowl games are cancelled forcing you to actually sit down and TALK to your relatives, including Uncle Joe who lives in a shack in Montana and has pictures of the Unabomber all over his walls.

- **Roofaphobia:** The fear that Santa Claus will actually land his sleigh on your house. All 12 reindeer weigh at least one ton and scientists have estimated that Santa's sleigh and payload weighs over 300,000 tons, not to mention Santa himself who is no light-weight. This weight will not only ruin your roof, but totally crush your house.

- **Fruitcakephobia:** You dream that you made a bet with your brother-in-law on who would win the football game and you lose, thus being forced to eat an entire fruitcake in ten minutes, washed down with moldy eggnog.

65

Here is a fun short Holiday Speech you can give at Toastmasters or a local civic club. It talks about safety and you can pick and choose just portions of the speech for an opening, then you can say, "Unfortunately, we all know someone who fell off the roof and got hurt while hanging lights. And at our company, we encourage you not only to be safe at home, but also safe at work. So let me take a second to cover some of the basic safety rules we must follow..."

Quote: Mail your packages early so the post office can lose them in time for Christmas.

~Johnny Carson

How to Hang Outdoor Holiday Lights: Survival Tips

- If you have a choice between staying inside and sipping a hot chocolate, or climbing onto a slippery, icy roof, stay inside and drink the hot chocolate.
- If your wife really wants the Christmas lights on the house, does she want them badly enough to climb a shaky ladder, crawl onto a roof when the wind chill is minus 30 degrees and the roof is covered with crusted snow and ice? It is her choice.
- Nothing ever good comes from climbing on a roof in the winter.
- To hang lights, you'll need a ladder, a tape measure, light clips/hooks, your lights, extension cords, a hammer, pliers and a screwdriver. Don't put too much vodka in the screwdriver.
- In winter the ground is frozen solid. So when you fall off the roof into the yard, it is like falling onto concrete. And you don't bounce but your bones do break.
- If your house is one story high, it might be okay to hang lights. If it is two stories high, think really hard about hanging lights. It if it's three stories high – what are you? Nuts?
- If your wife complains that your neighbors have a great light display and you have none, move her chair in front of the window, pour her a glass of wine and have her look at the neighbor's light display.
- Tell your kids that you are not hanging lights because Santa Claus' reindeer might get tangled up in them.
- There is snow outside. And snow is made out of water. And electricity and water do not mix. Why would you run an extension cord through water?
- Outdoor lights – $25 dollars. Lit-up reindeer on roof – $50. Fake Santa sleigh on roof – $50. Falling off roof, X-rays, cast, rehabili-

tation for broken bones – $35,000.

- If you must have Christmas lights on your house, hang them in July when there is more of a chance of getting sunburn than frostbite.
- Always have a person hold the ladder while climbing to put lights on your house. When you fall off, they will be able to call 911 and help will arrive quicker.
- Always check the roof for slick spots before climbing on the roof. Better yet have your son or daughter check for slick spots. They heal faster.
- It can be dangerous plugging in outdoor lights. Let your mother-in-law have the honor of 'lighting the house'.
- Measure the length of your house before hanging the lights. Nothing is worse than climbing on the roof to find that the string of lights is too short for the roof. But this will amuse your children while you sit on the roof and cuss.
- Before hanging the lights on the roof, plug them in to make sure they work. If they do not work, this is God's way of saying, "Forget the project, be safe, go inside and have some eggnog."
- Clark Griswold is not a role model.
- There are professional companies who charge $175 an hour to hang lights off your roof. Hmm, that is a lot cheaper than an emergency room visit – think about it.
- Do not hang your holiday lights if you have been drinking. If you have not been drinking, are not drunk and are in your right mind, why would you hang lights?

66

Another fun Holiday Speech which you can give in its entirety or pick and choose segments from it. You can then say, "One game we do not want to play with our customers is _____."

Quote: I once wanted to become an atheist, but I gave up – they have no holidays.

~Henny Youngman

Fun Holiday Games

- **Find Your Car:** This is a fun holiday game. You are so excited to go holiday shopping that you forget where you park your car. This is especially fun at a really big mall, like the Mall of America. Not only is the parking lot the size of Rhode Island, it is minus 40 degrees out with a chill wind blowing out of Canada. This is the segue to another holiday game – "Find Your Car Before Your Fingers Fall Off Due to Frostbite".

- **Re-gifting:** A great holiday game where you can get rid of all the junk someone gave you last Christmas. That scarf of many colors that looks like Walt Disney threw up on it. That fruitcake that has been sitting on your shelf all year. Which of course leads to another fun holiday game – "How Much Fruitcake Can You Throw Up?"

- **Find a Cheap Ticket:** Good luck with this holiday game. At the last minute, your mother announces this may be the last Christmas she can spend with her grandchildren thus giving the gift of guilt, the gift that keeps on giving. Your mother says this every year, and your wife falls for it every year, forcing you to look for cheap airplane fares or sell a kidney. Of course all the cheap airplane fares were gone by last June, taken by those inane people who actually plan six months ahead, when you just worry about getting out of bed every morning.

- **Find a Decent Tree:** Because I have an IQ of two, I play this holiday game every year, where I wait until the last possible moment to buy a tree. I know that the cost of Christmas trees will plummet before Christmas, because who buys a tree after Christmas? Of course every other male with an IQ of two, and there seems to be many of us, are all wandering the same Christmas tree lot , looking at trees that have been rejected by any normal human being. We find ourselves saying, "Gee, this tree is okay if we put that bare side against the wall and use a LOT of Christmas decorations to hide that bald spot in front." Your wife meanwhile is playing her busy holiday game of "I told you so".

- **Untangle the lights:** If you didn't have an IQ of two, this holiday game could be avoided by merely wrapping the lights every year around a rolled newspaper. But because you do have an IQ of two, you get so frustrated taking the lights off the tree that you just throw them in the box. This leads to another holiday game called "Screw the Untangling" – where you merely throw the tangled lights away and go to a drugstore and buy another string of lights.
- **Fall Off the Roof:** This is a holiday game better played by your teenage son because when he falls off the roof he will bounce better. Of course the ungrateful teenager will only have completed half the holiday decorations before he falls off, prompting another holiday game called "Have Grandma Climb the Roof". You are kind enough to hold the ladder.
- **Trick or Treat:** The holiday game played by your brain-damaged son after he falls off the roof and he doesn't realize Halloween is over and he goes door-to-door looking for Halloween treats. Your neighbors will just nod wisely and ask, "So you fell off the roof again?"
- **Visit the Emergency Room:** A holiday game played by males over 40 who live in a warm climate. After drinking too much beer and watching too many bowl games, someone decides it would be fun to go "outside and toss the old pigskin around". These men decide that it would be fun to play a game of touch football, ignoring the fact that the only exercise they have done for the past 15 years is get out of bed in the morning. This holiday game ends up with every male involved spraining every muscle (or the few muscles they have left) in their body and going to the Emergency Room.

- **Guess What Aunt Emma is Bringing to Dinner:** Every family has a member that should never be allowed to watch the food channel. This holiday game results from Aunt Emma watching the food channel, and instead of bringing something to the dinner that she is capable of making, say canned cranberries, she brings a dish called Diaper Delight, that looks like someone just changed a baby's diaper and you all stand around daring each other to taste it first. Thankfully, Aunt Emma is deaf so she does not know this holiday game is going on.
- **Hide the Good Liquor:** This holiday game involves hiding the good liquor from the dipsomaniac in your family who will drink anything if it even faintly resembles alcohol. It is a shame to waste your good liquor on him, so you use the old trick of buying the cheapest bourbon you can find and putting it in a decanter, fooling Uncle Ernie into thinking that he is drinking top-notch bourbon, even though he couldn't tell a good bourbon from cough syrup as he destroyed any taste buds he had 30 years ago. But the good thing about Uncle Ernie is that he is always the first to taste Aunt Emma's Diaper Delight. See the "Visit the Emergency Room" game listed above.

67

Even more grist for the mill, more fun Holiday Games you can work into a speech during the holidays.

Quote: Santa is very jolly because he knows where all the bad girls live.
~Dennis Miller

More Fun Games for the Holidays
- **Who's Dysfunctional:** The object of this holiday game is to go over to your relatives and survive six hours and pretend you are

a normal family. Enough said.

- **Find the Tape:** We have all played this holiday game. Let me say right now the best way to wrap presents is to go to the Dollar Store, buy gift bags and throw the presents in the bags and cover them up with crepe paper. Or you can forget this idea and play the holiday game of find the tape. You know that you have Scotch tape in the house somewhere, but it hides when it is time to wrap the presents. I have often been reduced, even after buying three rows of Scotch tape, to wrapping presents with duct or masking tape. Yes, the tape will show back up the day after Christmas.

- **Whoops! Stocking Stuffers:** This holiday game is played by optimists or people who simply wait until the last minute to buy stocking stuffers. Of course some people collect thoughtful stocking stuffers all year and place them neatly in a closet. These are the same people who buy their airplane tickets six months ahead of time, brag about it to everyone and then wonder why they have few friends. Then there are people like me, who rush to the Dollar Store at the last minute, only to discover that all the Christmas items are gone and the Dollar Store has stocked up on Easter items. You end up telling your child that purple bunny marshmallow Peeps are really cool to get in their stocking. It is a lot harder to explain the can of peas you threw in the stocking at the last minute during a panic attack where you were scared of being a bad parent and scarring your child for life as he has no stocking gifts except Peeps and more Peeps. And of course a can of peas.

- **The Assembly Game:** Probably the most famous holiday game of all time. It often starts with a father saying, "Hey, no problem, how hard can it be?" and ends with the same father curled up in a ball rocking back and forth saying, "But I can't read Chinese instructions." The extra player in the game is the mother who will say: 1) "I told you not to wait until the last minute." 2) "How come there are all these extra parts left over?" 3) "Here let me do it," and the mother will assembly the entire toy in under five minutes. This holiday game has lead many a father to drink, even though the five beers he had before assembling the toy really didn't help his cause.

- **Toy Breaking Record:** This holiday game is simple. How many toys can your child beak before bedtime? You know those toys you saved up all year to buy, so he or she can destroy them in less than six hours?

- **Forget the Batteries:** Face it. We have all played this holiday game at one time or another. Your kid has all these great toys and WHOOPS – no batteries. This often turns into another holiday game that mommy and daddy play called, 'I thought you bought the batteries'. Or yet another favorite holiday game for kids called, "Let's glare at my dumb parents".

- **Santa Wasn't Hungry:** A fun holiday game which starts when your darling child comes downstairs and notices that Santa Claus did not drink the milk or eat the cookies that he left out for Santa. This easily turns into Daddy's favorite holiday game, "Let Mommy explain".

- **Pretend It Is a Cool Present:** A holiday game we all learn to play at a very young age. For example, when you are expecting a cool new toy and you open your grandmother's gift which turns out to be a pair of pajamas. You play this game later in life when you wonder why your husband thought you had an urgent need for a chainsaw.

- **Rewrap the Presents:** Another holiday game learned in early childhood. When your parents are not around you shake the presents and can't figure out what it is, so you unwrap a corner – whoops, you just tore a hole in the wrapping and you are in BIG trouble – so you quickly get the Scotch tape and cover up the hole with about 15 layers of Scotch tape. This holiday game often turns into "I didn't do it" or "Blame my sister". Neither holiday game has ever turned out well.

- **The Real Stupid Present:** This holiday game is very simple. And stupid. Just give your wife a diet book for Christmas. This often leads to the Divorce Court Game.

- **Let's Ruin the Christmas Picture:** A holiday game often played by teenagers who get a piercing, a Mohawk hairstyle, or a tattoo just before the Christmas pictures.

68

Everyone travels on the holidays. You can use this as an entire speech, or pick and choose some holiday travel tips to weave into your speech. Then you can say, "Talking about travel, our company has traveled a long way this year. But I would like to take a few moments and talk about what we should expect on our journey next year…"

Quote: You got to be careful if you don't know where you're going, because you might not get there.

~Yogi Berra

Holiday Travel Tips

It's that time of year again. Uncle Ernie is getting out on parole. Whoops, that happens in the spring. What was I thinking? It's holiday time and many families, because they never learn their lesson, will take a road trip together. In fact many families spend more time traveling in November and December than they will the rest of the year. That is why daddy never gives up drinking for the New Year. He calls bourbon his "recovery tonic".

Well here are Uncle Ernie's tips: Never buy a Rolex from a man who is out of breath. No, here are some holiday travel tips for those of you who will be taking trips to visit friends and family.

- Don't go over 25 miles: Actually this is a very good holiday travel tip, as experts have noticed that after 25 miles, Daddy starts to grip the steering wheel too tight, Mother grits her teeth and stares ahead and little Susie and Jimmy are in danger of being dumped at a gas station in the middle of nowhere, if Daddy can figure out how to do it without getting caught. At this point he won't miss the kids, but does worry about possible jail time.

- Create a Family Travel Box with your family: Another good holiday travel tip. Fill the box with small books, magazines, maps, travel games, pens, crayons, etc. and leave your children home to play with it.

- Spend quality family time: Let's ignore the fact that there is nothing that is 'fun for the entire family' as the kids are too young to drink and instead, let's explore this holiday travel tip. Turn off the DVS player and Nintendo DS and play the travel games that you enjoyed as a kid. This should last oh five minutes, until you realize that there was a REASON they invented the DVS player and you put the Disney video back in that your brain-dead kids have only seen 535 times.

- The holidays are the busiest travel months for airports and airlines: This is why you must listen very carefully to this holiday travel tip. Never ever fly anywhere with any kid under 21. After 21, they can sit and drink with you in the airport bar. But you will ignore this holiday travel tip, won't you? So go ahead and sit in an airport for 20 hours while your flight is delayed, while your kids run up and down the airport seeking anything that contains sugar and your wife sits with her head in her hand, rocking back and forth, and moaning softly. The good news is that they will only play Frosty the Snowman one thousand times over the airport speaker system.

- Most importantly, when traveling during the holidays, be flexible: This is a great holiday travel tip. There are just some things that you will have no control over: traffic, flight delays, the screaming baby next to you, the very fat person flowing over into your seat, the bad breath of the flight attendant, the six hour wait on the runway as the toilet overflows and blue water floods the aisles. But, remember – this is the holidays and perhaps the best holiday travel tip of all is – don't pack a gun, just sit back and enjoy! Odds are that your firm resolve to "NEVER TO DO THIS AGAIN" will be forgotten by next November and you will be ready to create new holiday family memories, thanks, of course, to these holiday travel tips.

69

It's summertime and everyone is taking road trips. Here are some funny road tips you can work into the opening of a speech. And then you can say, "Now let's look at some tips on how we can make our trip to success…"

Quote: I told the doctor I broke my leg in two places. He told me to quit going to those places.
~Henny Youngman

30 Things Not to Say on a Road Trip: How to Survive a Road Trip with Your Spouse

Going on a road trip with your spouse? Here are the top 30 things not to say on a road trip. Or the top 30 subjects not to mention on a road trip. Or else your next road trip might be divorce court.

- His or her butt is taking up a lot more space than it used to.
- You are ONLY seeing her mother to stop her whining.
- The time he tried to save money by fixing the plumbing himself.
- The natural sunlight really highlights her wrinkles.
- He has to stop saying he has a 'bald spot'. Hell, the bald spot is bigger than a Frisbee. It is called being bald!
- Maybe Viagra would be a good idea for him.
- Maybe losing weight would be a good idea for her.
- The fact that he has trouble sliding his beer gut under the steering wheel.

- Quit being a cheap-ass and stop at a decent restaurant.
- Quit driving 20 miles out of your way to save one penny on gas.
- What was he thinking, eating chili on a long road trip?
- It is OKAY to stop the car to go to the bathroom every four hours.
- We don't need our car washed by the cheerleaders in bikinis.
- You would rather set your hair on fire than drive another five miles with him.
- It is okay to slow down around curves and when exiting the freeway. No one is going to take your 'macho license' away.
- Didn't he see that cop hiding?
- It is Highway 90. Not Speed Limit 90.
- I am in no hurry to get there and see your father drink.
- You were hoping that one day he would be promoted.
- Get over it. Quit driving around town looking for a motel under 40 bucks. Eisenhower isn't President anymore either.
- Why doesn't your team every get to the Super Bowl?
- Aren't you too old to be wearing jeans that tight?
- When you walk, it looks like two Volkswagens trying to pass each other.
- You really thought McCain had a chance of winning?
- What are you now? A size 14?
- My mother was right.
- College? Hell, your nephew should apply to reform schools.
- Only one lane per customer, dear.
- Diet Coke must make you GAIN weight.
- You really are too old to be driving after dark.

70

This is a great speech to give a group of students. You can easily modify it to fit the grade level you are speaking to. This speech uses humor to teach what employers expect from employees, a good solid work ethic. You can read some points off the list, then

point out, "These are more than ways to flunk a class. You take these same work habits and attitudes into any job, and you will be fired. So let's think of some positive attributes that employers look for. Any suggestions on how to make a positive impact at work?"

Quote: Thinking is the hardest work there is, which is the probable reason why so few engage in it.
~Henry Ford

How to Flunk Any College Class

Here is my advice on how to flunk English or any college class.

- Many English classrooms have computers and printers in them. This is for in-class writing assignments. Not for Facebook. But make sure you cruise Facebook while the teacher is lecturing. Also feel free to check your e-mail.
- Make sure you leave your phone on so it rings once or twice during class. You do not want to miss that important phone call from Obama or your doctor telling you that you have one day left to live.
- Text all your friends.
- Make sure you rush to class and print off your paper at the last minute. In fact make sure you do this in front of the instructor. This reassures him that you waited until the last minute to print off your paper and did not have the time to proofread it.
- Don't participate in class discussions, reassuring the instructor that you have no interest in the class and did not even read the chapters assigned.
- Whine and complain when you are assigned any paper over two pages.
- Cut and paste your paper directly from the Internet and pretend the instructor is really, really stupid and will not notice.
- Always be vague in your papers. Instead of having actual numbers simply say, "A lot of people", "Many people",

"Everyone agrees", "Most people", "As everyone knows", "We all agree". Your instructor will be dazzled by your utter lack of research.

- If you are forced to give a statistic, make it as vague as possible. Simply say that "crime has increased 25%." Do not give any actual numbers and avoid being specific, as in stating what crimes have increased, where they have increased, why they have increased, who the crime increase affects. In fact ignore the whole concept of 'who, what, why, when, where'. You know those boring five Ws.
- Even though the paper is due on Monday, buy yourself some extra time as you are special and should be treated differently than the rest of the class. Say, as if your instructor has never heard these excuses before, that your computer broke down, your printer didn't work, your flash drive did not work, you e-mailed him the paper, and did he get it?
- Always be late for class and blame the traffic, you couldn't find a parking spot, your alarm did not go off. This makes you look like a complete idiot who can't plan ahead and simply leave the house half an hour earlier.
- Make sure that your paper contains spelling mistakes, ensuring the instructor that you do not know how to use Spell-Check.
- Make sure that you make basic fifth grade mistakes, like mixing up 'their' and 'there' and 'it's' and 'its'. This will once again reassure the instructor that you are a VERY BUSY PERSON and do not have time to proofread your paper.
- When another student is making a presentation, don't pay attention. Instead do more important things like talking about the next party you are planning.
- Pretend that you are not really in college and always complain that the reading is too hard.
- Do not learn how to write a basic thesis or topic sentence. It is so much better making your reader guess what your paper is about.
- Place your head on your desk and say those early morning

workouts are wearing you out. Then go to sleep.

- Bring breakfast or lunch to class. Make sure you chew with your mouth open and the lunch contains something like sardines guaranteed to stink up the entire classroom.
- If you have to move your chairs into a circle for a group discussion, make sure you don't move the chair back. The teacher or the next class can move the chairs back. After all, they exist to serve you.
- Do not take the iPOD earphones out.
- Pretend it is not college and always ask if the paper needs to be typed.
- Even though it is a ten page paper, show up in class and ask the instructor if he has a stapler. God knows you are a busy person and did not have time to find a stapler. Why pay attention to details?
- Be sure you do not read your paper aloud before handing it in. This way it can be full of short, choppy sentences that makes it read like a one-note song. Can we say monotone?
- Make sure you use the passive voice whenever possible. Always write, "The ball was hit by John." Not, "John hit the ball." Go for the longest, most indirect way of getting your idea across.
- Act like you wouldn't know a verb if it bit you on the butt, and use is, was, have, has, got etc.
- Use vague words whenever possible. For instance use the word "thing" whenever possible.
- Even better, to make the paper longer use "that type of thing".
- Instructors also like when you use "There are". As in, "There are many people who smoke pot." It is much better than simply saying: "Many people smoke pot."
- Who needs paragraphs? Make sure your paragraphs run an entire page. Ignore that silly rule about topic sentences and one idea per paragraph.
- Make sure that when you hand in your rough draft and final draft that there are no changes. That they look exactly the same. This

always impresses the instructor with your attention to detail and your work ethic.

- When asked to hand in a detailed outline, make sure you stop at half a page.
- Show up every other week and promise that, "You will catch up."

71

Here is a list of how to tell if you are unemployed. You can use some of the tips in a funny opening. Then after the tips, you can say, "And to make sure that we all stay employed, _____." Note the way I introduced the topic, it is important to identify with your audience and let them know that you 'have been there, done that'. You too have been unemployed, and that way you don't come across as being insensitive.

Quote: The trouble with unemployment is that the minute you wake up in the morning you're on the job.
~Anon

You Might Be Unemployed If

Let it be known that I am NOT making fun of unemployed people. I have been unemployed, survived off Beanie-Weenies and slept in my van. But here are the ways you can tell if you are unemployed.

- You might be unemployed if you know the mailman by his first name.
- You might be unemployed if you think the Dollar Store overcharges.
- You might be unemployed if you break your piggy bank to buy a bottle of Two Buck Chuck from Trader Joe's.
- You might be unemployed if you look forward to watching reruns of *Two and a Half Men* every night.

- You might be unemployed if your tires are balder than your grandfather's head.
- You might be unemployed if pasta, pasta and more pasta is your main food source.
- You might be unemployed if creditors have you on speed dial.
- You might be unemployed if a big night out is 'two hot dogs for a dollar' at the local convenience store. Oh yes, and a Slurpee for 89 cents.
- You might be unemployed if every other e-mail is some fly-by-night college offering you a degree in Goldfish Training in just two easy months.
- You might be unemployed if you actually like the company of your mother-in-law.
- You might be unemployed if you think that soap operas are pretty cool now that you have time to follow them.
- You might be unemployed if you buy Kentucky Gentleman every other day and splurge on Jack Daniels for a Christmas present to yourself.
- You might be unemployed if you actually get tired of fishing.
- You might be unemployed if you keep moving happy hour up.
- You might be unemployed when every strange noise from your car sends you into a panic wondering how you will pay for ANY repairs.
- You might be unemployed if you have done more networking than NBC.
- You might be unemployed if you know that Oprah comes on at four.
- You might be unemployed if you walk your dog. A lot.
- You might be unemployed if you have given up on self-pity and are thinking about mailing homemade bombs to your ex-employers.
- You might be unemployed if you realize that life is about moving onto the next square and you are the only one who can roll the dice to get the game going.

- You might be unemployed if they know you by name at the Dollar Movie Theater. Especially on Tuesday when it is dollar popcorn!
- You might be unemployed if you wake up at three in the morning, hug your pillow and try not to worry about paying the mortgage.
- You might be unemployed if you realize that America is one tough town and when you're broke, no one gives a damn.
- You might be unemployed if you constantly wonder how long can you get away without paying the electric bill.
- You might be unemployed if you think about being a greeter at Wal-Mart.
- You might be unemployed if you wonder why people waste money on silly things, Like $300 sunglasses. That would pay your gas bill.
- You might be unemployed if you begin to think that it is okay to wear pajamas all day.
- You might be unemployed if you think the Free Trade Agreement sucks.
- You might be unemployed when you think that the definition of hell is when the average American hears 3,000 commercials a day and you can't buy a damn thing.
- You might be unemployed if you stop caring about athletes who earn over a million dollars a year.
- You might be unemployed if you throw out your alarm clock.
- You might be unemployed if you are still waiting for the economic stimulus to kick in.
- You might be unemployed if you agree to run away with Sarah Palin if she pays your bills.
- You might be employed if you are an economist explaining why everyone is unemployed.

72

Here is a speech on the best innovations in sports. It would make a good short speech for a civic club. You can also pick and choose some of the innovations for your opening. Then you can say, "And innovation is needed everywhere and here is what we need at our _____."

Quote: I believe in being an innovator.
~Walt Disney

The Best Innovations in Sports

Here are what I believe are the top innovations in sports. Feel free to add to the list:

- **Orange colored basketball:** Paul D. 'Tony' Hinkle, a coach at Butler, invented the orange colored basketball. Until the late 1950s, basketballs were dark brown, but Hinkle wanted a ball that could be better seen by players and fans. He worked with the Spalding Company and the orange ball up was tested at the 1958 NCAA Finals in Louisville. The NCAA was impressed and the new orange ball was adopted.
- **90 feet between bases:** The original Knickerbocker Rules of the 1840s established the distance between bases as 90 feet. Through trial and error, it was decided that 90 feet was the perfect distance. And it is! 100 feet would give the defense too much advantage and 80 feet would help the offense. Even today with bigger, stronger players 90 feet remains the perfect balance between a runner's speed and a fielder's throwing arm.
- **Soccer style field goal kicking:** Pete Gogolak, a Hungarian-born kicker, was made fun of in high school when he started kicking the ball soccer style. But he was the first man to kick a 50 yard field goal in college, and he changed the face of kicking. He joined the Buffalo Bills in 1964 and now everyone kicks soccer style.

- **Basketball shot clock:** The NBA introduced the shot clock in 1954, to speed up the game. Women's basketball adopted a 30-second clock in 1971. The NCAA adopted a 45-second shot clock for men which was reduced to 35 seconds in 1993 and to 24 seconds in 2000.
- **Invention of the baseball:** Ellis Drake was just a kid who never got paid for inventing the baseball. He invented the perfect ball with seams which enables curve balls, sliders and kinds of neat pitches. He lived in Stoughton, MA and played a game called 'round ball', where you threw the ball at the runner and if the runner was hit, he was out. The balls were made lead wrapped in yarn and covered in leather. These balls came apart easily and constant repairs held up the games.

  Sitting in class one day, Ellis scribbled out a design, then made a ball in his father's shoemaker shop that would not come apart easily. The two-piece, figure eight stitching ball is the same design used today. Within two years of Ellis' unpatented invention, Harry and George Wright took his designs and began selling balls to baseball teams for profit.
- **The forward pass:** The forward pass in football was legal in 1906, but rules stated it could only be thrown 20 yards. This rule changed in 1912 and you could throw it as far as you wanted. The Notre Dame–Army game of 1913 was the first extensive use of the pass after the rule changes and was the first time that long passes – 20, 30, and 40 yards – were thrown to receivers who caught them while on a dead run. The game received great publicity, and as one writer said, it "demonstrated the devastating potential of the forward pass."
- **The Three-Point Shot:** On November 29, 1980, Western Carolina's Ronnie Carr scored the first three pointer in college basketball history. Western Carolina was playing Middle Tennessee State. The Southern Conference introduced the three-point field goal by testing the experimental rule that other conferences had not adopted.

73

Sometimes it is good to get a little attitude into your speech. That 'attitude' shows you really care about the subject and are sick and tired of hearing nonsense. 'Attitude' sets a tone and makes the audience lean forward in their seats. This is also a great speech to use in front of any educators.

Also, this is a good speech to give to students. You can teach students about public speaking by saying, "I have heard many student speeches and I noticed that many student speeches lack one major ingredient. Passion. The students write and deliver speeches with all the passion of a nursing home patient on life support. Listening to most students speak is like having beer without alcohol, coffee without caffeine. What's the point? Who cares? If you want an A on that next speech, get angry, get upset. Attack the audience. Get them excited. How do you do that? Write the speech with an ATTITUDE! Here is an example of a speech with an ATTITUDE!"

Quote: If passion drives you, let reason hold the reins.
~Benjamin Franklin

Why Parents Are the Problem with Education

OK. Let's cut the nonsense. Let's throw out the stories on school vouchers and educational reform and teachers who are ill-equipped to deal with the modern world. Forget the garbage about a computer in every classroom and a bat wielding principal in every hallway. And if you dare mention back-to-basics, go lock yourself in a one-room schoolhouse and come out when you are ready to join the 21st Century.

Take every governmental tome on educational reform and make a nice doorstop with it.

The legislature can meet in special session all day long, pass every educational law they desire, and it won't make a difference.

Ladies and gentlemen, mothers and fathers, it's very, very basic. It is not the educational system that is failing our children. It's the parents. Parents simply do not know what it means to get involved in their kids' education.

Don't believe me when I say parents don't get involved? Quick – name all your kids' teachers. Name all the classes they are taking. Tell me exactly which classes they have weekly tests in. Tell me exactly what book they are reading in English, what they are studying in math, what science courses they are sweating through.

Name the last time you worked on a research project with your kid. When was the last time you did anything to encourage your kid to read, such as buying her or him a gift certificate from a bookstore? Instead of spending over $100 a month on cable TV, use that money to buy the book certificates.

When was the last time you and your kids went to the library together? When was the last time you made a point NOT to show up for his basketball game, but helped out with his lab experiment? When was the last time you walked in, turned off MTV, unplugged the video games, took away the cell phone, put a block on Facebook and kicked the kids upstairs to study?

Where did you go on the last family vacation? Did you visit some historical battlefields, a museum, or even have your kids draw a map of where you were driving? Or did you all traipse through some overpriced amusement parks cuddling up to cartoon characters while that giant sucking sound was money being siphoned out of your wallet? Money that could have brought your kid something more educational than a stuffed, copyrighted cartoon character.

Tell me – a rough estimate will do – how many hours a night does your kid spend doing homework, watching television or practicing sports? I'll make a bet that the TV and sport practices far outweigh the homework hours.

Yes, mom and dad. We all must take responsibility for our children's education. He isn't going to learn to read if he doesn't read at home. He's not going to struggle through math unless you sit down with him for an hour as he sweats through the math problems.

Forget the three days a week they spend at Pop Warner practice, Little League or hockey, I have a news flash for you. Johnny or Susie are not going to be pro athletes. Forget the three hours of television watching every night, forget the time they spend texting and talking on the phone. Take your kid, toss him into his room and say study.

If you want your kid to get a good education, it's up to you. Don't blame the teacher. In fact, if you can't remember the last time you visited your kid's classroom, you don't have much ground to complain about anything, especially teachers.

The truth is you can turn any corner and plow over a dedicated teacher. Dedicated teachers are everywhere and they are not in it for the money. They're in it because they care about kids.

But parents are not backing them up. One more quick quiz: When was the last time you went to a PTA meeting? When was the last time you made your child rewrite a paper because it did not measure up to your personal standards? When was the last time you thoroughly checked your child's homework?

If you can't answer all these questions with a strong, "Yes, I have done that," spare me the chatter about the lack of good educational facilities. When I walk onto a high school campus and see tennis courts, racquet ball courts, football stadiums, swimming pools and deluxe student theaters, I can pretty much figure out that it is not a lack of money holding back our educational system.

It is a lack of parental involvement.

So let's forget all this nonsense about education reform. We can reform the system from now until doomsday, we can pump all the money we want into the educational system, but the main problem, parental apathy, will still undermine every single reform that is undertaken.

74

Here is a list of some of the best nicknames and terms in baseball. You can pick and choose from the list and weave them into an opening. You could say: "One great thing about baseball is the nicknames and the terms. Let me share some with you." Then you can say, "They always say that a nickname is a sign of respect. Maybe our nickname should be 'Killer' as recently you all have been doing a great job and killing the competition..."

Quote: No orator can top the one who can give good nicknames. ~Ralph Waldo Emerson

Best Nicknames and Terms in Baseball

The best nicknames in baseball:
- Old Aches & Pains
- Cool Papa Bell
- Three Finger Brown
- Wahoo Sam
- Sliding Billy
- Schoolboy Hoyt
- Oil Can Boyd
- Sunday Teddy
- Say Hey
- Orator Jim
- Bucketfoot Al
- Memphis Bill
- Sweet Swinging Billy
- Eye Chart
- Steady Eddie
- Piano Legs
- The Human Rally Killer
- Toothpick Sam

- Fumblefoot Appling
- Bucky $#&*ing Dent
- Shoeless Joe
- Strawberry Bill
- Handsome Lou
- Sudden Sam
- Three Blind Weiss
- Showtime Shelton
- Twinkle Toes Bosco
- Sunday Charlie
- The Dead Milkman
- Sweet Lou
- Scrap Iron Hatfield
- Twilight Ed
- Bonham Bullet
- Double Barrel Darrel
- Hollywood Edmunds
- The Hebrew Hammer
- Mick the Quick
- Parkway Joe
- Reindeer Bill
- Brewery Jack Taylor
- Silent John
- Jump Steady
- Dimples Tate
- Slow Joe Doyle
- Goofy Gomez
- Jittery Joe Berry
- Biscuit Pants Gehrig
- Buttermilk Tony
- Doughnut Bill Carrick
- Half Pint Rye
- Meal Ticket Hubbell
- Sweetbreads Bailey

- Bird Dog Hopper
- Horse Belly Sargent
- Crazy Horse Meyers
- Muskrat Bill Shipke
- Pig Pen Dwyer
- Indian Bob Johnson
- Kickapoo Ed Summers
- Mother Watson
- Father Kelly
- Bomber Robays
- Motormouth Blair
- Steamboat Williams
- Bonehead Merkle
- Gettysburg Eddie
- Boom-Boom Beck
- Louisiana Lightning
- Bigfoot Stanley
- Walking Man Yost
- Big Puma Berkman
- Old Stubbleface
- Preacher Rowe
- Jumping Joe Dugan
- Shufflin' Phil Douglas
- Vinegar Bend
- Hippity-Hop
- The Hammerin' Hebrew
- Pronk

The best terms in baseball

- Yakker
- Uncle Charlie
- Texas Leaguer
- Tools of Ignorance
- Tater

- On the screws
- Chin music
- Can of corn,
- Baltimore chop,
- Captain Hook
- Dying quail
- Golden sombrero,
- A Lawrence Welk
- Lord Charles
- No room at the inn
- Scroogie
- Stank-eye
- Cement mixer
- Bugs Bunny change-up,
- Five and fly
- Banana
- Blind Tom
- Dead mackerel
- Ham and eggs
- Leading lady
- Bang
- Juiced!
- Merkle boner
- Pine pony
- Skillet
- A Peggy Lee, Linda Ronstadt
- Dialing eight
- Five o'clock hitter

75

Here are some facts on fat. These are good to weave into a speech
you may have to give employees or students about the importance

of good eating or being healthy. This can be used as an entire speech you can use at any health fair or rotary club. Think of this as your basic "Take Care of Yourself Speech" that fits numerous occasions. You can also weave these facts into an introduction and then say, "But we don't want to get fat here at our company; we want to stay lean and mean and to accomplish that we must _____."

> Quote: It is my theory that you can't get rid of fat. All you can do is move it around like furniture.
> ~Erma Bombeck

About two-thirds of US adults are overweight or obese. That means 134 million Americans. And there are more fat men than women. There are 65 million fat women and 68 fat men. Wow – that is a lot of fat people!

About one third of Americans are REALLY fat! The government is nice and calls them obese. About 64 million Americans are obese. But women win this one. There are 35 million obese women and only 29 million obese men.

And the news gets more depressing. When you look at Americans 20 years or older, less than one-third of them are at the right weight. About 65 million Americans are at the right weight. And here is where women make men look bad. There are 38 million women who are at the right weight. Only 27 million men are at the right weight.

In 1960 only about 44% of Americans were overweight. Not that that is something to brag about. But we have been super-sizing ourselves and today over 66% of Americans are overweight.

And it starts early. Seventeen percent of kids are overweight and 17% of teenagers are overweight.

What is the cost of all this fat? Fat people cost our economy about $117 billion dollars a year. Hmm that would pay for a few national health care plans.

Fat also equals lost productivity. About $40 million was lost in workdays, fat people spent about $63 million on doctor visits and had about $70 million worth of 'bed days'.

We could be fat because we don't do a damn thing. Only 26% of Americans participate in vigorous leisure time activities three or more times a week (getting off and on the bar stool does not count). What is really sad, "vigorous activity" is classified as "periods of vigorous physical activity lasting 10 minutes or more". Wow!

About 60% of Americans do not exercise at all. Except my ex mother-in-laws. They were very good at jumping to conclusions.

The direct cost of all this sitting round may be as high as $24.3 billion.

Oh by the way, here is what can happen when you are overweight:

Overweight and Obesity are Known Risk Factors for:

- diabetes
- coronary heart disease
- high blood cholesterol
- stroke
- hypertension
- gallbladder disease
- osteoarthritis (degeneration of cartilage and bone of joints)
- sleep apnea and other breathing problems
- some forms of cancer (breast, colorectal, endometrial, and kidney)

Obesity is also associated with:

- complications of pregnancy
- menstrual irregularities
- hirsutism (presence of excess body and facial hair)
- stress incontinence (urine leakage caused by weak pelvic floor muscles)
- psychological disorders, such as depression

- increased surgical risk
- increased mortality

So my advice is keep moving and the more you move, the further away you move from emergency rooms, diseases and other health risks.

76

Here is a short funny speech, again perfect for Toastmasters. But you can pick and choose some ideas from the speech and weave them into your opening. You could say, "Here are a few ideas for that perfect gift for the man in your life." Then you could say, "Of course those gifts may not be appreciated, but it does show the importance of knowing your audience and having the right product for the right customer..."

Quote: The Supreme Court has ruled that they cannot have a nativity scene in Washington DC. This wasn't for any religious reasons. They couldn't find three wise men and a virgin.
~Jay Leno

The Perfect Christmas Gifts for Your Man

Here are the thoughtful gifts that your man really wants for Christmas.

- Scrapbooking: What a delightful hobby to interest your hubby in. Start with the basics, a good scrapbook, some scissors, some cute materials to paste in and he can start his special project of doing a special scrapbook about YOU and all those special moments you share. But beware, your man might love scrapbooking so much that he will be home every night with you pasting and cutting and doing all sort of clever scrapbooking things instead of going bowling with the boys. How lovely.

- Dancing lessons: What a clever way to spend time together. Buy a gift certificate for free ballroom dancing lessons and slip it into his stocking. It might take away from your fun filled scrap-booking evenings, but what a lovely way to get out of the house and be together.
- Romance novels: Perhaps the gift he will treasure the most. Buy six romance novels at the bookstore and wrap up three for you and three for him. He will squeal with delight when he unwraps these heart-wrenching novels of love lost and regained and will eagerly look forward to cuddling with you every night for that special reading hour where you share the favorite parts of each book. Can it get more romantic?
- Fluffy bedroom slippers: Men hate to be seen shopping for these in public, Nothing more embarrassing that having fluffy bedroom slippers in your cart and then a buddy shows up and you have to explain that the bedroom slippers are for your wife. But once he opens these delightful slippers and wriggles his little toes into the soft, cuddly warmth of these slippers, you will have to remind him to take them off. Gosh, he might even wear them to work by accident.
- A nightshirt: Men really like nightshirts because they are easy to slip on and off and it is almost like wearing a dress. Plus they look real cool with the fuzzy bedroom slippers. Be sure to pick out a nightshirt with soft warm colors to match the glow in his eyes and the love in his heart when he opens this lovely gift.
- Romantic movies: It is very hard for men to go out and buy chick-flicks, even though deep down inside they love movies that revolve around romance and feelings and have zero action sequences. These heartfelt movies make great stocking stuffers and are great to snuggle up with and watch together on a Sunday afternoon. Who wants to watch those darn football games anyway?
- A nice bottle of red wine: Romantic movies and red wine. What a

perfect combination. It will give your man a good reason to stop drinking that beer or bourbon that he pretends to like. He will look forward to swirling the wine in the glass, sniffing its bouquet and then settling down to watch a good Meg Ryan movie.

- Oh yes – these gifts are surely heartwarming and thoughtful and are what every man secretly wants. If you relationship does not work out after my thoughtful advice, don't blame me. I will be busy scrapbooking and cannot take your calls.

77

Here is an analysis of President Obama's Nobel Prize Speech. Why is it in this list? Take the time and read the speech and the analysis and you will pick up at least three tricks you can use in your next speech. In fact the following is an entire speech course in five minutes.

Quote: I'm so overexposed, I'm making Paris Hilton look like a recluse.
~Obama

President Obama's Nobel Prize Speech: Key Writing Tips

I have been a corporate speech writer for over 12 years and key speechwriting techniques can be learned by studying President Obama's Nobel Peace Prize speech. These techniques include:

Start off by acknowledging your hosts:
Your majesties, your royal highnesses, distinguished members of the Norwegian Nobel Committee, citizens of America and citizens of the world.

Acknowledge the award you are receiving:
I receive this honor with deep gratitude and great humility. It is an

award that speaks to our highest aspirations – that for all the cruelty and hardship of our world, we are not mere prisoners of fate.

Use unusual verbs – everyone *shapes history* is a cliché. Note how he avoided the cliché by using the verb *bend*:
Our actions matter and can bend history in the direction of justice.

Make your verbs paint a picture:
Commerce has *stitched* much of the world together…
 A decade into a new century, this old architecture *is buckling* under the weight of new threats…
 Inaction *tears* at our conscience…
 Pent-up grievances *fester*…
 The absence of hope can *rot* a society from within…

Address any controversy right away:
And yet I would be remiss if I did not acknowledge the considerable controversy that your generous decision has generated. In part, this is because I am at the beginning, and not the end, of my labors on the world stage. Compared to some of the giants of history who have received this prize – Schweitzer and King; Marshall and Mandela – my accomplishments are slight…

A favorite trick – always throw in the name of the place where you are speaking:
… The other is a conflict that America did not seek; one in which we are joined by 43 other countries – including Norway – in an effort to defend ourselves and…

Remember Ethos, Pathos, and Logos – Establish your credibility, appeal to emotions then merge into logic – this section is a good example:
I am responsible for the deployment of thousands of young Americans to battle (**ethos**) a distant land. Some will kill. Some will

be killed. (**pathos**) And so I come here with an acute sense of the cost of armed conflict – filled with difficult questions about the relationship between war and peace, and our effort to replace one with the other. These questions are not new. War, in one form or another, appeared with the first man. (**logos**)

Use alliteration – note that *code* and *control* both begin with <u>co</u>:
Over time, as codes of law sought to control violence within groups...

We are the heirs of the *fortitude* and *foresight* of generations past...
The *service and sacrifice* of our men and women in uniform has *promoted peace and prosperity* from Germany...
We have *borne this burden* not...
... expressing devotion to country, to *cause and to comrades* in arms.
For when we don't, our *action* can appear *arbitrary*...

Repeat key words – note how he repeats *capacity* and *war*:
... The *capacity* of human beings to think up new ways to kill one another proved inexhaustible, as did our *capacity* to exempt from mercy those who look different or pray to a different God. *Wars* between armies gave way to *wars* between nations – total *wars* in which the distinction between combatant and civilian became blurred...

This is true in Afghanistan. *This is true* in failed states like Somalia, where terrorism and piracy is joined by famine and human suffering. And sadly, it will continue to *be true* in unstable regions for years to come.

Peace requires responsibility. *Peace* entails sacrifice.

Balance off the negative and positive forms of a word:
So part of our challenge *is reconciling* these two seemingly *irreconcilable* truths...

Think about word choice – *in the span of 30 years*, sounds better than *over 30 years*:
In the span of 30 years, such carnage would twice engulf this continent.

The old formula for a speech – tell them what you are going to say, say it, tell them what you said – note – here is where he tells the audience what his speech will cover:
I do not bring with me today a definitive solution to the problems of war. What I do know is that meeting these challenges will require the same vision, hard work and persistence of those men and women who acted so boldly decades ago. And it will require us to think in new ways about the notions of just war and the imperatives of a just peace.

Use transitional phrases – note the phrases in italics:
We must begin by acknowledging the hard truth that we will not eradicate violent conflict in our lifetimes…

To begin with, I believe that all nations…

Yet the world must remember that it was not simply international institutions – not just treaties and declarations…

Let me make one final point about the use of force…

But let me turn now to our effort to avoid such tragic choices…

This brings me to a second point – the nature of the peace that we seek…

Let me also say this: The promotion of human rights…

Use a famous person to endorse your ideas by quoting them:
I make this statement mindful of what Martin Luther King said in this same ceremony years ago: "Violence never brings permanent peace. It solves no social problem: it merely creates new and more complicated ones."

Ask key questions as a roadmap to let your audience know what

you will cover next:
What might this evolution look like? What might these practical steps be?

Begin a conclusion with a positive word:
So yes, the instruments of war do have a role to play in preserving the peace...

Use emotive language:
This is true in failed states like Somalia, where *terrorism* and *piracy* is joined by *famine* and *human suffering*...

And even as we confront a *vicious* adversary that abides by no rules...

Mix up your sentence structure – mix in short sentences with long sentences, establish a sense of rhythm, don't be monotone:
I believe that the United States of America must remain a standard bearer in the conduct of war. That is what makes us different from those whom we fight. That is a source of our strength. That is why I prohibited torture. That is why I ordered the prison at Guantanamo Bay closed. And that is why I have reaffirmed America's commitment to abide by the Geneva Conventions. We lose ourselves when we compromise the very ideals that we fight to defend. And we honor those ideals by upholding them not just when it is easy, but when it is hard.

Note how alliteration and repetition can be a powerful combination:
... I understand why war is not popular. But I also know this: The belief that peace is desirable is rarely enough to achieve it. Peace requires responsibility. Peace entails sacrifice. That is why NATO continues to be indispensable. That is why we must strengthen UN and regional peacekeeping, and not leave the task to a few countries. That is why we honor those who return home from peacekeeping

and training abroad to Oslo and Rome; to Ottawa and Sydney; to Dhaka and Kigali – we honor them not as makers of war, but as wagers of peace...

Use *urgen*t at least once:
One urgent example is the effort to prevent the spread of nuclear weapons...

Use language with biblical overtones a few times:
Those without nuclear weapons *will forsake them...*
Mix in a sense of obligation tinged with guilt. A key word to accomplish this is *responsible*:
And it is the responsibility of all free people and free nations to make clear to these movements that hope and history are on their side...

Back up your statement with specific examples:
No repressive regime can move down a new path unless it has the choice of an open door. (**statement**) In light of the Cultural Revolution's horrors, Nixon's meeting with Mao appeared inexcusable – and yet it surely helped set China on a path where millions of its citizens have been lifted from poverty, and connected to open societies. Pope John Paul's engagement with Poland created space not just for the Catholic Church, but for labor leaders like Lech Walesa. Ronald Reagan's efforts on arms control and embrace of perestroika not only improved relations with the Soviet Union, but empowered dissidents throughout Eastern Europe. (**examples**)

Use rhetorical fragments:
Agreements among nations. Strong institutions. Support for human rights. Investments in development. All of these are vital ingredients in bringing about...

78

**Here is a speech poking fun at blondes. The speech is packed with silly questions that you can lift from the speech and put into an opening, then you can say, "Now those questions were silly, but let's address some serious questions. These include _____."
And you don't have to poke fun at blondes. You can say Yankee fans, Cowboy fans... just make sure you are not offending anyone.**

Quote: Wal-Mart... do they like make walls there?
~Paris Hilton

Everyone is studying for the SATs but it is a little known fact that there is special SAT test for blondes. To apply to take the Blonde SAT test, you must take this sample test and mail it to Blondes, 101 Dismal Lane, Real World, California. The examiners will let you know if you are eligible to take the special Blonde SAT test. The test is similar to the one given to football players applying for college.
Here is the test:

- If one train is going east and one train is going west, when will they meet?
- The concept of Affirmative Action is based on nodding your head yes.
- What were the first words that Alexander Graham Bell texted to his assistant?
- Besides the Graham Cracker, what else did Alexander Graham Bell invent?
- If you buy five items at the Dollar Store and there is no tax, how much do you owe?
- If you have a Catholic mother and Jewish father, are you a Cashew?
- Is the K in knife silent? If so, why is it there?
- Who discovered Hudson's Bay?

- How many quarts of milk in a cow?
- Who takes care of the caretaker's daughter, while he's busy taking care?
- If you are driving across the desert one evening and the sun is in your eyes, are you going north or south?
- Fill in the blanks: Elvis the Pelvis had a brother called "Enis the _____".
- If olive oil is made from olives, what is baby oil made from?
- If someone with red hair is called a redhead, someone with black hair is called _____?
- Did Einstein include mothers-in-law in his theory of relativity?
- What finally ended the American Civil War in 1918?
- Who was President of the United States during Eisenhower's term?
- True or False: Cannibals don't eat clowns because they taste funny.
- True or False: Miniature golf was invented by a midget.
- True or False: Pasadena is 40 miles directly west of Los Angeles.
- True or False: Albuquerque was named after Mr. Al B. Querque, a land speculator.
- Write a short essay on why the North and South fought in the Civil War, but the East and West stayed neutral.
- True or False: Old McDonald raised the profitable eieio's on his farm.
- True or False: There are 25 answers to this test.
- When visiting Gettysburg, President Lincoln stayed at 200 Elm Street. This became known as his Gettysburg address.
- Canada is a street in New York City that is between Broadway and Park Avenue.
- True or False: Calvin Klein invented blue jeans.
- A scholar's 'body of work' is determined by a bathing suit contest.
- Does this question contain enough information for you to determine the answer: You are the bus driver. Two kids get on, one kid gets off, five kids get on and three kids get off. What color are the bus driver's eyes?

79

Here is a good informative speech you can give. Notice it contains advice about driving. You can also choose some tips from the speech and use them in an opening – for instance you could say, "Doesn't the way some people drive drive you crazy, you feel like telling them: insert tip from speech here." Then you can say, "Besides driving tips, here are some tips about our business that I would like to share with you _____." As you probably noticed, these tips can be used for teenage drivers if you have to speak at a school.

Quote: Never drive faster than your guardian angel can fly.
~Anon

Top Ten Driving Rules for ANYONE!

- If you fill your car up with gas, you cannot leave your car at the gas pump while you go in to buy a Coke. This makes everyone behind you wait for the gas pump.
- If you are not making a right turn, why are you in the right turn lane? That means the person behind you, you know the one who wants to turn right, you can tell because he has his blinker ON, has to wait for you and the light to change before he turns right.
- Do not speed up, cut in front of people, only to jam on your brakes at the red light. These other people might be actually coasting up to the red light, you know actually saving gas, while you are busy racing around like an idiot, cutting in front of people, just to stop at a red light.
- There is a long line of cars waiting to get on the freeway. You are not special. Do not race ahead to the front of the line and then try to merge at the last possible moment. This makes you look like an ass. Wait in line like everyone else.
- Cars slide and crash in rain, snow and ice. You cannot go full speed on rainy days when visibility is limited, when the ice is

covered with snow or black ice. You are the idiot that goes 70 miles an hour, passes everyone and then we all have to wait, tied up in a traffic jam, while the tow truck pulls you out of the ditch or you block three lanes of traffic after hitting a guard rail and spinning out and crashing into other cars.

- Walk through a junkyard and look at all the cars. Note the spider web patterns on many of the windshields. These are caused by people too dumb to wear seatbelts. That is where their heads met the windshield. By the way, hitting your head against a windshield in a car accident is like being dropped from an eight-story building. Not too promising for your future. Unless you like sitting in a wheelchair and drooling.

- It is a car. Not an extension of your penis. Don't be aggressive. A car is no place to prove your manhood. There are over six million crashes a year. Many caused by idiots who drive aggressively.

- Do not text while driving. It is worse than driving drunk. And the ten drivers lined up behind you at the stop light get pissed when they all miss the green light because you were texting.

- Your car has a back seat. This is like a bed. If you are drunk, use the back seat and go to sleep. When you are sober, in the morning, you can drive. If you think the back seat is uncomfortable to sleep on, try a jail cell. Or a hospital bed. Or a coffin.

- Your neck actually swivels. Isn't that amazing? Turn your neck and check your blind spot before changing lanes. Since you failed to use your blinker, it is the least you can do. Also use that special swivel feature your neck has to check behind you when backing up.

Bonus Tip: Read newspaper stories about teenagers who get killed in car crashes. It seems most of these kids die after 12 at night. Go home, do not drive after 12. Driving after 12 p.m. increases your chances of getting killed.

80

Here is a speech that makes fun of all the warnings we see every day. You can either use the entire speech for a short presentation, or pick one or two of these warnings and weave them into an opening. For example you can use the following warning signs about men and women:

Warning: Men are a species that may lead to the delusion that you can change them. Good luck on that. The basic idea when entering any relationship with a man is this: How bad can he get? Can I live with him the way he is? The basic thought process of any man is elementary. It is basically, "Will whatever I am about to do amuse me?"

Warning: Women are a species that may lead to logical thinking. They may actually make you question why you don't start saving your money and buy a house, instead of spending it on booze and women and bets on football, baseball and basketball. They will take control of your life because basically you need SOMEONE to take over your life, so you do not continue to act as a perpetual teenager with your long-term goals centering around happy hour and blondes.

Then you could say, "But I don't think I need to warn anyone about the danger of neglecting our customers ____."

Quote: Cigarette sales would drop to zero overnight if the warning said "Cigarettes contain fat".
~Dave Berry

Here is the speech:

We will start our speech on the power of love in a moment. But first we must satisfy the lawyers.

Warning: Love can be a powerful emotion leading to upset stomachs, diarrhea, obsessive behavior and broken hearts. It can also lead to irrational behavior including attending movies you never had ANY intention of seeing, shopping for curtains and matching sheets, which you never ever cared about, buying dead flowers and cheap candy, which you transfer to a fancy box. It also may result in rash decisions including getting engaged, getting married, having children, buying a house, getting divorced, giving away the house, paying alimony for many, many years.

Okay – now it is time to read about love – whoops another warning from the lawyers. Gotta love these guys.

Warning: Reading can be hazardous to your health. Might expose you to new ideas, make you realize that your current life sucks and there are other opportunities out there. As you increase your ability to read, you expose your mind to new ideas, open up new job opportunities and expand your intellectual horizons. Reading can also be dangerous to your health, because if you cross the street reading a book, you might get hit by a bus; this happens to about one out of a million readers.

Okay – back to our essay on love, which can be a powerful emotion in your life. What? Another warning? Okay.

Warning: Life can be hazardous to your health and ends 100% of the time in death.

As it often happens, love comes unexpectedly to many men and women. What? Another warning.

Warning: Men are a species that may lead to the delusion that you can change them. Good luck on that. The basic idea when entering any relationship with a man is this: How bad can he get? Can I live with him the way he is? The basic thought process of any man is elementary. It is basically, "Will whatever I am about to do amuse me?"

Warning: Women are a species that may lead to logical thinking. They may actually make you question why you don't start saving your money and buy a house, instead of spending it on booze and women and bets on football, baseball and basketball. They will take control of your life because basically you need SOMEONE to take over your life, so you do not continue to act as a perpetual teenager with your long-term goals centering around happy hour and blondes.

Okay back to the speech on love. You know on second thought, never mind.

81

Here are some key signs of growing old. Choose some and weave them into your opening. Then you can say, "But here at _____, we never want to grow old. We want to keep growing and developing new ideas. And to do that we must _____."

Quote: Middle age is when your age shows around your middle. ~Bob Hope

- You are getting old when you watch reruns of *The Golden Girls* and you think they are hot.
- You are getting old when you don't need a digital clock to tell time. You can read a real clock.
- You are getting old when you carry a flashlight to read menus in dark restaurants.
- You are getting old when you think you may have said the same thing twice, but you really aren't sure.
- You are getting old when the waitress says, "Do you want a coffee," and you think she said, "Do you want a hockey puck."
- You are getting old when your monthly medications cost more than your mortgage.
- You are getting old when it looks like you have a tan, but it is really your age spots connecting.
- You are getting old when you take pills on an hourly basis.
- You are getting old when you remember when MTV played music.
- You are getting old if your first car had a stick shift.

- You are getting old if you still believe that a phone was invented to talk on, not text, cruise the Internet, or tweet people.
- You are getting old if your first TV was black and white and only got three channels.
- You are getting old if you mistake the fire hydrant for a strangely dressed midget standing by the road.
- You are getting old when you remember when bowling scores were kept by people, not computers.
- You are getting old if you are the only one in your family who can still read a map.
- You are getting old when your kids take you to the *Antiques Roadshow* to see how much they can get for you.
- You are getting old if you remember when fast food was stealing a pie and getting out of the kitchen fast.
- You are getting old if you remember how to change the ribbon on a typewriter.
- You are getting old if you even remember typewriters.
- You are getting old if you remember putting leaded gas in your car.
- You are getting old if you remember when airlines actually served meals.
- You are getting old if you remember watching baseball players on TV smoking in the dugout.
- You are getting old when people perform the sign of the cross before getting in the car with you.
- You are getting old when you never see a newscaster your age.
- You are getting old when your grandkids have to help you with the child-proof caps.
- You are getting old when you worry if it is heartburn or a heart attack.
- You are getting old when you call everyone Buddy because you can't remember their names.
- You are getting old when you remember when Notre Dame was actually good in football.

- You are getting old if you have outlasted the last five Notre Dame coaches.
- You are getting old if you have given up on the Cubs ever winning.
- You are getting old when you buy your reading glasses at the Dollar Store and place them around the house. You also keep some in your car. And then you still lose half of them.
- You are getting old when you don't remember what Christmas present you are wrapping and who that present is for.
- You are getting old when you really don't want anything for Christmas that you can't drink. God knows you have enough clothes to last a lifetime, which at your age may not be that much longer.
- You are getting old when you creak when you sit down, you creak when you stand up, you creak when you walk...
- You are getting old when you remember chalkboards in classrooms.
- You are getting old when you remember school prayer.
- You are getting old when you shave by feel not by sight.
- You are getting old when it is getting tougher to see over the steering wheel.
- You are getting old when you get up the next morning and your car's blinker is still flashing.
- You are getting old when you avoid spicy food – burns going in, burns going out.
- You are getting old when you always carry Tums and Advil in your purse.
- You are getting old when the kids say you don't do a good job cleaning the dishes. There are still food spots on them. Heck, you are just glad you can see the dishes.
- You are getting old when you begin to think that big button remote might be a good idea.
- You are getting old when your main appointments are doctors' visits.

- You are getting old when ARRP sends you birthday greetings.
- You are getting old when all of your high school friends tend to look alike.
- You are getting old when you can't see the numbers on the scale.
- You are getting old when your idea of exercise is walking up the stairs to go to bed.
- You are getting old when you don't know or care about the latest TV shows.
- You are getting old when you look forward to Lawrence Welk on Public Television.
- You are getting old when you actually remember Harry Truman.
- You are getting old when the kids don't understand what a great singer Dean Martin was.
- You are getting old when your font is set at 18 on your computer.
- You are getting old when you give up worrying about your bald spot and start worrying about your prostate.
- You are getting old when every doctor looks like a kid.
- You are getting old when you give up dusting. Why clean what you can't see?
- You are getting old when you remember it took two people to carry your first microwave into the house.
- You are getting old when you remember cooking popcorn in a brown paper bag in the microwave.
- You are getting old if you tell your kids you had three channels of TV when you grew up and they were all black and white.
- You are getting old when you hide Christmas gifts so your husband won't peek, but you don't remember where you hid them.
- You are getting old when it is too much effort to add water to your bourbon and you just drink it straight.
- You are getting old when you never buy a sweater or sweatshirt that you have to pull over your head. Who can lift their arms that high?
- You are getting old when you twist your back just getting out of

bed.

- You are getting old when it would take a cement truck to deliver enough cream to 'smooth your wrinkles'.
- You are getting old when your main shopping worry is finding the closest bathroom.
- You are getting old if your main wardrobe consists of sweatpants.

82

Choose some of these signs for your speech opening. You can say, "Although divorce is not recommended, there are some signs that maybe it is time that you and your spouse should separate. Some of these signs include _____." Then you can say, "Divorce is no laughing matter. As they say, marriage is grand, divorce is a hundred grand. And we don't want our customers to divorce us. So how do we keep them?"

Quote: I'm an excellent housekeeper. Every time I get a divorce, I keep the house.
~Zsa Zsa Gabor

How to Tell When to Get Divorced

You know it is time to get divorced when you answer the marriage counselor's questions like this:

- What does he do that drives you crazy?
  Wakes up in the morning.
- What does she do that drives you crazy?
  Breathes.
- What is one thing you are willing to do to change things?
  Leave.
- What is your favorite activity together?

Hallway sex; we pass each other in the hallway and say screw you.

- What is the one thing you do to save your marriage?
  Don't keep guns around the house.
- What is your back-up plan?
  Put the car in reverse and hit him again.
- What issues have brought you to marriage counseling?
  His two girlfriends.
- What started this animosity?
  The words 'I do'.
- Do you feel distant from each other?
  Not distant enough – another state would be better.
- What did you expect to accomplish with this counseling?
  A guilt-free divorce.
- If you could change one thing in the relationship, what would you do?
  Get a new husband.
- How long have you been married?
  70 years.
- Are you sure?
  Okay, only ten but I use dog years for this relationship.
- What was the last fun time you two had?
  When we took separate vacations.
- How hard will it be save this marriage?
  It would be easier saving the Titanic.
- The church feels you should be married for life.
  Yeah, but that rule was created in the Middle Ages when people died at 30.
- Why do you say this marriage is like your saving account?
  I have very low interest in him too.
- What do you think about the institution of marriage? Should gay couples get married?
  Yes, they need to suffer to.
- So you say you never go to bed angry?

No, I sleep on the couch.

- What's your idea of the perfect living environment?
  A duplex.
- What part does religion play in your marriage?
  I pray everyday he will leave.
- Do you hold hands in public?
  Yes, if I let go, he cheats with any bimbo.
- Do you have sexual problems?
  Nope, my boyfriend is good in bed.
- Have you ever been happy?
  Yes, for twenty years, then we met.
- Do you ever speak to your husband about what worries you?
  I haven't spoken to him in ten years. I hate to interrupt his stories about his glory days when he wasn't bald with a potbelly.
- What would you think if she ran away with another man?
  Celebrate.
- What could you do to be more affectionate?
  Get two girlfriends.
- What is different about her since you got married?
  About thirty pounds.
- What is the main philosophy of your marriage?
  Never go to bed angry – stay up and fight.
- Why do you wear the wedding ring on your middle finger?
  That is the only thing that I can get up anymore around her.

83

Here is an ironic list you can share with a women's group or employees on how to find the perfect man. Or you can just pick and choose one or two items for your opening. Then you can say, "Okay, that was a semi-funny attempt at what makes the perfect man, but there is a more important question, we must ask. Who is our perfect customer? That is an important question, because we

don't want to waste our time and effort going after the wrong customers. Let's be smart and spend our time and resources going after customers that we are a good match with. What type of customers are those? We determine that by looking at our strengths. We ask questions. What makes us stand apart from the competition? I think – and I would like to hear your opinions – but I think our strengths include _____."

This can also be used a short stand alone speech for Toastmasters or other speaking groups.

Quote: Men should be like Kleenex, soft, strong and disposable.
~Cher

How to Find the Perfect Man

Having trouble finding the right man? Our new dating service, by using the below special list of male attributes, ensures that we do not just hook you up with anyone, but with someone who shares your same goals, interests and enthusiasm for life. To help us start finding that perfect man for you, let's look at a list of key male attributes. For your next mate, do you want?

- Someone who has an attractive comb-over.
- Someone who has an inability to hold a job.
- Someone who considers road kill "FREE FOOD!"
- Someone who has stained teeth from chewing tobacco.
- Someone who has the ability to blow his nose without using Kleenex. "Just hold one nostril..."
- Someone who has long greasy hair.
- Someone who has prison tattoos, nothing like a homemade tattoo.
- Someone who has smoker's breath.
- Someone who is 30 pounds overweight.
- Someone who has ex-wives.
- Someone who enjoys romantic dinners at Burger King.

- Someone who has an ability to talk about himself forever.
- Someone who has the ability to tell his high school football stories over and over.
- Someone who has the ability to multitask, drink beer, eat chips and click through 20 channels at once.
- Someone who has the ability to sit for hours on end on his fat rear end watching sporting events.
- Someone who is too lazy to PLAY golf but can watch it for hours on TV.
- Someone who thinks poker championships on television might be even better than pro wrestling.
- Someone whose height of ambition is to get disability checks for life.
- Someone who leers at all your friends and compares their breast size.
- Someone who never meets your eyes, but stays focused on your breasts.
- Someone who belongs to at least three Fantasy Football Leagues and two Fantasy Baseball Leagues.
- Someone who still has a bottle of High Karate which he splashes on for special occasions.
- Someone who can quote Homer Simpson but not Shakespeare.
- Someone whose potbelly hangs over his Speedo bathing suit.
- Someone who tells dirty jokes at the Thanksgiving dinner table.
- Someone who has spray painted his own car to save money. When he ran out of gray paint, he switched to red.
- Someone who thinks formal wear is a leisure suit he has been saving for special occasions.
- Someone whose favorite fabric is polyester.
- Someone who only leaves the house to go the unemployment office.
- Someone who drinks heavily and constantly.
- Someone who will get out of the halfway house soon.
- Someone who takes you to Thanksgiving dinner at the Salvation

Army.

- Someone who thinks moving up to a double-wide might be nice one day.
- Someone who thinks bowling shoes can be worn as dress shoes.
- Someone who sees nothing wrong with the three pit bulls he lets wander around the house.
- Someone whose breath smells like he swallowed a skunk.
- Someone who thinks only sissies use deodorant.
- Someone who thinks Ripple is fine wine. Not as good as Thunderbird, but still a fine wine.
- Someone who will hate to give out his address because of all the bench warrants.
- Someone who still lives at home and loves video games.

84

America is changing. One way to show how America is changing is to show how our health care system must adjust to deal with baby boomers. Just pick and choose some facts from the below speech to show how baby boomers will impact America and taxpayers. This speech is an excellent example of how you must examine trends and then prepare for them by changing the current system to deal with reality.

You can give the entire speech, then say, "I didn't mean to go on and on about baby boomers, but they do prove an important fact. Our economy is constantly changing and adjusting to meet the needs of our citizens. And that means we must all look ahead and make adjustments. What is coming down the road that will affect our business? What trends must we monitor and prepare for? How will these trends affect our business? Well, let me share with you a few trends we must monitor and then let me share some ways we can prepare for these trends to ensure our success..."

Quote: Look to the future, because that is where you'll spend the rest of your life.

~George Burns

It is called the Silver Tsunami. Over the next two decades, nearly 80 million Americans will become eligible for Social Security benefits, more than 10,000 per day.

That means, when you look at the trends, you will have more old people to support. Right now there are 3.3 workers supporting an old person. Soon, there will only be 2.1 people to support one old person. Hmm – I bet that this will increase what they take out of your paycheck.

And more good news, a lot of these baby boomers forgot to take care of themselves. More aging boomers are being hospitalized for heart attacks than people their age were a generation ago, and the increase in cases will place a big burden on cardiac care wards nationwide. And talking about increases – hmm think health care premiums, thanks to the baby boomers.

The 80 million baby boomers born between 1946 and 1964 now constitute a third of the US population, raising the specter of more disease and more costs for the health care system. Gotta love those baby boomers.

US hospitals already spent $56 billion in 2007 treating baby boomers ages 55 to 64. This isn't going to get better, only worse. Again, I know you can't wait to see how taking care of these baby boomers will increase your health premiums, leaving you even less to take home.

The average hospital cost for a baby boomer patient was $11,900 compared with $10,400 for 45 to 54 year olds.

Baby boomers were 2 to 3 times more likely than 45 to 54 year olds to be hospitalized for osteoarthritis, stroke, respiratory failure, irregular heartbeat, chronic obstructive pulmonary disorder, blood infections, and congestive heart failure as well as undergoing knee and hip replacements and to have heart bypass surgery.

About a quarter of baby-boomer households have so far failed to accumulate significant savings. They appear likely to depend entirely on government benefits in retirement. "The government" means the taxpayer, which means you – the young taxpayer.

Baby boomers in the United States may enter their 60s with far more physical disabilities than previous generations, which could spell trouble for an already overburdened health care system. Hey it is only money – thanks to the Baby "Doomers" you can keep sending the government more and more money.

The annual report on the financial health of the Social Security Trust Funds by the Social Security Board of Trustees stated that costs will exceed tax revenues by 2016. Oh boy – dig deeper Mr. Young Taxpayer.

More than half of working women do not have access to pensions or other retirement plans. And those who are fortunate enough to have access to health and retirement plans are now contributing to those plans out of their smaller paychecks leaving them less money to save for the future. Hmm – think TAXES for you to support these women.

Unlike Social Security, Medicare already spends more than it collects from payroll taxes. The numbers are numbing. Medicare spending has almost doubled over the past decade, from $148 billion to $283 billion. The prescription drug benefit added by Congress added almost $60 billion annually to the cost. Need I point out what this will cost you?

The cost of Social Security and Medicare will grow from nearly 7% of the economy today to around 14.5% by 2040. To put that number in context, if we spent 14.5% of GDP on these two programs today they would consume over 90% of all federal revenues. Unless we have more federal revenue. Hmm – where could that come from?

The Alzheimer's Association, based in Chicago, predicted that more than 7.7 million Americans will develop Alzheimer's by the year 2030, a 48% increase over today. That means the Baby "Doomers" won't remember what they are costing you.

85

We all have insecurities. And sharing a few of your insecurities with the audience makes you seem more human. They don't have to be deep insecurities like you "hated your mother". No one really wants to hear that anyway. So here is a lighthearted list – choose some insecurities. Then you can say, "Remember that our customers are like you and me. They have insecurities too. And it is our job to help them address their insecurities. Sure we are just a roofing company, but we can give them a secure feeling that they are getting a good product at a good price and they never have to worry about that roof, when they can worry about more important things like what was their son doing out so late…"

Quote: Each one of us requires the spur of insecurity to do our best.
~Robert Frost

My List of Insecurities: What Would Your List Look Like?

- How do you write email? Is it e-mail or email?
- Did I go through the yellow light too late and are there any cops around?
- Will my kids ever grow up and leave home or will they keep coming back?
- I am wearing blue jeans, blue shirt, blue jacket. Is that too much blue?
- No one seems to even notice or care that I am wearing too much blue. Have I turned into an invisible middle-aged man?
- Did I talk too much or not enough during that job interview?
- Do they all notice that even though it is a football party, I really could care less about football?
- She is asking for car advice. Should I admit that I can't tell a fuel pump from a radiator or fall back on that old standby, "Well, just remember to check your fluids"?

- I hate driving across this bridge. What happens if I get a flat tire or my car stalls? Where do I pull over?
- Am I getting to be one of those old people who talk too much about their aches and pains and I know that no one really gives a damn?
- Is there an important appointment somewhere that I am missing?
- Is this heartburn or a massive heart attack?
- Is a sign of old age that you hate video games because they are too complicated to learn?
- Is this a headache or a massive brain tumor?
- Are these just spots on my face or skin cancer that will kill me in less than a year?
- Is some mastermind stealing my identity, and if he is a mastermind, why is he wasting his time stealing my identity?
- If I was granted one person in history to talk to and if I chose Hitler, how would we communicate? I mean I can't speak German.
- Am I the only one that misses Microsoft Word 2003? Am I the only one still confused by Word 2007, 2011 ad nauseam?
- Am I the only one in the world that does not own an iPOD and sees no reason to?
- Am I the only one left in the world who still orders his coffee black? Should I give in and start ordering fancy espresso latte decaf mint julep coffees?
- Should I admit that sometimes I actually like Lawrence Welk on PBS? Is there a support group for that?
- Should I admit that I have not voted in the last five Presidential elections because it seems to make no difference?

86

Safety speeches, telling employees the importance of safety on the job, are one of the many speeches that executives must give on a

regular basis. A growing concern that must be covered in safety speeches is texting and driving. Here is a short speech telling your employees, or a group of teenagers, why they shouldn't text and drive. You can also pick and choose tips from this speech to incorporate into a longer speech about safety at the workplace.

Quote: When everything's coming your way, you're in the wrong lane.

~Anon

25 Reasons Not to Use a Cell Phone While Driving

- There are a thousand ways to die in a car crash and they are all permanent.
- No message is important enough to die for.
- Do you want a free nose job when your head hits the windshield?
- Everyone around you is texting. You need to watch out for them because they are not watching out for you.
- You may never make that great sale you been chatting about if you don't hang up and drive.
- Keep texting while driving and you won't have to worry where you and your friends are meeting.
- Do not call to ask what is for dinner. Hang up and worry about getting home safely to even eat dinner.
- Hit someone while texting and your next cell phone call will be from your jail cell.
- Drive and dial a cell phone and you are dialing the Grim Reaper. There are no cell phones in coffins.
- Would you let a blind person drive? Yet you are blind to the road when texting or dialing.
- If you saw the driver next to you reading a book and driving, would you think he was crazy? Yet, what are you doing when reading a text message?
- Do you want to trade in your set of wheels for a wheelchair? Half a million people are injured each year involving a distracted or

inattentive driver. Hmm, is a phone call that important?

- Every day, there are at least 800,000 people trying to kill you. On any given day, more than 800,000 vehicles were driven by someone using a hand-held cell phone.
- Would you like to be the one who explains to Jennifer Smith that you killed her mother while talking on the phone? She heads FocusDriven and got involved after a driver, talking on a cell phone, killed her mother.
- Would you like to talk to any parent who lost a kid because you were talking or texting on a cell phone?
- If texting is worse than driving drunk, only one questions remains. Are you an idiot?
- When driving, use your cell phone only for an emergency. Like when you get hit by another idiot who is talking on a cell phone.
- Is a two minute conversation worth two years of recovering from an accident?
- Would you read this list while you were driving? Think about it.
- It is hard dialing with a stump of an arm. Accidents cause amputations.
- Why would you let a two ounce cell phone cause you to crash a 2000 pound car?
- Cell phones kill.
- There are no cell phones in heaven.
- Your friends can share the video of your funeral on their cell phones.

87

Here is short tongue-in-cheek speech on the advantages of going to work tired. This is a fun speech to give at a Toastmasters or a local civic club. You can also pick and choose some ideas from the speech – maybe make a short list – "Three great things about going to work tired" and work it into your opening.

You could say, "I know many of you dislike early morning meetings, but there are some benefits to coming to work tired. Some of the benefits include _____. Of course, I am being facetious because we all need to come to work, prepared to do our best work, as our company and industry are facing challenges that we must all prepare to meet. Let me discuss some of these challenges and what we must do to prepare for these challenges."

Quote: If I didn't wake up, I'd still be sleeping.
~Yogi Berra

The Advantages of Going to Work Tired

There are a number of books out on Power and they are all designed to help get you ahead in the business world. For instance there is a new book out called *Power Sleep*, but I fell asleep halfway through reading it, but I think the essence was that if you get a good night's sleep, you will be "at the top of your game" – that is a phrase we Power Business writers like to use, "at the top of your game".

Anyway a good night sleep ensures that you will be bright-eyed and bushy-tailed (oh where, oh where are the cliché police when we need them). You will dominate in business and leap ahead to that vice president spot, thereby filling the American Dream of being a success and having to work 60 hours a week, instead of 40.

I actually do not know if it is a good idea to go to work fully awake, at least not in many of the jobs I have had. Sure, it might pay to be fully awake if you operate heavy equipment or perform brain surgery, but there are some jobs where it might help to be a little drowsy or at least a little brain damaged.

If you were fully awake and aware of what you were doing for a living, you might be tempted to jump out of a window.

The advantages of going to work half asleep and half conscious are that you have no desire to jump anywhere; you are content to stumble down the hallway and pour a cup of coffee without burning yourself or anyone around you.

Plus, if you go to work fully awake, you might realize that your corporation has not shown a profit in over ten years, many people around you seem to be disappearing and that the last CFO absconded to Brazil with all the retirement funds, leaving you to face the retirement choice of living with your children or working until you get up one morning and have to call in dead.

See, these are awful things to have to deal with. Whereas if you go to work half awake, your biggest worry is who forgot to make the coffee and why does the copy machine hate you and automatically jam up when you get anywhere near it?

And the other advantage of going to work half asleep is that you have the attention span of a gnat and cannot read more than 400 words, which is a blessing to you and your audience.

88

Here is an opening which tells how to avoid things you cannot change. You can change the speech around many ways, shorten it, add you own insights, but the key phrase to take away from this speech is "And you can't cure that."

After talking about "things you can't cure", you could say, "And the phrase 'and you can't cure that' also applies to work. There are many things we cannot change about the issues impacting our industry. Many industries, I am sure, are dissatisfied with issues and regulations that they must deal with. For instance, I am sure that the banking industry is not pleased with many of the new rules and regulations that Congress has passed. But the laws are passed. Signed, sealed and delivered. And any banker, worth his salt, knows 'and you can't cure that'. And once you realize 'you can't cure that', then you can move onto a more important step. A positive step. How do you deal with the things you cannot change? How can they make you a better company? How can they foster new ideas? In short, if you can't cure it, step back and put a plan in place to deal with it and become a better company, better prepared for the future."

Quote: When somebody tells you nothing is impossible, ask him to dribble a football.

~Anon

The Best Quote in the Entire World

I am driving home with my friend. He is listening to a message on his cell phone which goes on and on and on. He finally just hits delete. And then, and this is a historical moment, when that solid Midwestern common sense just reared its head and made sense of the whole world. My friend, who is from Iowa, turned to me and said, "God, that was my mother and she went on and on. But she is a woman and you can't cure that." (You can also use man.)

And then I realized my friend had hit the pinnacle, the apex of his career. Never in his lifetime could he top that quote.

"She's a woman and you can't cure that."

It was Dale Carnegie reincarnated. It was the classic Dale Carnegie quote, "You can't win an argument" reduced to its essence.

"She is a woman and you can't cure that."

It was a quote that you could tuck into your back pocket and bring out to deal with life's frustrations and it would fit every single damn time! I don't need to complain that I have arthritis. I don't need to complain that I am losing my hearing, eyesight and memory. It can all be summed up by – "I am getting old AND YOU CAN'T CURE THAT."

It is not resignation, it is not quitting, it is not giving up the good fight. That quote personifies acceptance, at some point, that we can only achieve peace and contentment when we realize "AND YOU CAN'T CURE THAT".

It is the old saying, "The only good thing about beating your head against a wall is when you quit." Because how many times do we complain and fight against things "WE CANNOT CURE"?

You no longer have to worry about your neighbor who has an IQ a point higher than a beaver. When your neighbor rages on and on about how Obama was elected because he was BLACK, all you have to say to yourself is, "My neighbor is an idiot AND YOU CAN'T CURE THAT."

You no longer have to worry about your son or daughter being teenagers, when they act like someone opened up their skulls, inserted an eggbeater and scrambled any common sense they possessed. All you have to say is, "They are teenagers AND YOU CAN'T CURE THAT."

The next time you hear some conservative rant and rant on some TV news show, you don't have to get upset. All you have to say is, "He was dropped on his head as a child AND YOU CAN'T CURE THAT."

So as you go through the day and you get frustrated by one idiot after another, simply repeat this: "They are an idiot AND YOU CAN'T CURE THAT."

89

Here is a list of annoying things. This is a great idea generator and maybe you can list annoying things at your workplace, in your industry, about the government, but it is a good theme to weave a speech around. You can pick out five annoying things, then tell your audience, "And let me touch upon our industry for a minute. I think we can agree that we don't agree with the way our competition is eating into our market share. How annoying is that? Now we can complain that it is annoying or we can actually take some positive steps to protect and grow our market share. These steps would include _____."

Quote: There is nothing so annoying as to have two people talking when you're busy interrupting.
~Mark Twain

List of 100 Annoying Things

- Red lights
- Athletes celebrating after making a tackle. Come on. It's your job!
- Conservatives
- Rap music
- Boston Red Sox fans
- Alabama football fans
- This list
- Ex-wives
- Loud commercials
- People who love their pets too much
- Men who watch EVERY football game
- Plastic bags that don't open
- Christmas music
- Christmas
- Valentine's Day
- Mother's Day
- Father's Day
- Cute female newscasters
- Coffee that is TOO hot
- Melted chocolate
- Congress
- National Health Care Debacle
- Expensive bourbon
- Couples holding hands in public
- Couples who "never fight"
- Marriage
- Flat tires
- Crooked eye glasses
- Chatty Pilots

- Taking off shoes at airport security
- People that don't cover their hands when coughing
- Harry Potter Sequels
- Diet root beer
- Warm beer
- People in front of you who don't sit down at games
- Cute cell phone rings
- People texting and driving
- Overpriced movie popcorn
- Cold McDonald's French fries
- Wet newspapers
- Bigots
- Mean people
- Tip jars at coffee shops. All you did was pour a cup of coffee.
- Cute cocktails with umbrellas in them
- People with more than two cats
- Any new *Spiderman* movie
- Air Guitar contests
- Clingy women
- Clingy men
- Comics who swear every other word
- Hooters – it drove back Women's Lib at least 50 years
- People who won't buy a book for $10 but will spend over a thousand on a big-screen TV
- Slow Internet service
- Women who don't drink martinis
- Judgmental people who write lists like this
- Conan O'Brien
- Any reality show
- *American Idol* – the 60th season
- Wal-Mart wages
- College professors who need a real job
- Mayonnaise
- Mustard

- Spell-check that has no idea how to spell that word I misspelled
- Any new update to any Microsoft software
- People who wear iPODS everywhere
- Celebrities who love Haiti even though they couldn't spell it two weeks ago.
- People who think the government owes them a living
- Waiting for any doctor
- The worried well
- Evangelists
- Cage fighting
- Poker on TV
- People who want their flood insurance covered by the government when they live in "The Flats"
- Bankers
- Relief pitchers who can't throw a strike
- Field goal kickers who choke
- Women who talk in baby voices
- Comb-overs
- Any ad for "enlargement"
- Career colleges who 'forget' to tell students credits don't transfer
- AOL
- English soccer fans
- People addicted to tooth whitening
- Tony Small
- Fox News
- Rush Limbaugh
- Men who play over 18 holes of golf.
- Skiing. It's cold and you can break bones.
- NHL All-Star Game – hockey without checking – PLEASE!
- The Pro Bowl – what's the point?
- Letting the winner of the MLB All-Star Game have home field. Shouldn't it be the best record?
- Pro teams which are too traditional to put the player's name on the jersey

- Cubs fans who think they actually have a chance
- Million dollar basketball players who can't even make a free throw
- Teachers who whine about being underpaid – they only work eight months a year!
- People who prejudge. Okay, you might have been wise to prejudge this list and not read it.
- Young love
- A list of annoying things that leaves off lawyers

90

Here is fun list of things you don't want to hear your doctor say. Makes for a fun opening and it is very easy to then say, "Well, those are some things that we don't want to hear our doctor say. But think about this, what are some of the things that we don't want our customers to say?"

You can also use this list as a creativity session. You could tell the employees to make a list of "Things you don't want to hear your customers say. Be creative with your lists, look upon this as brainstorming ideas, so we can improve our customer service. After you have made your lists, let's go around the room and have an open, honest discussion about the important changes we should make in customer service, so we can retain and recruit more customers."

Quote: The doctor gave me six months to live, but when I couldn't pay the bill, he gave me six months more.
~Walter Matthau

Whoops and Other Things You Don't Want to Hear Your Doctor Say

Going to the doctor is never fun. And you have to wonder about the sanity of doctors. Who wants to work around sick people all day? But here are some phrases you never want to hear from your doctor or from anyone on their staff.

- Whoops, normally I take off that diamond ring before giving a prostate exam. Sorry.
- Mrs. Watson, the good news is that it is not a tumor. You are pregnant. I don't get to say that to many women who are.
- Well don't be upset, Mr. Watson, vasectomies have a 2% failure rate and you hit the jackpot.
- If I gave you another facelift, Mrs. Jones, you would have hair on your chin.
- On no, our scales are very accurate. You're just fat. Maybe even obese.
- Well this sonogram shows that your baby might have a tail and horns. Who did you say the father was?
- How ugly is your wife, Mr. Thomas? Viagra normally works for everyone.
- This is my first day of drawing blood. It might take a few tries.
- We are sorry about that mastectomy; we got your files mixed up with Mrs. Brown's.
- Well you can cure your kid's behavior problems with Ritalin, or duct tape and a good locked closet.
- You might want to check with your husband to see how you got herpes. That is all I can say.
- Well, you know, Mrs. Smith, at your age bra sizes change due to gravity. You wear a 34 long now.
- Do you have a will?
- You might want to consider who will take over your business.
- The good news is that you have hemorrhoids and I don't.
- You will know why I am wearing a mask when you see your bill.
- We don't like to use the word deadly, we like to say fatal.
- When my nurse said CTD, she meant Circling the Drain. Just a little medical humor.

- Well, you won't have to worry about watching the Super Bowl next year.
- It's official, you will never see the Cubs win a World Series.
- It's prostate cancer, but at your age, something else will kill you before it does.
- Before I tell you what you have, can you pay in cash?
- So have you thought about cremation?
- WOW!
- Whoops!
- Damn!
- Heck, we all make mistakes.
- I have never seen a penis that infected before.
- Wow, your blood pressure is so high that any sex will kill you.
- The bad news is this is going to take extensive medical treatment. The good news is I can pay off my lake cabin.

91

How to be annoying. Here is a list that you can easily add to. It lists ways to annoy people. You can pick and choose some ideas, then add your own. Then you can say, "And what are some ways we can annoy our customers. Well some ways might include bad customer service, not delivering on time, not making a good product. And we don't want that to happen."

Quote: I don't have pet peeves. I have whole kennels of irritation. ~Whoopi Goldberg

How to Be Truly Annoying

- Don't go at a green light – stay still as long as you can and see how many people you can get to honk their horns.
- Call up a football fan during the Super Bowl and try to sell him something.

- When there is a long line of cars behind you at the gas pump, make sure you clean your windows, check your tire pressure, pump your gas, leave your car at the pump, go in and pay, walk to your car, stop, walk back in the store for a Coke, then walk back to your car, pretend it does not start, open the hood, check the battery, get back in the car and take off. Fast. Someone might be chasing you.
- When in your car, put your makeup on at a stop sign and see how many cars you can back up at the intersection.
- In a crowded parking lot, walk to your car, wave at the man waiting to take your parking place, sit in your car, listen to the radio, have a long cell phone chat, get out of your car and walk back into the store. Be sure to wave again at the nice man waiting for your parking space.
- When your girlfriend is watching the show she waits for all week, walk in and say, "We need to talk." Sees how she likes it.
- When you see someone with a flat tire, pull over and ask, "Going bowling, looks like you need a spare." Then drive off.
- Call up a store and say, "Why can't Dr. Pepper have babies? Cause he comes in a can."
- Pile 50 items on the express lane meant for 10 items.
- Tear the tag off something at Wal-Mart so there is no bar code. See how long the line behind you backs up while they do a price check.
- Wait until your wife has the worse day ever at work, wait until she is dead tired, then walk in and ask, "What are we having for dinner."
- Wash the whites and colors together. Tell your wife you were integrating the laundry because you believe in civil rights.
- Because you need something to do, tell the kids their curfew is now 8 p.m. and be amused for hours as they throw a fit.
- Unplug the mouse from the computer and see how long it takes your kid to figure it out.
- Pile a shopping cart full of frozen food, take it to the farthest

point away from the store's freezer, then abandon the cart and leave the store.

92

Here is a fun quiz that you can use in any speech that you give around St. Patrick's Day. Then you can say, "That was a fun quiz, but we must do more than depend on the 'luck of the Irish', if we want to improve our market share. We need to _____."

By the way, only # 1 in the quiz is false. The rest are true.

Quote: There are only two kinds of people in the world. The Irish and those who wish they were.

~Irish saying

- The day commemorates St. Patrick, who introduced beer to Ireland in the fifth century.
- There are 34 million US residents who claim Irish ancestry.
- There are nine times as many Irish in American than there are in Ireland (3.9 million).
- Irish is the nation's second most frequently reported ancestry, trailing only German.
- The percentage of Massachusetts residents of Irish ancestry are about double the national percentage.
- Irish is the leading ancestry group in Delaware, Massachusetts and New Hampshire.
- Irish is among the top five ancestries in every state but two (Hawaii and New Mexico).
- There are 54 counties where Irish is the largest observed ancestry group.
- Middlesex County, Massachusetts, claims 348,978 residents who are of Irish ancestry. Among the 54 counties where Irish is the largest observed ancestry group, Middlesex had the highest

population of Irish-Americans.

- There are currently 148,000 US residents born in Ireland.
- There were 4.8 million immigrants from Ireland admitted for lawful permanent residence since fiscal year 1820.
- Only Germany, Italy, the United Kingdom and Mexico have had more immigrants admitted for permanent residence to the United States than Ireland.
- Every year there are about 1,010 immigrants from Ireland admitted for lawful permanent residence to the United States.
- $23.0 billion is the value of US imports from the Republic of Ireland over a recent 10- month period.
- In ten months, the United States exported $6.6 billion worth of goods to Ireland.
- There are four places in the United States named Shamrock, the floral emblem of Ireland. Mount Gay-Shamrock, West Virginia, and Shamrock, Texas, were the most populous, with 2,623 and 1,828 residents, respectively. Shamrock Lakes, Indiana, had 164 residents and Shamrock, Oklahoma, 126.
- There are nine places in the United States that share the name of Ireland's capital, Dublin.
- Since Census 2000, Dublin, California, has surpassed Dublin, Ohio, as the most populous of these places (35,581 compared with 33,606 as of July 1, 2003).
- In Emerald Isle, North Carolina, with 3,528 residents, one out of six citizens is of Irish descent.
- Americans consume 22 gallons of beer per capita.
- California has the highest number of breweries (55); Colorado has the largest number of brewery employees, with more than 5,000.

93

If you have to give a speech about losing weight to any club or a

group of students, steal this speech. Note you can also take some diet myths from this speech and use them as an opening. You could say, "Let me quickly share several diet myths with you _____. But why do people believe in these myths? People want an easy quick way to lose weight. That is true with many things in life. But as you mature you realize that 'if it sounds too good to be true, it probably is'. In other words, there are no short cuts to losing weight or other challenges in life. It takes hard work. The same applies to sales. You are all professional salespeople and realize there are no shortcuts. You must follow some basic sales principles and I would like to touch upon some of those principles today."

> Quote: The second day of a diet is always easier than the first. By the second day you're off it.
> ~Jackie Gleason

Top Diet Myths

If you believe the claims in diet ads, please call me. I have a bridge in Brooklyn I am selling and I can get you a heck of a deal on it. The only thing that ends up lighter when you fall for a diet scam is your wallet. Here, according to the Federal Trade Commission, are the top seven diet ad lies:

1. Lose weight without diet or exercise:
Hmm, has it worked for you yet? Or are you still stuffing your butt into jeans and wondering why you can't lose weight when the only exercise you get is searching for the remote control. The FTC points out, "Achieving a healthy weight takes work. Take a pass on any product that promises miraculous results without the effort. Buy one and the only thing you'll lose is money."

2. Lose weight no matter how much you eat of your favorite foods:
Walk into McDonald's. Find the nearest skinniest person and sit next to her. It might take you a while, oh – three to four days – but one

will eventually walk in. And I bet she doesn't eat her favorite food of fatty burgers and calorie-packed fries. She probably has a SALAD! Again the FTC warns, "Beware of any product that claims that you can eat all you want of high-calorie foods and still lose weight. Losing weight requires sensible food choices. Filling up on healthy vegetables and fruits can make it easier to say no to fattening sweets and snacks."

3. Lose weight permanently! Never diet again!

Here's the part they leave out. Yes, it is possible to lose weight permanently and not diet or watch what you eat. It is called death. The weight drops right off. Trust me on this. Again the FTC wisely points out, "Even if you're successful in taking the weight off, permanent weight loss requires permanent lifestyle changes. Don't trust any product that promises once-and-for-all results without ongoing maintenance."

4. Blocks the absorption of fat, carbs, or calories!

Look, this is correct. There is a way to block the absorption of fats, carbs and calories. It can be summed up in three words. Eat a salad. Our friends at the FTC say, "Doctors, dieticians, and other experts agree that there's simply no magic non-prescription pill that will allow you to block the absorption of fat, carbs, or calories. The key to curbing your craving for those 'downfall foods' is portion control. Limit yourself to a smaller serving or a slimmer slice."

5. Lose 30 pounds in 30 days!

This can be accomplished by cutting off your head. You obviously aren't using it anyway if you fall for that "30 pounds in 30 days" crap. You aren't eating cabbage, you are using cabbage for a brain. The FTC states, "Losing weight at the rate of a pound or two a week is the most effective way to take it off and keep it off. At best, products promising lightning-fast weight loss are false. At worst, they can ruin your health."

6. Everybody will lose weight!

Sure, we will all lose weight. Everyone of us. Again, it is called death! But the FTC points out, "Your habits and health concerns are unique. There is simply no one-size-fits-all product guaranteed to work for everyone. Team up with your health care provider to design a personalized nutrition and exercise program suited to your lifestyle and metabolism."

7. Lose weight with our miracle diet patch or cream!

That makes a lot of sense. Like rubbing a steak on your hair to get shiny hair. There are no magic patches or cream. You gain weight because you eat too much and don't exercise. You lose weight when you eat LESS and EXERCISE. The experts at the FTC say, "You've seen the ads for diet patches or creams that claim to melt away the pounds. Don't believe them. There's nothing you can wear or apply to your skin that will cause you to lose weight."

94

Here is a short speech on possible business headlines. Or you can take some of the headlines, add a few of you own and use them in the opening. Then you can say, "Sure those headlines are amusing, if bad puns can be amusing, but think about this. If you could write a future headline for yourself, what would it say; where do you want to be in five years?"

You can also use this headline idea for your company. You can just say, "If we were to write a headline about our future sales, would it say our company exceeded the sales goals or fell short ?And that leads us to the essence of this speech; how can we make sure we exceed our sales goals, what must we do to prevent falling short?"

Quote: There's no business like show business, but there are several businesses like accounting.

~David Letterman

Business Headlines PUNish Readers

It all started when I heard a radio announcer say in a very serious voice – "Lumber mills cut back on production." And he did not realize that he had made a bad pun.

Then I realized that this could be the Ted Baxter of radio announcers and he had no idea what he was saying half the time and he had a wise guy writer, who was amusing himself, by making up puns and slipping them to the news announcer to read. And I thought that would be a great job. Here are some business stories I could amuse myself with and have Ted Baxter read on the air:

- Hearing aids at unheard of low prices
- Sheppard hires new staff
- Plane sales take off
- Bullet sales shoot up
- Glass sales shatter records
- Viagra sales on the rise
- Butcher company slicing employees
- Boat maker launches new products
- Molly Maids to sweep 600 employees out the door
- Jack Daniel's brewing financial trouble
- Issues at Budweiser coming to a head
- Toyota accelerates layoffs
- Nuclear plant gives employees glowing reviews
- Knife Company slashes costs
- Kite sales soar
- Undertakers face grave future
- Viagra sees rising sales
- Wrigley chewing up profits
- Drano production going down the drain

- Weight Watchers reducing employee count
- Lack of profits sickens hospital investors
- Airline profits crash on Wall Street
- Roofing company cutting overhead
- Ladder company stays one step ahead of the competition
- Banana sales slipping.
- Proctor & Gamble has clean balance sheet.
- Tree farm sprouts profits
- Local farmer outstanding in his field
- Funeral homes profit sheet dead on arrival
- Broom company reorganizes, makes clean sweep with past
- Optometry company eyes new business
- Cruise line profits sink
- Cigarette company profits go up in smoke
- Revlon makes up with investors
- Ski maker profits going downhill
- Telescope maker reflects on past year
- Mirror company seeks new image
- Clothing company profits tailor made for investors
- Dentists building bridges to new clients
- Veterinarians doggedly seek new business
- Candy maker snickers at financial skeptics
- Tractor sales plow ahead
- Light bulb sales brighten bottom line
- Gas sales explode
- Gasoline sales fuel economy
- Jacket maker zips up new markets
- Glue companies stick to financial game plan
- Ruler company measures up to Wall Street expectations
- Pencil company sees profits erased
- Ladder company posts higher profit margins
- Drug companies see no cure for financial pain ahead
- Sandpaper manufacturers face rough future
- Cake makers see rising profits

- Fireworks see booming market
- Car company puts brakes on expansion
- Orthopedic group thriving on bad breaks
- Orthodontists told to straighten up
- Saw maker cuts back
- Candy maker sweetens bottom line
- Bra maker boosts sales
- Proctologist group examines bottom line
- Rope company ties up market
- Shoe company operates on shoestring budget
- Boat company leaks insider information
- Door company encounters hard knocks
- Window maker says, "No pane, no gain"
- Glass company dreams shattered
- Gate company claims open and shut case
- Well company digging financial hole
- Bowling employees go on strike
- Theater screening new employees
- Economy still a major Headache for Bayer
- Dairy producers accused of milking the market
- Poultry producers squawk over price increases
- Hot dog sales cool off
- Anti wrinkle cream smoothes out sales
- Playground equipment sales seesaw.
- Chiropractor group to crunch numbers
- Electric company shocks consumers with price increase
- Ice cream sales face meltdown

95

Do you know college kids or high school kids who are going on Spring Break? Here is a short speech you can give them. It is also an example how you can weave research, tinged with a bit of

humor, to make your point. Almost any safety speech can give key tips, but the trick is to make the tips interesting; note how humor is used in this speech to accomplish that. This is a good template for future safety speeches.

Quote: Spring is nature's way of saying, "Let's party!"
~Robin Williams

Spring Break Safety Tips

Tip One – Pack Your Brain:

Spring Break is a wonderful time. You can plan your Spring Break vacation by taking all your money, placing it in a pile and realizing that $30.22 cents will get you nowhere. Time for that emergency back-up plan, called parents. After spending thousands on your books and tuition, they will be more than happy to give you EVEN more money, so you can go to some beach, drink heavily and chase women. If you do succeed in getting enough money to go on Spring Break, remember that there are certain safety tips you must follow.

And remember the number one cause of Spring Break accidents and bad incidents is stupidity, So along with that bathing suit, don't forget to pack a fully, functioning brain.

Be Careful about Drinking Too Much:

The Center for Disease and Control and Prevention (CDC) warns:

If drinking alcohol is part of your break, remember that it can impair your judgment and actions. Alcohol-related motor vehicle crashes kill someone every 31 minutes and non-fatally injure someone every two minutes. Don't drink and drive. There are plenty of non-alcoholic alternatives.

Another reason not to drink heavily is that many of my friends married people they met during Spring Break. All these friends are divorced now, because the booze-soaked blonde or the booze-soaked muscle boy turned out to be a great companion for drinking, but failed in the parent, work, responsibility department.

So remember it is not the drinking that can be dangerous but the people you may drink with and marry who are dangerous.

Be Careful about Getting a Sexual Disease:
The CDC, which seems intent on ruining any Spring Break fun you may have, unfortunately makes a vey good point about sexual diseases:

> Love is all around, and so are sexually transmitted diseases. The only 100% sure way to prevent sexually transmitted diseases and unintended pregnancy is by not having sex. If you choose to have sex, using latex condoms and having a monogamous, uninfected partner may help lower your risk.

Okay – so you shouldn't sleep around on Spring Break. Actually that is probably good advice anytime, as there is nothing worse than waking up in a strange place, tumbling out of bed and walking into a wall which was where the bathroom was suppose to be.

The CDC also makes a good point about trusting people. Don't!

The CDC wisely points out, and it is hard for me to agree with any governmental agency, but they WISELY point out:

> Women are more likely to be victims of sexual violence than men. Women who experience both sexual and physical abuse are significantly more likely to have sexually transmitted diseases. Take precautions and avoid situations or persons that may place you at risk for harm.

In other words, don't wander up the beach alone, drunk after midnight. Don't trust anyone in a bar, always take your drink with you, and never go home with some drunk you met in a bar an hour ago. Always travel in groups of friends.

Avoid Risky Activities

I always thought I would make a terrible ER doctor, because they deal with dumb people all day. About the second day on the job, after seeing drug overdoses, drunken driving accidents, injuries caused by skydiving, bungee jumping, jumping off balconies into pools, I would just quit.

In other words, the best way to end up in a wheelchair the rest of your life is to do something dumb. A key rule, if it involves a helmet, meaning possible BRAIN injuries, DON'T DO IT. If your friends are pressuring you, think, "Will they be around to push my wheelchair?"

As the CDC stated:

There may be temptations on your break that involve different or high-risk activity. Think twice before putting yourself at risk for injury. Be sure to use appropriate safety gear before venturing out, such as seat belts, life vests, or knee pads. Remember that unintentional injuries kill more Americans in their first three decades of life than any other cause of death. In fact, injuries (both unintentional and those caused by acts of violence) are among the top ten killers for Americans of all ages.

Hmm, sexual diseases, a lot of drunks, unsafe activities? Perhaps you should spend Spring Break at home, save some money, and maybe your life and sanity.

96

Here is a speech that looks into the future. You can use the whole speech or pick and choose some interesting facts about the future generation. Then you could say, "Well, those are some interesting facts about the future generation. But we also must remember that they are our future customers and how do we reach them? I would

like to discuss some marketing ideas..."

Quote: There is hope for the future because God has a sense of humor and we are funny to God.

~Bill Cosby

The 20 Something Generation

The Millennials are the American teens and twenty-somethings who are making the passage into adulthood at the start of a new millennium.

Feel sorry for them.

Can you imagine being stuck with a name like Millennials? I bet half of them can't even spell it. I know I can't. Makes the X and Y generations feel lucky. How long did it take them to learn to spell X or Y. Okay, it took me two years, but I had a problem with the "generation" part, not the X and Y.

According to Pew Research, the Millennials are "history's first 'always connected' generation... More than eight-in-ten say they sleep with a cell phone glowing by the bed, poised to disgorge texts, phone calls, e-mails, songs, news, videos, games and wake-up jingles."

Eight-in-ten? Something needs to be done about that. Let's make it easier for the next generation. Just graft a phone into their brains as soon as they are born. Sure they might have to plug their brains in every night to recharge the phone, but it would be tough for them to lose the phone. Of course taking a shower might be a problem.

In fact – WATCH OUT – pet peeve ahead. Why can they make a phone that texts someone in Hong Kong in one second, but it goes haywire the minute a drop of water touches it?

Nearly two-thirds of the Millennials admit to texting while driving. And that is okay. I have no problem being stuck behind a GREEN light for ten minutes until a Millennial looks up and goes through the light just as it turns red. I am glad for that extra time at the red light, as, at my age, I am too busy trying to turn off my blinker, turn on the windshield wipers while searching how to turn on the lights.

Actually, I am jealous that Millennials can text and drive. Someone sends me a text, I have to pull over, put on my bifocals, try to find the ^%^&** button to press and then try to read that text that is smaller than a Republican's heart.

By the way, there are over 50 million Millennials. Be prepared to be stuck at a lot of green lights.

And here is the part of the study that I love. The Pew research states, "Whether as a byproduct of protective parents, the age of terrorism or a media culture that focuses on dangers, the Millennials cast a wary eye on human nature. Two-thirds say 'you can't be too careful' when dealing with people."

Hmm, this is a generation that feels "you can't be too careful when dealing with people," but at the same time the report states, "Three-quarters have created a profile on a social networking site. One-in-five have posted a video of themselves online."

Anyone see a disconnect there? So much for that "too careful" part.

One lesson that the Millennials have not learned is that "No Pain means No Pain". This is a generation that loves to stick itself with needles. In fact, according to the report, "Nearly four-in-ten have a tattoo." (And for most who do, one is not enough: about half of those with tattoos have two to five and 18% have six or more).

I only have one word for that. OW!

97

Here is a beverage trivia quiz which is great for a breakfast or dinner meeting. While people are sipping their morning coffee or evening cocktail, you can say, "I thought it would be fun to start off with a beverage quiz."

You don't have to use the entire quiz, maybe just a few

questions. After asking the questions, you can ask, "Let's move beyond beverages and talk about something else that can be refreshing, at least to our customers. I am sure they appreciate a good cup of coffee, but they also appreciate good customer service. How can we provide that to them?"

Quote: Why does man kill? He kills for food. And not only for food: frequently there must be a beverage.
~Woody Allen

Beverage Quiz

- Which nation consumes the most beer per person per year?
  Ireland with 155 liters per person per year.
- Where does the United States stand in the list of beer consumption per capita?
  Only 8th. Americans drink 85 liters per person per year.
- Which country drinks the most bottled water?
  Italy – 155 liters per person per year.
- Where does the United States rank in bottled water consumption?
  7th with 46.8 liters per person per year.
- Which nation ranks first in soft drink consumption?
  The United States with 216 per person per year.
- Which nation ranks second in soft drink consumption?
  Ireland with 126 liters per person per year.
- Which nation drinks the most coffee?
  Norway with 10.7 kgs per person per year.
- Where does the United States rank in coffee consumption?
  12th, with 3 kg per person per year.
- Which nation drinks the most tea?
  The United Kingdom with 2.3 kgs per person per year.
- Where does the United States rank on tea drinking?
  12th with .02 kg per person per year.
- Which country drinks the most wine?

247

Italy with 54 liters per person per year.
- Where does the United States rank in wine drinking?
18th with 7 liters per person per year.
- Which nation drinks the most fruit juice?
Canada with 52.6 liters per person per year.
- Where does the United States rank in fruit juice consumption?
Second with 42.8 liters per person per year.
- Which nation leads in total spirit consumption?
Japan with 8.2 liters per person per year.

98

Here is a crime quiz which can lead into a speech on ethics. You could start by saying, "While we are all getting settled, here is a quick crime quiz. You can write the answers on your pad in front of you, if you want to play along."

After giving part or all of the quiz, you can say, "That may be an interesting quiz, but we must all obey the rules and regulations. As you know, the news has been rife with stories of corporate misconduct lately and I never want to see our name associated with any misconduct. That is why we must take ethics seriously. Now today, I would like to cover these key areas involving ethics..."

Quote: Organized crime in America takes in over forty billion dollars a year and spends very little on office supplies.
~Woody Allen

Crime Quiz
- Which country has the most murders per capita?
Columbia with 0.617847 per 1,000 people.
- Where does the United States rank on the murder list?
It is 24th with 0.042802 per 1,000 people.

- What country has the most prisoners per capita?
  The land of the free – The United States with 715 per 100,000 people.
- Which country is second on the list of prisoners?
  Russia with 584 per 100,000 people.
- Where does China rank on the prisoner list?
  71st with 119 prisoners per 100,000 people.
- Which country leads in total crimes per capita?
  Dominica with 113.822 per 1,000 people.
- Where does the United States rank on the crime per capita list?
  8th with 80.0645 per 1,000 people.
- Which nation leads in murders by firearms per capita?
  South Africa with 0.719782 per 1,000 people.
- What country has the most firearms?
  The United States with 90 guns for every 100 citizens.
- Who has the most police per capita?
  Montserrat with 7.81501 per 1,000 people.
- Which country has the most executions?
  China with 470 per year.
- Where is the United States on the execution list?
  Lucky number seven with 42 executions per year.
- Which nation has the most embezzlements per year?
  The Czech Republic with 1.00283 per 1,000 people.
- Where does the US rank on the embezzlement list?
  30th with 0.0584985 per 1,000 people.
- Which nation has the most car thefts per capita?
  Australia with 6.92354 per 1,000 people.
- Where does the United States rank on car thefts?
  9th with 3.8795 per 1,000 people.

99

Every day there is a new business crisis. Here is a funny speech

that looks at some business missteps. You can pick and choose of the examples and tell the new slogan the company can have. Then you can say, "Of course I am being facetious. It takes more than changing your slogan to handle a business crisis. Let's cover some steps in how to avoid a business crisis and, if it does happen, let's discuss some steps that you should take right away..."

Quote: Consultants have credibility because they are not dumb enough to work at your company.
~Dilbert

How to Become a Crisis Consultant in One Easy Step

When Toyota was facing some safety problems, you saw 'crisis management consultants' on every talk show offering Toyota free advice. Heck, the consultants offered complex solutions, and I have an easy solution. If you have a crisis with your product, just change your slogan. Here are some current recalls and my examples of how changing the slogan can solve the problem.

- West Missouri Beef is recalling approximately 14,000 pounds of fresh boneless beef products that may be contaminated with E. coli O157:H7. **My Slogan: Lose 30 pounds in one week.**
- Kidde Fire Extinguishers could lose pressure and fail to operate. In the event of a fire, this failure could put a consumer and property at risk. **My Slogan: We also sell fire insurance.**
- Blue Bird School Buses is recalling some buses because the battery cables may cause a fire. **My Slogan: It's not just a ride, it's an adventure.**
- Mazda is recalling certain models equipped with electrically heated front seats as the seat heater may overheat. **My Slogan: Mazda: We give you a warm feeling.**
- BMW is recalling certain models for failing to comply with the requirements of Federal Motor Vehicle Safety Standard Number 110. **My Slogan: BMW – Make Your Own Rules.**

- Cooper Tires is recalling certain Discovery tires because tread chunks may separate from the tire. **My slogan: We create excitement.**
- Dorel Juvenile Group is recalling certain infant child restraint systems. The child could be injured in a crash. **My Slogan: We teach your child to fly.**
- Climate Control is recalling some footrests because the footrest's fan can become blocked and overheat when used in the upright position, posing a fire hazard. **My Slogan: Give your loved one a hot foot.**
- Outdoor Lighting Fixtures is recalling some lights because "Improper wiring in the light fixtures poses a shock hazard to consumers." **My Slogan: Free Perms.**
- Randolph Packing Co. Inc, is recalling 96,000 pounds of beef products that may be contaminated with E. coli O157:H7. **My Slogan: Beef – the natural laxative.**
- Toyota is recalling some cars because of unintended acceleration. **My Slogan: The car that drives itself.**
- Toyota is recalling some cars because of braking problems. **My Slogan: There is no stopping us.**
- Wilson Trailer is recalling certain models of livestock trailers which lead to a loss of suspension and may cause a crash. **My slogan: We keep you in suspense.**
- The EPA ordered the Scotts Miracle-Gro Company to stop selling four pesticide products that were improperly labeled. **My Slogan: A surprise in every bag.**
- Daniels Western Meat Packers is recalling approximately 16,290 pounds of frozen turkey patty products because they were inadvertently mislabeled and may contain an undeclared allergen. **My Slogan: Daniels – More than you paid for.**
- Hyundai is recalling certain Tucson Vehicles because passengers weighing over 240 pounds cause the air bag warning light to come on. **My Slogan: Free weight check.**

100

Every now and then we have to remind workers that they don't have it that bad. This could be used as a pep talk, or like many of the speeches in this book, you can choose some stats from the speech that you can weave into other speeches. This would be a good "reality check" speech you can give to a group such as Junior Achievement. Remember before you give a speech – check the tone of the speech and adjust it for the audience you are chatting with. For instance this speech used the term "cry babies". You can choose different words ranging from "discontents" to "whiners" to "complainers".

Quote: Anyone who can walk to the welfare office can walk to work.
~Al Capp

55% of Americans Hate Their Jobs

It is official. America has turned into a nation of cry babies. We all need one big collective tissue we can all cry into.

Only 45% of Americans are satisfied with their jobs according to a report released by The Conference Board.

Hmm, as my father would say, in his kind, understanding way, "GET OVER IT!"

Hello! When was your boss supposed to make you happy? What? You want free lattes, backrubs and recess every day at work? How about milk time and a nap? And yes, it is cold outside, let me run outside and warm up your car before you go home. In fact, is it okay if I bring breakfast by your house tomorrow and warm up your car, before you come into work, as I care about your happiness?

NOT!

Hello??? Remember your great-granddad who went across country in a covered wagon with NO guarantees of a job when he reached California? How about your other great-grandfather who landed in America with a shabby suitcase full of old clothes and dreams of a better life. He couldn't even speak English. How about your grandfather whose first job in the Depression was selling apples on a street corner? Remember your dad who worked THREE jobs to put you through college? Do you think they were worried about job satisfaction?

What you don't like your job? Those nasty customers wanting service and complaining too much and getting you all upset? I could shoot them for you. Would that be okay? Would that make you happy?

Oh wait, those customers are the reason you GET A PAYCHECK!

Or as my grandfather would say, "The world does not owe you a living."

And Americans want their world to give them a living and a happy living at that. Oh please!

Whining – you want to hear whining? Gotta love this quote from The Conference Board:

"Our job satisfaction numbers have shown a consistent downward trend."

Hmm – excuse me – It is called work because you do not enjoy it. That is why they pay you. If you enjoyed it, it would be called PLAY.

And doesn't anyone remember that old saying, "I was upset I had no shoes until I met a man with no feet." If you have a job in today's economy and you are getting a regular paycheck, I don't see much reason for you to say, "Gosh, I am unhappy with my job."

Let's put this in perspective. While Americans are crying that their work does not make them happy, that their bosses don't live to serve them and their needs, most people in most countries would love to exchange jobs with any American worker.

An accountant in America makes an average of $3,370 a month. In China that same accountant makes $704 a month; in Thailand accountants make $621 a month; and in Mexico, accountants are living the high life, making $831 a month. How about office clerks? In America the average office clerk makes $1,921 a month. In

Mexico, they make $481 a month and in Thailand they make $349 a month. Garment cutters? In America they make $1,661 a month; in Thailand $333 a month; and in Russia a whopping $143 a month.

Hmm, and you wonder why I call America a nation of cry babies?

101

Here is a speech that talks about sensitivity and what not to say in certain circumstances. As always, feel free to add your own ideas. Or you can choose just a few examples from the speech, then say, "Well those are things NOT to say, but at _____, we need to focus on the right things to say to our customers to get them to use our products and services."

Quote: Sometimes being a friend means mastering the art of timing. There is a time for silence. A time to let go and allow people to hurl themselves into their own destiny. And a time to prepare to pick up the pieces when it's all over.

~Gloria Naylor

The One Minute "Be Sensitive" Course

Rule Number One: Shut Up

Many men say the wrong thing at the wrong time. But here at Being Sensitive, also known as B.S., we offer one-minute lessons in "How to be Sensitive". Rule number one is Shut Up. Rule number two is Shut Up. And rule number three is Shut Up. Here are ten situations and what you SHOULD NOT say in these sensitive moments. In other words – SHUT UP.

- When you bail your son out of jail for underage drinking, do not say on the way out of the police station, "At least they didn't find the drugs."
- When your car is in a ditch and there are empty beer bottles all

over the car do not say, "Something wrong, officer?"

- When your wife is trying on jeans at the store do not say, "The universe isn't the only thing expanding."
- If your son complains about the food at school, do not say, "Hey, it wasn't my idea to home school you."
- When you get divorced down South do not ask the judge, "Is she still my sister?"
- When your neighbor's house is burning down, do not ask, "Who brought the marshmallows?"
- When your daughter brings home her first boyfriend, do not wear your bubba teeth, scratch your crotch, wear your muscle shirt or say, "Normally we don't let her date outside the family."
- Even though you hate your mother-in-law, do not stop for road kill and ask: "Staying for dinner?"
- If your wife has gained a few pounds, do not say, "Let's go to the Halloween party as a couple. You be Shamu and I will be his trainer."
- When your wife brags about being married for ten years do not say, "Yeah, but I count it in dog years."
- When you hit the accelerator instead of the brake and crash through the convenience store wall, do not say, "Hey – when did you all get a drive-through?" or "I will take a Slurpee to go."
- When your wife is in bed with swine flu and a fever of 120, do not ask, "What is for dinner?" or say, "Why didn't you go to work today, we need the money."
- If you run over a Hell's Angel bike, do not say, "Hey how much will a new tricycle cost anyway?"
- When your wife bends over when bowling and her pants tear in back do not say, "Should I put that down as a split?"
- If you have teenagers, remember the worse advice you can give them is, "Just be yourself."

102

Many meetings kick off with employees giving skits. Here is a fun, short skit your managers can use to loosen the audience up and to give the managers a chance to bond with the audience, showing them that managers are human too. Plus it is a fun skit to do, as the managers get to dress up like mafia gang members. This is a perfect skit to open any environmental meeting.

Quote: If a tree falls in the woods, and there's no one there to hear it, how will the environmentalists react?
~Anon

The Mob Goes Green: Key Ways Organized Crime Can Help the Environment

Louie: Yo, Vinnie, I been thinking we need to go green.

Vinnie: What – you some sort of tree hugger or what?

Louie: No, Vinnie, really, we need to help our planet.

Vinnie: Okay wise guy – any ideas?

Louie: Well, Vinnie, I heard that for every extra pound a car carries, you waste gas.

Vinnie: Yeah, so?

Louie: So anyway, I'm thinking we got to get Big Al's body out of the trunk. He must weigh close to 300 pounds. Plus he is starting to stink.

Vinnie: That's good thinking, Louie, what else do you recommend?

Louie: Well, we need to start killing smaller people. Less weight in the trunk.

Vinnie: Good, Louie, anything else.

Louie: Well, Vinnie, we also need to buy one of them Green Cars, the Prius by Toyota.

Vinnie: Yeah, why?

Louie: Because they self-accelerate. So we don't have to tie no brick to the accelerator. We put the stiff in the car. It self-accelerates and it goes off the pier and into Lake Michigan. And the beauty is Toyota gotta explain itself to Congress, not us.

Vinnie: That is pure genius, Louie, I hate them Congressional hearings.

Louie: Yeah, Vinnie, and the Government recommends we use public transportation to cut down emissions.

Vinnie: I don't know, Louie. Using a bus for a drive-by shooting ain't easy.

Louie: That ain't what I was thinking, Vinnie. I got some friends in the bus drivers' union. We stop running people over with cars. Hit them with a bus and they're flat and dead.

Vinnie: Well, Louie, the government is right. Public transportation can be a thing of beauty.

Louie: And, Vinnie, remember those four guys we sent out on that hit the other day?

Vinnie: Yeah?

Louie: They was all riding in the same car. That's carpooling, Vinnie, carpooling. We done good. Also Vinnie, them plastic bags we use don't help the environment. They ain't degradable.

Vinnie: So?

Louie: So, we start wrapping the drugs in brown paper, not plastic. Just another little way we can be green.

Vinnie: That is touching, Louie, just touching.

Louie: Also, Vinnie, we got to stop polluting the river.

Vinnie: The river?

Louie: Yeah, we just can't be dumping bodies in the river. That ain't sanitary and the EPA might start investigating us. You know how them government agencies are. They can send you up for ten years for water pollution.

Vinnie: Damn, Louie, the EPA can use environmental laws to nail us, can't they?

Louie: But, Vinnie, I think the government should reward us. We have been green for years.

Vinnie: What?

Louie: Vinnie, global warming is caused by too many people in this world. And ain't we done our best to lower the population, if you know what I mean?

Vinnie: Louie, genius, pure genius, let's get one of them award forms and fill it out.

Louie: Also, Vinnie, them environmentals encourage us to buy in bulk. Cuts down on packaging.

Vinnie: But, Louie, we been doing that for years. We buy cocaine in bulk. See, Louie, we are good people. Them Feds just give us a bum rap.

Louie: But, Vinnie, we must use more green products. Think about some of those blood stains in the car. We gotta stop using bleach. It ain't good for the environment. I think we could use vinegar and water. And, Vinnie. We need to recycle.

Vinnie: Recycle?

Louie: Yeah. Big Al was wearing a real nice suit and we could have donated it to the thrift store.

Vinnie: But, Louie, how about the bullet holes and blood on the suit?

Louie: That there, Vinnie, is where we gotta start thinking ahead. We should have required of Big Al that he take his suit jacket off. Vinnie – I also heard that we can't be feeding wild animals. It makes them depend on humans.

Vinnie: Louie, that means we have to dump the bodies somewhere else, don't it?

Louie: It ain't easy being green, Vinnie, but we gotta try.

103

This is a fun quiz to use around NCAA Tournament time. Odds are that most of the teams listed below will be in the tournament. If not, you can begin the speech by saying, "I know it is Tournament Time and I thought we could have some fun, by testing your knowledge of college nicknames. I am going to give you a name of

a team that at one time has made the tournament and you shout out the nickname."

This is a great icebreaker and gets the audience involved. Then you can say, "All you sports fans know that only once in tournament history have all four top-seeded teams made the tournament. There is a lesson there for us. Today, we may be a leader in our industry, but that is no guarantee we will be a leader tomorrow. What do we have to do to stay on top? Let's discuss that..."

Quote: Many athletes have tremendous God-given gifts, but they don't focus on the development of those gifts. Who are these individuals? You've never heard of them – and you never will. It's true in sports and it's true everywhere in life. Hard work is the difference. Very hard work.

~John Wooden

Duke – Blue Devils

Villanova – Wildcats

Baylor – Bears

Purdue – Boilermakers

Texas A&M – Aggies

Notre Dame – Fighting Irish

Richmond – Spiders

California – Bears

Louisville – Cardinals

Saint Mary's – Gaels

Old Dominion – Monarchs

Utah State – Aggies

Siena – Saints

Sam Houston State – Bearkats

Robert Morris – Colonials

Winthrop – Eagles

Kentucky – Wildcats

West Virginia – Mountaineers
New Mexico - Lobos
Wisconsin – Badgers
Temple – Owls
Marquette – None (Formerly Warriors and Golden Eagles)
Clemson – Tigers
Texas – Longhorns
Wake Forest – Demon Deacons
Missouri – Tigers
Washington – Huskies
Cornell – Big Red
Wofford – Terriers
Montana – Grizzlies
Morgan State – Bears
Tennessee State – Tigers
Syracuse – Orangemen
Kansas State – Wildcats
Pittsburgh – Panthers
Vanderbilt – Commodores
Butler – Bulldogs
Xavier – Musketeers
BYU – Cougars
Gonzaga – Bulldogs
Florida State – Seminoles
Florida – Gators
Minnesota – Gophers
UTEP – Miners
Murray State – Racers
Oakland – Golden Grizzlies
North Texas – Eagles
Vermont – Catamounts
Kansas – Jayhawks
Ohio State – Buckeyes
Georgetown – Hoyas

Maryland – Terrapins
Michigan State – Spartans
Tennessee – Volunteers
Oklahoma State – Cowboys
UNLV – Running Rebels
Northern Iowa – Panthers
Georgia Tech – Yellow Jackets
San Diego State – Aztecs
New Mexico State – Aggies
Houston – Cougars
Ohio – Bobcats
UC Santa Barbara – Gauchos
Lehigh – Mountain Hawks

104

We are all in the business of selling ideas. This is a great speech to give to a sales staff. Or simply go through the speech and highlight the ideas you want to use, plus incorporate some of your own.

Quote: An idea that is developed and put into action is more important than an idea that only exists as an idea.
~Buddha

We are all in the business of selling ideas. How often do you sell ideas to your kids, boss, spouse, neighbors? You sell ideas every day. So here are three key ways to sell ideas.

• Think of an idea as a story. You have to set it up. Remember the basic plot. First you introduce the characters and storyline. That is the opening act and is necessary for your audience to under-stand what is going on.

- In the second act of any story, your hero must overcome objections, prove why he or she is worthy.
- And then finally, you must have a credible closing act that your readers buy into and accept.
- You sell an idea the same way.
- Introduce the idea. Let your audience become familiar with it.
- Put the idea through obstacles, objections and let the reader see how the idea overcomes and triumphs over these obstacles.
- Have a credible closing for your idea, a happy ending; let the audience see how much better they will be when they adopt your idea.
- Have a logical closing that the audience will accept, as the whole plot has been building to the credible conclusion.
  When selling ideas, remember people are either slow or quick. That sounds mean, but it is true; always consider who you are dealing with. Some people just can't think quickly or are averse to making quick decisions. Throw a lot of facts, figures, stats, ideas at them and their mind kicks into overload and shuts down. Talk fast and they think you are slick. With these people:
- Make one point at a time.
- Talk slowly.
- Make sure they understand it, let them ask questions.
- And only when they understand the first point are they able to move onto the next question.

The other type is the quick thinker. I have worked for many CEOs and they want you to get to the point. I have seen salesmen make PowerPoint presentations before a CEO and read each point aloud. Excuse me, but this person is a CEO because he is quick. He can read quicker than you can talk. I have seen CEOs excuse themselves from these meetings and never come back. In short, are you dealing with a slow (methodical) thinker or a quick thinker who wants you to get to the point? You better know your audience or your idea will sink quicker than a lead boat.

Also, do not begin to sell any idea unless you have a thesis statement worked out. Remember your essay writing class and the teacher always demanded a thesis statement? The thesis statement would tell what the paper was about and why the reader should care. For instance, you can't walk into your boss and say, "I want a raise. Now!"

That would be a dumb approach.

Think about it – Why do you want and deserve a raise? Prepare a thesis statement: "I would like to discuss a pay raise because I have increased my productivity by 20%, I have eliminated waste in my department and I have reduced expenses by 50. Plus I resisted your wife's advances at the Christmas party."

Remember – you sell your idea with a good opening thesis statement. Another example: Don't say, "We need a new deck." Explain why. "Honey, we need a new deck on the house as it will give the kids an extra place to play; when your relatives come over, they won't all be crowded in the kitchen; and you and I can enjoy the outdoors as we watch the sunset and drink wine."

There you go. Three key ways to sell your ideas.

105

Health care is always a topic for many speeches. Here is a funny health care form. You do not have to read it to the audience. Just add and delete questions, and then when you are satisfied, pass it out to the audience.

Then you can say, "Before I start, we have passed out a health care form to you all. Please take a minute to read it." After the audience reads it, you can say, "Unfortunately, some of those questions on the form are pretty close to reality. But putting aside the form for a second, let's talk about the health care issues that affect our company and how we are handling them."

Quote: If I knew I was going to live this long, I would have taken better care of myself.
~Mickey Mantle

New Government Health Care Form Released

Do You Qualify?

Do you qualify for the new Health Care Reform Act? Here is the official government form. Just answer the following questions to find out if you qualify for national health care. Here is the National Health Care Reform Form Reformed Form:

- Is your current health care package a box of Band-Aids, a tube of first aid cream, a can of chicken soup and free health advice from your mother-in-law?
- If the answer to number one is yes, turn around 50 times, click your heels. Do you feel dizzy? If the answer is yes, proceed to the next questions.
- Do you have problems with your memory?
- What was question number 3?
- Does it burn when you pee?
- Do you have any chronic pain in your life besides your spouse?
- Why are there two Dakotas? Isn't one enough?
- Do you have kids? WHY????
- Do you have eye-sight problems ?
- Did a priest ever tell you to turn your head and cough?
- Do you have **HEARING PROBLEMS?**
- Is your company's health care plan merely a list of free clinics in Mexico?
- Is your company's prescription plan a jug of moonshine and a free get-well card?
- Do you have an overwhelming desire to take out your wallet and give the government money?
- Have you ever had thoughts of suicide, buying a Toyota, quitting drinking, getting engaged, voting for Ralph Nader, running a

marathon, running for Congress or other self- destructive behavior?

- Do you believe in the Easter Bunny, Santa Claus and well-run government programs?
- Do you have problems keeping track of things?
- Do you have problems keeping track of things?
- Do you have problems keeping track of things?
- How many drinks do you have a day? How many cigarettes do you smoke? How much sex do you have? How many women or men have you slept with? Are you really a blonde? Do you really believe this is any of the government's business? If yes, sign below for your national health care card.

X_____

106

Here is a fun list of daily ambitions for someone who is not that ambitious. You can begin the speech by saying, "I thought I would share a list of my brother-in-law's ambitions." After reading a few items, from the list, you can say, "And you can see why I hide in the den when my brother-in-law comes over. But I think we have higher ambitions here at _____, and let's discuss what some of our goals are and how we plan to meet those goals."

Quote: If you aim at nothing, you will hit it every time.
~Anon

Daily Ambitions
- Make it through the day without spilling anything on a white shirt. Usually this ambition is thwarted by nine in the morning when I am driving and hit a bump and realized the coffee lid should have been put on just a little bit tighter. But on a good

day, I can almost make it to five without spilling anything. Yesterday was a good day, and then exactly at 5:02, I spilled salsa on my shirt, followed by a spot of cheese sauce at 5:09. I am proud to note that I did not spill a drop of the margarita.

- Don't burn myself on McDonald's coffee. I know McDonald's coffee is hot. It says so, right there on the cup. When I am thinking, I put ice in my coffee. But at least once a week, I forget, get in my car, take a sip, and hit the roof after blistering my lips. It is my own damn fault.

- Get up in the morning without hurting anything. I have gotten out of bed the wrong way and twisted my back. I have friends who have gotten out of bed and twisted knees, ankles, and toes – how you twist a toe, I am not sure, but she did it. In short, after a certain age, getting out of bed, standing up too quickly, or kneeling the wrong way can be dangerous.

- Stay up to watch Jay Leno. I have been able to accomplish that goal once this week. Next week, I might work my way up to two nights of Jay Leno.

- Listen to any friend describe any ailment and stifle the impulse to say, "Hey you're old. What did you expect?"

- Don't say anything stupid. Like asking in the Dollar Store how much something costs.

- Avoid answering the phone before 10 a.m. It will just be an ex-wife, a student or a bill collector, saying, "What are you going to do about me?"

- Watch the nightly news and not be interested in the arthritis medicine ads. But…

- Convince myself I am eating healthy because I am drinking a Bloody Mary which contains tomato juice.

- Check my online banking statement and have enough money to buy a hot dog at Circle K if I don't but that Snuggie advertised on TV.

- Try not to neurotically check my e-mail.

- Try not to misplace my reading glasses. Actually I now buy them

at the Dollar Store and put them all around the house. And I STILL lose every pair within two weeks.
- Try not to think that Walter Cronkite could kick any current newscaster's ass.
- Try not to tell anyone that Barney Fife was a comic genius. They'll just roll their eyes.
- Try to watch something hip on TV like *Survivor* or *American Idol,* but I always end up watching the History Channel.
- Try to watch old movies and not think, "They are all dead now."
- Try not to give any male under 30 a lecture on how they age bourbon for years and only a Philistine would mix Coke with it.
- Try to make it to bed without falling asleep on the couch first.
- Try to read at least a chapter of a book without falling asleep.
- Don't call up old girl friends while drinking.

107

Here is a fun speech that plays with the English language and talks about the dangers of clichés. A good speech to give to students, but you can also weave some of the silly questions into an opening. You could say, "I have been having some silly questions run through my mind lately and they include _____. But today I want to share a serious question with you. Where will this company be in five years? And what do we all have to do to achieve our goals. Well, to answer that question, we must _____."

Quote: If Wyle E. Coyote had enough money to buy all that ACME crap, why didn't he just buy dinner?
~Anon

Over 50 Questions About Clichés
- Should you tell an idiot "practice makes perfect"?

- Does "better late than never" apply to dying? Wouldn't never be better?
- Do rabbits have "bad hare days"?
- If you're married can you have other "bosom buddies"?
- If "familiarity breeds contempt" does it also breed restraining orders?
- "A good man is hard to find", but does Viagra make "a hard man good to find"?
- Does "divide and conquer" work when dating Siamese Twins?
- Does "dead men tell no tales" apply when CSI collects DNA evidence?
- Is it true that you can lead a skunk to water but you can't make it stink?
- Is "from the horse's mouth" a good thing to say about your mother-in-law?
- Are funny farms where they keep clowns?
- Doesn't "getting the short end of the stick" sound painful?
- Should you "gather rosebuds" before Rose's father gets home?
- If "happiness is a state of mind", you don't mind I am leaving you?
- If you "let the cat out of the bag", won't curiosity kill it?
- If you "lend me your ear", can I call you Van Gogh?
- Should "you look before you leap", as not everyone picks up after their dog?
- Does "love your neighbor as thyself" work until your wife comes home?
- Would "loose as a goose" make a good ad for Ex-lax?
- Can you please "make a long story short" and surprise everyone?
- If your husband "hesitates and is lost", will he stop and ask for directions?
- "Money doesn't grow on trees", but isn't money made of paper?
- If "mum's the word", what is the other word?
- If people like your mother-in-law are "few and far between" doesn't that offer hope for mankind?

- You can "peter out", but won't your peter out get you arrested?
- Sure "an apple a day keeps the doctor away", but what happens if "it is rotten to the core"?
- Has the person who said "Talk is cheap", checked his cell phone bill?
- Should "you fall from Grace" before her husband comes home?
- If she is as "tough as nails, as ugly as sin, and sweats like a pig" isn't it good that "love is blind"?
- If you are "as dumb as a stump or as dumb as a log" do you feel at home in the forest?
- Is it "waist not, wants not new jeans"?
- Is it really fair to encourage people to "just be themselves"?
- If "All things being equal" were true, wouldn't more woman look like Dolly Parton?
- Isn't "Any port in a storm" the worse pickup line ever?
- Doesn't "a bird in the hand" sound somewhat messy?
- What's so special about Newton finding that "apples don't fall far from the tree"?
- Shouldn't you worry about someone "who goes to bed with the chickens"?
- If you are as dumb as a "box of rocks" should you "rock the boat"?
- Doesn't "absence make the heart grow fonder" for someone else?
- Is it good to be "as honest as the day in long" when you live in wintertime Alaska?
- With free downloading of songs, can you still say "buy it for a song"?
- Does "Cardinal sin" involve small children?
- Can you "be caught with your pants down" and "caught between a rock and a hard place" at the same time?
- Wouldn't a hairdryer solve "still wet behind the ears"?
- If "Willy Nilly" married "Silly Billie" would she be Willy Nilly Silly Billie?
- Where do "the tough get going, when the going gets tough"? I

would leave town.

- If "ignorance is bliss", do I have the wrong kind of ignorance?
- If "a watched pot never boils", does a watched boil never pop?
- If "two heads are better than one" why do you only see two headed people at side shows?
- "There is more than one way to skin a cat" but it sure pisses off the cat.
- Don't you hope that the person who said the way to "a man's heart is through his stomach" never went to medical school?
- Did Bugs Bunny have "hare brain ideas"?
- Isn't "steady as a rock" an insult because rocks never move forward?
- If you keep "putting your foot in your mouth" do you get athlete's mouth?

108

Here are some of the world's worse headlines. You could say, " I have been thinking of some of the world's worse headlines and they include, "_____." Then you could say, "But headlines do a good job of capturing the main essence of a story. And if we wrote a headline about our customer service, what would it say? Would it be good or bad? Unfortunately, we need all our customer service headlines to be good, as we are in a very competitive business and one bad headline can drive customers away. So how do we keep writing good customer service headlines?"

Quote: If Thomas Edison invented electric light today, Dan Rather would report it on CBS News as "candle making industry threatened."
~Newt Gingrich

World's Worse Headlines

- Headline when insane man escapes and rapes women: Nut Bolts and Screws
- Headline for Catholic Sex Scandal: Bottoms Up
- Headline for man buried in fertilizer: Came Up Smelling Like Roses
- Headline for 250 baseball hitter: Blind as his bat
- Headline about man complaining to his doctor that his Viagra did not work: Bone of Contention
- Headline about Tiger Woods' wife attacking his car: Back Seat Driver
- Headline for feature story on cook: A Man for all Seasonings
- Ad for Porno Movie: April Showers with May Flowers
- Ad for Viagra: As stiff as a poker
- Headline for stolen sports cars: Police Trying to Catch Some Z's
- Headline for Policeman caught stealing: Jones Cops a Plea
- Headline about murderer wearing a tuxedo: Dressed Fit To Kill
- Headline about overweight woman called Mary: Eat, Drink and be Mary
- Headline about man who hangs himself: Man Reaches End of his Rope
- Headline for suspicious fire: Fire Marshall has Burning Question
- Headline about two egg trucks colliding: It's a Crack Up
- Headline about Joan Cream being promoted: Cream Rises to the Top
- Headline about Mr. Watson, the new grade school principal: Elementary, My Dear Watson
- Headline about John Fancy released from prison: Fancy Free
- Feature story about retired Army band drummer: Drummed out of the Army
- Headline about a woman weight lifter: Faith can Move Mountains
- Headline about California legalizing marijuana: State Goes to Pot
- Headline about man who hangs himself: Jones Hangs in There

- Headline about leader of a group of jewelry thieves: Jones named as Ring Leader
- Headline about champion angler: Jones has Bigger Fish to Fry

109

A funny speech to give at a Wedding Shower for the groom.

Quote: I feel like Zsa Zsa Gabor's eighth husband on her wedding night: I know what I'm supposed to do… I just have to figure out a way to make it interesting.
~Johnny Carson

Ten Top Honeymoon Tips for Him

Many men are unsure how to act on their honeymoons. Here are the ten Honeymoon tips for men:

- Do not invite your girlfriend.
- Miller Highlight is not real champagne. It is just the champagne of beer.
- "Pull my finger" is not considered foreplay.
- Do not say, "The good news is she comes with a 30 day no hassle return policy."
- If on a cruise, a muscle shirt with a bola tie is not considered formal attire.
- Lingerie is nice for a honeymoon, but you might look funny in a teddy.
- Turning on ESPN is not 'setting the mood'.
- Any motel with a Six or Eight attached to its name may not be the best choice.
- Take long walks on the beach. Remember to invite her along.
- Do not ask if her mother is the star of the whale show.

110

Here is a quick list you can use for the opening of a speech. You can say, "Here are ten miracles I would like to see." And then you can say, "I have often said that we have miracle workers here at work and I want to single some of you out to praise..."

Quote: Mama always said miracles happen everyday. Some people don't think so, but they DO!
~Forrest Gump

Ten Miracles

- Miracle One: The government balances the budget while reducing taxes.
- Miracle Two: For the second time in history, all number one seeds in the NCAA Tournament make the Final Four.
- Miracle Three: There is a rap video not talking about money or degrading women.
- Miracle Four: The Minnesota Vikings win a Super Bowl.
- Miracle Five: Bankers actually take responsibility for their bad lending habits.
- Miracle Six: In keeping with the hard times, Congress takes a pay cut.
- Miracle Seven: Your Toyota actually stops.
- Miracle Eight: Wal-Mart provides affordable family health care for its workers.
- Miracle Nine: Gas below one dollar again.
- Miracle Ten: You can actually retire at 65.

111

Here again is good list about aging. You can use it when speaking to a senior citizen group. Of course it helps if you, the speaker, are over 50. You can use some ideas from the list for an employee meeting and say, "That is a humorous list, but I don't believe one saying about old age. They say, 'You can't teach an old dog new tricks.' Well, our company is over _____ years old and we keep changing with the times. In fact, I would like to share several changes that we will soon make to ensure we are competitive in today's market."

Quote: If you live to be one hundred, you've got it made. Very few people die past that age. ~George Burns

Ten Signs That You Are Getting Old – Or was that 30 signs? What 10:30? I should be in bed.

- You keep looking for the TV remote and it is in your pocket.
- Someone keeps hiding your cup of coffee.
- You need trifocals to read your cell phone.
- You remember what you were doing the day JFK got shot.
- You could start smoking at your age and not die of cancer.
- Your memory has more holes than a screen door.
- You keep hoping they eliminate Jay and play reruns of Johnny Carson.
- You remember when TV actors kept their clothes on.
- Blink, blink, blink, blink – until your passenger tells you to turn off your blinker and you say, "What?"
- Pong was your first video game.
- You forgot this list was "Ten Signs You are Growing Old".
- Hot food burns going in and going out.
- Was this 15 Signs You Are Growing Old? Let me find my reading glasses.
- When they say "feel the burn", you don't think exercise, you think heartburn.
- You can read this list tomorrow and think you have never read it before.
- The only state you visit is Confusion.

- You remember when being a Catholic alter boy was not the most dangerous job in the world.
- You are older than the combined ages of the two cute blonde newscasters on TV.
- You are against something, and you will write your congressman when you can remember his name and when you can remember what you were against.
- You think that a girl in a skimpy bikini must be cold and you offer her your sweatshirt.
- You are in bed by ten and wonder why you stayed up so late.
- Was this 25 signs you are growing old? Better check the title.
- You climb the stairs just to hear heavy breathing.
- You wonder if ironing your face will remove the wrinkles. Now where did I put that iron?
- Your metabolism has slowed down so much you gain weight just by looking at a PICTURE of cheesecake.
  You suspect your warranty is wearing out.
- You put on your resume that you are biodegradable. Just in case. What was I writing about?
- You are convinced that CRAFT stands for Can't Remember A Freaking Thing.
- You have actually read Raymond Chandler, James Thurber, E.B. White and Damon Runyon.
- You have trouble counting – so there are my top 30. I will now try to go pee.
- You have a sneaking suspicion that you have already told that person that joke. But if he or she is over 50, they won't remember anyway.
- Your cell phone is ringing. You pick up the TV remote and start talking into it.

112

Here is a funny list of the top twenty questions that dating sites should ask. You can use some of the questions, then say, "Those are humorous questions, but it is always important to ask the right questions. It is a good way of finding out how you can do a better job. And we should ask the businesses we serve how we can do a better job of serving them."

Quote: The trouble with women is that they get all excited about nothing… and then marry him!
~Henny Youngman

Your Personal Profile: The Top Twenty Questions That Dating Sites Need to Ask Men

- Do you clip your toe nails and leave the clippings on the floor?
- Are you over 40 and still haven't learned to put the toilet seat down?
- Do you pick your nose while you are driving because you think no one can see you?
- Do you drink directly out of the milk carton?
- Do you ever do the dishes or wait for someone else to do them?
- Do you decide if your socks are clean by sniffing them?
- Do you think it is okay to hound someone for sex on the first date?
- Do you leave your shirt unbuttoned to show off your gold chains and hairy chest?
- Do you bite your fingernails and swallow them?
- Do you ALWAYS wash your hand after using the bathroom?
- Are you overweight, over 40 and still expect to date a slim attractive woman in her twenties?
- Did you spend more money on rims for your tires than you did for higher education?
- Do you think that grabbing your crouch while dancing is a sexy

move?
- Do you compete with Donald Trump for the "comb-over of the year" award?
- Do you think that it is okay to brush your teeth "every now and then"?
- Does your personal hygiene consist of one shower a week and lots of cologne and deodorant?
- Does your mother still do your laundry?
- Do you have any relatives called Bubba?
- When was the last time you held a job for over a year?
- Do you know what MMORPG stands for and, if you do, how many hours a day do you spend online?

113

Here is a list of "When you need to buy a new car". This is a great list as everyone in the audience has owned the car from hell and can identify with the list. After reading the list you can say, "I know that we have all, at one time or another, owned one of those cars. Just like we've all had bad customer service experiences. I want our customer service department to be like a smooth-running dependable car, a pleasant experience for anyone who walks through our doors. How do we accomplish that?"

Quote: Middle Age – When you want to see how long your car will last instead of how fast it will go.
~Anon

Signs You Have a Bad Car
- You are afraid to shut your engine off as the car may not start again.
- You always back into parking places just in case you have to jump-start the car.

- Your ceiling cloth is held up by staples.
- The car has more dimples than a golf ball.
- You cleaned it out and found the newspaper saying the Titanic sank.
- Your car doesn't leak oil; it just has a self-changing oil system.
- Your bumper is held on by a bungee cord.
- You leave the keys in it and still nobody steals it.
- You always park at the top of a hill, so you can roll down the hill and pop the clutch to get it started.
- Your kids rather take the bus.
- Your feet get wet when it rains because of that dang hole in the floor.
- Your car is so old it only has an AM radio.
- Your antenna is a coat hanger.
- Your tires are as slick as ice.
- Your car is a Rolls Hardly – rolls down one hill, hardly makes it up the next.
- Who needs blinkers? Just stick your hand out the window.
- Your sunroof is where your roof rusted out.
- Who needs brakes?
- You turn the radio up loud to cover that irritating grinding noise.
- You have a plastic sheet for a back window.
- One wiper works – kind of.
- Your dates always make you pick them up a block away from their house.
- When going up hill, your car sounds asthmatic.
- You have a flashlight to hold out the window just in case the headlights go out again.
- Your air conditioning is a fan on the dashboard plugged into your lighter.
- Your GPS system is a ten year old map on the back seat of the car which you can't reach when you need it.
- You can drive okay if you look below or above the crack in the windshield.

- You threaten your kids that if they don't behave, you will drive them around town.
- One mirror is duct taped on, the other one is missing the glass.
- Cops have to stop laughing before they give you a ticket.
- Your dog won't even ride in your car.
- You save money on car washes. I mean, why bother.
- The heat works well, in the summer.
- The spray paint you used on that dent actually improved the look of the car.
- You would put a bumper sticker on your car saying, "Don't laugh, it's paid for", but the bumper fell off five years ago.
- You once had to drive home backwards as your transmission got stuck in reverse.
- Hubcaps? Who has hubcaps?
- You have to crawl in through the window on the driver's side.
- Your interior light dangles from the ceiling. That is okay as it doesn't work anyway.
- There is no cover on your brake or gas pedal. They are just bare metal.
- Triple AAA laughs when you try to join.
- Your car is so old it has its own AARP card.
- The demolition derby turned your car down.
- Your speedometer is stuck at 30. All the time.
- Your gas gauge does not work, so you have to check the gas level with a stick.
- New tires cost more than your car is worth.
- You think about calling Dr. Kevorkian to put your car out of its misery.
- Neighbors pay you to park your car on the next block.
- The engine keeps shuttering and shaking twenty minutes after you turn it off.
- You repaired the holes in your muffler with aluminum foil and duct tape. It didn't work.

114

Another good list you can use when you are talking to an older crowd. This is a list that can be even used when speaking to a weight watcher's group. After presenting the list or part of it, you can say, "I don't want to talk about how slow we get as we age, but I want to focus on the positive and share some ideas on how we can keep our edge."

Quote: It's okay to be fat. So you're fat. Just be fat and shut up about it.
~Roseanne Barr

One of the reasons you gain weight as you age is because your metabolism slows down. Let me offer 20 examples on how slow your metabolism is:

- A young metabolism is a super-charged speedboat. Your metabolism is sitting in a canoe still looking for the oars.
- If your metabolism were in the Kentucky Derby, it would still be approaching the finish line.
- Young fast metabolisms are like NASCAR; your metabolism is like NAGCR – National Association of Golf Cart Racing.
- A young metabolism can eat five Big Macs, three orders of fries and three milkshakes and lose five pounds. With your metabolism, a senior coffee adds five pounds.
- A young metabolism can eat a whole box of cookies and lose weight. Your metabolism gains five pounds just by looking at the picture on the box.
- A young metabolism races like a greyhound. Your metabolism races like a dachshund.
- A young metabolism can climb a flight of stairs without even breathing hard. Your metabolism crawls up the stairs and needs an oxygen mask at every landing.

- A young metabolism can do ten laps in the pool while your metabolism is still trying to find its bathing suit.
- A young metabolism works out at the gym and runs five miles home. Your metabolism is trying to figure out why they are talking about Jim.
- A young metabolism is as quick as Einstein. Your metabolism is as quick as a remedial hamster.
- A young metabolism is a Porsche. Your metabolism sits on the porch.
- A young metabolism is the high speed lane. Your metabolism is still trying to find the freeway entrance.
- A young metabolism is as quick as a rabbit. Your metabolism is quicksand, sucking up every calorie.
- A young metabolism is a high energy metal rock band. Your metabolism is Lawrence Welk on Prozac.
- A young metabolism is like an I-Phone. Your metabolism is like a party line.
- A young metabolism is a speed reader. Your metabolism is still trying to find a crayon to color in the picture.
- When you were a kid, you were a race car. Now you are a Model T.
- A young metabolism has the power of a car battery. Your metabolism has the power of a dead battery in a flashlight.
- While a young metabolism is burning off 10,000 calories in an hour, your metabolism is thinking about crawling out of bed.
- A young metabolism has to slow down for speed bumps. Your metabolism sees a speed bump and wonders how it is going to climb that big hill.

115

The economy is no laughing matter, but here is a lighthearted approach to a serious subject. You can read some items from the list below and then say, "I know it is not easy to face financial trouble and sometimes you don't know if you should laugh or cry. But in these difficult times, we must ask ourselves how we can make it easier for our customers."

Quote: If you think nobody cares if you're alive, try missing a couple of car payments. ~Anon

The Top Ten Signs You are in Financial Trouble

- A man named Guido shows up at your doorstep with a smirk and a baseball bat.
- You know the repo men by their first names.
- The bank sends you mail addressed to "Former Residence".
- You call your alma mater asking THEM for a donation.
- You begin to think that you could live in a storage shed and shower at the YMCA.
- MasterCard doesn't think it's funny when you say, "Cost of not paying your monthly bill: 21% interest; cost of meeting new friends called bill collectors: ulcers; cost of telling MasterCard to go screw itself: Priceless."
- You find that "Your Friendly Neighbor Bank" isn't so neighborly and charges you $38 for a $1.75 overdraft, making it the most expensive cup of coffee you ever had.
- The electric company sends you a month supply of candles with a note saying, "You will be soon lighting up your own life."
- Your assets are a can of beans, two cases of Top Ramen and a digital watch that stopped running two years ago.
- You now watch cable TV with a pair of binoculars aimed at your neighbor's window. Wish he would quit watching *The Simpsons* so much.

116

This is a good list to emphasize that "many things are too good to be true". It is also a funny way to show that many people stretch the truth a little. And after you read the list, or part of it, you can say, "As you can see, there are many ways to hide the truth. But we don't do that at _____. We believe in the straightforward way of doing business. Screw them the first time. Just kidding, we tell the truth the first time."

Quote: Men occasionally stumble over the truth, but most of them pick themselves up and hurry off like nothing has happened.
~Winston Churchill

Don't Believe Every Man's Dating Profile

Women, when you go to a dating site, looking for that special someone, beware. This may come as a shock, but some men out there do not tell the whole truth. Okay, they flat out lie. But hey – women do the same thing. When a woman puts down "curvy" as a body type, that just might mean she is a bit overweight.

Below are some phrases that you will commonly see on a man's dating site profile. As a public service I have translated the phrases to let you know what the man really means.

• I am a very loving caring man with a zest for life looking for that special someone.
  Translation: My ex-wives kicked me out because my "zest for life" consisted of chasing women and drinking.
• I am an entrepreneur and am pursuing several business endeavors.
  Translation: I have not held a steady job for ten years and am currently suing my ex- wives, hoping I can get them to pay me alimony.

- Body type: Husky.
  Translation: I have a beer belly that won't quit. It stops jiggling three days after I sit down.
- I try to stay in shape and eat right.
  Translation: Hey round is a shape. And eating right means lots of protein, aka Big Macs.
- Love to take long walks on the beach, spend time over a romantic dinner at a seafood restaurant getting to know you.
  Translation: Don't mean a word of it. That's just the crap women want to hear. The last seafood restaurant I took a date to was Long John Silver's. And that %^%& ordered the expensive three-piece fish dinner.
- Just got out of a long-term relationship and am making major changes in my life.
  Translation: Just got out of jail and promise that I will not embezzle anymore. Unless I can get away with it.
- Recently ran a marathon.
  Translation: That was what my last marriage felt like, one long freaking marathon with that crazy woman who didn't accept my other girlfriends.
- Love to travel and see new places.
  Translation: I have outstanding warrants in three states and had to leave town fast.
- Am an avid sportsman. Looking for a companion to go hiking with me.
  Translation: I sit on my butt all weekend watching sports. I want you to hike to the bar with me and pay my tab.
- The first thing that people notice about me – I love art.
  Translation: The only place I don't have a tattoo is my butt.

117

Were you an unwanted kid? Here are some ideas that might give

you a hint. After reading part of the list to the audience, you could say, "Sure, those are some signs that you may have been an unwanted kid, but I want all of you employees to know that you are wanted and needed, and much appreciated."

Quote: My uncle's dying wish was to have me sit in his lap – he was in the electric chair.
~Rodney Dangerfield

Signs You Were an Unwanted Kid

- Your dad said that tornadoes had real cool winds that you could fly your kite in.
- Your family had a "secret place" to meet during a disaster. They let you play "Hide and Seek" or "Find Your Parents", two fun games.
- If a tornado hit, there was only room in the storm shelter for your parents and the dogs. But they would leave a shovel outside for you to dig your own shelter.
- When a flood came, your dad said, "It's an excellent opportunity to test your swimming skills."
- If a forest fire came, they let you stay and spray the house with water.
- If a nuclear bomb struck, your parents bought you a desk you could hide under.
- Dad always kept a full tank of gas, because in emergencies gas stations were closed. But he let you ride your bike "for exercise".
- In an emergency, your family would leave. You were in charge of turning off the electricity, gas and water. Then you could find that "secret meeting place".
- After a disaster, structures are weakened and damaged. Poisonous snakes slither in flooded structures. Your dad let you enter the home first.
- The roof is weakened during a disaster. Your dad let you walk on the roof "just so the roof doesn't fall in on the dogs".

- A damaged home may have leaking gas. But your dad said that was a bunch of "government nonsense" and you could enter, carrying a torch.
- He told you to pick up any damaged electric wires you saw in the house.
- He said wet appliances wouldn't shock you when you plugged them in. They still call you "Curly".
- You got to "test" the milk left for two weeks in the broken refrigerator after the disaster.
- Your father didn't want you to ruin your new shoes, so you went barefoot to pick up the broken glass in the house.

118

Below is a vice president quiz. You can use this quiz by picking the names of five vice presidents and asking the audience who the vice presidents served under. No one will know. Then you can say, "I would like to talk a moment about obscurity, how people who think they are important are quickly forgotten. I think we just proved how quickly people can be forgotten. But, I never want our company to become obscure, out-of-date, forgotten. So what can we do to maintain our high profile; what can we do so our customers never forget us?

Quote: I've always wanted to be somebody, but I should have been more specific.
~George Carlin

Vice President Quiz: Who Did They Serve Under?

Do you know your Vice Presidents? Here is a list of 20 Vice Presidents. Who did they serve under?

- John Adams

- George Clinton
- Martin Van Buren
- Daniel Tomkins
- Elbridge Gerry
- John Tyler
- William Rufus King
- Hannibal Hamlin
- Schuyler Colfax
- Levi Parsons Morton
- Adlai Ewing Stevenson
- James S. Sherman
- Charles G. Dawes
- Charles Curtis
- Alben W. Barkley
- Henry Agard Wallace
- Charles Warren Fairbanks
- George Mifflin Dallas
- Aaron Burr
- William A. Wheeler

Answers

- Adams – Washington
- Clinton – Madison
- Van Buren – Jackson
- Tompkins – Monroe
- Gerry – Madison
- Tyler – Harrison
- King – Pierce
- Hamlin – Lincoln
- Colfax – Grant
- Morton – Harrison
- Stevenson – Cleveland
- Sherman – Taft
- Dawes – Coolidge

- Curtis – Hoover
- Barkley – Truman
- Wallace – FDR
- Fairbanks – Teddy Roosevelt
- Dallas – Polk
- Burr – Jefferson
- Wheeler – Hayes

119

Here is a list of some common delusions many of us share. You can choose a few for your opening, then say, "But I have no delusion, and neither should you, that our competition is going to go away. They are going to keep searching for ways to steal our market share. But we will fight back and these are some of the steps we will take."

Quote: It is far better to grasp the universe as it really is than to persist in delusion, however satisfying and reassuring.
~Carl Sagan

Do You Have These Common Delusions?

- **Cubs Delusion:** An unhealthy optimism that the Cubs might actually win a World Series in your lifetime. Characterized by repeatedly saying, "Wait Until Next Year."
- **Commitment Delusion:** An unhealthy ability to form any lasting meaningful relationship with any woman. Often found in men who are living in a studio apartment, eating Top Ramen, while their ex-wives are gleefully opening the alimony check and living in their former house.
- **Red Sox Delusion:** An avoidance of reality. Often caused by supernatural events, such as the Red Sox actually winning a World Series. Red Sox fans also actually expect another such

miracle to occur again. They have a better chance of marrying the Tooth Fairy or finding out where the Easter Bunny lives.

- **Soccer Matters Delusion:** Occurs every four years when the US soccer team actually makes a World Cup Tournament. Newscasts proclaim that Americans actually care about soccer, while the average American flips through the channel wishing that football season would begin soon.
- **Government Help Delusion:** The strange belief that if the government takes over everything from health care to banks to car companies the economy will actually improve. Characterized by an avoidance of any economic data that deals with reality, such as the monthly unemployment reports.
- **Fill the Jail Delusion:** Another strange belief that if we fill the jails with anyone that even stumbles across a marijuana cigarette, we can win the war on drugs. Characterized by an avoidance of reality, a denial that wealthy drug lords will always exist, no matter how many you kill.
- **Jay Leno Delusion:** A strange belief that when Jay Leno came back, people would actually watch NBC. Rumor has that it that NBC is working on resurrecting Johnny Carson.
- **Newspapers Are Alive Delusion:** A belief that people will actually wait for a newspaper to arrive on their doorstep, just to read news that they saw on the Internet a week ago.
- **The Weather Channel Delusion:** Shared by over 100 million Americans, this delusion is characterized by a strange belief that watching weather on TV is more exciting than taking a walk and experiencing real weather.
- **BP Delusion:** The strange belief that when a major corporation causes a major environmental crisis, the corporation will be honest and forthcoming about the extent of the crisis and the damage caused by the crisis.
- **Commercial Delusion:** Related to the BP Delusion. Characterized by the delusion that if your CEO comes on TV and acts sincere, all will be forgiven.

- **Helpless American Delusion:** A common belief often found in politicians, characterized by the delusion that Americans are not grown up and incapable of taking care of themselves, so the government must babysit them. Closely related to the Government Help Delusion.
- **Middle East Delusion:** A strange belief that if we keep getting involved in the Middle East, all animosity will disappear, and that religious sects that have been fighting for years will join hands and sing Kumbaya, then all go out for ice cream together and never exchange a cross word again.
- **Movie Stars Are Happily Married Delusion:** You are actually shocked when that "perfect Hollywood couple" breaks up less than two months after their marriage.
- **The Bank Delusion:** Characterized by a belief that a bank is your friend. Closely allied with the Electric Company Delusion, that the electric company will let you go three months without paying your bill and still keep the lights on.
- **Kids Will Leave Home Delusion:** Characterized by the belief that after your kid spends $100,000 earning a degree in either history, political science, communications, English, humanities or sociology, he will NOT move back in with you when he graduates.
- **Love Is All you Need Delusion:** Characterized by constantly asking mommy and daddy for money.

120

There are ways that you can tell a person is NTB or Not That Bright. Here are some of the ways you can tell. After reading part of the list, you can say, "But at _____, we want to be recognized as one of the smartest companies in the business. And we will continue to build our reputation by..."

Quote: Just think how stupid the average person is and then realize half of them are even stupider.

~George Carlin

NTB

- She marries him thinking he will change. Come on, he can't even put the toilet seat down. What signs of change are you looking for?
- Believes British Petroleum's press releases.
- Believes that Sarah Palin represents the future of American politics.
- Believes that the United States can bring peace to the Middle East, solve the immigration problem and win the war on drugs.
- Watches poker, golf, then fishing on television for five hours straight.
- Doesn't understand why the *National Enquirer* never wins a Pulitzer Prize.
- After three divorces, finally believes he has "found the one".
- Actually thinks her husband will save money by not calling a plumber.
- Actually believes her teenage son when he says, "To reduce our stress, the school has a new policy of no homework."
- Thinks that the oil spill is Obama's fault.
- Believes that Congress will actually reduce the federal deficit.
- Supports "Made in America" but buys everything at Wal-Mart.
- Takes another puff and says, "I will never get lung cancer, I have good genes."
- She thinks that he will never run off with a younger woman, so she keeps eating.
- He thinks that a flabby belly hanging over skintight Speedos is actually sexy.
- He thinks the younger woman, with two kids, actually loves him for his mind and body, not his checking account.
- Thinks that the corporation needs him and will never lay him off.

- Thinks that Toyota planned the BP oil spill to get the news off of Toyota. Hmm, it did work.
- Believes that a politician will actually be elected and "reform Washington".
- Believes that Americans actually care about the World Cup, the Tour de France and Wimbledon. Come on, we have NASCAR.
- Watches *Cops*, followed by *Operation Repo*, followed by reruns of *American Idol*.
- Keeps rooting for the Cubs. Actually this borders more on pathetic than brain damage.
- Lets their son go on an overnight camping trip with the local priest.
- Thinks that Hulk Hogan might actually make a good California governor.

121

And another list of bad cars. After picking and choosing what you want to use for an opening, you can say, "We have all put up with cars like that. But customers do not have to put up with bad customer service. We have plenty of competitors out there waiting to steal our customers away – so to keep customers we must..."

Quote: I drive way too fast to worry about cholesterol.
~Anon

- The car is the only thing your ex-wives didn't want in the divorce.
- You try to give the car to your teenage son but he would "rather walk".
- Bank officers laugh when you put the car down as an "asset".
- The muffler is held on by wire and hope.
- When you hit a speed bump, parts keep falling off the car.
- Hail damage actually improves the look of your car.

- The car has made you religious – you pray it starts every morning.
- You can't park it by the curb or the junkman hauls it away.
- You keep pretending the hole in the exhaust makes it sound like a race car.
- Like a dog, it marks its territory with oil, transmission and radiator leaks.
- You hope you never have a flat tire; the lug nuts are rusted onto the car.
- When you take your car into the garage to get it repaired, the mechanic asks, "Why?"
- Your daily work out is turning the steering wheel because the power steering pump went out 20,000 miles ago.
- You will never be injured by an airbag going off. Airbags?
- You never have to worry about being stopped for speeding.
- Horn? You stick your head out the window and yell, "LOOK OUT."
- Your eight-track stopped working twenty years ago.
- Your dashboard has a crack deeper than the Grand Canyon.
- You can't adjust the seat. One size fits all drivers.
- Your parking place at work is by the dumpster.
- The car has more leaks than the CIA.
- Even a crash test dummy doesn't feel safe in your car.
- They stopped making replacement parts for your car ten years ago.
- You couldn't even trade up to a Yugo.
- Cash for Junkers program? The government wanted you to pay THEM.
- You stay away from car washes, because the last time you drove through your bumper fell off.
- The only air conditioning is from all the rust holes in the car.
- Your radio dial fell off and you use a dime inserted in the old radio dial to change stations.
- So who wants to go over 50; three cylinders work just as well as

four.
- Your car's name is Wheezer.
- You seriously consider paying more than $400 for your next car.
- You know she is not dating you for your money.

122

Some more good material for a safety speech. You can use this list and say, very tongue-in-cheek, "Everyone says it is bad to text and drive. But I disagree. There are some very good reasons to text and drive." And right there you have grabbed your audience. You are not lecturing them; you have put a new twist on the speech telling them it is okay to violate safety rules.

The audience is now paying attention. After you share the list or parts of the list with the audience, you can say, "Seriously, it is a bad idea to text and drive and we must all do all we can to ensure our safety and the safety of those around us. That is why we have issued this new safety manual..."

Quote: Hug your kids at home, but belt them in the car.
~Unknown

The Top Ten Reasons to Text and Drive!
- You drive a Toyota. You're used to living dangerously.
- Hey, that's what you bought auto insurance for.
- Come on – too few cops, too many people texting – what are the chances of getting caught?
- Gives you something to do with your hands when you're not drinking a beer in the car.
- Texting? Who's texting, you're cruising the Internet on the interstate, Baby!
- Hey, you think I can wait another hour to find out what kind of new shoes my friend bought? I wonder if she bought the red

pumps?
- If they didn't want you to text in the car, why can you recharge your phone in the car?
- Show off your multitasking abilities. Text, listen to the iPOD and still have a hand free to flip off that crazed driver next to you. Wish he'd get off the phone and pay attention.
- Hello?? When else do you have time to update your Facebook page?
- Aren't red lights really just text-sending time?

123

Often people don't face reality and they blame everyone but themselves. The following list illustrates that point and after reading some of the list, you can say, "It is obvious it is easier to blame others, and not ourselves. But sometimes we need to take a hard look at ourselves and see what we can do better. That also relates to our company and the recent downturn in sales. What can we do better?"

Quote: I want a man who's kind and understanding. Is that too much to ask of a millionaire?
~Zsa Zsa Gabor

Men often to accept it might be their own fault. Let's face it, men are stable and reasonable human beings. Women have MOOD SWINGS and you have to put up with their mood swings. In fact, here are typical scenarios which show how unstable MOOD SWINGS make women:

- You just spent the rent money at a bar. Your wife is screaming at you. Blame it on MOOD SWINGS.
- You are unemployed. Your wife has just found out that instead of

looking for a job, you spend every day looking at porn sites. Your wife is screaming at you. Blame it on MOOD SWINGS.

- Your girlfriend just called your house. Your wife is screaming at you. Blame it in MOOD SWINGS.
- You paid the cable bill so you could watch football games. But you forgot to pay the electric bill and they turned off the power. Your wife is screaming at you. Blame it on MOOD SWINGS.
- You still leave the toilet seat up, even after ten years of marriage. Your wife is screaming at you. Blame it on MOOD SWINGS.
- Your wife wants a second honeymoon. You book a Motel Six in downtown Detroit. Your wife is screaming at you. Blame it on MOOD SWINGS.
- Your wife has a car accident. She finds out that she has no car insurance as you used the money to support your gambling habit. Your wife is screaming at you. Blame it on MOOD SWINGS.
- You have spent the whole day on the couch watching football games. Your wife has done all the laundry, washed the cars, painted the front porch and mowed the lawn. You ask her what is for dinner. Your wife is screaming at you. Blame it on MOOD SWINGS.
- Instead of looking for a job, you have spent the day drinking beer. You are now out of beer. Your wife comes home at 9 p.m. from her second job. You ask her if she remembered to pick up more beer. Your wife is screaming at you. Blame it on MOOD SWINGS.
- Your shirts are looking dingy lately. You know your wife is doing something wrong. Maybe it is the washing machine. You would get up and look at it, but you aren't quire sure what it looks like or where it is located. You mention to your wife she might want to a better job on the laundry. Your wife is screaming at you. Blame it on MOOD SWINGS.
- Your wife is trying to get her college degree. She is taking night classes. She walks in at 10 p.m. and the phone is ringing. It is your son. Basketball practice ended two hours ago and you forgot to pick him up because you admit you were "a bit drunk". Your wife

is screaming at you. Blame it on MOOD SWINGS.

- You have just won the lottery – $244 million dollars. Except you can't remember where you put the ticket. Then you remember you were a bit drunk and flushed the ticket down the toilet last night, thinking it was LAST week's ticket. Your wife is screaming at you. Blame it on MOOD SWINGS.
- Your wedding anniversary was last week. You forgot it. To make up for it, you buy your wife two presents – a blender and a subscription to the MLB channel. Your wife is screaming at you. Blame it on MOOD SWINGS.
- Your wife has been throwing up all night with the flu. Since she is up anyway, you ask her to make breakfast, but don't breathe on the food. You don't want to get sick. Your wife is screaming at you. Blame it on MOOD SWINGS.
- You have enough money in your pocket to buy your wife flowers and candy. Or you can buy some top-notch Scotch. You buy the Scotch. Your wife is screaming at you. Blame it on MOOD SWINGS.

124

It is summertime and you have to give an informative speech for your speech class or Toastmasters or at your local Civic Club. Here is a quick funny speech on barbecuing:

Quote: Always wear something sensible when cooking at the barbecue.
~Lady Godiva

How to Barbecue and Singe Your Hair

It is summer and that means it is time to singe your eyebrows, set the house on fire and see if you can really start a fire with bourbon. In other words, it is barbecue season. Of course for many men, barbecue season can be any time of year. I have friends who barbecue when it is 20 below in Minnesota. Of course this may be because their mother-in-law is visiting and they are looking for some reason to get out of the house These same men stare at a dark hole in the lake and call it ice fishing. Normal cannot apply to anyone living in Minnesota, North Dakota or Canada. Residents of the Michigan Upper Peninsula are also a bit suspect.

But it's barbecue season and the debate rages: Are you a true pyromaniac if you use a gas grill? Whoops, I mean are you a true barbecue connoisseur if you use a gas grill? With a gas grill, where is the pleasure of dousing the coals with way too much charcoal fluid, throwing in a match and jumping back before your hair catches on fire? You can always tell a true pyromaniac, I mean barbecue expert, because they walk around all summer with singed eyebrows.

When you shoot that fluid onto the coals and get that flame ripping into the air, make sure your wife is not around because she will say, "Are you trying to burn the house down?"

And because you owe the bank $50,000 more than your home is worth, because you are working two jobs to pay off that adjustable rape, I mean rate mortgage, and you feel that you are single-handedly bailing out the banks, the thought of burning down your home sounds very attractive for a second. A very long, fleeting second.

But I digress. If there is a principle difference between men and women, it is this. Women will come out and cringe at the charcoal, gritty, soot-covered grill you are cooking the meat on. Meat that your family will soon digest. They will take the grill and clean it, use oven cleaner on it, soak it and it comes back looking like new.

A man looks at the grill and thinks that, sure it looks a bit dirty, but there are very hot coals right underneath the grill and that sanitizes the grill. Any germ that can survive the 400 degree temperature deserves respect. Also black lines on the steak, caused by the soot on the grill, give meat that All-American barbecue look. Plus the grit that gets tangled up in the hamburger and gives it that crunchy taste – well heck, this is barbecue, BABY!

One useful tip. Despite what you think, you have no culinary skills. Your expertise applies to throwing meat on the grill and it takes all your talent not to burn it. So do not make your own hamburger patties. They will fall apart as soon as they hit the grill, and half the patty will fall into the coals, sparking a mini-fire that will torch the half patty still on the grill. Buy the patties that are preformed. These patties were formed by experts who went to years of patty-forming school and these patties will not fall into the fire. Plus they will make you look semi-competent at grilling. For other useful tips go to www.litmyhaironfireagain.idiot.

By the way, if you are out of charcoal fluid, you can start a fire with bourbon, but you have to use the high octane bourbon, 100 proof. Of course if you take a few sips of the bourbon, then pour it on the fire, expect to spend a few days in the burn unit, but the good news is that hair and eyebrows do grow back. And they can do amazing things with skin grafts these days.

125

One rule of giving a speech is if you have to make fun of someone, make fun of yourself. That the way the joke is at your expense, you have not hurt anyone's feelings, and the audience bonds with you, thinking, "Hey this guy is okay, he makes fun of himself."

One way to poke fun at yourself is to list "your talents". The following list gives you an example of what I mean. You can, of course, change the list, to poke fun at your own shortcomings. And after you read some items from the list, you can say, "I admit that I have my shortcomings. But one strength I do have is that I believe in this company and its employees..."

Quote: I have no special talents. I am only passionately curious.
~Albert Einstein

What I am Semi-competent At...

There are many things I am incompetent at. Marriage for instance. Throwing a knuckleball. Jump Shots. Remembering birthdays. But I must give myself credit for being competent at a few things. Here is a Baker's Dozen of things I am, if not good at, at least semi-competent.

- Hiding the remote control from myself. And then I wonder why I spend half an hour looking for it, instead of, GOD FORBID, actually manually pushing the buttons on the TV.
- Burning noodles. A singular talent. Not quite sure how I do it, but I do know that when the noodles get stuck on the bottom of the pan and burn, all the noodles have a slight smoky flavor. Which is good if you are cooking steak, not so good when it comes to spaghetti.
- Procrastinating – hang on. I will explain that in a minute.
- Mispleeing, Misp[elling. I mean misspelling words so that even my spell-checker says, "What the hell?"
- Annoying my children. Who are GROWN UP but still don't like to be told to clean up, get a job, date someone who does not have any felony convictions, avoid tongue piercings...
- Rooting against the Red Sox. Come on – someone has to!
- Taking care of myself. This may be a matter of debate, but my standard is I am doing okay if I merely wake up every morning.
- Being able to do magic tricks which amaze and mystify anyone below the age of three.
- Being able to ignore phone calls from ex-wives for days at a time.
- Cutting my own hair when drinking. Again a matter of debate. I am the only one who believes I have this talent. Other people buy me hats.
- The ability to stand by my conviction that "Oil Can Boyd" is the best nickname for any ballplayer ever. Yet to be proven wrong. And as an aside – is "Can" his middle name or part of his first name?

- The ability to shoot myself in the foot, reload and do it again.
- Have always resisted the temptation to mix good bourbon with Coke. Of course, this is easy, as I always buy cheap bourbon.

126

Here is an explanation of why nothing is made in America anymore. You can read it, then say, "But we and our customers know that is not true. If you want the finest _____, you just have to come to our company and we will provide it."

Quote: This country will not be a good place for any of us to live in unless we make it a good place for all of us to live in.
~Theodore Roosevelt

Here is why nothing is made in America anymore. We don't have time. In fact, no one in America even has time to work. That is why everything is being outsourced. **Think about this. These are the Average Times Spent During the Typical Workday**

- 1 hour getting ready for work. You know getting up in the morning, taking a shower, getting dressed, warming up your car, getting the kids off to school…
- 6 hours watching television. Not a surprising number, but the average person spends six hours a day watching TV.
- 2 hours on the Internet. This includes time spent on Twitter, Facebook, e-mail, goofing around.
- 4 hours a day on the cell phone. I was a bit amazed at this too, but when you think about texting and calling and checking messages…
- 2 hours in traffic: And this is probably a low estimate. Think about the time spent commuting, time spent at red lights, time looking for a parking space…

- 2 hours eating and drinking: Probably another low estimate. This includes breakfast, lunch, dinner, snacks, coffee with friends...
- 1 hour doing chores: This number could probably be doubled for women. This just covers household chores including dishes, dusting, laundry, mopping, sweeping, making beds... Okay this number could be tripled for women.
- 1 hour a day waiting in line – actually this makes sense, go out for coffee, you wait in line; go out to dinner, you wait in line; go to the grocery store, you wait in line; go to the bank, you wait in line...
- 1 hour wasted: This hour includes various activities like waiting for elevators, waiting for your kids to slowly walk to the car, slowly get in the car...
- 8 hours sleeping

Okay let's add these hours up – hmm – they equal 28 hours! And note I did not include grocery shopping, soccer practice, video games, pumping gas...

So there you have it. Americans spend 28 hours a day doing everything but working. And you wonder why we outsource everything?

127

Here are some tips for a successful garage sale. After you read some or all of the tips, you can say, "Of course I wouldn't recommend trying any of those ideas. But I was at a yard sale the other day, and there was a box labeled "electronic dog and cat caller". I opened it and it was an electric can opener. Anyway, yard sales can be fun, but I would not suggest using any of the sales ideas I just read. However, when you want good sales ideas, all you have to do is go to our sales staff..."

Quote: Said at Prof. Frink's yard sale: "Three dollars and it only transports matter?!"

~Homer Simpson

The 12 Step Program for a Successful Garage Sale

- Put stickers on the kids. Say about two dollars apiece. If they expressed alarm that you are willing to sell them, tell them that you will only sell them to a nice home. But if you get a good offer, you will also consider a bad home. If they express further alarm, tell them that, "Okay, we will keep you around, but you better keep your rooms clean."
- The rule of thumb is if you have not used it for a year, sell it or throw it away. This may apply to your husband or wife.
- If it is not working anymore, sell it for a discount. This may apply to your brother-in-law.
- Charge 50 cents for the lemonade. $2.50 for the gin and tonics.
- If your neighbor is having a wedding reception at his house, that is a good time for a garage sale, as there will be lots of traffic up and down the street. The same applies to funerals.
- Ask your mother-in-law to help. She can carry all the heavy stuff to the cars for the buyers.
- Your kid is at college. Sell everything in his bedroom. Even the bed and dresser. That way he won't be tempted to move back in after he finds out that there is not a strong job demand for philosophy majors.
- Make sure it is your lawnmower you are selling and not your neighbor's, which you forgot to return. But if your neighbor has moved away or is suffering from dementia sell the mower anyway.
- Do not sit in a lawn chair in Speedos with your stomach hanging over. This tends to drive away customers.
- Accept the fact that you will never fit into a size two ever again. Sell the damn clothes.
- If you think it might have been an anniversary gift, don't push

fate. Hang onto it.

- You can sell your husband's ratty flannel shirt for a $1 or watch him wear it again. Easy decision.
- Don't think of it as a trophy. Think of it as one more thing you have to dust. Sell all the trophies in the house. If your kids and spouse complain, tell them that if they are that good, they can always win another trophy.

Okay, I lied – there are really 13 steps. But I will make you a deal. You know that old baseball with Babe Ruth scrawled across it. Look old baseballs are worthless and this Ruth guy is dead. Give me a call and I will buy it for $1.

128

It's back to school time and here is a list you can share with your audience about how times have changed and here is the checklist teachers really need at the beginning of school. You can then say, "I know that that this list made fun of the hassles that teachers had to go through just to get their jobs done. Well, here at _____, management's job is not to put up barricades to your success, but rather to find ways to help you."

Quote: My education was dismal. I went to a series of schools for mentally disturbed teachers.
~Woody Allen

Teacher Back To School List

It's time for students and teachers to head back to school. And like every prepared professional, every teacher needs a back to school checklist, to make sure he or she has everything they need to survive, I mean enjoy, another school year.

So here is the back to school checklist for teachers:

- Fake sympathy for the parents who can't understand why Johnny is flunking out. You know why – stupid parents, stupid kid.
- One BIG bottle of aspirin.
- One small flask of bourbon.
- Complete set of lesson plans to meet every FREAKING GUIDELINE Congress has imposed on education, even though NOT ONE FREAKING SENATOR has EVER spent an entire week trying to teach a class.
- Earplugs for staff meetings. Like the administration is going to say anything new this year.
- Cleaning supplies for the classroom. The superintendent got another raise this year and she was "so sorry" to have to lay off the janitors. So you get to spend a week cleaning up the classroom.
- Big bottle of No-Doz for all those evenings you get to spend grading papers.
- Extra pair of walking shoes for those evenings you get to go door-to-door campaigning for the override election so the kids can have books next year.
- A big sign saying NO CELL PHONE USE in classroom which the students will ignore as they are too busy texting to read the sign.
- One thousand extra pens to help you fill out all the paperwork which you suspect goes to a chimpanzee at the district office who stamps it and sends it to his boss, a monkey who stamps it, who sends it to her boss, an orangutan who stamps it and sends it to his boss, an ape who stares dumbly at it, wads it up and eats it.

129

There are times that you might have to speak before a group of teachers. Many businesses have such opportunities and more and more businesses are forming educational partnerships with local schools. To break the ice, here is a funny letter you can read to teachers.

Quote: If you think education is expensive, try ignorance.
~Anon

Teachers:

Welcome back to school.

You will note that you have no textbooks this year. We are trying a new experiment where you write out the information each day on the whiteboard and the students take notes. This will help you to reinforce the key information to the students. To be honest, it was either buy textbooks or pay your salary every week. Note that you will have to write a lot of information on the board so you might want to get to school early. We recommend about 4:30 a.m.

You will also note that your floor needs to be mopped, your whiteboard needs to be scrubbed and the desks need to be, at the very least, dusted. The good news is that, although we miss our friends on the janitorial staff, this does give us a chance to get together early this year and have a cleaning party. Of course, it might take a few days to clean up your classroom which has been pretty much ignored all summer, so we request you come to school a week before classes begin. Of course you will not get paid for this week, but we do thank you for volunteering.

As you know a learning plan, due to new federal guidelines, must be developed for each student in your class. Each class has about 40 students, so that means you must develop a comprehensive, ten page learning program for each student. We ask that these plans be written in long hand, helping you to avoid the temptation to cut and paste and say the same thing for every student.

Please do not plan any out of town trips this fall as we have scheduled a fund raiser for every weekend this fall. We hope these fundraisers will help us pay the water, electric and gas bills. These fund raisers may be somewhat labor intensive, as many of them will be bake sales and we hope you can provide five cakes, two dozen cookies and, of course, a smile and can-do attitude, every weekend.

Unfortunately, your leaders, aka the administrators, will not be available to help with these fund raisers as we are have conventions these weekends in Las Vegas, the Bahamas, New Orleans and Orlando. So we will be out of town the first four weekends.

Well, that is a quick update and I hope you are looking forward to the new school year. Hope to see your smiling face soon.

Sincerely

John J. Durfess

Principal

PS 66666

P.S. You have to be delirious if you think the school can make copies of tests for your classroom. Find your nearest Kinkos.

130

Here is a letter you can pass out to the audience if you have to give a speech about your company's health care plan. After they have read the letter, you can say, "Thank God that letter is not talking about the health care plan at our company. We continue to strive to find the best health care benefits for you and we strive to keep your monthly premiums down. Now let's talk about the steps we can all take together to keep comprehensive coverage for every employee, while reducing costs..."

Quote: My doctor is wonderful. Once, when I couldn't afford an operation, he touched up the X-rays.

~Rodney Dangerfield

An Open Letter to All Employees

Dear Employee:

As you know the cost of health insurance keeps rising and to keep your premiums below $1,000 a month, we have been searching for a policy that will meet your needs and your wallet's needs.

We have been able to limit your premiums to $999.00 a month. This is, of course, just for you. If you have a family, we suggest you move to Canada or some other country with national health care.

The good news is that with this new policy, there is no co-pay when you go to a doctor. That is because no doctors accept Blue Death insurance, except for a few in Nogales, and Tijuana, Mexico. You may try using a doctor in the United States; they need a good laugh and they will have one when you show them your new insurance card.

Your new health policy does contain a free medical kit which includes bandages, aspirin and a saw for any emergency amputations you might have to perform. Your new health policy also supplies a great book called *Do it Yourself Medical Care*. You will find that setting your own broken arm or leg is relatively easy, taking out your own appendix might be a bit more complicated and we do not recommend doing open-heart surgery on yourself unless you have had a few drinks.

Actually the book is packed with easy to follow diagrams and has a companion website where you can watch the operation step by step and duplicate the doctor's moves. We do anticipate losing a few employees who botch the self-surgery, but fewer employees mean more job security for you.

Many employees want to know if the new policy covers pregnancy. Actually we recommend filling your evening hours with crossword puzzles, television and a good book. That way none of us will have to worry about that silly pregnancy clause buried in the policy which states you must have your baby on February 31st to qualify for full coverage.

Anyway, your executive team is striving to make this an

enjoyable workplace and we aim to give you the best benefits this side of a Siberian prison farm. We think we have succeeded in keeping your premiums down and just a quick note. The premiums will be taken directly out of your paycheck and if you end up every month owing us money, look on the bright side. It will help our profit margin and keep the shareholders happy.

If you have any questions please call your local Blue Death insurance rep who is either located at an Asian or Indian call center. They keep switching, so you can understand our confusion.

Sincerely Yours in Good Health,

Your Management Team

131

Everyone has a cell phone and many feature apps. Yet have the right apps been developed? Here is a list you can add to of apps that you would like to see.

Then you can say, "Just like those proposed apps, we are always working on new ideas at _____." And thankfully, they are much more practical than the apps I proposed. Here are some of the latest ideas, we are working on..."

Quote: New ideas pass through three periods: 1) It can't be done. 2) It probably can be done, but it's not worth doing. 3) I knew it was a good idea all along!

~Arthur Clarke

Apps I Want to See

Okay, I do not have a I-Phone. That is because I am not quite sure if I-Phone stands for Idiot Phone or Intelligent Phone.

But I will rush out tomorrow and buy an I-Phone if they add some apps I can actually use. Currently the I-Phone has an app for finding your way around town. I call that a bit less than underwhelming.

Gee, I would like to pay $100 a month for that app, but wait! I can get a map for FREE.

But here are some apps that I can use. And if they are added to any I-Phone, I will stop my incessant whining and BUY an I-Phone.

So here are the Apps I want to see:

- An App that pays alimony to my ex-wives.
- An App that reminds me that getting married is never a really good idea for me.
- An App that gives me the winning lottery numbers.
- An App that gives me the winning football teams every week and the correct point spread. Look out Vegas, here I come.
- An App that explains women to me. Of course that App would have to be developed by a woman genius.
- An App that delivers free bourbon and pizza to my house when I click on it.
- An App that would let me fly over all traffic jams.
- An App that would not charge me for extra luggage on an airplane.
- An App that would pay my rent.
- An App that would run my bath, iron my clothes, warm up my car, and even put gas in the tank.
- An App that would let me time-travel.
- An App that would make me invisible.
- An App that would explain the meaning of life to me.
- An App that would help the Cubs win a World Series.
- An App that would earn me an MBA and I never have to go to class.
- An App that would explain why I would want an MBA and become a criminal. I think they call them bankers.
- An App that would let me be a major league knuckleball pitcher.
- An App that would let me take pictures like Ansel Adams.

132

Following is a complete speech on self-deception and how it can harm us, and lead to expensive, self-destructive decisions. You can also shorten this speech and use it as an introduction which talks about self-deception and how many companies fail, because they don't face reality, keep deceiving themselves and keep doing things the same old way.

You have to ask yourself and your management team are you all facing reality or are you all deceiving yourselves, thinking that your company does not need to change, that things will improve.

After giving the introduction below, you can then talk about your own company and ask everyone the hard questions: "Are we deceiving ourselves and what do we need to do to change?"

Quote: Chicago Cub fans are ninety percent scar tissue.
~George Will

The Chicago Cub Syndrome: Is Self-Deception Holding You Back

It is called the Chicago Cub Syndrome. It is rooting for a lost cause year after year, hoping things will change. Look, the Cubs have not won a World Series for over 100 years. Pick up the clue phone, it is ringing. They will never win one.

But it gets scary when the Chicago Cub Syndrome takes hold of our politicians and they continue to throw good money after bad. Examples of the Chicago Cub Syndrome in politics? We can win the war on drugs. Hmm – how is that working out? We have more people in jail than any other nation, we have not made a dent in illegal drugs being sold in the United States and drugs lords are killing each other to capture the lucrative US drug market.

Another example of the Chicago Cub Syndrome, an example of an astonishing lack of connection with reality. How about "Peace in the Middle East". How is that working out?

The Chicago Cub Syndrome? Tougher laws will take care of immigration. Hello – desperate people take desperate measures when it comes to supporting their family. They will take any risk to improve the lives of their children. That is not a bad thing.

Here is a classic example of the Chicago Cub Syndrome. "We can clean up politics with new campaign funding laws." Good luck. As they say in Chicago, "Vote early and vote often."

But the Chicago Cub Syndrome also works in relationships. How many women and men stay in God awful marriages, because "things will change"? She will stop drinking, he will stop running around, someone will get a "good job", someone will quit getting fired, will take personal responsibility and not blame their boss, he will quit golf and pay attention to me, she will quit running up credit card debt (I know, men do that too).

Hello – most people do not change. And buying into the concept that someone will change is buying into the Chicago Cub Syndrome. Do not go into a relationship thinking you can change someone, rather ask how bad can they get. If anything, people get worse.

And the Chicago Cub Syndrome, very analogous to Charlie Brown and Lucy and the football, applies to simple things in everyday life. You know that friend who swears she will be on time next time – NO SHE WON'T. You know that person who is going on a diet next week? That person who will call soon? That person who will pay you back? Welcome to the Chicago Cub Syndrome. The Cubs won't win a World Series and don't wait by the phone. He ain't calling.

The Chicago Cub Syndrome represents our belief in unreality. Sure the Cubs will win a World Series; if I keep smoking, I won't get cancer; if I am obese, nothing will happen; I am just a little tipsy, I can drive…

Think about this. It is very hard to deal with reality and to see through the myths we deceive ourselves with, on so many levels, in so many ways. We can stop global warming (until everyone in China owns a car), racism is over, the downtown of any city will be revitalized... ENOUGH!!!! Our lives cannot be based on deception.

The Chicago Cub Syndrome can be humorous, and deception may be how we all have to stop from going insane. But in what areas of your life does the Chicago Cub Syndrome apply and would your life be better if you acknowledged you were deceiving yourself and moved on?

Would our politics improve on every level if we stopped and said, "Are we applying 'The Chicago Cub Syndrome' here and I better deal with this situation based on reality and not wishful thinking."

Ah. The Chicago Cub Syndrome. How is it affecting us all?

133

Here are some fortune cookies from hell. Feel free to add to the list. After reading them to the audience, you can say, "Well we would all like to predict the future and I feel that our future here at _____ will be very strong because we _____."

Quote: Trying to predict the future is like trying to drive down a country road at night with no lights while looking out the back window.

~Peter Drucker

Fortune Cookies from Hell

- Your priest will invite your son for a sleepover.
- Your mother-in-law will have a LONG healthy life and move in with you.
- The Cubs and you share the same fate. Can you say loser?
- You will not have a heart attack. A bus will run you over first.
- Your ex-wife wants to get back together and "work it out".
- The IRS has you on Speed Dial.
- That cute girl you met last night has an STD.

- You will discover your husband wearing your pantyhose.
- Your son has something special to tell you about his sexuality.
- Your TV will break down on Super Bowl Sunday, when you are having that big party.
- You will not need a witch costume for Halloween. Just be yourself.
- The scale is NOT wrong.
- Your stock broker will make it to Brazil safely before anyone notices your funds are missing.
- Food stamps, welfare and a homeless shelter in your future.
- Your wife will not leave you. You have another 30 years together.
- You will win the special Michael Jackson DVD.
- The FBI wants to talk to you.
- God is pissed at you and you will pay. My advice – don't die.

134

A humorous introduction about what photos should be banned. After reading the introduction, you can say, "And I think that we should ban several things from our company including bad service, sloppy production..."

Quote: A photograph is usually looked at – seldom looked into.
~Ansel Adams

The problem with digital cameras is that it is way too easy to take photos. If you grew up in the fifties, sixties or seventies, there are probably very few photos of you as a kid. There might be a few team photos from Little League, a prom photo or two, even maybe one of you on a new bike you got for Christmas and a real dorky one of you playing a shepherd in a Christmas play. That is about it.

But now, because of digital cameras, every instance of every kid's life is photographed. There are WAY too many photos these days. So Congress needs to ban at least several types of photos. These include:

- No more baby pictures. Look it is a baby. Red skin, big ears, bald head. All baby pictures look alike and we all hate it when you show us a picture of a baby. We are just forced to say, "How cute," when we are really thinking, "I hope that kid grows into those ears." Face it, all babies are FLKs. Funny Looking Kids.
- No more photos of anyone giving birth. Please keep the miracle of birth to yourself.
- No more pet photos. A dog is a dog and a cat is a cat and if you take photos of a pet and put them on Facebook or show them to people at the office, get a life. And it is not cute when you put a doggie sweater or funny hat on the pet. I just end up feeling sorry for the pet.
- The first time little Susie sits on the big people's toilet. Please!
- No more stadium photos. Why do people go to a stadium, sit in the upper deck which is about a mile from home plate, then take a picture of someone batting? These photos are about as exciting as the last photo you took of an airplane wing.
- No more 30th, 40th, 50th anniversary photos. No one ever looks happy in them. The couples always have a sad, resigned look on their face like they expected something bigger and better out of their lives.
- No more photos of any kid in any sports uniform. Show me a picture of kid in a soccer, baseball, basketball, football, karate, ballet uniform and guess what? They all look the same. See baby photos above.
- No more photos of anyone attending an eighth grade prom. Why the hell would they even have an eighth grade prom? Let's take a photo of kids at the most awkward stage of their lives and torture them with it forever. We all know what the photos will look like. Some tall lanky girl with braces and pimples towering over some eight grade boy in an ill-fitting suit and a haircut that looks like a maniac took some scissors and just started chopping. WHY would we ever take a picture of such a pathetic-looking couple?

- That is just a partial list of photos that should be banned. But I must end this as I must go take a photo of my six month year old niece drooling. Let me know if you want a copy.

135

It is always good to tie your speech into the time of year. For instance, if it is baseball season, to loosen up the crowd, to bond with them, it is fun to have an audience participation quiz.

Here is a quiz where you give them the nickname of a minor league team and they have to guess what major league team they are affiliated with. After giving the names of maybe five or six teams, you can then say, "Well, that is enough about minor leagues. I just want to say that I think all of you are major leaguers and I appreciate your efforts..."

Quote: When I played, they didn't use fancy words like 'emotionally distressed'. They just said I couldn't hit.
~Bob Uecker

- Norfolk Tides – Baltimore
- Bowie Baysox – Baltimore
- Reno Aces – Diamondbacks
- Mobile BayBears – Diamondbacks
- Las Vegas 51s – Toronto
- New Hampshire Fisher Cats –Toronto
- Syracuse Chiefs – Washington
- Harrisburg Senators – Washington
- Memphis Redbirds – St. Louis
- Springfield Cardinals – St. Louis
- Durham Bulls – Tampa Bay
- Montgomery Biscuits – Tampa Bay
- Portland Beavers – San Diego

- San Antonio Missions – San Diego
- Indianapolis Indians – Pittsburgh
- Altoona Curve – Pittsburgh
- Oklahoma City RoughRiders – Texas Rangers
- Frisco RoughRiders – Texas Rangers
- Fresno Grizzlies – San Francisco
- Connecticut Defenders – San Francisco
- Tacoma Rainiers – Seattle
- West Tennessee Jaxx – Seattle
- Lehigh Valley IronPigs – Philadelphia
- Sacramento River Cats – Oakland
- Midland RockHounds – Oakland
- Rochester Red Wings – Minnesota
- New Britain Rock Cats – Minnesota
- Salt Lake Bees – Angels
- Arkansas Travelers –Angels
- Round Rock Express – Houston
- Corpus Christi Hooks – Houston
- Trenton Thunder – Yankees
- Albuquerque Isotopes – Dodgers
- Chattanooga Lookouts – Dodgers
- Nashville Sounds – Milwaukee
- Huntsville Sounds – Milwaukee
- Northwest Arkansas Naturals – Kansas City
- New Orleans Zephyrs – Marlins
- Jacksonville Suns – Marlins
- Colorado Springs Sky Sox – Rockies
- Tulsa Drillers – Rockies
- Columbus Clippers – Indians
- Akron Aeros – Indians
- Tennessee Smokies – Cubs
- Toledo Mud Hens – Detroit
- Erie SeaWolves – Detroit
- Louisville Bats – Cincinnati

- Carolina Mudcats – Cincinnati
- Charlotte Knights – White Sox
- Birmingham Barons – White Sox
- Buffalo Bisons – Mets

136

Here is a short speech about launching a new program. No one likes change and when you launch a new program, you will meet resistance. The best way to overcome resistance is to fire everyone and start over.

Okay, just kidding, the best way to overcome resistance is to explain exactly what the new program will accomplish and give as many details as possible. People are anxious about the unknown and you can help relieve their anxiety by offering as many facts as possible about the new program.

So you can take the following template, fill in the blanks, and help employees be more informed and more comfortable with the change you are suggesting.

Quote: A baby is the only one that likes change.
~Anon

"Plain Speaking" Template for CEOs and Politicians

That famous philosopher, Yogi Berra, once, during Photo Day at Yankee Stadium, offered his team this advice, "Everyone line up alphabetically by height." Of course there was confusion. I am committed to eliminating confusion by stating clearly what our new program (insert name of program) will accomplish. It is designed to accomplish these key objectives.

- Objective One
- Objective Two

- Objective Three
- Objective Four

When Robert Fulton introduced the steamboat, people were lined up on shore and as the steamboat huffed and puffed and cranked and cranked, trying to start, the skeptics yelled, "It will never start, it will never start..."

To their surprise the steamboat started slowly upriver and the skeptics shouted, "It will never stop, it will never stop..."

My new program, _____, is viewed with skepticism by many critics. But to make it work, we will take the following steps.

- Step One
- Step Two
- Step Three
- Step Four

Once, a little girl in Sunday school was drawing a picture. The teachers asked her what she was drawing. The little girl said, "A picture of God." The teacher said, "But no one knows what God looks like." The little girl said "They will now."

In the same vein, how will we know what success will look like? How will we know when it is time to make corrections in our program?

We have established key ways to monitor and measure each step of the program. We will measure the success or failure of this program by putting these measurement steps in place:

- Measurement One
- Measurement Two
- Measurement Three
- Measurement Four

Frank Lloyd Wright said, "I know the price of success, dedication, hard work and an unremitting devotion to the things you want to see happen."

I am dedicated to seeing this program achieve these specific goals:

- Goal One
- Goal Two
- Goal Three
- Goal Four

These goals will be reached by _____. The program will cost _____. It will be paid for by _____.

Finally a schoolboy wrote about Socrates, "Socrates was a man who went around giving advice and they poisoned him."

I am dedicated to more than lip service. I am dedicated to seeing this program succeed.

Thank you.

137

Here is a good opening that pokes fun at men.

Then you can say, "To be honest, many men are very mature. When I think of maturity, I think of someone who can set high goals and achieve them. In sort, I think of our sales force and what they accomplish on a daily basis to make this company successful..."

Quote: *Three* wise men – are you serious?

~Anon

How to Tell a Man is Growing Mature

- He stops wearing his super hero underwear.
- He no longer says, "Pull my finger."
- He can actually say the word "commitment" without having a

coughing spell.

- He only watches football four hours every Sunday.
- He takes time out for the important things in life – like you.
- He no longer thinks beer is a breakfast drink.
- He thinks that pro wrestling might be fake after all.
- He will actually go to a movie which does not feature explosions every two minutes.
- He realizes there are other channels besides ESPN and Spike.
- He cancels his subscription to the *Sports Illustrated Swimsuit Issue*.
- He realizes that a Bloody Mary is not really "eating his vegetables".
- He actually takes you to a restaurant that features white table-cloths, good food and wine instead of waitresses wearing tight shirts that feature cleavage.
- He realizes that putting money into the kids' college funds is more important than the big screen TV.
- He realizes that your mother is a human being too.
- There are better ways to communicate with his brothers than giving each other wedgies.
- He learns that he can say more romantic things than, "Hubba, hubba, ring a ding ding, baby, you've got everything."
- He knows that picking up a second job to support his family is more important than "hanging with his friends".
- He knows that "long-term" investing is more than saving enough money to buy beer on Saturday night.
- He knows that most things are not worth staying up for. Few things are worth being tired all day at work.
- He learns that saving money involves buying his own bottle of bourbon for nine dollars instead of spending $40 at the bar for four shots.
- He learns that mowing the lawns means more to you than his conquest of the latest video game.
- He discovers that operating the washer and dryer are actually within his capabilities.

- Instead of picking up the TV remote, he picks up a book to read.
- He realizes that going to doctor for annual checkups might actually be a good idea.
- He realizes that swear words are not real communication.

138

Here are new terms that we need. You can also make up some new terms that you can share with your audience. Or as a creativity exercise, you can have the audience make up terms and share them with each other.

After using the introduction, you can say, "Although those were some new words we could use, there are several words that already do a great job of describing our employees. They include professional, dedicated..."

Quote: The difference between the right word and the almost right word is the difference between lightning and a lightning bug.
~Mark Twain

Six New Words and Phrases We Need

It is time to add some new words to our language. Here are six new words or phrases that we need:

Redding: If you are redding it, you are hoping that the red light does not change. There are reasons you want to be stuck at a red light. You want to finish that text message, you want to put that contact back into your eye, you need to finish putting on makeup, you have just spilled coffee on yourself and you need to clean it up, you need to turn around and get something out of the backseat. People who are redding it can also be called redders – people who actually hope for a red light. But redders find that when you are hoping for a red light, all you get is clear sailing, one green light after another.

Cubber: Someone who does not face reality. Named after Cubs fans who actually think that this year the Cubs will win. A Cubber could be that woman who dates a man thinking she will change him, the man who thinks he can find the restaurant without asking for directions, the sales manager who thinks "sales will pick up in the spring". You are a Cubber if you have false hopes and don't face reality. A perfect example of a Cubber is someone who opens a restaurant in the same location where five other restaurants have failed.

Singles Hitter: This applies to someone who never scores, never hits homeruns, just manages to get on base. An example would be the salesperson who always gets the appointment, but can never close the deal. Someone who always gets invited to the interview, but never gets the job. A woman who is always a bridesmaid, but not a bride. A man who gets the first date but is frozen out of the second date.

Eeyoring It: Taken from the donkey in *Winnie the Pooh* who always sees the dark side, who is always pessimistic. This is anyone who always takes the doom and gloom approach, who always has reasons for not taking a proactive role because "something bad will happen". This is the guy who is afraid to ask that girl for a date, the salesperson who does not call on the big client, the boss who is scared to expand his business. The thought process is, "Why should I call her, she will just turn me down." That is Eeyoring it.

A Bag Shopper: A woman that buys everything, then takes it home and never wears it. She leaves it "in the bag". Such women have closets full of clothes and shoes they never wear.

Congressing: If you are congressing someone you are flattering them, telling them what they want to hear, just so you get what you want. A salesperson is congressing if he or she tells you that suit looks great on you. They really don't care; they are congressing you because they want the commission. A real estate agent may tell you that you better buy this house before "someone else snaps it up". She or he is just congressing you as you are the first person to view that house in two months (the cobwebs in the house should be a clue). She is congressing you for her commission.

139

Remember it is always good to tie a speech in with the time of year. Here is a fun football quiz you can give your audience. You can choose the questions you want to ask.

Then you can say, "Well here at _____, even though we find football fun to watch, our main priority is _____."

Quote: Anybody who watches three games of football in a row should be declared brain dead.
~Erma Bombeck

Do You Watch Too Much Football?

A Football Quiz for Men: How to Tell If You are in A Football Coma

Football season has begun. Have you checked out of reality? See if you can answer these questions.

- Did you hear what your wife just said?
- Do you care about what your wife just said?
- So you know how expensive divorces are?
- Do you now care about what your wife said?
- If you were listening, who did she invite over Saturday night?

- If you said the Green Bay Packers, would it be a good idea to turn off the TV and pay more attention to what your wife said?
- Beer? No she did not say have a beer. She said, "Can you HEAR?"
- If you turn off the volume on the TV and just watch the game, is that really listening?
- Do you know how much it will cost to repair the car? Do you even know what happened to the car? Perhaps the next time your teenage son comes into the room carrying a steering wheel, you might want to pay attention.
- Did you know that your wife and daughter are out shopping with the credit cards you handed to them while you were in your football coma? Do you know why your wife needs a new dress?
- You should know why she needs a new dress. Do the words anniversary, Broadway play, plane tickets and the Ritz mean anything to you? They will soon.
- Do you remember what you just promised to your teenage son? Do you even know why you just handed your 16 year old, who has a love for fast cars, beer and girls, your credit card?
- When are you going to paint the house, remember that promise you made to your wife during the football game's overtime?
- Your biggest worry is not the next game. It might be the policemen and your son who are ringing the doorbell.
- Do you know that your biggest worry is not where the chips are? It might be your teenage daughter and her boyfriend Spike, alone in her room. Can you say Granddad?

140

I hate roller coasters and I suspect so do many other people. Here is a list of what they should really name roller coasters. You can weave some of these names into your opening, then you can say, "I think we can agree that roller coasters can be scary. But there is an old saying, the only ones that get hurt on roller coasters are the ones that jump off. Well, I just want to thank all of you who have stuck with us this past year – it has been one hell of a ride. But how does the future look?"

Quote: Being head of the church is like putting together a jigsaw puzzle while riding on a roller coaster.
~John M. Allin

I don't like roller coasters. My idea of a good day at the amusement park is to sip coffee and watch other people ride. Anyway here are my –

Top Names for Roller Coasters

- The Wet Your Pants Express
- The Chiropractor Special
- The Snapped Neck Express
- The Vomit Comet
- The Paralyzer
- Scream like a Little Girl Express
- The Coma Causer
- How Stupid Can You Be Ride
- The Blackout Special
- Kiss Your Spine Goodbye
- The Spleen Splitter
- The Brain Bouncer
- The Sphincter Tester
- The Serial Killer
- The Heart Attack Express
- The Dizzy Whizzy
- Whiplash Express
- There Goes Breakfast
- OHHHH God
- I Wanna Go Home

141

Here are 15 ways to tell you are having a bad Valentine's Day. This is a fun list to use around Valentine's Day. Then you can say, "Thank God, things aren't that depressing at our company. In fact, we're looking forward to a good year because..."

Quote: Today is Valentine's Day. Or, as men like to call it, extortion day.
~Jay Leno

You Know You are Having a Bad Valentine's Day When

- Your girlfriend sends you an electronic Valentine's Day Card, which is also sent to 10 other recipients.
- Your Valentine's Day Card is a Dear John Letter.
- Your Valentine's Day Card is a summons from court saying your wife has filed for divorce.
- Your wife takes an ocean cruise with her boss.
- The police deliver a restraining order from your girlfriend.
- You go home and your stuff is piled up on the lawn.
- Your girlfriend knows you are allergic to peanuts and buys you a Snickers.
- Dinner is McDonald's and a bottle of Ripple.
- The locks are changed.
- Your girlfriend unfriends you on Facebook.
- The herpes test comes back positive.
- You're in a firefight in Iraq.
- She sends you black roses.
- Your girlfriend has moved and left no forwarding address.
- You are invited to appear on Jerry Springer.

142

Here is a list of clichés. You can say, "A while back I was listening to the President's State of the Union address. I am not making this up; he actually used all the following clichés."

Read some clichés, then say, "But, I am not here to pack my speech with clichés. Rather, I am here, as Harry Truman said, to do some 'plain speaking'."

Quote: In every election in American history both parties have their clichés. The party that has the clichés that ring true wins. ~Newt Gingrich

Here are the Clichés

- That American dream
- In the greatest nation on earth
- We should have no illusions about the work ahead of us
- The great task of building our nation
- Ordinary people who dare to dream
- In the greatest nation on earth
- Our destiny remains our choice
- That American dream
- None of this will be easy
- This is a country where anything is possible
- Let's speak with one voice
- We must never forget our struggles and forge ahead
- We sent a message
- Let us be clear
- We will not relent, we will not waver
- Shaping a world of peace and prosperity
- Made great strides
- Cut through the red tape
- Need to think big
- A more competitive America

- I will veto earmarks
- Will require innovation
- Facing a changing world
- How and when your tax dollars are spent
- Simplify tax code
- Make government more efficient
- What sets us apart as a nation (or a people)
- The dreams of a little girl (or boy depending on the example)
- We share common hopes
- We are poised for progress
- We have more work to do
- We must take on new challenges
- Shape our own destiny
- Meet the demand of a new age
- Let's invest in tomorrow
- I urge Democrats and Republicans to work together
- Meaningful reform
- I saw the promise of _____
- I strongly believe that _____
- Let's agree to make that effort
- Winning the future
- Knock down barriers
- We set a goal
- Keep faith with American workers
- So now is the time to act
- This new and changing world
- God bless the United States of America

143

You see IQ tests everywhere. You cannot open your computer without one flashing at you. Here is a silly IQ test you can give your audience and just have them write the answers down.

After you have had fun with the audience and the test, you can say, "Obviously, that was very tongue-in-cheek, but I think you are all very bright, as you are competing and excelling in a very tough business climate."

Quote: I can is 100% more important than IQ.

~Anon

What is Your IQ?

Every time I turn on my computer, I see an IQ test. I never take them. Why would I want to know that some third grader in China has a higher IQ than I do? But not to be outdone – I have created my own IQ test. Here it is.

- What part of a fish weighs the most?
  The scales.
- Which side is the left side of a pie?
  The side that isn't eaten.
- What starts with a T, ends with a T, and is full of T?
  A teapot.
- I can run, but can't walk. What am I?
  A nose.
- Mr. Brown is a butcher. He is six feet two inches tall and has a size 40 waist. What does he weigh?
  Meat.
- What grows down while growing up?
  A duck
- What dress do you never wear?
  Your address.
- What is a dog after it is seven years old?
  Eight years old.
- Which has more legs – a horse or no horse?
  No horse. No horse has eight legs, but a horse has four legs.
- What has the head of a cat, the tail of cat, but is not a cat?

A kitten.
- Why would a truck driver drive off a cliff?
  To test the air brakes.
- Why would you take a cigarette out of the box?
  To make it a cigarette lighter.
- If candy bars are one dollar in Boston, what are window panes in Los Angeles?
  Glass.
- What can speak every word in the world?
  An echo.
- What runs around a pasture, but never moves?
  A fence.
- Why was the Medieval Era called the Dark Ages?
  Because it was knight-time.
- Which month has 28 days in it?
  They all do.
- What did Paul Revere say at the end of his ride?
  Whoa.
- If you throw a black stone into the Red Sea, what will it become?
  Wet.
- Why is a crow?
  Caws.

144

Start off the speech by saying, "Every had one of those days when you feel like a _____, then choose some items from the list below or add your own. Then you can say, "I admit that we have had some bad days at our company, but those are behind us now and we are looking towards a future which will _____."

Quote: I told my wife the truth. I told her I was seeing a psychiatrist. Then she told me the truth: that she was seeing a

psychiatrist, two plumbers, and a bartender.
~Rodney Dangerfield

Bad Days

Do you ever have those days when you feel just a bit off? When you feel like:

- A rose without petals
- A chip over the golf green
- A missed field goal
- A line drive curving foul
- A free throw off the rim
- A throw over the first baseman's head
- A crashed race car
- A soccer kick off the goalpost
- A flat tennis ball
- A cracked bat
- A hanging curveball
- A note off
- A wrong word
- A flat tire
- A burnt steak
- A pen without ink
- A pencil with a broken point
- A jammed printer
- A spoiled banana
- A stain on a white shirt
- Cold coffee
- Melting ice cream
- A toothache
- Stuck in neutral
- A blister
- A cracked windshield
- An oil leak on a new driveway

- A clock with a dead battery
- A car with no gas
- A clogged drain
- A leaking faucet
- A warm refrigerator
- Flat soda
- A migraine
- A deflated balloon
- Black ice on the highway of life
- Sour milk
- A broken mirror
- A rip in a prom dress
- A root canal
- A dog that can't bark
- A frog that can't jump
- A tiger that can't growl
- A shanked punt
- A hangnail
- A derailed train
- A grounded ship
- A burned-out bulb
- A bad haircut
- A TV with one channel
- A scratched record
- A one color rainbow
- A bad poker hand
- A one song jukebox
- An overflowing toilet
- A broken taillight
- A banned book
- An unwanted mother-in-law
- A cell phone with no service
- A watch with no hour hand
- A lawn mower with no blades

- A dull razor
- Wilted lettuce
- A bent nail
- Third down and 20 yards to go
- A bike with a broken chain
- Eyeglasses with one lens
- A blank page
- A frozen computer screen
- A missed fly ball
- A jammed gun
- Squeaky fan belt
- A frozen TV dinner at a gourmet restaurant
- Stale bread
- A fireman in the ash hauling department
- A fork with two prongs
- Sweet tea with no sugar
- An I-Phone with one app
- An uneven pool table
- A warped board
- An unopened parachute
- A one-wheel drive Jeep
- An infomercial with no product to sell
- A Halloween pumpkin on Thanksgiving
- A wrinkled shirt
- Hemorrhoids on a Tour de France rider
- A Speedo on a fat man
- A marathon runner with lead shoes
- Heartburn at a ten course dinner
- Flu on your honeymoon
- Ice skates with no blade
- A ski slope with no snow
- A mountain climber scared of heights
- A cracked engine block
- A liberal on Fox News

- A Republican in favor of health reform
- Obama after the last election
- A dancer with flat feet
- A test with all wrong answers
- A conductor with no rhythm
- A percussion section with no drums
- A cat with only five lives
- The inventor of Preparation J
- A candle without a wick
- A shotgun with no shells
- A turkey on Thanksgiving
- Rudolph the Reindeer with a black nose
- A one song i-Pod
- A chipped tooth
- A pimple on a beauty contestant
- An empty swimming pool
- Sneakers with no soles
- Nike with no swoosh
- A greenhouse made of concrete
- A clogged fuel injector
- A soggy cigar
- A police car with no siren
- A comedian with no jokes
- A knock joke
- Coffee without caffeine
  Wine without alcohol
- A blind boxer
- An ice cube in a furnace
- A Chevette among Corvettes
- A drill with no bits
- A flat head screwdriver in a world of Phillips screws
- A baseball player with no mitt
- A mule at the Kentucky Derby
- A Model T at the Indianapolis 500

- The Lone Ranger with no mask
- Superman without a cape
- Batman without Robin
- A congressman facing a lie detector test
- A corn on the cob tester with no teeth
- A miniature golf course with no windmill

145

We must find new ways to measure things. Here are some new measurement indexes we can use. You can use these in your introduction and, of course, you can create your own humorous measurement indexes.

Then you can say, "A favorite saying of executives is, 'If you cannot measure it, you cannot manage it.' I doubt any good manager would use the management indexes I have just suggested. But we measure many things at our company, and one that I have been concerned about is sales. We must look at ways we can _____."

Quote: If a man smiles all the time he's probably selling something that doesn't work.
~George Carlin

Here are Some New Indexes to Measure Key Areas in Our Life

Hunches Index: This index is for people who live in cold climates. Whenever you are about to open the door and step into the cold, you always hunch your shoulders. Hunches are rated on a scale of one to five. If it is really cold outside, say minus five, that would be a five hunch factor.

Shots Index: This is a new movie reviewing system. I, for medicinal purposes, tend to take a flask with me to theaters. If it is a real bad movie, I might need five shots of bourbon to get through it. Thus a five shot movie stinks. But if it is a good movie and keeps my attention the whole way, that is a no-shot movie. A three shot movie would be a so-so movie.

The Palin Index: Named for the woman who can say with a straight face:

"But obviously, we've got to stand with our North Korean allies."

"They are also building schools for the Afghan children so that there is hope and opportunity in our neighboring country of Afghanistan."

The Palin Index measures how stupid a politician's remarks are. A real dumb remark would rank a 10 on the Palin Index. Some quotes that would rank a 10 would include:

Senator Harry Reid: "Today is a big day in America. Only 36,000 people lost their jobs today."

Nancy Pelosi: "We have to pass the (health care) bill so you can find out what is in it."

The Arnold Index: An index to measure the stupidity of laws that are passed. Named after Arnold Schwarzenegger who said about the Arizona Immigration law:

"I was also going to give a graduation speech in Arizona this weekend. But with my accent, I was afraid they would try to deport me."

And yes, the Arizona Immigration law would rank a 10 on the Arnold Index.

The Favre Index: Named in honor of Brett Favre who retires and retires and retires. This index measures the credibility of a person. If you rank 10 on the Favre Index, you have zero credibility.

146

Valentine's Day – here is a fun list you can share with your audience about gifts they can buy at the Dollar Store, then you can

say, "Well I am not sure that list will guarantee you have a good Valentine's Day. Sure you are saving money, but at what cost? That same thought applies to our business processes – we must invest wisely..."

Quote: Hopefully you get what you pay for, because you always pay for what you get.
~Anon

But here are the Top 35 Cool Presents that you can buy at the Dollar Store for that special someone in your life. I had a broom and mop on the list but on second thought, I am all about romance:

Top 35 Dollar Store Presents
- Valentine Musical Water Globe
- Valentine's Day Sandwich Zipper Bags
- Heart Throb Earrings which light up
- The Petite Rosebud Pin: Red Rosebud Pin with Lifelike Petals
- Light of my Heart Pen that lights up
- Be Mine Bell Necklace with Jingling heart dangle charms
- Jumbo Jewel flashing lights ring. One size fits all.
- Stuck on You Hearts Glitter Tattoo
- Heart Shaped Love Tokens
- "I love You" Bear with rose in tube
- Heart Yo-Yo: A fun Valentine's Day keepsake. This yo-yo features a heat design and a shiny metallic sheen
- Vinyl Heart Key Chains
- I love you window clings
- Valentine Glitter Magnets
- Polyester Musical Rose
- Furry Handcuffs
- Smile Face Heart Glitter Tattoos
- Whoooo Loves You – "Plush Valentine Owl"
- Mini Relax-able Squeeze Hearts

- Valentine Lei with Medallion
- Kids Valentine Socks
- Glitter Heart Sunglasses
- Valentine Rock N Roll Peanut Butter Candy
- Plastic animal Valentine pins
- Vinyl Valentine Finger Puppets
- Gods Heart pin. This heart spells the love of God
- Naughty or Nice Mood Pendant
- Whipped Cream
- Stay Awake Pills
- Imitation Perfume Fragrances
- Gas Relief Pills
- Breath Spray
- Snore Relief
- Stuffed Animals with crooked eye
- Scrunchies in red, pink or purple

147

Here is why it is good to be in a coma. After reading some items from the list, you can say, "I don't recommend being in a coma, and we certainly want to stay on our toes, especially since we're facing very tough competition. Let's discuss some ways we can improve our market share..."

Quote: Why don't you slip into something more comfortable, like a coma.
~Anon

Good Things about Being in a Coma
- It is very difficult to carry on a conversation with your mother-in-law.
- You get to miss episodes of *American Idol*.

- You get to avoid laundry conversations about mixing whites and colors and the water temperature.
- You don't have to take out the trash.
- Your son gets to drive around town in your car and use your credit card to fill it with gas.
- When you wake up, the Cubs still haven't won a World Series.
- You have to skip Happy Hour.
- When you wake up, the Clippers are still losing.
- When you wake up, your daughter has tons of new outfits bought with the credit card she borrowed from her brother who borrowed it from your wallet.
- Good news: You have been lucky enough to miss Sarah Palin's reality show. Bad news: You are awake to hear that they have renewed the show for a second season. If you are lucky, this will drive you back into another coma.
- No more rush hour traffic – if you are in a coma and in bed, you are at work.
- You get to file your taxes late.
- You don't have to sit through *It's a Wonderful Life* anymore during the holidays.
- For all you know you could be in a retirement community in Florida. Isn't that just like being a coma? Except in a coma, you miss the shuffleboard game on Tuesday at 11:00 a.m.
- No Fox news.
- When you wake up, Conan will be host of *The Tonight Show*.
- You don't need a two o'clock nap.
- Even though your wife is in the room, it's hard to be wrong when you are in a coma.
- You have a good excuse for missing anniversaries.
- You miss that wonderful e-mail opportunity to send money to an African bank and collect your inheritance.
- You get to skip that root canal.
- Save money on buying Christmas gifts.
- No more special offers to enlarge any area of your body

- No one expects any New Year's resolutions from you, so you can pretty much be your obnoxious self all next year too.
- You won't be able to remember the Super Bowl, but you never remember that anyway. Quick, name the last three winners of the Super Bowl. See!
- Your brother-in-law can't ask you for a loan.
- Your son can pay his own bail.

148

Here are some fun dumb Christmas jokes you can open a speech with around Christmas time.

Quote: What I don't like about office Christmas parties is looking for a job the next day.
~Phyllis Diller

Real Dumb Christmas Jokes
- **Why did the stripper visit Santa?**
She wanted to see the North Pole.
- **Why did Santa and Mrs. Santa get divorced?**
They were Polar opposites.
- **Why does Santa get so angry at the elves?**
He's Bi-Polar.
- **What kind of sunglasses does Santa wear?**
Polarized.
- **How many elves does it take to change a light bulb?**
Watt?
- **Where was Santa born?**
Pole-land.
- **What is the favorite sport at the North Pole?**
Pole vaulting.
- **How does Santa keep his boots so shiny?**

Shoe Pole-ish.
- **Why was the elf named employee of the year?**
His accomplishments dwarfed all others.
- **Why can Santa beat jets in a race around the world?**
He has the pole position.
- **How many elves does it take to change a light bulb?**
None. Rudolph lights the way.

Bonus Jokes!!!
- Where does Santa go to learn how to slide down chimneys? The Chimnasium.
- What does Rudolph want for Christmas? Sleighstation 3.
- Why does Santa always enter a house through the chimney? Because it soots him.
- What do you get when Santa goes down a lit chimney? Krisp Kringle.
- Why do Dancer and Dasher get to take frequent coffee breaks? Because they are Santa's Star Bucks.
- How do canines in Mexico say Merry Christmas? Fleas Navidog.

149

Here are ten reasons men hate Valentine's Day. Then you can say, "But despite the fact that many men hate Valentine's Day, we eagerly go through with it, because we don't want to sleep on the couch. No, because we know that to please our significant others, we often have to step outside our comfort zone, and do something that will make us look like heroes. Think about it, isn't that the same way we should look at customer service? Don't get too comfortable with the 'way we always do things' and go out of our way to help customers."

Quote: No man is truly married until he understands every word his wife is NOT saying.

~Anon

Ten Reasons Why Men Hate Valentine's Day

- It is another chance for your girlfriend to call you insensitive.
- You spend money on dead flowers. You could have spent the same money on MLB 2013 for your Play Station.
- There is the jewelry quandary. You know she wants jewelry, yet it is hard to find nice jewelry that says, "I am NOT ready to make a commitment." A belly button ring or a nose ring might make good 'no commitment' jewelry.
- Burger King, in HER world, does not qualify as a romantic restaurant.
- You go to a French restaurant where you have to order a fancy wine, but all the wines are listed in French, so you point at one and who knew the French made "Snail Wine..." Certainly not you.
- You can't get away with that line, "But honey, every day with you is a special day."
- Your date does not consider conversation about the Red Sox's strong bullpen romantic.
- You always buy the wrong candy. When you visit her in the ER, don't ask, "How was I suppose to know you had a peanut allergy."
- So who knew kitchen appliances didn't make good gifts.
- February 14th often falls on Monday, ensuring you will miss Monday Night Football Headlines.

150

We have had some tough winters lately and here is a list to cheer your audience up. Then you can say, "At the risk of using a very

bad pun, this winter has been tough sledding. And, as you know, our business has been facing tough sledding too..."

Quote: Laughter is the sun that drives winter from the human face.
~Victor Hugo

Winter Survival Kit Contains

- A plane ticket to Florida.
- Cash reserves to pay the heating bill.
- A down-filled Snuggie.
- A flamethrower – beats shoveling.
- A heated garage – not for the car, for you. The garage is cheaper to heat than the house and you can sleep in the garage.
- An endless supply of optimism that winter will end soon. It won't.
- Bourbon.
- A new job in Arizona.
- Antidepressants.
- A ski mask. Serves a double purpose. Keeps you face warm and comes in handy if you need to pick up some extra cash from the bank.

151

Here is a funny annual meeting letter you can copy and put at everyone's place. After they read it, you can say, "I am happy to say that our company is doing much better than the company in the letter."

Quote: My formula for success is rise early, work late and strike oil.
~J.P. Getty

Dear Stockholder:

As you can tell from reading the papers, it has been an exciting year here at Big Business Inc. and we are sorry to see that events at our company have negatively impacted your stock, which is dropping faster than a man without a parachute. But on the bright side, isn't it fun to play "How Low Can It Go"?

Labor costs have risen through the roof this year, cutting into our annual profits and adding an additional burden to our cost of doing business. As you know our labor costs were competitive when we operated that factory in China with the kids. Of course that little explosion forced us to close the factory, meaning we had to lay off all the children, bring our manufacturing back to the US, and pay actual, living wages.

And of course our legal costs have dramatically risen since our factory in Minneapolis was charged with polluting the water. Our stance is and always will be, "Look, it is Minneapolis. The damn river is frozen 10 months a year, covered with ice at least four feet thick, so who even notices the red water? And there is no putrid smell, well at least until spring, when all the water melts."

Plus additional costs were incurred when the Federal Government, strongly 'encouraged' us to recall all of the Baby-Wet-Her-Pants-Dolls. It seems, for some strange reason, we had filled the dolls with toxic Chinese water with a lead content high enough to cut your IQ in half. Our argument, which the government rejected, was "How high can the kid's IQ be anyway, if the parents buy our product?"

In fact lead poisoning might improve the kids' IQs. And certainly couldn't hurt the parents' IQ any either.

Upper management did not help our cause when a substantial amount of cash went missing the same time as our Chief Financial Officer, accompanied by his 23 year old secretary, took a trip to Brazil. Which is odd, as last time I checked, we have no factories in Brazil, but this could change if we can find inexpensive child labor – I mean if we can find 'a well-trained labor' force in Brazil.

We do have a number of sexual harassment suits pending against us. It might have been a bad idea to erect that pole in the office and encourage potential employees to show their dancing skills. Whoops!

But the year is behind us, and we would be remiss if we did not look ahead. There is a good chance that we can avoid future indictments and lawsuits as our business plans to transition into the auto business, declare bankruptcy and have the government bail us out. Either that or start a bank.

Be assured that your upper management is always here working for you, which between you and me, may not be a good thing.

Sincerely

Nathan B. Fuddpucker

CEO

P.S. – I may be taking a business trip to Brazil. If I do not return, rest assured you will be in good hands with the rest of our management team, at least with those remaining, who have not packed their bags and joined me in Brazil.

152

Here are some new holiday traditions. This will make a short funny speech or you can pick and choose your favorite two or three games and say, "Well, we have a holiday tradition around here and that is honoring our employees..."

Quote: Did you ever notice that life seems to follow certain patterns? Like I noticed that every year around this time, I hear Christmas music.

~Anon

New Holiday Games

- **New Game:** Lock mother-in-law in the closet.
- **New Game:** Kids find your gifts. Let's face it, how tough is it for a kid to go to the tree, see his gift under the tree and unwrap it. Let's make it more fun. Hide the gifts outside. This will be especially fun if it is 30 below, the wind is blowing and the snowdrifts are six feet high. This can lead to a few more games such as "Find Johnny in the Snowdrift", "How Long Does it Take Susie to Get Frostbite", and "Quit Crying, Bobbie, Find Your Damn Gifts".
- **A Betting Game:** How long will it take "Uncle Charlie to Get Drunk?" A variation of this game might be "How Many Drinks Will Uncle Charlie Have?" or "What Time Will Uncle Charlie Pass Out?"
- **The Worst Gift Award:** Let's face it, some people give terrible gifts. Every freaking year. Just once you would like to get a good gift from Aunt Edith; how many Barry Manilow CDs can a man stand? If Aunt Edith got the Worst Gift Award, maybe she would wake up and give someone a decent gift.
- **Blow up the Fruitcake:** You all get to take every fruitcake you got, take them into the backyard, stick a firecracker in them and blow them to hell, but the Devil will probably send them back when you are sleeping back and you will find a fruitcake, much like a horse's head, next to you when you wake up in the morning.
- **The Re-gift Award:** Let's face it, we all re-gift. And this is not a talent that should be slighted, rather it should be celebrated. So let's give the best re-gifter a re-gift, such as some very seldom played Barry Manilow CDs.
- **Whiskey in the Morning:** You are going to have to face Aunt Jane, who is a bit of a religious nut, who says "Grace" for twenty minutes, while the turkey gets cold and you just want to slap her silly; Aunt Alice, who is 45, single and, while she scratches her armpits, blows her nose on her sleeve, rips off a few farts and

wonders why she can't find a man; Uncle Bob, who dropped out of high school, but will spend the entire day solving the world's problems; Uncle Billy, who is the walking definition of insecurity, but will tell you about his next "great deal"; Aunt Lucy, who frowns every time someone drinks; Grandmother Lucy who tells everyone her husband is gay; Grandfather Roy, who is drunk by noon, because he lives with Grandmother Lucy and Aunt Connie, who has to leave the table 13 times to wash her hands, because there are "germs everywhere". And let's not forget Aunt Sally, who wants to talk about, "How it's a wonder she is sane, after the childhood she had." And you stifle the urge to ask her how she defines sanity, because in your book, she makes Charles Mason look sane. Of course, there is Aunt Susie, who has the IQ of a turnip, who will tell you how she joined a book club and they are all struggling through *Winnie the Pooh* and she wonders if THE is really his middle name. All of this is to say that "Whiskey in the Morning" is probably a tradition that you should have started years ago. And all the husbands and wives who married this collection of fruitcakes would be glad to join you in another game called "Drink Heavily All Day".

153

Poking fun at warning labels is always a good way to start a speech. Here are some proposed warning labels for caffeine and alcohol. After reading one or both of these labels, you can say, "Well, I have a warning label, that I borrowed from my rear view mirror. Warning: Competition may be closer than it seems."

Quote: It may be that your whole purpose in life is to serve as a warning to others.
~Anon

New Warning Labels for Alcohol and Caffeine

Most drugs now come with warnings. Like do not take this drug if you like breathing, eating and basically staying alive.

Everyone says caffeine and alcohol are drugs. Hello – why not add warnings to caffeine and alcohol.

The warning for caffeine might read:

WARNING! Caffeine can create a false sense of euphoria and make you actually want to go to work, instead of going back to bed, waking up at three in the afternoon, mixing a few Bloody Marys, watching *Jeopardy*, congratulating yourself for being a genius and going back to bed. Caffeine can also pep you up, make you enthusiastic and volunteer for projects at work such as planning the office Christmas party. Caffeine can also make you excited about your work, make you actually think you are doing something worthwhile, when the truth is your bosses are just waiting for you to resign or die, whichever comes first, so they can ship your job to India.

The warning for alcohol might read:

WARNING! Alcohol can make you do real stupid things like waking up in Las Vegas, staring at the woman next to you, wondering who she is, then realizing that she is your new wife. It can make you tell very funny jokes about your boss at the Christmas party, kiss the CEO's wife a little TOO long under the mistletoe, and then tell the Vice President that his wife really does need braces and the last overbite you saw that was THAT bad was on a monkey at the zoo. Side effects of alcohol including vomiting, waking up with a small man inside your head who has installed a bowling alley in your head and is now bowling a VERY LOUD perfect game. Alcohol increases the temptation to get a tattoo, makes you think you look good in a Mohawk, and makes you think – "Hey who needs clothes?" Do not drink if pregnant, but can help you get pregnant.

Of course these warnings could go on and on, but there is only so much space on the labels for coffee and booze and we must save some room for the actual product's name.

154

It is college bowl season and here is a complete speech you can use or devise a good opening from. You choose one or two of the bowls, then say, "And at our company, we have our own bowl, The Success Bowl, and you are the team that has gotten us there..."

Quote: Nobody in football should be called a genius. A genius is a guy like Norman Einstein.
~Joe Theismann

I think we need a new line-up of College Football Bowl games to reflect the current state of America. Here are some suggestions.

The Bail-Out Bowl: You find the two football teams with the worst record in college football and whose football programs are going down the drain due to bad management and a lack of foresight. This could also be called the GM bowl. But each team gets a million dollars for participating, courtesy of you, the taxpayer.

The Unemployment Bowl: You take two teams of economists. Of course each team has a theory on how to create jobs for America. I am not saying that there will be a lot of talent on each team. But remember these are economists who are suiting up. But it does give a whole new meaning to the term 'red zone'. And, of course, the quarterback will not be thrown for a loss. He will be thrown for a deficit. And we know that economists can't agree on anything. That should make for interesting play calling in the huddle. And after each quarter, the economists will have to study the numbers and issue quarterly reports.

Each team can have a graph chart on their helmets. And the scoreboard can feature graph charts showing if each team's fortunes are going up or down.

The Jesus Bowl: Was Jesus a savior or just some guy with a long beard and sandals? Let's end this ongoing debate between Christians and Jews once and for all. Have the Christians play the Jews and the winner gets to decide the Jesus debate. The Jesus Bowl will give a whole new meaning to a 'Hail Mary' pass.

The Christians can have a Cross on their helmets and the Jews can have a Star of David. The snacks in the stands can be communion wafers or unleavened bread. Rosary beads and menorahs will be the souvenirs. And there will be a special section for Jewish and Catholic mothers to sit, wring their hands and say, "We will never win, we will never win."

The Terrorist Bowl: Let's face it. Terrorists just have too much time on their hands sitting around plotting to blow up airplanes, buildings and the occasional ship. We need to keep them occupied. So have two teams of terrorists play each other and the winning team gets to blow up the losing team. Plus the game will give a whole new meaning to the term 'long bomb'. To make the game interesting, plant land mines around the sidelines. That way you will know if a Terrorist caught the ball in-bounds or out of bounds. The big BOOM will be your clue.

To enter the stands the fans must undergo a strip search by TSA agents.

The Iraq/Afghanistan Bowl: Have veterans from the wars in Afghanistan and Iraq form two teams. But the key to this bowl is there is no clock. You don't know when the game ends. It just goes on and on and on. Even if you get hurt, the coach can keep putting you back in.

155

Have to give a Holiday Speech? Simply use this humorous letter as an icebreaker. Then you can say, "I am all sure that we get gifts that we wonder about, but let's hope our customers never view our products the way we view Aunt Martha's gifts. Let me quickly discuss some ways we can keep turning out quality products."

Quote: Oh, for the good old days when people would stop Christmas shopping when they ran out of money.
~Anon

Share those special homemade Christmas gifts with friends and family.

Dear Aunt Margaret:

Thank you for that Christmas vest. There is nothing quite like a homemade present during Christmas and I love the big red buttons you sewed on the vest with green thread. What a clever idea.

And few people would be imaginative enough to make a red Christmas vest and cover it with green glitter. It surely does sparkle under the Christmas lights. Also making the fake pockets out of real Christmas bows was a nice touch too.

And I can't say enough about the little reindeer and Santa Clauses you glued on top of the glitter. Is that called applique?

I also enjoyed the collar you glued to the vest with the bright red and green Christmas ribbons hanging down. Again, a delightful touch! And of course, I also loved the real candy canes you glued to the vest, on top of the Santas and reindeers and glitter. That is nice because if I get hungry, I can just pull off a candy cane and eat it!

Of course, I love the felt Christmas tree you glued on the back of the vest and the little red and white felt Christmas packages you glued under the tree. I can tell you are really enjoying that hot glue gun we got you for Christmas last year.

I always say a glue gun, a few sips of wine and there's no telling what the creative mind will come up with.

All in all, it is a snappy vest and there is nothing quite like a real homemade gift. I hope you don't mind, but I passed the vest onto my brother, the lawyer, who wanted a vest just like it and I will make sure he wears it to all his court dates to spread Christmas cheer throughout the legal system.

By the way, my brother, although he is too shy to ask, really did love that homemade fruitcake with the broccoli sprinkles and I am sure he would be delighted, just delighted, if you sent him another one.

Regarding the vest, I was especially pleased to hear that you bought the felt for a steal at the Dollar Store and have enough left over to make me a Christmas hat. Yes I do think that a bright red hat, decorated with little green Christmas trees and topped off with reindeer antlers covered with glitter, would be the perfect accessory to go with the vest. I may also let my brother borrow that and wear it to client meetings.

You said you have enough felt to make me some green and red Christmas pants. I do believe that my brother would love to have the green and red pants to go with the vest. In fact, I will take a picture of my brother in his Christmas outfit, put it on Facebook and share it with the world.

Thanks again for all your homemade gifts. And keep enjoying that glue gin. I mean gun. It makes crafts so much more fun and enjoyable.

Your Favorite Nephew
Philip

156

Some fun holiday Elf Jokes you can throw into a speech. Then you can say, "Excuse the pun, but we don't want to short our customers. We want to give them full service..."

Quote: Christmas is the Disneyfication of Christianity.
~Anon

- Why do elves make good listeners?
  They are all ears.
- Why do elves make good house guests?

They only stay for a short time.
- What is an elf's favorite sport?
Miniature golf.
- When will an elf arrive?
He will arrive shortly.
- What is an elf's favorite Christmas carol?
Have yourself a merry, little Christmas.
- Why was the elf mad?
Santa shorted him on his paycheck.
- What is an elf's favorite food?
Shrimp.
- What is an elf's favorite dessert?
Short Cake.
- What is an elf's other job?
Short Order cook.
- Why was the elf's sled repossessed?
He was a little behind on his payments.
- Why couldn't the elf pay rent?
He was a little short this month.
- Why did the elf have to buy a new lamp?
The other one kept shorting out.
- Why don't elves read long books?
They like short stories better.
- Why did the elf flunk out of school?
He had a short attention span.
- Why do all elves look alike?
Because there is little difference between them.
- What is an elf, who is about to retire, called?
A short timer.
- Why do elves make terrible stockbrokers?
They always want to sell short.
- What is an elf's favorite book?
Little Women.
- What is an elf's favorite children's book?

Stuart Little.
- What do elves like to start?
Small businesses.
- What do many elves die of?
Small pox.
- What did the dying elf say?
I only have a little time left.
- Why do elves like Ken dolls?
They can share clothes.
- Why does no elf name being with S?
Then he would be Selfish.
- What do elves watch in the summer?
Little League games.
- What do elves do on holidays?
Take a short vacation.
- What do elves have with tea?
Shortbread.
- What do elves play in baseball?
Shortstop.

157

Here are some business signs that you would like to see. Pick a few from the list and weave them into an opening. Then say, "And there is one sign I would like to see on our competition's door – Going Out of Business. But that is not going to happen, so we need to _____."

Quote: Why join the navy if you can be a pirate?
~Steve Jobs

Okay this list could go on forever but –

Here are Some Businesses I Would Like to See

Feel free to add you own:

- Lindsay Lohan Rehab Center
- Jesus Christ School of Pain Management
- Lady GaGa School Uniform Design Group
- Elmer Fudd School of Gun Control
- Bobby Knight School of Anger Management
- Sarah Palin School of Reality
- Fred Flintstone School of Car Design
- Donald Duck School of Elocution
- Scooby Doo School of Heroism
- Saddam School of Ethics
- Los Angeles Clippers School of Champions
- Tiger Wood School of Fidelity
- Einstein's School of Basic Math
- Eminem's School of Marriage Counseling
- Bill Clinton School for Interns
- Chicago Cubs School of Eternal Hope
- Ben Roethlisberger School of Respecting Women
- Alabama School of Political Correctness
- The Three Stooges School of Drama
- The Bozo School of Footwear
- The Hindenburg School of Flight
- The Post Office School of Customer Service
- The Wall Street School of Business Ethics
- The Turkey School of Aerodynamics
- Coyote and Roadrunner School of Couple Therapy
- Mr. Magoo's School of Optometry
- The Priest Day Care Center
- The Congressional School of Budget Cutting
- Gillian's School of Nautical Navigation
- Kevorkian's School of Health Care Management
- George Bush Book of Military Tactics

- Nick Saban School of Good Losers
- Dentist School of "This won't hurt"
- Hemingway Depression Counseling
- General Custer School of Indian Management
- Christopher Columbus School of Where Am I?
- Napoleon's Tall Men's Clothing Shop
- Paris Hilton School of Talent
- Brett Favre School of Retirement Planning

158

Here is a good opening that you can use at a breakfast meeting where everyone is drinking coffee. The point of the opening is "You get what you pay for". After giving this opening about how you saved money, but almost gagged to death on cheap coffee, you can say, "And are we being penny wise and pound foolish with our customers, are we saving pennies, but costing ourselves thousands...?"

Quote: Decaffeinated coffee is kind of like kissing your sister.
~Bob Irwin

The Coffee Opening

I must admit that I have a secret guilt.

When it comes to buying coffee, I pinch pennies. I always try to buy the cheapest coffee I can find because I figure – what the heck, coffee is coffee. Hmm, of course not a lot of people stop by my house for a cup of coffee. That might be a hint.

But when it comes to buying cheap coffee, I have found my boundaries. I have discovered how low I will go in buying cheap coffee. And, me, yes me, who would drink mud, is about to tell you about the worse coffee ever.

This coffee is so bad, that we should brew it, give it our enemies and they would surrender. We could threaten to give it to Republicans and they would vote for health care; we could give this coffee to Dr. Phil and he would send it to rehab.

I bought the discount store brand of coffee because it was only two bucks. Let me say that this coffee was so bitter that after my first taste, I spit it out. This was not coffee in that can. They must have taken ashes from a crematorium and put them in the can.

This was not coffee, it was swamp water, sewer water, ground up mucus, and those are the nice things I can say about this coffee.

I could not believe how bad it was. So I cleaned out my coffee maker, which I firmly believe you should do once a year anyway, and made another pot of Hell's Own Coffee the next day. Same effect. It was as bitter as an ex-wife.

So the next day, I added less coffee and it was just as bad. Then the next day, I mixed sugar in the coffee before brewing it and it tasted just as bad. Perhaps brewing is the wrong word. This coffee is so bad, it needs to be exorcised, you need to take the last rites before drinking it, you should write your will before drinking it.

The next day, I thought about tossing in a ground-up squirrel but realized that might actually make the coffee taste better.

The safest place to drink the discount store coffee? I would suggest outside the Emergency Room, so you can get your stomach pumped if necessary. This coffee should not be served in a cup; it should be used as an enema. This coffee is so toxic, it should be delivered to stores in Hazardous Waste Trucks. They should sell it as paint thinner, rat poison or weed killer, not coffee. I wouldn't call this coffee robust, I would call it Dead on Arrival. Like you will be if you drink more than two cups.

159

Here are the ten best stories and quotes to use in a graduation speech.

Quote: I have never been jealous. Not even when my dad finished fifth grade a year before I did.

~ Jeff Foxworthy

- Once a schoolboy wrote: "Socrates was a man who walked around giving people advice and they poisoned him." Well today, I do not mean to stand up and give you advice. I just want to share some experiences with you.
- When Robert Fulton was first demonstrating the steamboat, people crowded the bank. And as Fulton tried to get the steamboat going, it wheezed and clanked and shuttered; the skeptics on the bank shouted, "It will never start, it will never start." But the steamboat did start and with some huffing and puffing, it started up the river. And the skeptics cried, "It will never stop, it will never stop." The point is, that when you undertake any important task in life, there will be skeptics. Ignore them and, like the steamboat, move ahead.
- Once a little girl was drawing a picture in class. The teacher stopped by and asked her what she was drawing. Without hesitation, the little girl replied, "God." "But," said the teacher, "no one knows what God looks like." The little girl said, "They will now." The point of that joke is always have a sense of confidence in your abilities. Do not be afraid to try new things.
- For many seasons, Wayne Gretzky was the leading score scorer in professional hockey. Once, someone asked him, how he could score so many goals. Wayne replied, "I learned early that you miss 100% of the shots you do not take." So do not be afraid to take shots in life; you must try new things, take shots, to succeed.
- Another Wayne Gretzky story. A broadcaster was analyzing why Gretzky was so good. And he summed it up this way. "He does not skate where the puck has been, he skates to where the puck is going to be." Remember that "you cannot drive by the rear view mirror". To steer yourself into the future, anticipate where the puck is going to be.

- I graduated many years ago. And I am sure that my graduation speaker offered us many words of advice. Yet, only one piece of advice stuck out in my mind and I have carried it with me for many years. The advice was merely two words, "Be flexible". And that is so true; your generation, unlike others, will never hold the same job for 30 years and receive a pension. Things have changed and you must always and adjust with the times. Be flexible.

- Whenever I think of commencement exercises, I am always reminded of Bob Hope's legendary commencement speech. As he warned of the dangers and disappointments of the cold, cruel, hard world outside, he gave his audience just two words of advice – "Don't go!"

- To quote George Bush, "To those of you who received honors, awards and distinctions, I say well done. And to the C students, I say you too may one day be President of the United States."

- Do not ask the meaning of life. Rather give meaning to your life. Define life for yourself and those around you by your actions. The world needs heroes. Be one.

- A little baseball advice: "You are young. You can afford to take chances. But that means, at times, not being worried about security. Remember, you can't steal second with a foot on first."

160

Here is a funny list to use when talking to parents or anyone involved with children.

Quote: My childhood should have taught me lessons for my own parenthood, but it didn't because parenting can be learned only by people who have no children.
~Bill Cosby

New Childhood Diseases Announced

- Noiseitis – The inability to use an inside voice
- Shotgun Fever – The uncontrollable urge to yell "Shotgun" every time he and his sister race for the front seat.
- Soggy Syndrome – Characterized by a constant complaint her cereal is soggy, just after she spent ten minutes on the phone with friend deciding what to wear.
- WHATEVER Infection – The inability to have any conversation with any parent without saying "WHATEVER".
- TMI Rash – The inability to spell out any word. OMG – LOL – TTFN.
- One-thought Syndrome – The inability to have a second thought. For example, your son is inside and his brother is standing in front of a window. He throws a baseball at his brother and his brother ducks. What will happen next?"
- Pickup Avoidance – The inability to pick anything up within the confines of their room.
- Cell Phone Ear – Characterized by a strange red glowing of her ear, caused by pressing a cell phone against the ear for 12 hours straight.
- Insanity – Very contagious and easily passed to parents, characterized by parents standing in the corner, gulping down bourbon and asking, "Why did I have kids?"
- VideoMath Phobia – Characterized by the ability to master a complex video game within ten minutes, but be stumped by the simplest math problem.
- Magicitis – The belief that if you wait until the last minute, homework will do itself.
- Gas Fairy Delusion – The belief that you can drive on fumes and that when you bring the car home empty, the Gas Fairy will fill it up for you.
- Facebookitis – A constant compulsion to check Facebook every five seconds.
- TextThumbs – A gradual wearing down of the thumbs by

constant texting, often resulting in a 14 year old with thumbs the size of a two year old.

161

If you are giving a speech about relationships, here is a good list for the opening. Again you can pick and choose the items you want to use.

This is also a fun list to point out that, "Often, the warning signs are there, but we ignore them. That will not happen in this company. In fact, there are several trends in our industry that I am concerned about and would like to discuss with you today."

Quote: I have had so many blind dates, I need a Seeing Eye dog. ~Anon

A word to the wise. If you are using an online dating service and see any of these phrases on his profile, run – run as far as you can, as fast as you can.

- I am very needy and will text message you 20 times a day as a sign of my dependence.
- Love movies and dinner, but I am not wealthy so you can buy your own damn dinner.
- Been divorced three times, continue to take no responsibility for a failed relationship. Ex- wives were just plain ass crazy.
- Own three pit bulls.
- Do you have a fishing boat?
- Are you a deaf mute who owns a liquor store?
- Like to celebrate anniversaries every week. Sure call me neurotic.
- Do not call me at home. The wife might answer.
- Last wife disappeared. They have not found the body.
- That sex offender thing was just a misunderstanding.

- I thought of it as being concerned. She called it stalking.
- Do you know how to file a restraining order?
- I was 'away' for a few years.
- Sunday is the best day to meet as that is when they have extended visiting hours.
- Can meet you for drinks after my AA meeting.
- I am not obsessive. I am not obsessive. I am not obsessive.
- Hobbies include gun shows, pro wrestling and strip clubs.
- I am not a control freak, but you must call me at 8 a.m., 10 a.m., 12 a.m., 2 a.m., 4 a.m. Texting is not acceptable.
- Do you have nice breasts?
- If the guards find my cell phone, I may not be able to answer.
- I have a panty collection.
- I DO NOT HAVE ANGER MANAGEMENT ISSUES.
- I miss my mommy.
- I believe that being bisexual doubles your chances of getting a date.
- My favorite game is "Hide the Weenie".
- Do you mind sharing underwear?
- I have switched to crack as cocaine is too expensive.
- I was once a Catholic priest.
- I think Charles Manson was misunderstood.
- Do you mind wearing a burka?

162

A good list to use in a speech to educators. Again you may pick and choose the items you like. This speech can also be used to any gathering of employees and you can say, "I just shared a few warning signs, that it might be time to change schools. The question, then arises, what warning signs are we missing about customer service. What warning signs are our employees seeing, and thinking that it might be time to change companies?"

Quote: The only thing that interferes with my learning is my education.

~Albert Einstein

The Top 20 Signs It is Time to Change Schools

- For your science project, the teacher gives you a skunk to descent.
- Your phys ed teacher makes you carry an anvil across the pool.
- Your physics teacher encourages you to jump from a high building to measure your rate of fall.
- Your chemistry teacher lets you take the uranium home.
- Your track coach appoints you as official javelin catcher.
- In botany class, you are the only one assigned to collect poison ivy.
- The football coach saves money by using you as the tackling dummy.
- In a play about Socrates, the drama teacher encourages you to "taste the hemlock".
- In shop, you ARE the safety demonstration for the band saw.
- During band practice, you carry the piano.
- The bus driver tests the brake by having you stand in front of the bus.
- The cafeteria lady saves chipped beef on cream toast leftovers from two weeks ago just for you.
- The janitor uses your head for a mop.
- The hockey coach makes you play goalie with no pads to "build character".
- Nobody told you that the new school opened up last month. Or where it is.
- The biology class plans to dissect you.
- The inside of your locker is your second home.
- You are the only one in computer lab with an abacus.
- The biology teacher uses you as an example of how evolution often fails.

- The English teacher assigns *War and Peace* for the class to read. She assigns you *The Little Lost Puppy*.

163

Sometimes you may be asked to give a speech on Memorial Day, President's Day, July Fourth or some other historic holiday. Your opening doesn't have to be too serious. Shake up the crowd and get them laughing with this opening.

Quote: Rarely is the question asked: Is our children learning? ~George W. Bush

On April 12, 1861 the Civil War began.

Here are Some Little Known Facts about the Civil War

- Brett Favre retired and unretired three times as a general of the Confederacy.
- Abe Lincoln wore a top hat because he had a comb-over like Donald Trump.
- The South lost at Gettysburg because AT&T was their carrier and they couldn't get any signals, thus disrupting their cell phone service and all communication.
- The Civil War was fought to protect and preserve Justin Bieber's hair.
- Regis Philbin was the first reporter on the scene at the Battle of Bull Run. He was only 22 at the time.
- "Who is buried in Grant's Tomb?" still keeps historical researchers busy for hours.
- Abe Lincoln wanted to stay home and watch *Desperate Housewives*, but his wife dragged him to Ford's Theater.
- Lincoln's bodyguard was at the Star Saloon, right next door to Ford's Theater, having drinks with Charlie Sheen, when the

President got shot.

- John Wilkes Booth was scheduled to be a guest on the Lettermen Show to promote his new play, but he was unable to make it due to a broken leg.
- The first shot of the Civil War was taken by Tipsy McDowell in a saloon in Boston. It was reported to be Irish whiskey.

164

If you have to talk to a group during the summer, use these funny boat buying tips. Then you can say, "But instead of buying a boat, let me offer some wiser investment tips."

Quote: A lot of people ask me if I were shipwrecked and could only have one book, what would it be? I always say How To Build a Boat.
~Stephen Wright

Top Used Boat Buying Tips

- Avoid a boat that is too old; if it is called the Niña, Pinta or Santa María, this might be a clue.
- Check for previous damage; if is called the S.S. Minnow, this could be a problem.
- Check the sleeping quarters for seaweed. Ask yourself how did it get there?
- If the owner makes a joke, "Well, you can have the Titanic now," this is not a good sign.
- Are there two extra set of oars in the boat, to "increase the power", if anyone wants to go waterskiing?
- Financier J.P. Morgan was asked by a reporter how much Morgan's yacht cost to operate. "If you have to ask, you can't afford it," was Morgan's reply. Remember expenses like storage, personal property taxes, slip rental, maintenance, insurance and

divorce lawyers.

- What are those bailing buckets doing on board?
- Boats need trailers. How much will a trailer cost? And how much will the repairs cost when you back up and hit a wall the first few times?
- Ask why they say, "The happiest two days in a boat owner's life are when he buys and sells his boat."
- Check for holes, in the boat and in your head.

165

Below is the foundation for a good graduation speech. You can add some personal stories, perhaps include a story about a person or two who you admire. This speech, with a little editing, can also be an inspirational speech to give to any youth group, or even to motivate a sales group.

Quote: You cannot get to the top by sitting on your bottom.
~Anon

Make Something Happen

This is something I did not know when I graduated from college.

You can make things happen.

I did not know that when I graduated from college and you may not either. Because the last few years, you have not been *making things happen*. You have been in a reactive mode. The teacher assigns a paper, you write it. There is a chemistry test tomorrow, you study for it. There is a lecture, you attend it.

But you can *make things happen*.

Unfortunately, people go to college to "get a good job". Again, that is a reactive mode. You go to college, you get a good job, you do what the boss wants. Not unlike college, your bosses speak, they order you around, you react.

But you can *make things happen*.

You can open your own accounting firm. Create jobs for hundreds of college graduates.

You can open your own ad agency. Create jobs for all those English and art majors.

You can start your own volunteer organization. Help people who are too tired and desperate, at the moment, to help themselves. Give them a chance, like you had, to make something of their lives.

You can go out and build a house for a homeless person.

You can change a child's life by becoming a mentor.

You can take a weed-covered vacant lot in the inner city, turn it into housing for the homeless, a garden, a playground.

You can run for city council, mayor, the State Legislature, Congress, even President.

You can change the world, even when you are dead, by having children who carry, into the next century, your morals and values and belief that *you can make things happen*.

In short, *you can make things happen*.

How can this mindset help you in life? A quick example. A good salesperson does not wait for the phone to ring. He goes out and *makes things happen*. A small business owner does not wait for people to knock on his door, he goes out and knocks on doors, creates opportunities for himself and his business, *he makes things happen*.

But you have to escape the mindset that college instilled in you all. You have to quit being reactive. Start being proactive. You no longer have to worry about what is due Monday, how much homework you have this weekend, what does Dr. Babble want for the final thesis.

Now you have to shift into another mode. The mode, the belief that *you can make things happen*, that you can make life better for people. And if each one of you makes life better for just one person this year, you have started a lifelong career of *making things happen*.

Henry Ford made things happen. Bill Gates made things happen. Steve Jobs made things happen. The connection between all three is that none of them had a college degree, because they were anxious to get out in the world and *make things happen.*

Hopefully hours of studying, hours of mind-numbing lectures and hours of busy work have not buried your entrepreneurial spirit.

America will not continue to be strong if we all work for the government. Our economy always has and always will depend on people who *make things happen.* Every major corporation has been founded by someone *who made things happen.*

Every major invention that has launched new industries, the car and the computer are two obvious examples, were launched by people who made things happen.

To be blunt, I firmly believe that we need less people wringing their hands, moaning about the economy, and complaining they can't find a job. We need more people *who make things happen.*

One final thought – ask yourself as you leave college: What can I make happen? And how do I start accomplishing that?

166

Here is a list of silly science projects. You can pick and choose from the list or use the entire list as an opening. Then you can say, "Our education system is in trouble and, in spite of that humorous list, it is time for all of us in business to take our responsibility seriously and do what we can to help our local school."

Quote: In the first place God made idiots; that was for practice; then he made school boards.

~Mark Twain

- Energy of the Sun: Put on a bathing suit. Go sit by the pool. See how long it takes to get a good tan.
- Evolution of Man: Go to a redneck bar and disprove the theory of evolution by filming drunken rednecks.

- The Search for Life: Go to a fraternity house on Sunday morning. Step over the drunks sleeping in the hallway and search for any sign of intelligent life.
- Method of Pest Control: Lock the door when your mother-in-law comes over. See what happens to your relationship with your wife.
- Exploring Extinction: Call up Joan Rivers and ask her how the dinosaurs died.
- Causes of Air Pollution: Go to a political convention.
- Effects of alcohol on the brain: See "Search for Life: Number 3".
- Effect of UV Radiation on Human Skin: Put on a bathing suit. Go sit by the pool. I know this sounds a lot like Number One, but trust me, it is.
- Fiber in the Diet: Slip Ex-Lax into a friend's cereal. Do not measure the results.
- Dental Health: Take meth for a week or two. See how many teeth fall out.
- The Effects of Lightning: Give your mother-in-law a kite and a key.
- The Effectiveness of Corporal Punishment: Walk around college and say to women "Spank me, baby." Warning: This might involve sexual harassment charges.

167

Even great people give bad advice – here is a complete graduation speech making fun of bad advice. And it encourages graduates to think for themselves and to make their own choices.

Quote: Education is what you get after you leave college.
~Anon

The World's Best Graduation Speech

- Look I'm the guy who told Lincoln to go to the play
- Who advised Columbus the earth was flat
- Who told Copernicus the sun revolved around the earth
- Who suggested Newton stay away from apple trees
- Who told Leonardo to change the smile on the Mona Lisa
- Who told Custer it was just a few Indians
- Who told Ford to call the car Edsel
- Who thought Prohibition was a good idea
- Who wondered what harm can a few cigarettes do
- Who invented Preparation J
- Who told the Wright Brothers to stick to making bicycles
- Who told my brother-in-law the IRS would never find out
- Who predicted a good year for stocks in 1929
- Who said "Go East, young man"
- Who told Elvis "Stick to driving a truck"
- Who thought "moving picture talkies" were a silly idea
- Who thought that Louis Pasteur made up the concept of germs
- Who told Charlie Sheen a few drinks couldn't hurt
- Who told Caesar to go to the Forum
- Who told GM the Japanese could never take over the auto market
- Who suggested Hemingway give up writing
- Who told Picasso he couldn't paint
- Who told Van Gogh not to seek therapy
- Who told Eve, "Hey, it's just an apple"
- Who told Texans the Alamo was bulletproof
- Who told the Light Brigade to charge
- Who told General Picket to advance
- Who thought Television was just a passing fad
- Who told Jesus to trust Judas
- Who told Americans not to worry about Hitler
- Who said Pearl Harbor was well protected
- Who thought Babe Ruth was too fat to be any good
- Who thought the Beatles were just another garage band

- Who told Colonel Sanders there was no future in chickens
- Who told Napoleon that the English were nothing but a nation of shopkeepers
- Who told the McDonald's brothers Americans preferred cooking at home
- Who told the Japanese the Americans were just kidding about that nuclear bomb
- Who advised Bill Gates to stay in college
- Who thought the Red Sox would never win a World Series
- That Facebook was just plain silly
- Who never saw a future for I-Phones.
- So I was wrong sometimes
- So sue me
- But remember the world is full of bad advice
- And many of the adults who will speak today at graduations across the country may be wrong too.
- Keep that in mind and remember it is your life.
- You only get one
- So do what you damn well please with it.

168

How do you give someone bad news? Here is a funny bit that can open a speech on Communication. After reading all or parts of this bit to your audience, you can say, "Well we all hope we can communicate with our employees better than that. Let me share some communication tips with you."

Quote: Bad news is not like wine. It doesn't improve with age
~Colin Powell

Well I am Mr. Euphemism.

I don't lie, but I may be creative every now and then. Let's just say I believe in being economical with the truth and economy is a good thing:

- You can always trust me. In fact, you are not being fired you are merely being downsized, while our company is being right-sized.
- You are being given the opportunity to seek better opportunities, you are being furloughed. Or should we say outplaced or if you prefer outsourced, given an opportunity to visit the relocation center. When asked, just say "you are between jobs". Consider yourself a transitioned employee.
- Think of yourself as being displaced, that your job was redundant, your job was optimized, you were realigned, released back into the talent pool.
- Look at yourself as being self-employed, a freelancer, a consultant. You can tell your friends you are taking an unpaid sabbatical.
- You are merely starting a career as a professional blogger, domestic engineer, a job market researcher, or best of all, you are embarking on a journey of self-discovery.
- Yes, I am sorry to inform you, we are having a reduction in force and you have just been reduced. You have been RIFTed. You have been, shall we say, decruited, freed up for the future, reshuffled.
- If we look at it strategically, you are merely participating in our "synergy-related headcount restructuring." Or you have been reengineered. Consider yourself part of a workforce imbalance correction. Consider yourself part of our skill-mix adjustment.
- But remember you are not being fired. You are just enduring a career downgrade. Facing a career alternative enhancement. You are at work investigating the efficiency of our unemployment system.
- Your job is being restructured without you in it.

- I am not saying you were stealing. That would be a bad reflection on my management. We merely seem to have some "inventory leakage". You did not provide bad customer service, you did seem to have "negative customer outcome". I would never say you were late for work, but you were "chronologically challenged".

Can I make it any clearer?

169

Here is a humorous speech on the black holes of life. You can easily adapt it with some stories of your own. Or else you can just talk about a few dark holes of life, then say, "Well, a black hole is something you stumble into and never get out of. Bad management has caused many black holes that companies stumble into and never recover from. Is our company facing any black holes? We might be and let's discuss how to avoid them. "

The Scientific Find of the Week Has to Be

"Contrary to established scientific thinking, you'd be roasted and not "spaghettified" if you stumbled into a super massive black hole."

Well I have some experience with black holes and my theory is that you are neither spaghettified nor roasted. You keep spinning around like you are in a big clothes dryer and you can't get out.

Plus, we don't need to have super powerful telescopes to search outer space for black holes. There are plenty here in earth. Five quick examples? The federal budget, a lawyer's heart, a used Yugo, alimony and a puppy's stomach.

What is my experience with black holes?

First, I am a Cub's fan. And they have not won a World Series for 100 years. And every season, Cub fans step in the same black hole and think the outcome will be difference. Nothing escapes from a black hole. The Cubs are in the biggest black hole in baseball history.

If they do escape and win a World Series, every physics book will have to be rewritten.

And I have a daughter. Who is going and going and going to college. As she says, "College, the best seven years of your life." But that is okay. What I am concerned about is that college loans may be so expensive, they will be financial dark holes which kids will never escape.

By the way, I know who invented black holes. I am sharing this with you, but you already know. Lawyers. They even appear to have black holes in their offices. I have no idea where they keep the black holes. But I KNOW they are there, because they keep sucking me dry.

I am a taxpayer. And I can quickly name some black holes that keep sucking in gigantic wads of money. I have been on this earth for over 50 years. And I remember that when I was a kid, the government would solve the immigration problem, bring peace to the Middle East, win the drug war and balance the federal budget.

Hmm, unless I have missed something, these four items are definitely the black holes of government, which keep sucking money in and spitting no results back out.

Concerning the black holes of immigration, Middle East, drugs and a balanced budget, I offer the government two pieces of advice.

One, the only good thing about hitting your head against the wall is it feels so good when you stop. And the definition of insanity is doing the same thing over and over again and expecting different results.

I suspect that the government may be creating some new black holes, where the taxpayer may be roasted and not 'spaghettified'. Three that come to mind are endless bail out programs, a national health care system and continual 'stimulus' programs.

But I could be wrong. And of course the Cubs may win the World Series this year.

170

Here are ten silly interview questions. You can use these by saying, "I am a bit disappointed in HR; they would not let me write any interview questions and I had a list prepared. Here it is." After reading the list you can say, "But let's cover some job interview questions you should be prepared to answer."

Quote: Doing the job right the first time gets the job done. Doing the job wrong 14 times gives you job security.
~Anon

Here are My Top Ten Job Interview Questions

- What is the meaning of life?
- Why is there a South Dakota and North Dakota? Isn't one Dakota Enough?
- Do you have trouble opening trash bags?
- Do you think I am attractive?
- Do you have a boyfriend?
- Is broccoli a fruit or a vegetable?
- Do you know that this company will file for bankruptcy at noon today?
- What is your pet peeve? And why do you have a pet peeve? Don't dogs and cats make better pets?
- If you have a Ford Focus and I have a Ford Focus and we get married – do we have Foci?
- If patting a fellow worker's bottom is sexual harassment, why aren't football players sued?

171

At first this appears like a humorous quiz. But you can use the quiz for a speech about drugs or alcoholism. After reading the quiz and the surprise answer, you can say, "That is a funny quiz, but there is a strong element of truth in that quiz. When you are on drugs or alcohol, you cannot be trusted. That is why we have a strong drug and alcohol policy here at work and let me cover some specific areas of that."

Quote: It only takes one drink to get me drunk. The trouble is I can't remember if it is the 13th or the 14th.
~George Burns

Do you have memory loss? This is a serious condition and can be determined by the following questions.

The good news is that if you do have memory loss, there are three simple solutions that may help solve the problem. They are revealed at the end:

Memory Loss Test

- Do you have problems remembering where you parked?
- Do you have problems remembering your address?
- Do you meet people and the next day do not remember their names?
- Do you look at your credit card bill and cannot identify half the charges?
- Do you go up to houses that kind of look like yours and try to fit the key in the lock?
- Do you wake up late at night and try to remember where you are?
- Do you have trouble remembering the lyrics to songs?
- Do you often push the wrong floor in the elevator?
- Do you have to look at your business card to remember your phone number?
- If you carry on a conversation, can you repeat the main points of the conversation to someone 24 hours later?
- Does your mind wander and do you occasionally lose track of

time?
- Do you daydream a lot about being someone famous and lose touch with reality?
- Do you hear a funny joke or story, but cannot remember it 24 hours later?
- Do you find business cards or receipts in your wallet or pocket, and wonder where they came from.
- If someone asks you to describe what you had for dinner, can you easily tell them? Or do you really have to think about it?
- Do you often have a bruise on your body but cannot remember how it happened?
- Can you remember the name of your third grade teacher, but not the name of someone you met less than ten minutes ago?
- Do you often call people "Buddy" because you cannot remember their names?
- When traveling, do you have problems remembering the name of your hotel. Or your room number?
- Do you *misplace* your rings, wedding, engagement?
- Do you wander into a store, often late at night when you are tired, and struggle to remember what you are there for?
- You are supposed to meet someone. But you forget who?

Often coordination and physical symptoms problems accompany memory loss, indicating a degeneration of neurologic function.

- Do you often feel dizzy when you stand up?
- Do you sometimes stumble when you walk?
- At times do you tend to slur your words?
- Do you have headaches, especially in the morning?
- Does your mouth feel very fuzzy in the morning?
- Do you ever have blurred vision?
- Do you accidently bump into inanimate objects?

Solution

As promised here are the three solutions. Quit drinking. Stop drinking. Give up drinking.

172

Often times, you may be called upon to give an auto safety speech to parents, teenagers, even workers. You can use the below stats to open an auto safety speech or use the stats as an entire speech.

Quote: It takes 8,460 bolts to assemble an automobile, and one nut to scatter it all over the road.

~Anon

To make your teenager, workers or friends aware of how dangerous driving is, have them take this true-false test. The answers are at the end.

- Half of all fatal crashes in 2007 occurred on roads with posted speed limits of 55 mph or more.
- In 2007, it was a criminal offense to operate a motor vehicle at a blood alcohol concentration (BAC) of .08 or above in all 50 States.
- About 43,000 people a year are killed in car accidents.
- There are over 257 million registered vehicles in the US.
- Americans drive over 3 billion miles a year.
- In 2006, 29,722 male drivers and 29,722 female drivers were killed.
- There are about 1.5 million car accidents with deer each year that result in $1 billion in vehicle damage, about 150 human fatalities, and over 10,000 personal injuries.
- You are most likely to hit a deer in Pennsylvania.
- There are about seven million car accidents a year in the US.
- Almost 3 million people a year are injured in car crashes in the

US every year.
- There is one death every 13 minutes from a car crash in the United States.
- The costs of car accidents in the US is over 200 billion a year.
- Older drivers, over 65, only account for 8% of people injured in car accidents.
- Crashes are the leading cause of death in teenagers aged 16 to 18, and account for one third of all deaths in this age group.
- When you encounter an aggressive driver, your best defensive move is to flick him off.
- There are close to a million cars on the road at one time being driven by someone holding a cell phone.
- Most drivers need at least 1.5 seconds to react.
- Over 5,000 people a year die in motorcycle crashes.
- Car accidents cost each American more than $1,000 a year.
- About 30% of people killed in car crashes are speeding.
- You are thinking that death happens to other people.

Okay – number 15 is false. The rest are all sobering stats.

173

Graduation time? Here is a funny poem you can share with parents. You can say, "This is a very touching moment for many parents and I would like to share a poem, that another parent shared with me. The poem is from his son, the philosophy major. Here it is:

Quote: Poetry is an echo, asking an echo to dance.
~Carl Sandburg

Graduation Poem

I am somewhat a scholar
Just received my college degree
Know all the great philosophers
I am not confused
by Confucius
I can pick a Locke
With the best of them
Kant you?
Let's open a can of Plato
Fry some Bacon
maybe Russell some feathers
Marx my words,
I can pronounce
Nietzsche with the very best accent
All this is to say
that I may move back home
for just a little bit.

174

Here is a funny list of things that you will never hear men say. You can choose the items you like for a humorous introduction, then say, "But we all have things we don't like to hear..." Then you can pause and ask for audience participation. "What are some of the things we don't want our customers to say?"

Quote: If you want to sacrifice the admiration of many men for the criticism of one, go ahead, get married.
~Katharine Hepburn

Things Most Men Will Never Say

- Of course, I have no idea what I'm doing.

- You're right. Riding in a golf cart isn't really exercise.
- It is ONLY a fantasy league.
- Of course it's not PMS. You're just very sensitive.
- Fine, you go out with your girlfriends. I will go out with my boyfriends.
- I love those prostate exams.
- That woman is showing way too much cleavage.
- Where are all the great Broadway plays like *CATS*?
- Let's snuggle and watch *Sex in the City*.
- Honey, we need to talk.
- Do I look fat in this?
- I would love our daughter to work at Hooters.
- Marriage sounds like a good idea.
- Let's invite your mother over for the weekend.
- It's only a game; I'd rather talk with you, Honey.
- You didn't even notice my new hairstyle.
- I'll do the dishes.
- Let me change the diapers.
- I think our daughter's date is a bright young man with a future.
- Not tonight, dear, I have a headache.
- I just can't find jeans that fit.
- No problem, it's only a car bumper.
- Those cheerleaders need to cover up more. Those poor girls must be freezing.
- Bridge sounds great. I'll cancel the poker game.
- There is way too much action in this movie. I wish they had more dialogue.
- I don't mind if my daughter stays out past midnight.
- Sure, go charge as much as you want. That's why we have credit cards.
- Forget golf, I'm going to a yoga class.
- Boy I love that movie *The Notebook*.
- That Danielle Steele sure can write.
- Do we get the Soap Opera Channel?

- Hallmark Channel has SUCH good shows.
- Forget whiskey. I'm really a wine man.
- Oh boy – a musical.
- Tofu – great – beats steak and beans any night.
- T.J. Maxx is my favorite store.
- Pink looks pretty good on me
- No problem. My golf clubs do make great weed whackers.
- I did look at the calorie content of the beer and I will switch to Evian water.
- I would love to stop and ask for directions. Good advice dear.
- You are so right. I will go for yearly checkups.
- I don't need that fishing trip. Let's buy new curtains instead.
- This is our one month anniversary. We have been dating for one month.
- I don't want to give advice. I just want to listen.
- I will never say "Pull my finger" again.
- I am so sorry that I passed gas. It is not funny.
- Wow – I was hoping you suggest the ballet.
- Of course a good haircut costs at least $100.
- How did you know I always wanted a manicure for my birthday?
- I miss Barry Manilow.
- I understand why you like *The View*.
- It is so embarrassing how some women show off their legs. Hot pants should be banned.
- Pick up some yogurt at the store. Thanks.
- Wow – AVON lets men go to the parties too!
- Of course I can find a date for your 40 year old girlfriend with five ex-husbands who looks like a walking blimp and has a drinking problem, three teenagers living at home and the personality of a barracuda. Love to!

175

It is always fun to poke fun at the "Battle Between the Sexes". Here are Men and Women light bulb jokes. But be careful about how you use them. Make sure your audience has a sense of humor. After using a few of these jokes, you can say, "Sure there is a trace of humor in those jokes, but I am proud that in this company we pride ourselves on working together. And here is what we need to pull together to accomplish..."

Quote: Whenever I date a guy, I think, is this the man that I want my children to spend their weekends with?
~Rita Rudner

- How many men and women does it take to change a light bulb? One man to change the light bulb – one woman to ask if he stopped for directions.
- How many men does it take to change a light bulb? Why change it – the TV still works.
- How many men and women does it take to change a light bulb? One man to screw in the light bulb – one woman to ask if before screwing it in has he considered the bulb's inner feelings.
- How many women does it take to change a light bulb? Five. One to screw it in and four to say a man would get paid more for that same job.
- How many women does it take to screw in a light bulb? Five – one to screw it in and four to form a support group. How many men does it take to change a light bulb? None, why sit in the dark. Let's go fishing. How many women on PMS does it take to change a light bulb. None – CHANGE THE DAMN THING YOURSELF.
- How many women does it take to change a light bulb? None – I changed the damn kids' diapers. You change the bulb.
- How many men does it take to change a light bulb?

None, they're smart enough to plug in the lamp.
- How many men does it take to change a light bulb?
One – but he will brag all week about how he helps around the house.
- How many men does it take to change a light bulb?
One – but first he will explain all about electricity and how it works and the wiring in the house and the electric bill and how the kids need to turn off the lights and how he is not made of money and you just want to scream – CHANGE the damn bulb.
- How many men and women does it take to change a light bulb?
One man to screw it in and one woman to ask if there are other bulbs in his life.
- How many men does it take to change a light bulb?
None – the best housekeeping is a dark room. No more dusting.
- How many men does it take to change a light bulb?
None – they thought you said Lite Beer.
- How many men and women does it take to change a light bulb?
One woman to change it and one man to ask her when she is done, will she wash his shirt.
- How many men and women does it take to change a light bulb?
One woman to put it on the Honey-Do list and one man to change it six months later.
- How many men and women does it take to change a light bulb?
One woman to request it and one man to wonder if this is one of those "commitment, long-term things"?
- How many men does it take to change a light bulb?
One – and he is going to take his time because his spouse in the other room just said "Honey we need to talk."
- How many men does it take to change a light bulb?
Two – a man and his friend Jack Daniels. When the room starts spinning the bulb can change itself.
- How many men and women does it take to change a light bulb?
One man to change the bulb and one woman to hold the ladder, then call her friends and try to discuss "how we are finally

working together and what is the next step in the relationship."
- How many men does it take to change a light bulb?
One, but it will take him three trips to the hardware store to get the right size. Then three more trips to get the right wattage. Then three more trips to get the lamp fixture he broke.

176

What! More light bulb jokes. More jokes you can pick and choose from for a great opening.

Quote: Every woman should have four pets in her life. A mink in her closet, a Jaguar in her garage, a tiger in her bed, and a jackass to pay for it all.
~Mae West

- How many pessimists does it take to change a light bulb?
None – things never change.
- How many Cub fans does it take to change a light bulb?
None. They just "wait till next year".
- How many Amish does it take to change a light bulb?
Change? You gotta be kidding.
- How many bankers does it take to screw in a light bulb?
None, they are too busy screwing up the financial system.
- How many GM stockholders does it take to screw in a light bulb?
None. They have had enough screwing this year.
- How many teachers does it take to change a life bulb?
None, they just wait for it "to live up to its potential".
- How many politicians does it take to change a light bulb?
None. Why shed light on our activities?
- How many English professors does it take to change a light bulb?
None. But they get a great discussion going on how the light bulb represents Conrad's *Heart of Darkness*.

- How many cops does it take to change a light bulb?
  Two – one to change the bulb and one to give you a ticket for having a light out.
- How many auto workers does it take to change a light bulb?
  None. They just get laid off, then get paid until the light bulb starts working again.
- How many auto workers does it take to change a light bulb?
  Why? Is there overtime involved?
- How many doctors does it take to change a light bulb?
  One, but to make sure the light bulb is dead, he has to order an MRI, X-rays, CAT scans, blood tests...
- How many Congressmen does it take to change a light bulb?
  None. They like keeping you in the dark.
- How many HMOs does it take to change a light bulb?
  Thank for you calling. If this is an emergency please call 911. Please listen closely to the available options. Press one if...
- How many conservatives does it take to change a light bulb?
  "Do we really need change?"
- How many Cub fans does it take to change a light bulb?
  None. They are used to things burning out. Like their team.

177

This is a great quiz on "the average child" to give when parents are in the audience. And most of the time, parents are in the audience. After picking a few items from the quiz, you can say, "Now, it is time to move onto some important facts about..."

Quote: Give me the strength to change the things I can, the grace to accept the things I cannot, and a great big bag of money.
~13 year old

How many children live in poverty? How many children do not

have enough to eat? How many use drugs? How many hours of TV does the average child watch? Take this quiz and find out! Answer each question true or false – the answers are at the end.

- 47% of high school students report having had sex.
- Over 20% of high school seniors report using drugs.
- 13% of high school seniors smoke.
- 4% of eight graders smoke.
- 87% of young adults 18–24 have completed high school.
- 66% of all students enroll in college after completing high school.
- 20% of all children, ages 5 to 17, speak a language other than English at home.
- 68% of children 0–17 live with married parents.
- There are 74 million children ages 0–17 in the United States.
- 55% of all children live in counties where air pollution rises above acceptable levels.
- 10% of all children drink from unhealthy water systems.
- 40% of children live in inadequate housing.
- 80% of teenagers never talk back to their parents.
- 18% of children live in poverty.
- 18% of children do not get enough to eat.
- 60% of children 3–5 are read to by a family member everyday.
- The average child spends over four hours a day watching television.
- The average American kid spends 900 hours in school each year and 1500 hours watching television.
- The average child has seen 8,000 murders on TV by the time he finishes elementary school.
- The average child has seen 200,000 acts of violence on TV by the time she is 18.
- The average child sees over 20,000 thirty second TV commercials a year.
- According to a recent Nielsen study, the typical teen sends nearly 80 text messages every day.

- 300 kids a year are killed by falling furniture – e.g. a dresser tips over and crushes them.
- A child will go through an average of 7,000–9,000 diapers from birth to being potty trained.
- The average cost of raising a child from birth to the age of 21 is $165,000.

Yes – of course number 13 is wrong. All the others are true.

178

We are surrounded by guilt every day. There are experts telling us not to smoke, not to drink, not to eat, exercise more, save more... Here is a funny speech about The Guilt Museum. You can use all of it, or pick and choose some excerpts for an opening. Then you can say, "But despite all those people out there trying to make me feel guilty, I never feel guilty when I say we have the best employees in the business."

Quote: Guilt – the gift that keeps on giving.
~Erma Bombeck

I was (or a friend was) driving through Paducah, Kentucky because that is the best thing to do – keep driving through Paducah – when I saw a sign National Guilt Museum. Talk about the coolest museum ever. But then I saw that the sign really said National Quilt Museum.

But I started to plan a National Guilt Museum.

Anyway – here is my rough layout of the National Guild Museum. Of course there will be a room featuring mothers and the loudspeaker will say, "So nice of you finally to stop by. Your brother Murray, the doctor, is out saving people and you are wandering around a museum?"

Tour guides will include a mechanic asking when was the last time you changed your oil, a dentist asking when you had your last checkup and a lawyer asking if you have a will.

There will be exhibits featuring starving children in Africa who you have sent NO money to, an anti-smoking exhibit showing lungs that are blacker than the inside of a coal mine and a sweet child saying, "Daddy, oh Daddy, please stop." The alcohol exhibit will portray a homeless man under a bridge and the sign says, "He couldn't stop drinking either." On the way out of the liquor exhibit, there will be a picture of your liver with more holes in it than a golf course and of course a sweet child saying, again, "Daddy, please stop, please stop."

I have worked out a few more exhibits in detail.

The Guilt Museum could be like a little town. You walk into the museum and you first enter a McDonald's. But as you enter it, a loudspeaker turns on. "Hello Lard Ass, do you really need to be eating here. Your arteries are already as clogged as the LA freeway. You might want to sit over there in that EXTRA-WIDE booth where we have created extra space for your extra BUTT – oh I'm sorry I thought that was two butts, not one. We hope you enjoy your meal today as you get your yearly intake of salt from one order of French fries. And don't even think how many cows we kill, oh about a million or two each day, just so you can go buy some extra large pants. And don't worry about the planet, just pile that trash up on your tray and then we will dump it in some landfill where it will disintegrate in about a thousand years."

Then the next stop in the National Guilt Museum is the bottled water exhibit. As you walk in the bottled water exhibit, the loudspeaker comes on and says – "Well hello, welcome to Destroy the Planet Land. What, you are too good to drink out of the water fountain, which is RIGHT outside the door? You have to have your water in a PLASTIC bottle which takes about 10,000 gallons of gasoline to make and deliver. Did you know that over one billion water bottles are thrown away EVERY day because you are TOO DAMN LAZY to drink out of the water fountain? And come on –

what the hell are you carrying around a bottle water for anyway. Where do you think you are – the Mohave Desert. You are going to die of thirst just walking around this museum for 30 minutes, as that is all your limited attention span can handle? Oh, and on the way, just toss the bottle in the flower bed, as you obviously don't give a rip about OUR planet earth."

The next stop is the Starbucks. The loudspeaker turns on, "Hello Mr. Drug Addict. Oh we both know that caffeine is a drug, why don't you just shoot it directly INTO YOUR veins. And you must be MR. RICH, paying three bucks for a cup of coffee. The worker who picked the coffee beans for you to enjoy your HABIT makes three bucks a month. But that doesn't bother you. OH NO – like most druggies, you are just happy to get your fix."

As you can tell, I am still working on the idea for the National Guilt Museum and soon will form a foundation to collect donations. What? You are too good to donate? You have better things to do with your money? Waste it on booze and betting?

179

Here is a list of different types of parents. It is a good list to present to a group of parents and ask them to evaluate themselves. You can also use part of this list for a creativity exercise at work. After reading or handing out the list, you can have your employees make up lists of different types of employees.

> Quote: When my kids become wild and unruly, I use a nice safe playpen. When they're finished, I climb out.
> ~Erma Bombeck

Everyone is talking about *helicopter parents*, you know those parents that 'hover' over their children. Why not make up some name for other parents?

- **The Conan O'Brien Parent:** Your child whines about everything and you still reward him.
- **The Nancy Pelosi Parent:** You don't teach your kids financial responsibility. No matter what the cost, your kids can always get someone else to pay for it.
- **The Tiger Woods Parent:** You forget your main role as a parent and go out and play as many holes as you can.
- **The Joan Rivers Parent:** No matter what the cost, you try to look as young as your daughters.
- **The Care Bear Parent:** Instead of sitting down and talking with your kids, you think hugs will take care of everything.
- **The Obama Parent:** You promise your kids everything but don't deliver.
- **The Titanic Parent:** Your kid has a drug and drinking problem, and he is going to run into an iceberg but you ignore it.
- **The Peter Pan Parent:** You won't let your boy grow up. He is 30 years old and still bringing his laundry home for you to wash.
- **The Humpty Dumpty Parent:** Your child has emotional issues and you try to put him or her back together again, without seeking the professional help he needs.
- **Soccer Mom:** She gets a kick out of watching her kids play. Sorry – I could not resist that one pun.
- **The Mark McGuire Parent:** He wants his kid to be the next star athlete so that he is willing to ANYTHING to help the kid succeed. Even look the other way when the kid uses steroids.
- **The Van Winkle Parent:** It takes you 20 years to wake up to the fact that you need to be a parent, not a friend.
- **The Savior Parent:** You think you're Jesus Christ and can take of your kid in any situation. Closely aligned with the Peter Pan Parent.
- **The Judas Parent:** Your kid smokes pot and you think you have to turn him into the authorities instead of dealing with the problem yourself.
- **The Barbie Mother:** You enter your kid, at the age of four, into

beauty pageants.

- **The Gloria Steinem Parent:** You are determined that your children will NEVER depend on a man.
- **The Low Jump Parent:** You don't set high expectations. A trailer park is good enough for me and should be good enough for you.
- **The Einstein Parent:** You can't understand why teachers don't realize what a genius your child is.
- **The Vampire Parent:** You encourage your kids to take a "bite" out of life. Okay – really I promise that is the LAST pun.
- **The Paris Hilton Parent:** You ignore the spiritual side of your kids and only teach them, "You can't be too skinny or too rich."

180

Major Events of Year _____announced. This is a fun list to use around the beginning of the year. You can offer these "predictions", then you can say, "But what can we predict for our company's future for the next year. Let's discuss that right now."

Quote: Look to the future, because that is where you'll spend the rest of your life.
~George Burns

- Some Third World country, which couldn't even build a battle tank, will announce they are building a nuclear bomb, send the UN into emergency session and then agree to abandon their nuclear ambitions after the US sends them billions in foreign aid.
- Several former acting stars, whose careers are in the toilet, will admit they are gay, battled a drug addiction or suffered an abusive relationship. They will write a book about their traumas, and appear on talk shows in a vain attempt to sell the books and to regenerate their career.
- Microsoft will admit that, even though it went through extensive

testing, there is a glitch in its new operating system, which for some strange reason will not allow access to Google searches.

- There will be at least over a thousand new stories on TV about global warming. They will all show the same polar bear stranded on some chunk of ice floating in the ocean. Hasn't that hunk of ice melted yet?

- A person who builds his house in California, on an unstable mountain, will be shocked when it slides down the hill in a mudslide.

- Not one person will be killed in a double-wide trailer this year, due to a tornado. That is because all the double-wides have been foreclosed on by the banks and no one lives there anymore. The owners have all moved underneath a freeway bridge.

- Some person who lives next door to a serial killer will say, "But he seemed so normal."

- Congress will debate what to do about illegal immigration, while their Hispanic yard man is at their house mowing their yard.

- Somebody, after the hurricane causes a BIG wave, which washes away their house, will complain about the government not providing flood insurance.

- The Cubs will not make the World Series.

- The government will announce the creation of new jobs, neglecting to add that the jobs are at fast food places or Wal-Mart, don't provide benefits and pay $8 an hour.

- A major sports star will be caught cheating on his wife.

- A major college football star will be sent to court on a felony charge.

- A major league baseball player will admit using steroids.

- A politician caught having an affair will check into a rehab treatment center.

- People who build in the foothills in California, close to tons of trees, will be shocked when they have to evacuate due to a major forest fire.

- Too many teenagers who do not know that it is just not safe to drive after 12 at night will be killed in car accidents.

- Some politician will not raise taxes, but will establish extra "fees".
- Congress will still be debating National Health Care.
- Some crazy gunman will shoot up a school, college, a factory where he got fired or a post office... pick a location. The next day the NRA will issue a press release about "our right to bear arms."
- There will be a movie about some disaster hitting the earth.
- There will be movie about vampires, who, if we are lucky, will be killed off in the disaster movie.
- Even newer plans will be announced on how we plan to win in Afghanistan and Iraq.
- At least ten marketplaces in the Middle East will be blown up by suicidal bombers. The next day some politician will announce that the United States has stabilized the Middle East.
- There will be at least three financial stories about how some shyster scammed people out of millions. Congress will spring into action by establishing committees to study our current financial system. The committees will blame the Federal Reserve Board or the SEC and then disband after the American public has moved onto the next scandal.
- There will be several interviews with prisoners who claim they are innocent and who have found Jesus while in prison.
- There will be a multi-million recall of some car for some silly reason like the left door handle gets stuck on Tuesday evenings when there is a full moon.
- Despite the ongoing recession, colleges will announce even more tuition hikes.
- There will be thousands of students who sign up for career colleges, only to find their credits will not transfer to any other college.
- There will be an earthquake in a Third World country destroying thousands of buildings and killing thousands of people because there are no building codes.

- An evangelist who proclaims the Glory of God will be caught in an affair or embezzling from the church.
- Mothers Against Drunk Driving will push for what they really want – the return of prohibition and actually find some congressman dumb enough to support the bill.
- We will be shocked to find that millions of dollars of foreign aid have financed a dictator's fancy lifestyle and have not been actually used to help the starving people.

181

Here is a funny list of things you do not want to hear from your babysitter. You can read the entire list, then say, "And here are some things we do not want to hear from our customers..."

Quote: Grandmas are great babysitters, and they're less likely to sneak boys over.
~Anon

Things Your Babysitter Should Never Say

- Hi – I am just sweeping up something.
- Susie spit that out – hey Mrs. Jones, are poinsettias really poisonous?
- How old was your cat?
- First of all. I told Tommy not to climb on the roof.
- Hmm, where exactly is the water cut-off valve?
- Man – do you know how fast a grease fire can start?
- I know my boyfriend had NO business driving your car.
- You know how you told Tommy not to use his dad's clippers on the dog?
- Hey, let me turn down the music...
- Well. I told my boyfriend to come over, but don't bring any friends...

- Hmm, where is your health insurance card?
- So, I'm just calling to see how your dinner is going and by the way, can you pick up some Band-Aids on the way home?
- Man, we didn't know the knife was that sharp and...
- Hmm, how do you make the smoke alarm quit going off?
- Well Tommy wanted to know if he could play tennis in the house and I was thinking – you know – like COMPUTER tennis, like that FAKE TENNIS, but...
- The good news is if I can get your credit card number, they can fix the front picture window before it rains tonight...
- So Tommy thought he would dye Susie's hair but that didn't work, so he tried to cut the color out of her hair – hey let me take a picture with my phone and send it to you. Hey, how is your dinner going?
- No problem, we're just sitting here watching the news about that escaped killer who is hiding somewhere in your neighborhood – whoops someone is at the door...
- Hi Mrsss. Joneees, do you know you are out of borbonn, bourbon, bourbon. I just thought I would tell youu, so Mr. Jonesy can pick some burb-on up on his way home. Okay gotta goo...

182

Twittering is the newest fad. But most twitters are nonsense. What if wise historical figures used Twitter? Here is a list of what Abe Lincoln might twitter. Then you can say, "Lincoln would have had wise twitters, but I suspect he also might not use Twitter at all. Because Twitter and any electronic communication has a serious drawback. It is not safe, anyone can tap into it, and once you send it, you cannot get it back. So having said that, here is what we all need to know when keeping our company information secure..."

Quote: There is nothing either good or bad but twittering makes it so.

~William Shakespeare

So what would happen if Abraham Lincoln could twitter? Perhaps the twitters would look like this?

- **On lawyers:** "Discourage litigation. Persuade your neighbors to compromise whenever you can. As a peacemaker the lawyer has superior opportunity of being a good man. There will still be business enough."
- **On Speeches:** Keep it short, an example: "Fourscore and seven years ago our fathers brought forth on this continent a new nation, conceived in Liberty, and dedicated to the proposition that all men are created equal."
- **On Learning from Experience:** "I do not think much of a man who is not wiser today than he was yesterday."
- **On Honesty:** "If I were two-faced, would I be wearing this one?"
- **On Bad Coffee:** "If this is coffee, please bring me some tea; but if this is tea, please bring me some coffee."
- **On Marriage:** "Marriage is neither heaven nor hell, it is simply purgatory."
- **On Self Fulfillment:** "Most folks are as happy as they make up their minds to be."
- **On Ambition:** "Someday I shall be President."
- **Political Advice:** "The time comes upon every public man when it is best for him to keep his lips closed."
- **Work Ethic:** "Things may come to those who wait, but only the things left by those who hustle."
- **Communication:** "When I am getting ready to reason with a man, I spend one-third of my time thinking about myself and what I am going to say and two-thirds about him and what he is going to say."
- **Common Sense:** "When you have got an elephant by the hind

legs and he is trying to run away, it's best to let him run."

- **Laughter:** "With the fearful strain that is on me night and day, if I did not laugh I should die."
- **Conservatives:** "What is conservatism? Is it not adherence to the old and tried, against the new and untried?"
- **Alcohol:** "Tell me what brand of whiskey that Grant drinks. I would like to send a barrel of it to my other generals."
- **Slavery:** "Whenever I hear anyone arguing for slavery I feel a strong impulse to see it tried on him personally."
- **Capitalism:** "These capitalists generally act harmoniously and in concert, to fleece the people."
- **Commitment:** "Be sure you put your feet in the right place, then stand firm."
- **Character:** "My great concern is not whether you have failed, but whether you are content with your failure."

183

Are you addicted to lifeing? Here is a speech that discusses a new term – lifeing. This is a great speech to give to any gathering of young people. Also it makes a great sermon for church. After talking about "lifeing", you can say, "But I hope that all of us in this church avoid lifeing and go deeper in our commitments to and with each other.

Quote: I hear YouTube, Twitter and Facebook are merging to form a super Social Media site – YouTwitFace.
~Conan O'Brien

I have been thinking about terms that we need and the obvious one is Lifeing.

What is lifeing? It is pretending that someone cares about your life and you spend your whole day lifeing. E-mailing, texting,

Facebooking, Twittering – well you get the idea.

And lifeing is not that you care about anyone else. You just want to tell the world about your life. That is why you twitter inane things every half hour. Just took a shower, **Am** eating breakfast, Driving to Work. Whoops there is a lot of traffic. At work. I have a lot of work to do.

And when you are 'lifeing', you really aren't communicating. You merely are lifeing people to tell them about your life. One sign of someone who is addicted to lifeing is someone who brags about how many "friends" they have on Facebook. There is no way they talk to 1,000 friends in one day. But when someone is addicted to 'lifeing', they just like to send messages to show how popular and important they are. One of their inane lifeing twitters might read, "Today, I have over 1000 friends on Facebook."

Another sign that you are addicted to lifeing is the number of text messages you send. I can understand sending maybe three text messages a day, but when you send over 400 text messages a day, all centered around your life and what you had for lunch and what you had for dinner and what show you are watching and what movies you like and what boys or girls you are attracted to, again, that is sure sign that you are addicted to lifeing.

Someone who is always 'lifeing' always has an electronic device in his or her hands. This is the person who will be an hour from home, discover they have forgotten their cell phone, and drive an hour back home. They need their cell phone, because without it they can't be 'lifeing' people all day about exciting events in their life. "Have to get some gas." "Boy, gas is almost $3 a gallon. I also checked my oil." "You won't believe what song I just heard." "Whoops left my iPOD at home."

Are you addicted to lifeing? If your computer homepage is Facebook and you have sent over 100 messages a day to your friends, telling them silly things about your life, you are addicted to lifeing. If every time you do something, even take the dog for a walk, you have to twitter a thousand people, you are addicted to lifeing.

In short, if you spend your whole days twittering, Facebooking, texting just to tell people about your life, you spend way too much time 'lifeing', and really need to get a life.

184

Here is a funny speech on How to Eliminate Obesity in Kids. Again, this can be used as an entire speech before a club gathering or Toastmasters, or you can choose some of the ideas for an opening. Then you can say, "We do need to eliminate obesity among our children, but we also need to work on health issues here at work. So let me tell you about some incentives we have put in place to help all employees lead a more active, healthy lifestyle."

Quote: The second day of a diet is always easier than the first. By the second day you're off it.
~Jackie Gleason

How to Help Obese Children

People say that today kids are too fat, obese is the politically correct term, because kids don't get enough exercise. Well, once again, I am ready to leap ahead of the crowd and offer some suggestions to halt the runaway obesity epidemic in America. And after that I will stop a runaway train, leap a few buildings with a single bound and stop a speeding bullet or two.

But my super-feat today is to stop obesity among our children.

- Serve nothing but broccoli and peanut butter sandwiches for an entire week – at home and in the school cafeteria. Anyone that gobbles those down deserves to be fat and there isn't a damn thing we can do to help them. But if the food is really bad, like broccoli and peanut butter, we can reduce the calorie intake of our YOUNG AMERICANS. (You are supposed to whistle *Yankee Doodle* and wave a flag every time I say YOUNG AMERICANS. Please try to keep up.)

- Eliminate the bus. Kids get fat when they sit. So eliminate the school bus and everyone has to run or walk to school. Sure some kids might live five miles away, but think what great shape they will be in at the end of the year.

- Put a bear in the parking lot during recess. The bear will chase the kids and they will be busy running and screaming and climbing to get away from the bear. Sure a few kids might be eaten, but these will be the slower heavier kids which will make the obesity stats look a lot better!

- Put the classrooms on the roof and in the basement. This means the kids will have to climb stairs, a lot of them, to get back and forth to class.

- Eliminate the janitor staff (which budget cuts are doing already). Make the kids mop and clean and push a broom and paint classrooms and mow the school grass with push mowers and we have accomplished three goals. The school maintenance budget drops (kids are free labor), kids learn a job skill and also lose weight. This is not abusing kids, but rather a career training program for our YOUNG AMERICANS. Sure, you scoff at this brilliant idea, but let's face it, pushing a broom and cutting grass are jobs we cannot export or off-shore, and they may be the only jobs left in our GREAT COUNTRY.

- Make every kid carry five bricks in their backpacks, in addition to the heavy books. Make those kids almost sink to the ground under the weight of these backpacks. This will again accomplish two objectives. The kids will lose weight and will be ready for those forced hikes when they join the Marines.

- Of course I have many other ideas to help stop the obesity epidemic that is SPREADING across America (when it is a really BAD pun, you have to say it loudly, so your audience can understand your subtle humor).

- But I am hanging onto my other ideas until they make me Chairman of the President's Council on Physical Fitness. I can see it happening soon, just after I go on that date with Lady GaGa, find the flaw in the Theory of Relativity, and climb backwards up Mt. Everest.

185

Eulogies are not easy to give. I have provided a sample one below. The secret to a eulogy is to tell sad, funny, true stories about the person. Do not make them a saint. We all know he or she was human and we want to be reminded of that, of their interaction with other people. After hearing your eulogy, we want to walk out of that ceremony feeling that we really knew the person. Here is the sample eulogy:

Quote: I am always relieved when someone is delivering a eulogy and I realize I am listening to it.
~George Carlin

Sample Eulogy:

Memories of My Father

My dad was a college baseball coach, athletic director at Brown and other universities, a cartoonist, an artist, a leading expert on athletic facilities, a war hero and a father, a father above all. Here are my memories:

First and foremost, my father always had a sense of humor. I remember when we first moved to Providence, Brown football was not good. In fact, terrible would have been a step up for them. But my dad maintained his sense of humor. He loved telling the story of how he had some Brown football tickets on the dashboard of his car and someone broke into the car. And his friends asked if they stole the tickets. My father would always say, "No, they left four more."

And my father had patience. I must have been six or seven and I saw a TV show about Thomas Edison and how he was a boy genius and he could take stuff apart and put it back together. Well, if those were the qualifications for a boy genius, I could do that. So I found a screwdriver and found a door and took the lock out and the doorknob off and all of a sudden, I am sitting surrounded by these parts, and I realize that I have no idea how to put them back together. At that point my father walked in and just shook his head.

It was a historical moment because that is the first time he said to me, "Phil, you need to have the second thought," a phrase I would hear often through my life.

When we were bat boys for Chapman College my number was 00 and my brother's number was 01. He once said that he chose those numbers because it represented our combined IQs. Of course at the time my brother and I were in the dugout, happily throwing water on each other.

He had other phrases. I would come home from walking our dog Moxie, who always managed to get the leash tangled around me and trip me. I would be upset and my father would say, "Phil, you have to be smarter than the dog."

Not that my father was perfect. He had delusions, like thinking the Cubs might actually win. He never realized that when he was coaching baseball umpires get annoyed when you show them the rulebook. That never ends well. And it took him a while to learn that Peggy was always right.

He never understood some things. Like why TV programmers didn't just throw all the crap out and just show Westerns and ballgames all the time. He might have been right.

And he thought it was okay for us to be in the dugout when Ralph Cripe struck out. I don't know if that was a good idea, but we did learn some interesting words that season.

He was a forgiving man. He forgave his daughter for marrying a Dodger fan. And he always bragged about how smart Anne was.

And he knew that one day she would realize that Brooks Robinson was no Ernie Banks. We are all amazed that not one of the girls was named Brooks.

He always wanted the best for us. He worked two or three jobs just to ensure that we went to the best schools. But sometimes it backfired on him. He sent us to summer camps and before he knew it I would be back home happily lying on the floor watching TV, eating cheese doodles and drinking orange soda, which I thought was a heck of a lot better than people bossing me around at summer camp. He would get that resigned look on his face and next year try another camp. I went to hiking camp, baseball camp and hockey camp, only to end up at home happily eating cheese doodles.

I think he tried to sign me up for the Marines, but I was only 12.

He was an idea man. And he was a good idea man and I am proud of that. This man was hired by the Ford Foundation, featured on the cover of magazines, wrote a book – he was the leading expert on athletic facilities in the nation. And at the same time, he loved to paint and shows were held around the country featuring his paintings. How creative was he? Let it be said that he had to be the only athletic director in the country with a Masters in Art. And perhaps the only one that ever wrote a children's book. It was called *You're The Reason I Drink* and dedicated to me. Actually it was *Snow Shoe the Camel*.

In fact, the last letter I got from him was a great idea of how to drastically reduce the cost of building a Wright designed home. And to us it was perfectly normal growing up in a home with Astro Turf and to take paper bed sheets to camp. Of course, I was always home before my supply of paper sheets wore out.

And as I said, he was a patient man. He and my sister would go to my school just to clean out my desk. Of course when he discovered that was where I hid all my D papers, I got a spanking that night. But after a while, I think he just gave up. But not before hanging the paddle in my room and reminding me to look at it and to have the second thought before DOING ANYTHING.

And he was a walking contradiction at times. War was hard on him and he never let us have toy guns when we were kids. But his favorite TV show, next to *Gunsmoke* of course, was *Combat*. And he never pretended to be a hero, even though he was always my hero. When I asked him for memories of World War Two and being a bombardier, all he would say, "I just remember being scared, just scared every time we went up."

When he returned from his first mission, he thought they would be heroes. It was a rainy muddy night in Italy and they walked around the B-24 and there were over 400 bullet holes. So they radioed the colonel and told him they were home and could they send a truck to pick them up. The colonel basically asked them which legs were broken and they could damn well walk back to base.

And once I asked did he take aim and shoot down German fighters. And he said, "Heck we just filled the sky with machine gun fire and red tracers, so the Germans wouldn't get near our plane."

When he went to Italy on a ship, he and his crew were supposed to stay below deck with all the other flyboys and sailors. But below deck smelled of vomit and sweat and he and his friend "Skinny" Ennis just went on deck and slept in the plane that was tied on deck.

That was Skinny's idea and Skinny got shot down and died in a Prisoner of War camp, and at 18 my father learned how hard it was to lose people. This past week we have all learned that lesson, because it was hard to lose Dad.

He loved crosswords puzzles but he started doing them when he was on the tarmac before flying missions in World War Two. It was a way a scared 18 year old, miles away from Hudson, Ohio, could stay sane.

But I think World War Two shaped my dad and his generation in ways we can't even begin to understand. Today people panic when they get a flat tire. To Dad, that was no big deal. A big deal was being shot out of the air at 20,000 feet and falling to your death.

And the war made him appreciate life. I remember him telling me once, "Phil, you can't believe how nice it was to get home and to walk to the drug store and pick up a magazine and read it." He knew the pleasure of simple things.

And he was good with words. Even when he was well into his eighties, he would whip through the Word Jumble, while I was trying to figure out the first word. I remember struggling over the word donut; he walked by and said, "Oh that is donut."

"Sure, why didn't you tell me ten minutes ago?"

He just shrugged.

There were moments he was just a kid. I must have been in fourth grade and we were living in Orange, California and he was painting on the front porch. A fire engine went by and he said "Let's go!" And all of a sudden we were two kids running through backyards, climbing over fences, chasing a fire truck down the street to find a fire. By the time we got there, the fire was in full glory and we stood and watched it. What made him stop painting that watercolor and just take off with me to chase a fire truck?

His mother was always worried about him. When he was little, he kept telling his parents he wanted to be a garbage man. That was his life's ambition. Why? Because in 1929, the garbage men drove wagons pulled by horses – and that was the life. Imagine having a job where you can drive a horse all day!

And he was the glue that held our family together. No matter where we were – at summer camp, school, college, he would always send us weekly letters. The best one I ever received was merely a cartoon. It was a kid at camp and it showed the Suggestion Box. And the kid was dropping a snake into the box.

My dad loved his family and he was always bragging about his grandchildren. Even his grandson who was always kind enough to point out that the Twins had won a few World Series and how many had the Cubs won?

Above all – he made a difference in people's lives. And I can't even begin to say how many, because I just don't know. But I know that when we lived in Providence, he was on the Board of Directors of the Boys and Girls Club and how many children did he help then that we will never know about?

There are a million more stories I can tell but the most important thing I can say is, Thank You, Peggy. I can never even begin to tell you how much you meant to my dad and how you showed us what true love was. At times he was not easy to live with (not that any of his children inherited that trait), but THANK YOU for always being there when our family and my dad needed you.

Finally I think my dad would like this joke. A man and his friends are great baseball fans. The man dies and goes to heaven. He contacts his friend. His friend says, "Wow – do they have baseball in heaven?" And the man says, "Good News and Bad News. They have baseball in heaven. But tomorrow you are the starting pitcher."

186

Here are some twitters from the future. What happens when all those young kids turn old and still depend on Twitter? You can read some of these and then say, "Although these twitters are humorous, they are also warning signs that we should listen to. Over 80 million Americans will soon be 65 and older. What will these new senior citizens want and how can our company meet the demands of this growing market?"

Quote: Many people die when they are 25, but are not buried until they are 75.

~Benjamin Franklin

Thirty years when all the kids using Facebook are old, will it be called Wrinkle book?

Another thought. What happens when all the kids who use Twitter now turn 70? What will their messages look like? Here is a glimpse of their 'twitters' when all these kids turn 70:

- Twitter: Hello, it is nine o'clock and I must go to bed.
- Twitter: Have to pee.
- Twitter: I heard that Obama the Third is promising we will pull out of Iraq soon.
- Twitter: Thank God for Global Warming. Can finally suntan in Minnesota during February.
- Twitter: Am running to the store. I am out of Depends.
- Twitter: Checked out Nursing Homes today. Happy Valley has a nice cocktail hour featuring prune juice.
- Twitter: Have to pee.
- Twitter: I have torublle typioing on Twiotter. Can't see the keeys.
- Twitter: Is that oil leak in the Gulf ever going to stop?
- Twitter: I think I hear the phone ringing. Or is that the doorbell?
- Twitter: Have to pee.
- Twitter: Congress is discussing Universal Health Care.
- Twitter: How old is Dick Clark? Looks good for his age.
- Twitter: How about Joan Rivers?
- Twitter: No, they just prop her up. As long as she keeps selling junk, she is not 'dead'.
- Twitter: If she has another facelift, she will have hair on her chin.
- Twitter: I think I will stay up late and watch the *Jay Leno the Third Show*. I remember his grandfather.
- Twitter: Am going to watch *The 50th Anniversary of Saturday Night Live*.
- Twitter: Remember CDs?
- Twitter: What? Need to find my trifocals.
- Twitter: Have to pee.
- Twitter: Whoops didn't make it.
- Twitter: Remember Hannah Montana? I heard she passed away. Or passed a kidney stone. Those announcers need to talk louder,
- Twitter: Time for my – hang on, it's time for my?? Get back to you.
- Twitter: Looking for my cane.
- Twitter: How do they expect you to live on social security

payments of $25,000 a month. Heck bread alone costs $260 a loaf.

- Twitter: Have to... damn, not again.
- Twitter: Have to admire Charlie Sheen. It is his official 100th trip to rehab.
- Twitter: What, the Cubs didn't make the World Series ?
- Twitter: Was going to run to the store, but the golf cart is out of power. Must remember to plug it in. Also must remember where I put the golf cart.
- Twitter: My grandkids laughed at the picture of my cell phone. They can't believe we didn't have microchips transplants like they have today.
- Twitter: Have to pee.
- Twitter: How old is Dick Clark? Looks good for his age. Wait a minute, did I say that already?
- Twitter: How about Joan Rivers?
- Twitter: No they just prop her up. As long as she keeps selling junk, she is not 'dead'.
- Twitter: Why does this twitter sound so familair, famlaoor, damn wish I could seee the keyss.
- Twitter: If she has another facelift, she will have hair on her chin.
- Twitter: Good one – never heard that before.
- Twitter: Have to...
- Twitter: Oh shut up and tie it in a knot

187

I think we all have road rage and here are some things you would like to say to other drivers. Choose some items from the following list and share them with your audience. Then say, "Being a good driver means knowing how to handle your road rage. And to provide good service, we often have to contain our emotions when dealing with customers. Can anyone start this discussion off with some examples on how to handle a difficult customer?"

Quote: Until you've learned to drive, you've never really learned how to swear.

~Anon

Driving Lessons

- Are you making a right turn? NO? Then get out of this lane so the other 20 drivers lined up BEHIND you can make a right turn.
- See that sign. It says DO NOT WALK. So what the hell are you doing? Are you SO special that you get to walk anytime you please and HOLD up traffic?
- No U-Turn. Do you even know what a U looks like? Do you know your alphabet? It is one simple letter. U. So don't make a U-Turn.
- The light is GREEN. That means GO. It means quit texting, put down the phone, step on that magic device called a gas pedal and GO.
- That light is red. As in STOP you IDIOT. Yellow may mean "go like hell", but RED means STOP. Put your foot on the freaking brake and quit trying to kill someone.
- This is a school zone. That mean kids, who have an IQ of two and the attention span of a monkey on cocaine, tend to wander across the street whenever they please. BECAUSE THEY ARE KIDS and YOU ARE THE ADULT and the whole secret in going through a school zone is NOT to kill a kid. Or even bump a kid. So SLOW DOWN.
- That solid yellow line means DO NOT PASS. Because you are going up a hill and you are not God. You cannot see what is coming up the other side of the big hill. It might be a BIG truck which will squash you like a bug on a windshield. The last thing that will go through your mind will be your ass. Do not pass as BIG trucks and little cars driven by people with little brains do not mix. The truck will always win.
- See the blue sign? See the wheelchair on the blue sign? See the words handicapped? Can you read? Let us make this easy. If you

are NOT handicapped, you should NOT park in a place for the handicapped. Again, you are NOT special, you are probably fat and a little walk won't hurt you. So park somewhere else.

- See that flashing red light in your mirror? Whoops – you don't because you are texting. Hear that noise. It is called a siren. Whoops, you have your iPOD on and your favorite song, *Why Am I so Stupid* is playing. And your windows are rolled up and the air conditioning is going full blast. I hope you are COMFORTABLE!!! The person in the ambulance may die, but that is okay as it is ALL about YOU!

- I am so GLAD that you are in far left lane of the freeway. The lane meant for passing. But you are helping us all save gas, as you are going 50 miles per hour in the passing lane. Do not worry about that semi riding your butt. He is not trying to tell you anything. He is very happy that you are going 50 in the passing lane. Maybe you can go 40. That might make that angry, red-faced truck driver calm down.

- See the ditch? Whoops, you are in the ditch. So sorry. What have we learned about ice on the road? Maybe we should SLOW DOWN, YOU IDIOT! When you have a four-wheel drive, it means you slide on all four wheels and end up in a ditch. Wasn't that a fun lesson? You wanted a new car anyway and you should be out of traction in about four months.

- You are special. Park anywhere you want. It is okay to double-park and take up a whole lane and let people back up behind you. You will learn a whole new bunch of swear words. Why is that man pounding on your window?

188

Here is a funny list of what to say to your older friends who date women way too young for them. This list contains great quotes you can use at a bachelor party or a roast. Especially for that friend

whose eyesight is so bad, he can't see she is too young for him.

> Quote: I have the body of an 18 year old and she is waiting in the car.
> ~Milton Berle

I think my over 40 friends need to stop dating women who are WAY too young for them. I have started to drop hints. For instance I tell them:

- So after the movies do you go out for a senior coffee and a Happy Meal? Who gets the toy?
- So after you discuss *Spongebob Squarepants* – what else do you talk about?
- Does she know your birth certificate is in Roman numerals?
- So she uses beauty cream and you use dental cream?
- So when are you taking that Disney Cruise?
- Are you amazed that the movies are in color now?
- So she has a Facebook page and you have a Where Am I page?
- When she is ready to go out dancing, you're ready for Metamucil and bed.
- Get yourself one of those electric wheelchairs. That way she won't strain herself pushing you up that ramp.
- Man, your date is so young they check her ID at R rated movies, while they're making sure your bottled oxygen will last through the movie.
- Must be "Take a senior-to-dinner day".
- Do you pick her up in the nursing home shuttle?
- She's skipping her homework to go out with you?
- Did you ever tell her you're so old you sat behind Jesus in the third grade.
- So which golf cart do you pick her up in? The one with the rims?
- So is she your designated organ donor?
- Does she make sure that you turn off your blinker before you go

into the restaurant?
- So her curfew is when?
- I thought Bambi was the name of a deer.
- What time do you drop her off at Sesame Street?
- Do you kiss her good night or burp her?
- Does she know that Fix-A-Dent is your dental cream, not a car repair shop?
- She's just stopped wearing diapers and you just started wearing diapers.
- Maybe you remind her of Oscar the Grouch.
- So what is her favorite show on Nickelodeon?
- Do you get her a high chair at the restaurant?
- Do you know that you can add her age to her friend's age, and you are older than both of them combined?
- She's almost 30, you're almost dead.

189

How about those disclaimers that you see everywhere, for example, that if you take a certain pill, your chances of living next Tuesday are slim. Here is a funny list of disclaimers that should accompany every political ad. After sharing these disclaimers with your audience, you can say, "But I hope that we are always honest with our suppliers, shareholders and customers, so we do not need disclaimers. We believe that honesty is the best way of dealing with stakeholders."

Quote: A society where such disclaimers are needed is saddening. ~Anon

- Warning – this guy is not that bright. He is spending over three million dollars of his father's money to land a Senate job that pays about $174,000 a year. Amounts may vary depending on bribes and other incentives such as free fact-finding trips to Bermuda in the winter.

- Any decisions that this candidate makes can affect your personal freedoms, quality of life, health care, taxes, child's education, personal income, job security, present and future invasions of small non-threatening countries, immigration policy, where you can and cannot smoke, what you can and cannot smoke, what age you can drink, how much you can drink, the Federal Deficit, what you can wear on Tuesdays, if you can or cannot admit you are gay, how many clothes you have to take off at the airport and other personal freedoms.

- This candidate is probably lying to you, his lips are moving.

- He is a Christian, but may not believe in welfare, he is a happily married man, but may have an 18 year old boy/girlfriend on the side.

- This candidate will pass laws that affect your small business, although he has been a government employee his whole life and never had to meet a payroll.

- He is not running for the public good, but because he likes to dress up in suits, have people call him Senator and drive around in a big car and get retirement pay after only serving five years.

- Chances are his concern will shift from helping you make your house payments to seeing how many free lunches he can get from lobbyists.

190

There is a new term that covers everything, "Generalized Anxiety Disorder". So you can share a list with the audience that covers your "Generalized Anxiety Disorders. You can use the following list, and are encouraged to add your own. Then you can say, "The term "Generalized Anxiety Order" may be a bit humorous, but I am serious when I say I want our customers to not be anxious and feel like we take care of them. Let's look at some ways we can achieve that."

Quote: I try not to worry about the future, so I take each day, one anxiety attack at a time.
~Cartoon character Ziggy

A Partial List of My Generalized Anxiety Disorder Would Include:

- Sarah Palin being elected to anything
- People taking the Tea Party seriously
- Congress tackling Health Care yet again
- Congress tackling anything
- Being stuck in an elevator and listening to Barry Manilow over and over and over
- Bankers getting even more bailout money
- The IRS
- Gas prices
- College tuition
- Drunk drivers
- Lack of steady paychecks
- Invading another country
- Lady GaGa as First Lady
- Snoop Dog being named United States Poet Laureate
- Roger Clemens being named Major League Baseball Drug Czar
- Ozzy Osbourne School of Speech Therapy
- Chinese calling in their US Bonds
- Having my day disturbed by having a small meteorite hitting the earth
- They find Christ's body
- Trying to keep up with Martha Stewart if she were my neighbor
- Holidays
- America's education system
- Who is building the fence to keep illegal aliens out?

- Somewhere a defense attorney is reading this article and rubbing his hands together as he has just found a perfect way to free that axe murderer – he had Generalized Anxiety Disorder

191

Another funny list that you can use around the holidays. You can share these holiday survival tips with your audience, and then say to employees, "These tips are a bit funny because the holidays are a stressful time. And that is why our health plan has ways to help you handle stress including..."

Quote: Stress – The confusion created when one's mind overrides the body's basic desire to choke the living daylights out of some jerk who desperately deserves it.
~Anon

Let's Put Together Some Holiday Survival Tips

- Buy knee and elbow pads, as well as a helmet for that crowded mall shopping.
- Taser gun: Can be used to stop kids from looking at presents. Taser the cat to show the kids what will happen if they touch the presents. Chances are this will not kill the cat. If it does, the good news is that the kids will get a new kitty for Christmas. Another option is to test the Taser on a large animal, such as an ex-husband, who will flop around the floor after being Tasered. This will really scare the kids not to shake their presents.
- 25 Rolls of Invisible Tape: Ask your obnoxious nephew if he wants to be invisible. Wrap him in invisible tape than say, "Whoops it didn't work. I can still see you." Go shopping then come back and untape him.
- A machine gun that you can mount on your hood and spray cars with bullets when they try to steal your parking place. This

might be illegal. You might want to check with your local public officials. But it is still a good idea.

- Ear Plugs: Needed to survive all the Christmas Music. Especially any version of *Feliz Navidad*, the worst Christmas song ever.
- Hire a personal food taster: His or her job is to eat every fruitcake that comes to your door.
- Take a cruise: You can return when the holidays are over.
- Break the television. It can be repaired when all the sappy Christmas shows and Christmas ads yelling "Buy Me" are over.
- Buy a Fire Extinguisher so you are prepared when your husband shows you, "How to really smoke a turkey" with his new smoker.

192

If you have to give a speech around July Fourth, here is a great list to use as an opening.

Quote: Police arrested two kids yesterday, one was drinking battery acid, the other was eating fireworks. They charged one and let the other one off.
~Tommy Cooper

The Top Ten Phrases You Hate to Hear on July Fourth
- Whoops
- Can you hold this for a minute?
- How many fingers do you need?
- Hey you didn't want kids anyway.
- Catch
- The burn unit is open
- Hey they can do wonders with plastic surgery
- Wow, that was a short fuse
- Trust me – hold this between your legs
- You needed a new cat anyway

193

Here is a great list of funny and true firework names. Pick a few you like and use them in an opening. Then you can say, "Well, those are great firework names, and I am warning your right now, I fully intend to use a pun. I used those names because I wanted to start this meeting with a bang. Okay I apologize. But we have a full day ahead of us and some of the things we will cover include..."

Quote: You may be a redneck if... your lifetime goal is to own a fireworks stand.
~Jeff Foxworthy

Just in time for July 4th...

The Best Firework Names Ever!
- 10,000 Degree Sunburn
- Dragon Farts
- What No Beer?
- The Roof is On Fire
- Martinis at 11
- Fan Blastic
- Echo from Hell
- A Very Dear Man
- Monkees Violate the Heaven Palace
- Fertile Homestead
- Ass Kickin' Mule Hoof Crackers
- Neighbor Annoyer
- Financiers' Choice
- Newton's Nightmare
- Atomic Afterglow
- Gimmie Shimmy
- Nada Zip Zilch

- Edge of Madness
- Naughty Elephant
- Moonshine Cocktail
- Get Into the Movies
- Glimmer Glamour
- Attitude Adjustment
- Hillbilly Heaven
- Flip Flop Fly
- Enchanted Urn
- Hicktown Heaven
- Grizzly Growler
- Make It a Double
- J.A.S.F. (Just Another Stinking Fountain)
- Insanamania
- Larry
- Mad Cow Capers
- Kaleidoscope Kandle
- James Bomb
- Illegal as Hell
- Gold Diggin' Blonde
- Enough Said
- Fast and Loose
- BAMboozle
- Blue Me Up
- Bomb Voyage
- Foreign Policy Maker
- Cats in the Cupboard
- General Custer's Last Atano
- Hoot and Holler
- Sizzle Drizzle
- Ritzy Glitzy Blue
- Lie, Cheat and Steal
- Wacko
- Wailing Jenny

- Shagadelic Mojo
- Behind the Barn (Country Style)
- So #*@! Good
- Loud Little Sucka
- Crackling Balls
- Shock It To Me
- So What Are You Look'n At
- Crackle Jackle
- Sippin' Sunday
- Cold War Ethics
- Chemical Romance
- Run Like Hell
- Serial Killer
- Pyro Gyro
- Craizy Daizy
- Chirping Oriole
- Chitty Chitty Bang Bang
- Burn Baby Burn
- Surprise Surprise
- Stimulus Package
- Tabloid Rumors
- Squealing Pig
- That is Your Problem
- Wake the Neighbors
- Warlord of the Rings
- Weeble Wobble Bobble
- Fatal Error
- Blue Rush
- Creole Crackle
- Cruel Mistress
- Crush Hour
- Deadman's Party
- Twitter Glitter
- Refiner's Fire

- One Bad Mother-in-Law
- Coco Loco
- Redneck Rowdy
- Parrot's Prattle
- Toot and Twirl
- Pyroholics Anonymous
- Raging Rottweilers
- Nightmare on Your Street
- Plumber's CRACKLE
- Requiem for a Scream
- Sphincter Splitter
- Palms Away
- Nukes of Hazard
- Oh My Pretty
- On Dark and Stormy Nights

194

Here are the rules of Southern Grammar. You can use this list as an opening and then say, "I don't mean to make fun of any Southerner, because they have one thing that every customer service department can learn from – Southern hospitality."

Quote: I used to say that whenever people heard my Southern accent, they always wanted to deduct 100 IQ points.
~Jeff Foxworthy

Here are Some of the Rules of Southern Grammar

You are not about to do something. You are "fixing to". As in, "I am fixing to go to the store."

You never ask the question "Where is it?" You ask "Where's it at?" Many questions end with at.

You do not "make some toast". You need to throw in an extra

pronoun whenever possible. As in, "I am going to make me some toast." To be completely proper, you can say, "I am fixing to make me some toast. Where is the bread at?"

Do not greet someone by someone by saying "Hello". You need to say "Roll Tide."

And of course there is the ubiquitous Y'all. And many Southern Grammar Conventions are centered around the crucial question – is it spelled y'all or ya'all. In fact, and I can not make this stuff up, Birmingham once had a campaign called "Pick it up, Ya'all". But as much as I poke fun at Y'all, it beats the "Youse Guys" I always heard in New York.

When you go shopping, you do not get a cart. You get a buggy. It is never summer, you must always say "The long hot summer."

It is never the Civil War, it is the War for States' Rights.

Never use the word "soon". Use the word "Directly" as in "Directly, we are going to the store."

Never use the word "think". Use the word "reckon", as in "I reckon he is late again."

Always try to make a sentence longer by using "go on". Never say, "Give it your best shot". Say, "You go on and give it your best shot."

Don't say "It is cold." Say it is "cold as all git out."

Forget using the word almost. Use "near bout" – Bob "near bout broke his neck the other day."

Don't say distance. Say apiece as in, "That is a far piece from here" or "I am fixing to go down the road apiece."

195

Here are the real rules of golf. This is a great list to use at any business retreat where golf is involved. You can also use several items from this list and then say to employees, "Let's talk about another set of rules. The real rules of competition and how we

must adjust to rules that, quite frankly, always seem to be changing."

Quote: It took me seventeen years to get 3,000 hits in baseball. I did it in one afternoon on the golf course.

~Hank Aaron

The Real Rules of Golf

- Do not hit the 19th hole too early.
- Golf balls don't float.
- Expensive clubs break easily – especially when wrapped around a tree.
- The easy putt isn't.
- The hole is either farther or closer than it looks.
- Golfing lessons only make you realize you have bad habits. Your wife can tell you about your bad habits for free.
- A divot is God's way of telling you, you stink.
- A short straight shot is better than a long shot in the woods.
- The best invention on the golf course is the beverage cart.
- If your best short game is off the tee, you may want to quit.
- Why do you want a low score? With the price of green fees, get your money's worth – hit the golf ball as often as possible.
- The hole gets smaller as you get closer.
- The only places God put sand was on the beach and in the desert. The Devil put sand on golf courses.
- Golf is the only sport you pay for to get frustrated.
- The best shot is at the 19th hole.
- Putting a powerful wood in the hand of a bad golfer is like handing a baby a shotgun. The ball could go anywhere.
- Even the most successful man is humbled by chipping over the green.
- It is time to give up golf when the sand wedge is your most used club.
- The definition of insanity is always hitting the ball the same way

and expecting different results.

- It's best to keep your head down – that way you won't see your friends laughing.
- When a bad golfer says he broke 90, he is talking about clubs.
- Only golfers and madmen go out in the midday sun.
- The Front Nine should not describe the number of shots on the first hole.
- Hackers belong in the computer lab, not the golf course.
- Some golfers are so bad – their handicap is showing up.
- Hazards on golf courses include water, sand traps and beginners.
- A lie is either how the ball is resting on the ground or the score you tell your friends Monday morning.
- Match Play means a bad day where you should light your clubs on fire.
- A Mulligan is either a do-over or a drunken Irish caddy.
- A putter is a special golf club that makes the ball keep rolling right by the hole.
- Rough can either describe the grass that borders the course or describe your game.
- A scratch golfer makes all the other golfers scratch their heads and wonder why he is playing.
- A turkey can be three consecutive birdies during one round of golf or the person you are playing with.
- Only golfers and cavemen use clubs.
- A man's true character is revealed when he is out of bounds and no one is looking.
- When someone says, "It's a long shot," they are talking about your chances of making par.
- While men worry about their golf grip, they should worry about the grip golf has on them.
- The most expensive part of golf is the money your wife is spending, while you're spending time golfing.
- While you are playing a round, your wife could be playing around.

- "Clean your balls" is always a funny line.

196

Have to give a graduation speech? No worries. Here is a short course in how to do exactly that!

Quote: You cannot get to the top by sitting on your bottom. ~Anon

How to Write and Give the Shortest and Best Graduation Speech

You have been invited to speak at a graduation because they want to hear *lessons from your life*. The audience does not want clichés. They do not need quotes from other people. They invited YOU because they want to hear what YOU have to say.

So here is your speech:

- **Opening:** I am here to share three important lessons from my life which I will hope you will keep in mind in the years to come.
- **Lesson Number One:** Tell a story and the lesson you learned.
- **Lesson Number Two:** Tell a story and the lesson you learned.
- **Lesson Number Three:** Tell a story and the lesson you learned.
- **Conclusion:** Review the lessons learned, emphasize why they are important, wish the graduates luck and get the hell off the stage. They have parties to go to and you are the only one standing between them and the parties.

197

Here are two graduation speeches. Actually they are the same, but one is longer and the other shows how you can shorten a speech to

fit the time they have given you to speak. This speech also offers some great quotes you can use for an opening. Note the speech revolves around baseball. This is an easy technique and you can craft a speech, complete with quotes and advice, around your favorite sport.

> Quote: Education is an admirable thing, but it is well to remember from time to time that nothing worth knowing can be taught.
> ~Oscar Wilde

Now, I am going to look to those great American Philosophers – baseball players and managers – for wisdom I hope you can use your whole life.

For instance, never sit down wind from someone chewing tobacco. The only way to catch a knuckleball is wait until it stops rolling and pick it up. Whoops – wrong notes!

Here is some serious advice that should help you as you enter that cold cruel world.

Stay hungry. Don't settle for a job that makes you comfortable. Sure we all need to work, but the way to get ahead is stay hungry. As Leo Durocher once said, "Give me some scratching, diving, hungry ballplayers who come to kill you."

And always set high expectations for yourself. Perhaps this was best summed up by baseball manager Sparky Anderson who said, "I don't know whether I'm a big leaguer or not, but I want to find out, and if I can't do it, then I'll be a minor leaguer the rest of my life."

What do you need to do to prove you belong in the big leagues? And that is not just a rhetorical question. You must really ask yourself, no matter what profession you are in, what do you have to do, to be in the big leagues of your profession?

Take chances. Okay, okay I know Wayne Gretzky was not a baseball player, but he did offer some of the best advice I ever heard. Someone asked him why he was the leading goal scorer on his team.

His answer was simple and direct. He said, "I learned early that you miss 100% of the shots you don't take." '

So take your shots.

In short, do you want to be a minor leaguer all your life? I am going to use a cliché here. I think I am allowed one per speech, but shoot for the stars. You have nothing to lose.

Stick up for what is right. Let me quote Leo again as he defended Jackie Robinson, "I don't care if the guy is yellow or black, or if he has stripes like a god-damn zebra. I'm the manager of this team and I say he plays."

Tommy Lasorda also had some excellent advice on how to excel. He said, "There are three types of baseball players: those who make it happen, those who watch it happen, and those who wonder what happened."

Always ask yourself – "What are you making happen?"

And, I know this is hard to believe, but you will make mistakes. I know, I am shocked too, that you are not all perfect. But don't dwell on the mistakes – take them as a learning experience and move on. As Sparky Anderson said, "People who live in the past generally are afraid to compete in the present. I've got my faults, but living in the past is not one of them. There's no future in it."

And Tommy Lasorda hit the nail on the head when he said, "About the only problem with success is that it does not teach you how to deal with failure."

Perhaps the best way to deal with failure was summed up by baseball manager Gene Mauch who said, " I have an amazing ability to forget."

Having a strong work ethic isn't bad either. I think every employer can identify with Casey Stengel who said, "All I ask is that you bust your heiny on that field." But knowing Casey's reputation, I doubt he said "heiny".

Now here is a very deep thought. Perhaps the deepest one you will hear in this speech, so I urge you to all to wake up for a minute and pay attention.

Nolan Ryan once said, "One of the beautiful things about baseball is that every once in a while you come into a situation where you want to, and where you have to, reach down and prove something."

You too will be in situations like that in life – where you must reach down and prove something – to your boss, to yourself, to your spouse, to your children. And at that point "when you have to reach down and prove something", that is when you find out who you really are.

Of course, at this point, I must throw in a quote from that truly great American philosopher, Yogi Berra, who said, "Ninety percent of this game is half mental."

There is a lesson buried in there somewhere, but I will let you figure it out yourself.

However, I also am always amused by what Joaquin Andujar once said, "My favorite word in English is 'youneverknow'."

Let me start to wrap this up with the best advice I ever heard in a speech. "Stay flexible."

Because Joaquin was so right; the amazing thing about life is "you never know". So stay flexible, stay open to new ideas and avoid running into parked cars.

You see, I even added a safety tip for you all.

Finally Bob Feller once said, "Every day is a new opportunity. You can build on yesterday's success or put its failures behind and start over again. That's the way life is, with a new game every day, and that's the way baseball is."

And you are all blessed that, as you graduate, you will face new opportunities. And remember there will be a "new game" everyday.

Go out there and enjoy life. And do it now, because "Youneverknow".

Now here is a shortened version of the same speech.
It allows you to get on and off stage quicker and be less of a
target for rotten eggs. Just kidding. Normally they
throw tomatoes.

I am going to look to those great American Philosophers, baseball players and managers, for wisdom.

Stay hungry. The way to get ahead is stay hungry. As Leo Durocher said, "Give me some scratching, diving, hungry ballplayers who come to kill you."

Set high expectations. Sparky Anderson said, "I don't know whether I'm a big leaguer or not, but I want to find out, and if I can't do it, then I'll be a minor leaguer the rest of my life."

What do you have to do to be in the big leagues of your profession?

Take chances. Wayne Gretzky was not a baseball player, but said, "I learned early that you miss 100% of the shots you don't take."

So take your shots.

Also, stick up for what is right. When defending Jackie Robinson, Durocher said, "I don't care if the guy is yellow or black, or if he has stripes like a god-damn zebra. I'm the manager of this team and I say he plays."

You will make mistakes. But take them as a learning experience and move into the future. As Sparky Anderson said, "People who live in the past generally are afraid to compete in the present. I've got my faults, but living in the past is not one of them. There's no future in it."

Have a strong work ethic. Every employer can identify with Casey Stengel who said, "All I ask is that you bust your heiny on that field."

Nolan Ryan said, "One of the beautiful things about baseball is that you come into a situation where you have to reach down and prove something."

You too will have to reach down and prove something – to your boss, to yourself, to your spouse, to your children. That is when you find out who you really are.

Joaquin Andujar once said, "My favorite word in English is 'youneverknow'."

And Joaquin was so right, in life "you never know". So stay flexible, stay open to new ideas.

Finally Bob Feller once said, "Every day is a new opportunity. That's the way life is, with a new game every day, and that's the way baseball is."

And there will be a "new game" every day. Go out there and enjoy life. And do it now, because "Youneverknow".

198

You can take a preface to any word and use it for an opening. Here is an example of how you can take the preface 'sub', play around with it and create an opening. Then you can say, "Well, perhaps we should ban the word 'sub' around here, as none of us want our service to be subpar. So how do we maintain excellent customer service?"

Quote: There are no traffic jams along the extra mile.
~Robert Staubach

Think about the preface 'sub'. If you submit, you give in. Who wants to be subpar or sub average? Beware of sub cults, you might be subjected to anything. Being submerged can drown you. Being substandard isn't good and who wants a bare subsistence? A substitute is not the real thing. Subversive is not a great trait, who likes a subversive employee? Subzero will kill you. Well, and I am going to end this with a pun, so I am warning you now, but let's move onto another SUBject.

199

When you have to speak before a gathering of mothers or a group of parents, here is an original poem they have never heard before and it will get a few laughs. This is also a good poem to use for fundraising. You can say, "Despite the clichés we all tell our kids, they must know one thing. That we really do care about them. And that is why <u>name of charity</u> is seeking your help."

Quote: No one in the world can take the place of your mother. Right or wrong, from her viewpoint you are always right. She may scold you for little things, but never for the big ones. ~Harry Truman

Poem

It was a bad day for mothers
John tripped over his laces
and broke his leg
Sally crossed her eyes and
they stayed that way
Bob was in an accident
with dirty underwear
Joey went out with wet hair
caught his death from cold
(the funeral is this Friday)
All of Harold's friends jumped
off a cliff and he followed them
Tom didn't wait until
his father got home
Jeff played with a stick
poked his eye out
Sarah sat too close to the TV
went blind
Dave didn't look at his mother

when she was talking to him
but Betsy did find money
growing on a tree.

200

Here is a funny speech about on-line dating and how truth-in-advertising may not be the best thing for some people. This is a fun speech to present to a singles group or a gathering of young professionals.

Quote: Keep your eyes wide open before marriage, half shut afterwards.
~Benjamin Franklin

Here is my dating profile that I will soon post on E-Hammy.Com. I expect good results.

Well this is outside my comfort zone, but then again being a free man has also taken some getting used to. I kept telling them that the meth lab was not mine, I was just letting Billie Bob use my trailer. And ain't that life, they stick me in prison and then Billie Bob blows up the trailer so now I am in this homeless shelter, while I look for a new double-wide and a job.

I was thinking maybe a truck driver, but they frown on anyone with DWIs and I have a fine collection of DWIs, almost 20. I know that is nothing to brag about, but a when a man sets a record, that is something he should be proud of.

I am a good cook and a good provider. When I was living with Mary Sue, afore she went and married that no-account Billie Bob, because he had a full set of teeth, I always brought home some fine road kill and was an expert at making possum and squirrel stew. The secret behind squirrel stew is you got to clean the brains out as they is too salty and a bit hard to digest. Also you have to cut off their little claws, but the rest of the squirrel is just fine to eat.

If I meet the right lady, I can relocate, if it is okay with my probation office. I am looking for a woman with at least 20 teeth, no more than three tattoos and who washes her hair at least once a month. I do like a clean lady, so if you don't wash your overalls more than once a month, do not apply to be my sweetie.

I am educated, spent over ten years in school, of course most of it was in fifth grade, that addition and subtraction was hard on me. So that kinda ruled out my accounting career, but I is good enough with numbers to be a member of Congress.

Anyway, I is looking for a lady and we could be sweethearts. I am a kind loving man who drinks a bit too much, likes taking other people's cars for joyrides, likes wrestle mania, and have no kids, excepting that my cousin's kid's eyes are a bit too close together and he has an overbite just like me, so you never know.

We can meet at Burger King or McDonald's as I like them fancy restaurants for a first date. Plus maybe I might be able to sneak in some moonshine, which is better than paying for drinks at one of them bars.

201

Here is a list of funny place names, just a fun opening or a full speech you can use around Holiday Time.

Quote: Once again, we come to the Holiday Season, a deeply religious time that each of us observes, in his own way, by going to the mall of his choice.
~Dave Barry

The US Census Bureau, because they obviously have nothing better to do with your tax money, has shared these place names associated with the holiday season. They include:

- North Pole, Alaska
- Santa Claus, Indiana
- Santa Claus, Georgia
- Noel, Missouri
- Rudolph, Wisconsin
- Dasher, Georgia
- Snowflake, Arizona
- A dozen places named Holly, including Holly Springs, Mississippi. and Mount Holly, North Carolina

But wait, there is more! In keeping with the holiday spirits, here are some holiday names the Census Bureau left off the list.

- Over the Limit, Arizona
- Fruitcake, Rhode Island
- Reindeer Stew, Idaho
- Elf Bowling, Alabama
- Frosty Melt, Missouri
- Returns, Nebraska
- Re-gift, Minnesota
- Dead Tree, Iowa
- Shattered Dreams, Nebraska
- Spiced Punch, Florida
- Is Your Mother Leaving, New Mexico
- Empty Wallet, Wisconsin
- Debt Mountain, Colorado
- Dead Elf, Oklahoma
- Overdrawn, Texas
- Drunken Elf, Montana
- Drowning in Debt Lake, South Dakota
- Recovery, Georgia
- Hangover, Mississippi
- Empty Stocking, Missouri
- Cheap Skate, Ohio

- Poverty Row, Illinois
- Reindeer Farts, Alaska
- Bounced Check, California
- Plummeting Reindeer, South Dakota
- Rum Center, Louisiana
- Bah Humbug, Rhode Island
- Busted Toy, Washington
- Choking Hazard, Nevada
- Coal Lump, Arkansas
- Tacky Red Suit, Michigan
- Charred Reindeer, Oklahoma
- Busted Sleigh, Utah
- Red Splatter, Vermont
- Clogged Chimney, Maine
- Ticking Gift, Montana
- Reindeer Falls, New York

202

Here is a list of the Top Ten Things Not To Say in Court. You can read off this list, then say, "As you know, these are funny, unless you are facing a lawsuit. And many companies today face lawsuits and today I want to discuss what we expect out of employees, so we don't spend all our company's money defending frivolous lawsuits."

Quote: Make Crime pay, Become a Lawyer.
~ Bumper Sticker

Top Ten Things Not to Say in Court
- You call yourself a man – come off that bench and fight.
- When do I get my whiskey back?
- Does that robe hide your fat?

- You can't throw me in jail. They're overcrowded.
- Prostitution? Judge, I thought she was your sister.
- Judge, I am being judged by people too dumb to get out of jury duty,
- Why do I need to go to drunk driving class? I already know how to drive drunk.
- Pardon me, but you have obviously mistaken me for someone who gives a damn.
- If I agreed with you, we'd both be wrong.
- Do I have a ride? My other ride is your mom.

203

Here is a list of what each professional should know. After reading off some items from the list, you can say "And what do customers expect us to know. Let's discuss that today."

Quote: If I had my life to live over again, I'd be a plumber.
~Albert Einstein

- Plumber: Hot is on the left and payday is on Friday.
- Roofer: Don't fall off the roof.
- Fireman: Let the rookie enter the burning house first.
- Cop: Don't get shot.
- Doctor: 80% of your patients will cure themselves. Don't kill the rest.
- Teacher: Act like you care and you are not counting the days until vacation.
- Nurse: After the doctor leaves, do it the right way.
- Politician: Always promise to never raise taxes.
- Electrician: Turn off the power.
- News cameraman: Always point towards the flame.
- TV newsperson: You can never have too many trench coats.

- Lawyer: You client only tells you 80% of the truth.
- Computer Repair: Ask if the computer is plugged in.
- Cell phone repair: Check for the red tag in back that shows the client dropped the phone in the toilet.
- CEO: Wall Street judges you by profits not by the number of employees you have.
- Carpenter: Keep your thumb out of the way.
- Accountant: When in doubt, depreciate something.
- Machinist: Always count your fingers before you go home.
- Sailor: A leak never gets better.
- Public Relations Exec: When you are in a hole, quit digging.
- Football Coach: You get judged by winning, not ethics.
- Racecar Driver: Always steer left.
- Mechanic: Why sell a water pump when you can sell a whole cooling system?
- Priest: God will provide but pass the collection plate anyway.
- Pilot: Pull the stick back, houses get smaller. Push the stick down, houses get bigger.
- Forest Ranger: Don't play with matches.
- Fitness Coach: Stay off the Twinkies.
- Cowboy: You gotta be smarter than the cows.
- Stockbroker: Ain't my money I'm playing with.
- Rapper: Everything rhymes.
- Appliance Repair Man: Gas goes BOOM.

204

Here is an extensive list of businesses that cartoon characters might run. Pick and choose some names for a great opening and then you can say, "Those are funny business names, but we must ensure that our business name always means quality and value to our customers. How can we do that? "

Quote: I am a bear of very little brain and long words bother me. ~Winnie-the-Pooh

- Mr. Magoo's Eye Doctor
- Porky Pig's Speech Therapy
- Donald Duck Anger Management
- Elmer Fudd Gun Safety Classes
- Sylvester's Bird Appreciation Society
- Goofy's Learning Academy
- Tigger's ADHA Management Counseling
- Captain Hook's Clock Repair
- The Coyote's "How To Cook a Road Runner" Course
- Fat Albert's Weight Loss Clinic
- Alvin's Singing Lessons
- Homer Simpson Child Psychologist
- Eeyore's Depression Clinic
- Fred Flintstone's Fine Men's Clothing Shop
- The Shaggy Electric Razor
- Casper the Ghost's Assertive Training Center
- Jughead's Fine Hat Shop
- Bugs Bunny Modesty Training
- Olive Oyl Vitamins
- Scooby Doo Real Estate Office
- Kenny's Health Clinic
- Popeye Food Channel
- Marge Simpson Hair Salon
- Pepe Le Pew Dating Service
- Krusty the Clown Day Care Center
- Beavis and Butthead Attorneys at Law
- Mighty Mouse – Rodent Exterminators
- Pinky and the Brain Science Academy
- Lisa Simpson's Butcher Shop
- Eric Cartman's Political Correctness Workshop

205

Here is a humorous list of how to get along with your mother-in-law. Warning – use this at your own risk.

Quote: I just took a pleasure trip. I took my mother-in-law to the airport.
~Henny Youngman

- Do not ask when she got out of rehab.
- Do not ask her to move to a sturdier chair.
- Do not say, "I haven't seen a dress like that since the fifties."
- Do not ask, "So do you really have a dead puppy collection?"
- Do not ask to borrow her broom to ride home.
- Do not ask, "Have you all considered family therapy?"
- Do not say, when she makes a surprise visit, "Are all the bars closed today?"
- Do not say, "I never thought Spandex could stretch that much, but on you it looks good."
- Do not say, "Your husband says Home Improvement means you moved out."
- Do not yell, "Hide the kids, your mother is here."
- Do not ask, "Who does your makeup, Shrek?"
- Do not say, "We chilled the Ripple just for you."
- Do not say, "Gosh, I can't guess why your husband would drink so much."
- Do not say, "Does the museum know a mummy is missing."
- Do not say, "Beauty mark? Looks like a wart to me."

206

Here is another list on how to survive the holidays. Then you can say, "That may be a funny list on how to survive the holidays, but

I would like to discuss a more serious subject, what we must do to survive as a business.

Quote: A lovely thing about Christmas is that it's compulsory, like a thunderstorm, and we all go through it together.
~Garrison Keillor

- Even though they have been obnoxious all day, do not encourage your kids to run with sharp knives.
- Stuff the turkey, not yourself.
- After cooking the turkey, do not show guests your finger and ask, "Does this look infected to you?"
- Add one shot of bourbon, three shots of club soda and drink.
- Ignore your mother-in-law when she says your neck bears a resemblance to the turkey's neck.
- "Good food, good meat, Good God, let's eat" is not a proper blessing.
- Pretend you have not heard Uncle Ernie's joke ten times, "Two elves walk into a bar…"
- Do not sharpen the carving knife and stare at your mother-in-law.
- Do not embarrass your kids with your stupid jokes such as, "You cannot see the turkey now, it's getting dressed."
- Again, when you are carving the turkey, do not embarrass your kids by saying, "I am a real cutup."
- Do not feel obligated to tell your guests that a 160 pound person would have to run for four hours, swim for five hours or walk 30 miles to burn off the average 3,000 calorie holiday dinner.
- Do not use those plastic spoons and forks you have been sneaking out of fast food places.
- When your 40 year old brother brings an 18 year old date, don't ask if she wants to sit at the kid's table.
- Do not ask your bulimic sister which bathroom she plans to throw up in.

- Add three shots of bourbon, no club soda and gulp it down.

207

Everyone is social networking today and here is a list of "netiquette" rules you can share with your audience. Then you can say, "Although that was a funny list, we must be serious about what we do and do not send on the computer from our offices. Let's talk about what the true netiquette rules are around here."

Quote: After you die, your fingernails and hair keeps growing. But e-mails drop off.
~Anon

The word *netiquette* is short for 'Internet etiquette'.

Here are Some Common Rules of Netiquette

- Write to the level of your audience so you do not confuse or offend them. If you are sending a message to your congressman, use short simple words. Hello Mr. Congressman. I am upset. Here is why I am upset...
- Do not drink heavily and text people or e-mail people. Also, when drinking heavily, do not send messages to ex-girlfriends. This never works out. Also do not join dating sites when drinking heavily.
- If someone gets a restraining order against you, you might want to check the tone of your e-mails.
- Do not say anything negative about anyone in e-mails. They can go viral and that picture you photoshopped of your male boss wearing garters and stockings means you will be looking for a new job.
- Be respectful and treat everyone as you would want to be treated. Except for those idiots who actually LIKE the Red Sox. Netiquette

says that Red Sox fans can be abused for thinking that the bandbox the team plays in is a real ballpark.

- Wait to respond to a message that upsets you and be careful of what you say and how you say it. While you are waiting call the person, offer to buy him or her a drink, then give him or her a hot foot at the bar.
- Be considerate. Rude or threatening language, inflammatory assertions, personal attacks, and other inappropriate communication should not be tolerated. However, remember that Red Sox fans and politicians are exempt from this rule.
- Emoticons can be used to emphasize meaning. But if you have a brain, you realize that using emoticons leads to emasculation and before you know it, you are sipping drinks with little umbrellas in them and crying through chick flicks.
- Never post a message that is in all capital letters – it comes across to the reader as SHOUTING! Use boldface and italics sparingly, as they can denote sarcasm. *DO YOU GET THAT, RED SOX FANS?*
- Keep messages relevant to the topic being discussed. I totally agree with this and always stay on subject and have you noticed that you never see a baby squirrel and that abbreviation is a long word and shouldn't it be shorter and…
- Always practice good grammar, punctuation, and composition. This shows that you've taken the time to craft your response and that you respect your audience. Ain't that a swell tip?
- Use spell-check! Of course if you are like me, spell-check will not recognize half the words you spell which is why I am a Spelling Chimp.

208

Another humorous list, The Top Ten Rules for Nudists. After reading this list as an opening, you can say, "You can all relax, I am

going to keep my clothes on. Our latest sales figures are depressing enough, but let's discuss ways we can increase sales."

Quote: Nudists are people who wear one button suits.
~Anon

- Always wear sunscreen.
- When hiking be able to identify poison ivy.
- Get a tummy tuck.
- If you are over 60 and your bra size is 32 long, reconsider your nudist career.
- Avoid cactus.
- Use ChapStick on your nipples.
- Standing at attention takes on a whole new meaning.
- You have no place to put your keys, cell phone or wallet.
- If you are male, do not play flag football. The other team might grab the wrong thing.
- Do not slide when playing softball.

209

Many men worry about becoming bald. But here is a list of what is good about being bald. Then you can say, "It does not matter if you are bald, it is your attitude about it. And attitude is important in many areas of life. Now I would like to chat about attitudes in the workplace..."

Quote: I am not bald, I am just taller than my hair.
~Anon

- No more bad hair days
- Save tons of money on hair products
- Bald doesn't turn grey

- Start a great collection of hats
- People rub your head for good luck
- A new use for sunscreen
- No more hair clogged drains
- Can sell advertisements on your head
- Don't have to worry about losing your hair
- No stupid comb-overs

210

Here are the Top 25 Things when a meteorite hits the earth. You can read all or part of this list and then say, "See, there can be even good news when the earth is destroyed. But it is hard to find good news in our latest safety records and here is what we must all do to improve..."

Quote: Jesus is coming. Look busy.
~Anon

The Top 25 Things That Happen When a Meteorite Hits the Earth

- Your cell phone service reception really drops off.
- Completely ruins the Cubs chances of ever winning a World Series.
- No more traffic jams on the LA Freeway.
- Free cremation for everyone.
- Takes the spotlight off any politician having an affair.
- Don't have to worry about what to wear tomorrow.
- Completely wrecks the value of your home.
- Screws up your chances of winning the lottery.
- No more worries about Greece, Italy and the Euro.
- Makes God the biggest Terrorist of all.
- No more worries about capital punishment being ethical.

- No more worries about Global Warming.
- FEMA can't be blamed for slow reaction.
- Skip final exams.
- Prevent the Kardashians from making any more shows
- The NBA season is REALLY canceled
- Gives the EARTH a hell of a hangover.
- Get to test that Hide Under Your Desk theory.
- No more worries about OPEC.
- All Middle East Problem solved.
- The price of gas finally stops rising.
- Ruins the Holiday Shopping Season.
- No more student loans to pay back.
- No more alimony.
- The social security system does not run out of money.

211

Here are the ten worst home repair books. It is a quick list you can use for an opening and have fun adding some of your own. They you can say, "And of course, I do not want to see any customer service book about our company written by "Shea Cares Less".

Quote: Do what you do so well that they will want to see it again and bring their friends.
~Walt Disney

- How to Use a Saw – by Three Fingers McKee
- How to Use a Blow Torch – by Skin Graft Jones
- How to Clean Out a Septic Tank – by Stinky Smith
- How to Pick a Lock – by Jailhouse Eddie
- How to Patch a Roof – by Jim Leaky
- How to Fix a Toilet – by Elmer Flood
- How to Fix a Gas Heater – by Boom Boom James

- How to Plant a Garden – by Susie Wilting
- How to Build a Deck – by Jim Splinters
- How to Use a Hammer – by Thumbs Dickerson

212

Here are the Top Ten Names for a Nudist Camp. A fun opening to read, then you can say, "But we do not want to EXPOSE our employees to danger. That is why this is a good time to review safety rules."

Quote: Thought for the day – where do nudists carry their cell phones?
~Anon

- The Crack of Dawn
- Danglers
- Peek City
- The Booby Trap
- Balls In Play
- Flabulous
- Cheeks
- Hidden Bush
- Hanging Out
- Right to Bare

213

What messages do Christmas gifts really send? Here is a short list, perfect for an opening, about what certain gifts mean. Then you can say, "Now I'll feel bad, after reading that list, if any of you receive those gifts this year. Almost makes me want to take that

scarf I bought for my wife back. But let's take a moment and explore the real gifts of the season, the gifts that we can't buy in stores..."

Quote: Three phrases that sum up Christmas are: Peace on Earth, Goodwill to Men, and Batteries not Included.
~English Proverb

When You Unwrap That Special Gift, Here is What the Person is Really Saying

- Snuggie – The last minute gift
- Boston Red Sox hat – You are a loser too
- Flask – For the traveling alcoholic
- Cardigan sweater – We all get old
- Scarf – The easy way to cover up that chicken neck
- Ripple wine – The cheapest way to destroy your kidneys
- Avon Perfume – I had to buy something from Betty Lou; she has been bugging me all year
- Fishing Rod – Get out of the damn house
- Rubik's Cube – I bought your gift at a garage sale
- Wal-Mart PJs – Why waste money on you at Victoria's Secret

214

The following list makes a great opening, then you can say, "But when it comes to customer service, we do not want to short our customers..."

Quote: The worst gift is a fruitcake. There is only one fruitcake in the entire world, and people keep sending it to each other.
~Johnny Carson

The Top Ten Names That Will Start a Fight With an Elf

- Sir Shortsalot
- Stubs
- Bridget the Midget
- Munchkin
- Smurf
- Frodo
- Troll
- Thumbelina
- Kickstand
- Squeak

215

A good question to ask your audience is "Are you an average American?", then read them part of this entire list. Then you can say, "But I am pleased to say there is nothing average about our sales department..."

Quote: In America, anyone can be President, that's one of the risks you take.
~Adlai Stevenson

- You might be an average American if you don't answer the phone because bill collectors keep calling.
- You might be an average American if that friendly loan officer is foreclosing on your home.
- You might be an average American if you think splurging is filling up your car with gas.
- You might be an average American if you have spent over six months looking for work.
- You might be an average American if you are worried sick about getting sick.

- You might be an average American if your savings account is your kids' piggy bank.
- You might be an average American if you wonder where the money is coming from to fix that oil leak in your car.
- You might be an average American if a regular dental checkup is a luxury you can't afford.
- You might be an average American if you wait for sales at the thrift store.
- You might be an average American if your congressman has health insurance and you don't.
- You might be an average American if a night out is Happy Meals all around.
- You might be an average American if you have $30,000 in student debt, but no job.
- You might be an average American if you wonder why millionaire pro basketball players are striking and you can't even afford a ticket to a game.
- You might be an average American if you thank K-Mart and Wal-Mart for bringing back lay-away.
- You might be an average American if you decide that your car can last another year, or two, or three…
- You might be an average American if you think that the Free Trade Agreement wasn't that good of an idea, as you watch your job outsourced overseas.
- You might be an average American if you will never see a pension plan.
- You might be an average American if you only buy generic brands.
- You might be an average American whose idea of vacation means having time to find a second job. Or any job.
- You might be an average American if you watch your kids' standard of living sink faster that the Titanic.
- You might be an average American if Top Ramen is considered a staple in your house.

216

Having bad luck with the ladies? Maybe these redneck pickup lines might help. After reading these you can say, "Those pickup lines are humorous, but at our company, we have better ways of picking up new customers, including quality service and great products."

Quote: He fell out of the ugly tree and hit every branch on the way down.
~Anon

Okay, Here are the Top 35 Redneck Pickup Lines to Meet a Woman at the Talladega Speedway

- Nice tattoo.
- Nice tooth.
- I have never seen a nose ring so infected. Can I help you to the first aid tent?
- Did you know Talle Dega was named after one of them famous French painters?
- Double-wide? Oh I was just talking about my ex-wife. I'm single now.
- It's amazing how these race car drivers can drive 500 laps and never get lost.
- How do you keep your eyes crossed like that?
- You are so smart using shoe polish as hair dye. I bet that saves lots of money.
- Them bathrooms have indoor plumbing. Let me show you.
- It ain't often that you meet a lady who drinks imported beer from St. Louis.
- I am a night watchman. Get me alone at night, you'd better watch me.
- I agree – deodorant is overrated.
- I think hot pant overalls look so sexy.

- Eau de Moonshine smells good on you.
- I got me some stocks investments. Two cows and a goat.
- I would stick to you like crime scene tape.
- You don't often see a duct tape belt as pretty as that.
- Don't this motor oil make my hair look slick?
- Didn't I see you at our last family reunion?
- I don't know which is more exciting. This here race or WWF.
- I have never seen a dress made out of beer cans.
- That is a good idea – using whiteout to cover the tobacco stains on your teeth.
- I bet that gap in your teeth is mighty handy for opening beer cans.
- I ain't seen no woman with such a fine flea collection in her hair.
- I agree underarm hair braiding is a lost art.
- Like to share a can of Vienna sausage?
- I am the only one on the campground with a duct tape tent. Ain't that impressive?
- How many dogs you think they kilt to make them corn dogs?
- Wow, you really named your tooth Old Yeller?
- You want to share some road kill stew?
- A purty woman like you is harder to find than a good coon dog.
- Well you is prettier than a freshly stuffed possum.
- You make me feel higher than my pickup truck.
- Your eyes are as green as pond slime.
- You make my shotgun go off.

217

Here is a funny list you can share with your audience. It is how cell phones can make you sick. You can say, "As I walked in here today, I saw many of you on your cell phones, so I thought I would brighten your day with a true list of how cell phones can make you sick. You can thank me later."

Quote: Apparently we love our own cell phones but we hate everyone else's.
~Joe Bob Briggs

The good news is that your cell phone does not cause brain cancer: "In what is described as the largest study on the subject to date, Danish researchers found no evidence that the risk of brain In what is described as the largest study on the subject to date, Danish researchers found no evidence that the risk of brain tumors was raised among 358,403 mobile phone subscribers over an 18-year period." But their blood pressure did increase dramatically when they received their cell phone bills.

The bad news is I have found ten other symptoms associated with cell phones. These include:

- **Cell Phone Rash** – Symptoms of cell phone allergy include a red, bumpy, itchy rash in areas where the nickel-containing parts of a cell phone touch the face. It can even affect fingertips of those who text continuously on buttons containing nickel. In severe cases, blisters and itchy sores can develop.
- **Insomnia** – Results of a new study suggest that using a cell phone shortly before going to bed can lead to sleep disturbances and a number of other symptoms. "The study found that radiation from cell phones can cause insomnia and interfere with stage-4 sleep (meaning users wake up feeling unrefreshed)."
- **Cell Phone Addiction** – If you can't get through dinner without sending text messages or furiously typing on a personal digital assistant during a meeting, it may be time to take a step back. Frequent users often become anxious when they are forced to turn off the phone or if they forget it at home, so much so that they can't enjoy whatever they're doing, Often, cell phone addicts compulsively check their phones for voicemails and text messages.
- **Death Wish** – Not caused by depression, but by stupidity. Often

manifests itself when a teenager is driving over the speed limit, putting on makeup and texting all at the same time.

- **Cell Phone Elbow** – Cubital tunnel syndrome is a nerve compression syndrome (like carpal tunnel syndrome). In the case of cubital tunnel syndrome, the nerve involved is the ulnar nerve. The location of the compression is at the elbow as the ulnar nerve's course wraps around the posterior elbow along the medial condyle of the humerus. This is the area often called the 'funny bone' when it gets hit. When people hold their elbow flexed for a prolonged period, such as when speaking on the phone or sleeping at night, the ulnar nerve is placed in tension.

- **Phantom Vibration Syndrome** – When you think your phone is vibrating and pick it up and no one is there. This behavior is often exhibited by teenagers who cannot believe that they have actually received NO texts in the last three minutes.

- **Cell Phone Vision Syndrome** – Cell Phone Vision Syndrome, also known as Computer Vision Syndrome, is real. "A new problem that some eye experts are calling computer vision syndrome (CVS) is sweeping the country; it can affect up to 90% of people who spend two or more continuous hours a day with their eyes glued to a screen, whether it's that of a computer, an e-reader, or a smart phone. The symptoms, which can include blurry vision, headaches, dry eyes, or even long-term nearsight-edness, may accrue over a period of days or months..."

- **More bacteria than a toilet** – Mobile phone retailer Dial-a-Phone conducted the study taking swabs from everyday objects and analyzing the bacteria found on them. The shocking results found that there's more muck on our mobiles than the average door handle, keyboard, and bottom of a shoe or even a toilet seat.

- **Repetitive Stress Injuries** – Your sore thumb from texting is really repetitive strain injuries or a repetitive motion disorder. It can also lead to serious medical problems.

- **Deafness** – According to statistics from the US Centers for Disease Control and Prevention about 12.5% of children and adolescents 6 to 19 years old and 17% of adults between 20 and 69 years of age have suffered permanent damage to their hearing from excessive exposure to noise. Sounds louder than 85 decibels can damage hearing. Normal conversation is about 60 decibels, and stereo headphones out of our MP3-enabled devices including cell phones often reach 100 decibels.

218

I have a friend who lives in Alabama and he can't understand why people poke fun at his state. Then he sent me the most recent vital stats for Alabama and said, "I understand now." You can then read some of the following vital stats about Alabama, and then say, "Now the question becomes, when it concerns our company, what vital stats should we be following?"

Quote: Don't corner somethin' that you know is meaner than you.
~Old cowboy saying

Well the Vital Stats for Alabama are in and it's time to pass out a few awards:

- **It's Never Too Late Award**
  The oldest man to father a child was 84, the oldest mother to give birth last year was 53.
- **It's Never Too Early Award**
  The youngest father was 14. The youngest mother was 12. 12.4% of babies were born to women 19 and younger.
- **Stop it. Right Now!!! Award**
  The baby with the most siblings went home to 13 brothers and sisters.
- **Better Put a Ring On It Award**

Of the 59,979 live births a year in Alabama, 42% are to unmarried mothers.

- **Wouldn't It be Cheaper to Watch Cable Award?**
  There are about 81,907 pregnancies a year in Alabama.
- **They Should Know Better Award**
  The oldest groom was 92 and the oldest bride 91.
- **Get the Kids Out of House Award**
  The youngest groom was 16 and the youngest bride 13.
- **But He Doesn't Look His Age or Can You Say Sugar Daddy Award**
  The greatest age difference between a groom and bride in Alabama this year was 53 years.
- **There's Always Next Time Award**
  The youngest male to divorce this year was and the youngest female divorcee was 16.
- **I Just Got Sick of Him Award**
  The longest marriage to end in divorce this year lasted 58 years.
- **Whoops I Made a Mistake Award**
  The shortest marriage to end in divorce this year lasted 13 days.
- **The Just Don't Learn Award**
  The greatest number of previous marriages for a divorcee, both male and female, in Alabama this year was 10.
- **I Got a New Boyfriend/Girlfriend Award**
  The oldest man to divorce this year was 104. The oldest female divorcee was 90.

219

What should you get your child for Christmas? Here are some gift ideas for that little darling. After you read the list, you can say, "Okay, those may not be the best gift ideas, but let's think of some ideas that will help our customers through the holidays..."

Quote: Everyone is gifted but some people never open their package.

~Anon

Top Electronic and Science Gifts for Kids

- Shock the babysitter – this is NOT a cattle prod. It merely looks like one and kids will have hours of fun sneaking up on the babysitter and shocking her.
- Electronic tattoo kits – avoid the rush and let your child tattoo himself and his friends. Not only will your kid learn a valuable skill, but he can go into business for himself. Operating right out of his own basement!
- Electronic eavesdropping kit – what are mommy and daddy really saying about you after you go off to bed. A simple receiver, the size of a watch battery, can be hidden in mommy and daddy's room. Find out what your parents really think about you.
- Home cloning kit. Tired of your brother. Well, you could ship him off to an orphanage but wouldn't your parents notice him missing? Problem solved, with the home cloning kit. Make a clone of your brother, before he disappears. No one will suspect a thing!
- Home counterfeiting kit. Mom and Dad a bit stingy on the allowance? Now make your own money with this high tech scanner. Makes $20 and $50 bills so real that not even your junior drug dealer will know. Warning: Make sure the ink is dry before passing the money around.

220

If you are talking to an audience of men, two good topics are always fishing and golf. Here is a short list of fishing rules. After sharing this list, you can say, "And we always hear that fish story, about the big one that got away. As you know we are always looking for new business and we don't want the 'big ones' to get away. So what can we do to ensure we are successful at attracting new customers?"

Quote: The fishing is always better on the other side of the lake. ~Anon

Key Rules of Fishing

- No matter how much you spend on fancy lures, a worm is still the best for catching fish.
- You can buy a $500 sonar device, a $200 fishing rod, and a $20,000 boat and the kid fishing off his dock with a $5 bamboo pole will still kick your butt.
- Fish are swimming food. They have no brains. But yet they are smart enough to avoid you. Think about that.
- The best way to catch a fish is to use a green hook, aka on the way home, buy fish at Safeway.
- If there is a submerged tree, your boat bottom will find it.
- Just when you find a great fishing spot, some kid on a Jet Ski will go by hollering. I do believe in some states it is legal to shoot him. But you might want to double-check on that.
- There is no easy way to explain how your line got caught in a tree.
- The minute you take a break and hand your girlfriend the line, she will catch the biggest fish of the day.
- Every fish you catch is a big fish if you use Photoshop.
- Be patient. Patience really is the key to good fishing. So is an ice chest full of beer.

221

Again, if you have to give a quick speech during a golf retreat, here is a good list to use for your opening. And then you can say, "Golf is a frustrating game, and it is tempting to stretch the rules a bit, as that list shows. But in life and in our business, we will not tolerate any stretching of the rules by any employee..."

Quote: Golf is a game in which you yell "fore", shoot six, and write down five.
~Paul Harvey

Ten Tips to Improve Your Golf Game
- Get a pencil with a good eraser.
- When you're drunk, don't drive. Don't even putt.
- No ball is in the rough if no one is around.
- You can subtract a stroke for any ball in the lake. Only Jesus can walk on water and they have no business putting lakes on a golf course. What do they think? This is a fishing resort?
- If you land in a sand trap, you can pick the ball up and throw it on the green. If you wanted to play on sand you would go to the Mohave Desert. Hell with them.
- If the ball is close to the green, that is close enough. Why slow down play by putting? Give yourself one stroke for a great putt which you would have made and continue onto the next hole.
- When you get home, brag about having two strokes on every hole. Do not tell them about the windmill on hole three or the dragon on hole four. Let them assume you played a real golf course.
- Go to the bar and order a drink called a Hole In One. Then go home and tell your wife you had a Hole In One.
- When asked what your handicap is, do not say My Mother-In-Law. This is not really a tip, but somewhat funny.
- Throw your clubs in the lake and take up bowling.

222

Here are jokes you can use about any team you want to make fun of. We use "Red Sox" but you can easily change Red Sox to any team. After picking one or two jokes, you can say, "Today, I want to talk about our winning team."

> Quote: Beethoven can't really be great because his picture isn't on a bubble gum card.
> ~Charles Schulz

- What is the difference between a Yankee hotdog and a Red Sox hotdog? They still serve Yankee hotdogs in October.
- The Red Sox have to expand their payroll to hire a Heimlich coach.
- The Seven Dwarfs fell in a deep ravine. Snow White peered into the steep chasm and called out to the dwarfs. From the depths of the dark hole a voice returned, "The Red Sox are playoff contenders." Snow White thought, "Thank God! Dopey survived!"
- The American bobsled team is recruiting Red Sox players. No one goes downhill faster.
- What do you a call a Red Sox player with a bottle of champagne in his hand? A waiter.
- What's the height of optimism? A Red Sox fan buying playoff tickets.
- What do Red Sox infielders have in common with Michael Jackson? They both wear one glove for no apparent reason.
- What do you call a Red Sox player who can make a catch? A fisherman.
- What do you call 25 millionaires around a TV watching the playoffs? The Red Sox.
- What does a Boston Red Sox fan do after his team wins the World Series? He turns off the video game.
- What do you call a Red Sox player wearing a 2011 World Series ring? A thief.
- They are going to call the next hurricane The Red Sox. They hope

it doesn't hit anything either.

- It was so rainy in Baltimore, the Red Sox couldn't see who was beating them.
- The Red Sox just beat the Titanic's record for sinking.
- The Red Sox's best pitch is the sinker.
- The teacher asks, "Does anyone know where Pittsburgh is?" Billy and says, "Yeah, Pennsylvania!" The teacher replies, "Now where is Detroit?" Suzy says, "That's in Michigan!" Trying to confuse the children, the teacher asks, "Where's Boston?" Tommy raises his hand and says, "Third place."
- On Take Your Daughter to Work Day, the Red Sox played against their daughters and lost, 12–3.
- You heard about the big oil spill off the Atlantic coast? Well they've hired the Red Sox to help clean it up. Yeah, they just go out there and throw in the towel.
- They had to close the Red Sox Restaurant – too many players where choking.

223

Here is a list of where not to meet that special person. After choosing some ideas from the list, you can say, "And if our customers want to meet great customer service, they can come to our shops..."

Quote: Redneck after getting divorced – Judge, is she still my sister?

~Anon

The Top 25 Places NOT to Pick Up a Date

- Family Reunions
- Tattoo Parlor
- Sex Addict Meetings

- Drunk tank at local jail
- Sexual Disease Testing Center
- By her father's moonshine still
- Strip Clubs
- Narcotics Anonymous
- Skinhead rallies
- State hospitals
- Homeless shelter
- Food Bank
- Cult meetings
- Trailer Parks
- Meth Labs
- Probation Office
- Divorce Court
- Thunderbird and Ripple Wine tasting
- Hell's Angels Clubhouse
- Satanic Worshippers' Convention
- Bi-Polar Conventions
- Any Southern Gun Show
- Nursing Home
- At any graveside service
- Halfway houses

224

This is a good list to use around election time. You can say, "I would like to share some quotes with our local politicians..."

Quote: Politics is show business for ugly people.
~Anon

- Let them hate as long as they fear.
  – Accius, Latin poet, 86 BC

- I will undoubtedly have to seek what is known as gainful employment, which I am glad to say does not describe holding public office.
  – Dean Acheson
- Power tends to corrupt and absolute power corrupts absolutely.
  – Lord Acton
- When the political columnists say "Every thinking man", they mean themselves and when candidates appeal to "every intelligent voter" they mean anyone who will vote for them.
  – Franklin Adams
- Politics, as a practice, has always been the systematic organization of hatreds.
  – Henry Adams
- Written laws are like spider webs: they will catch the weak and poor, but will be torn in pieces by the rich and powerful.
  – Anacharsis, Scythian prince 16th Century
- The best defense against the atom bomb is not to be there when it goes off. – Anon
- The silly, flat, dishwatery utterances of the man who has to be pointed out to intelligent observers as the President of the United States
  – The *Chicago Times* review of Lincoln's Gettysburg address.
- Under capitalism, man exploits man. And under communism, it is just the reverse.
  – Anon
- The most perfect political community is one in which the middle class is in control, and outnumbers both of the other classes.
  – Aristotle
- The business of the civil service is the orderly management of decline.
  – William Armstrong
- I am not in Washington as a statesman. I am there as a very well-paid messenger boy doing your errands. My chief occupation is going around with a forked stick picking up little fragments of

patronage for my constituents.

– Henry Ashurst

- Fame is like a river, that beareth up things light and swollen, and drowns things weighty and solid.

  – Francis Bacon

- Politics is the art of looking for trouble, finding it whether it exists of not, diagnosing it incorrectly, and applying the wrong remedy.

  – Ernest Benn

- Broadcasting is really too important to be left to the broadcasters.

  – Tony Benn

- There is a providence that protects idiots, drunkards, children and the United States of America.

  – Anon

- The prestige of government has undoubtedly been lowered considerably by the Prohibition laws. For nothing is more destructive of respect for the government and the law of the land than passing laws which cannot be enforced. It is an open secret that the dangerous increase of crime in this country is closely connected with this.

  – Albert Einstein

- Governments are far more stupid than their people.

  – Eisenhower

- I must say the John Kennedy's victory in Wisconsin was a triumph for democracy. It proves that a millionaire has just as good a chance as anybody else.

  – Bob Hope

- Citizens, first acquire wealth; you can practice virtue afterwards.

  – Horace, 8 BC

- What is conservatism? Is it not adherence to the old and tried, against the new and untried?

  – Lincoln

- For a politician to complain about the press is like a ship's captain complaining about the sea.

  – Enoch Powell

225

The weather is always a good topic to start a speech with. Here are some "How Hot Is It?" jokes that you can fit into the opening of a speech. Then you can say, "The only thing hotter than the weather have been our sales..."

Quote: If you saw a heat wave, would you wave back?
~Steven Wright

How Hot is It?

- It is so hot that Satan goes to hell to cool off.
- It is so hot that cows are giving off steamed milk.
- It is hot that they installed a fan in the debt ceiling.
- It is so hot that Global Warming has been replaced by Global Melting.
- It is hotter that the Republicans' rhetoric.
- It is so hot that Obama gets credit for 'cooling off' the economy.
- It is so hot that Global Warming is now Global Melting.
- It is so hot that McDonald's is frying burgers on parked cars.
- It is so hot that the catfish are already fried when you catch them.
- It is so hot that all the beach sand has turned into glass.
- It is so hot that you are actually inside reading this.
- It is hotter than your ex-wives' tongues.
- It is so hot that polar bears are wearing sunscreen.
- It is so hot that firemen go to fires to cool off.
- It is so hot that 'burn baby burn' describes more than your wife's cooking.
- It is so hot that brides wear bikinis to weddings.
- It is so hot that Coors brags about its warm-filtered beer
- It is so hot that sweats are the only thing your kid breaks.
- It is so hot you needed a second mortgage to pay your air conditioning bill.
- It is so hot that Ronald McDonald is wearing a Speedo.

- It is so hot that everyone is wearing 'sweat' pants
- It is hot that even Minnesota had to cancel their July ice-fishing events
- It is so hot your clothes iron themselves.
- It is hot that cats climb onto tin roofs to cool off.
- It is so hot that even white collar workers are rednecks.
- It is so hot that fire crackers light themselves.
- It is so hot that Alaska is now known as Dante's Inferno
- It is so hot that 'fire balls' to men describes more than a candy.

226

Know Thy Audience: Here is a quick article to help you prepare your speech.

Quote: It takes about three weeks to prepare a good impromptu speech.
~Mark Twain

Purpose of a Speech

First remember that any speech must:

- Establish and maintain a purpose
- Be understood by the audience
- Organize the ideas and develop supporting details
- Build effective sentences and paragraphs
- Use appropriate and effective transitions to provide coherence
- Choose words carefully

Critical Thinking is Key to Any Speech

Also remember that a good speech is based on critical thinking. Critical thinking is important in all areas of writing, but especially when giving a speech. An effective speech depends on your audience receiving your message and then acting upon it appropriately.

To ensure your speech is effective, there are three key questions you must ask, before you start any speech. The first is: "Who is my audience?" The second is: "What objectives do I want them to achieve?" The third is: "What is the best way to help them achieve their objectives?"

Did you note that the three key questions are not focused on you, but rather on the audience?

Let's explore these questions further.

The first question is "Who is my audience?" It is not a big imper-sonal audience, but rather a group of individuals listening to your speech. Think if you were in the audience. What would make you feel more kindly to the speaker; want to work with the speaker?

The second question is "What objectives do I want them to achieve?" In other words, when the audience gets up to leave, what do you want them to do? Be specific in your requests and be sure the listeners understand they are reasonable requests. Remember, it is not important that you think your requests are reasonable. It is important that your audience thinks they are reasonable.

Finally, the third question is "What is the best way to help them achieve their objectives?" So, you want the audience to take action. But what actions should they take and how can you make it easier for them? That's important; your speech must include how your audience can achieve the objectives you have established for them.

Never Assume

Do not assume that your audience has the same training or background as you. What is obvious to you may not be obvious to them. Here's an example.

One summer, a friend, Kathy, and I went on a cross-country trip in a Honda car. One day we met another couple walking along a creek at a campground. We started chatting and discovered we both were driving Hondas.

But then, it got a little weird. The other woman asked, "Don't you find it's tough to pack stuff?" Kathy replied, "It's a bit cramped, but we do okay" Then the other woman said, "How about those bugs, don't they drive you crazy?"

Well, by this time I had figured out that while we were talking about our Honda car, the other couple was talking about their Honda motorcycle. Yet neither Kathy nor the other woman ever realized they weren't sharing the same experience. About two minutes later, they both walked away, very satisfied that they had bonded and had a nice conversation.

No harm done, of course. But if you are addressing an audience, or presenting a report to upper management, you better make sure that they understand the terms you are using.

227

The Ten Key Rules for Speeches:

Quote: Speech is power, speech is to persuade, to convert, to compel.
~Ralph Waldo Emerson

Ten Rules for Speeches

- All speeches follow a basic pattern, "Tell them what you are going to say, say it, tell them what you said."
- You do not need to open with a joke, despite what everyone tells you. Chances are the audience has heard the joke before and will laugh politely – and they are really thinking is, "What a lame joke." Plus why waste time looking for jokes to open your speech, when you should be focusing on what message you want them to walk away with?
- The best opening is to compliment your audience. This creates an instance rapport with your audience. For instance, "I am very flattered to be asked to speak to you tonight. I recognize that you are all outstanding professionals and am honored to share some

thoughts with you tonight about _____."

- Know the organization you are speaking to. For instance if you are addressing the Society of Professional Engineers, do some research and find out how long the organization has been in existence, some milestones it has accomplished, some famous members and perhaps its future goals. You can add these to your opening, showing that you care about the organization they thought it was important to join.

- Know your audience. Why did they invite you? What are their main concerns? What do they want to learn from your speech? You cannot guess at what they want. Talk to someone who scheduled the speech and find out what THEY want you to discuss. Not what YOU want to discuss.

- Don't get fancy. Simply say, "I am here tonight to talk about _____." For instance you might say, "I am here to talk about the importance of sales training to an organization."

- Next – don't cover too much in a speech. Cover three key points. After you introduce your topic – break it into three key points. For example: There are three important reasons that you should have a comprehensive training program for your salespeople. First, a comprehensive training session will help them to use their time wisely. Two, it will help them identify leads they might miss. And third, it will teach them the importance of follow-up and closing the sales.

- The three key points are the outline of the speech. Let's look at our example of why organizations need a comprehensive sales training program. You will cover:
  - Using time wisely.
  - Identifying and finding leads
  - Follow up and closing a sales.

Bingo – there are the three main parts of your speech.

- Back up each section with specific examples, stats and a good war story. For instance – look at the first point you want to make,

Using Time More Wisely. How to be 50% more efficient. Tell the audience the key ways that salespeople waste time. Then tell a story. Audiences love stories. Tell a specific story about someone who went through sales training and how he or she increased the use of their time, how they became more efficient.

- The ending. Tell them what you said. Simply repeat the three key points you covered, emphasize why they are important. Then thank the audience for letting you speak and once again tell them how great they are and how honored you were to speak with them. Politeness goes a long way!

228

Here is a list of "new generation" excuses that students use in schools these days. After sharing this list, you can say, "Well, the excuses might have changed over the years, but one thing has not changed in our company. We do not give our customers excuses, rather we supply the right product at the right time on time."

Quote: Don't make excuses, make good.
~Elbert Hubbard

New Age Excuses

What a blessing, the computer has given students a new generation of excuses. No more, "The dog ate my homework." Now we have:

- My computer broke.
- The Internet was down.
- I e-mailed it, what happened?
- My printer was out of ink.
- My printer was broken.
- I need to buy a new keyboard.
- I can't afford a Word program.

- My computer caught a virus.
- I left my computer at the repair shop.
- Someone hacked in and took my essay.
- My screen went all black.
- I lost my power cord.
- Someone stole my laptop.
- I dropped my laptop.
- I know I saved the essay, but...
- My sister deleted my essay.
- I poured Coke on the keyboard.
- I lost the flash drive I saved it on.
- My computer lost power and I have to start over.
- And of course, the classic – My computer ate my homework.

229

Here is a short inspirational poem you read as an opening. Then you can say, "That poem is so true. We do choose our own attitudes..."

Quote: Our attitude towards life determines life's attitude towards us.

~John Mitchell

Which Bus are You Taking Today

Which bus are you going to catch today?
The Stress Express,
the Uptown I am Misunderstood,
the Crosstown Pity Party.
the Downtown Monday Blues.
or the Cubicle Shuttle
which you catch at the corner
of Discontent and Reality

Maybe the popular I Hate My Boss Bus?
The Procrastination Bus
is a bit late
and the Ennui Bus
arrives whenever.
The Enjoy Life Bus
runs every hour on the hour
even on weekends
I really don't care.
You choose your bus
and attitude.

230

You can begin this opening by saying, "I just received this letter from Pundit School, where we teach you to be an expert in everything." After sharing the letter, you say, "Well, we get plenty of advice on how to run our business, but I would like to hear from the real experts – our employees."

Quote: An expert is anyone who is five miles from home with a briefcase.
~Anon

Welcome to Pundit School

Welcome to Pundit School, where in a week, or less, you become an expert in everything. You can solve immigration, the budget, the economy, social security, the health care system, the trade deficit and even win a few wars, all while dispensing valuable, moral advice to all of us who need your wisdom and guidance. You can coach teams to the Super Bowl, the World Series and the NBA Finals. On the sixth day, while attending Pundit School, you will cure cancer, reach full employment, eliminate poverty, halt obesity, and reform education, with No Politician Left Behind. On the seventh day, you will rest. When graduating from Pundit School, you are well qualified to be a talk show host, a leading editorial writer, an economist, a stock analyst or a top notch blogger. Entry requirements for Pundit School include an inflated ego and a sense of superiority. If you wish to proceed to graduate school, we will teach you to heal the sick, walk on water, part the occasional sea and make wine out of water.

231

You can start this opening by saying, "I was able to peek at the greeting they give TV people when they enter journalism school. I would like to share it with you." After reading the short list, you can say, "Well journalists may go for the sensational news story now and then and endanger their credibility. What must we do at our company to build our credibility, not destroy it?"

Quote: You know, we all have our inner demons. I, for one – I can't speak for you, but I'm on the verge of moral collapse at any time. It can happen by the end of the show.
~Glen Beck

Welcome to Broadcasting School

I would like to welcome you to Broadcasting School. You will be taking:

- Trench Coat 101
- Smiling with Very White Teeth 102
- How to Point the Camera at the Flames 310
- Faking Sincerity 200
- Using Children to Wrench Hearts 205
- How to Look Young and Pretty (to take away that old hag's job, she is over 30)

- How to make the 1,000th story on trailers being destroyed by tornadoes still sound interesting.
- How to push a microphone in front of a grieving widow whose husband just died in a car accident. Be sure to ask, "How do you feel?"
- How to make any storm sound like the "storm of the century".
- A quick aside, all ugly people in class, I suggest you become weathermen or sportscasters
- That is all and remember practice being humble.

232

I love pleonasms. A pleonasm is when you say the same thing twice, as in 'sharp point'. Below is a list of pleonasms you can weave into an opening. Then you can say, "And at our company I want the phrase 'good customer service' to be a pleonasm.

Quote: It was déjà vu all over again.
~Yogi Berra

- All-time record
- Advance forward
- Actual facts
- Affirmative yes
- Best ever
- Attach together
- Brief summary
- Cash money
- Connect together
- Cooperate together
- Current trend
- Descend down
- Drop down

- Disappear from sight
- Hot water heater
- Woman pregnant with child
- Female hen
- Empty hole
- Enter in
- Final outcome
- Free gift
- Grow in size
- Join together
- Kneel down
- Look ahead to the future
- Mutual respect for each other
- New invention
- Open up
- Overused cliché
- Pair of twins
- Proceed ahead
- Protest against
- RAM memory
- Regular routine
- Retreat back
- Round in shape
- Serious danger
- Sharp point
- Sudden impulse
- Sum total
- True facts
- Usual custom
- Very unique
- Very pregnant
- Past records
- Past history
- PIN number

- Palm of the hand
- Outside in the yard
- Past experience

233

With over 20 years' experience as a speechwriter, I know what quotes will and will not work in a speech. Here are my top 50 customer service quotes that I have seen work every time. Not to state the obvious, but pick and choose the ones you like and weave them into an opening for a speech for customer service. If you have a meeting of customer service reps, you can print these quotes out, and then for a creativity exercise, beak the reps into groups of five and have them read the quotes, then create at least five of their own which they have to read to the entire group. Having them write and read quotes helps to engrain the concept of good customer service.

- Be everywhere, do everything, and never fail to astonish the customer. – Macy's Motto
- Do right. Do your best. Treat others as you want to be treated. – Lou Holtz
- Excellent firms don't believe in excellence – only in constant improvement and constant change. – Tom Peters
- If we don't take care of our customers someone else will. – Anon
- If you want to lift yourself up, lift up someone else. – Booker T. Washington
- It is not the employer who pays the wages. Employers only handle the money. It is the customer who pays the wages. – Henry Ford
- It is not the strongest of the species that survives, nor the most intelligent, but the one most responsive to change. – Charles Darwin

- Learn to say thank you every time. – Anon
- More business is lost every year through neglect than through any other. – Anon
- No enterprise can exist for itself alone. It ministers to some great need, it performs some great service, not for itself, but for others; or failing therein, it ceases to be profitable and ceases to exist. – Calvin Coolidge
- Politeness goes far, yet costs nothing. – Anon
- Remember, the deepest principle of human nature is the craving to be appreciated. – William James
- Spend a lot of time talking to customers face to face. You'd be amazed how many companies don't listen to their customers. – Ross Perot
- The aim of marketing is to know and understand the customer so well the product or service fits him and sells itself. – Peter Drucker
- The customer is king. – Anon
- The customer's perception is your reality. – Kate Zabriskie
- The goal as a company is to have customer service that is not just the best but legendary. – Sam Walton
- The price of greatness is responsibility. – Winston Churchill
- The purpose of business is to create and keep a customer. – Peter Drucker
- There is only one boss. The customer. And he can fire everybody in the company from the chairman on down simply by spending his money somewhere else. – Sam Walton
- To keep a customer demands as much skill as to win one. – American Proverb
- Treat every customer as if they sign your paycheck... because they do. – Anon
- Undertake not what you cannot perform but be careful to keep your promise. – George Washington
- Washrooms will always tell if your company cares about its customers. – Anon

- Watch your thoughts, for they become words, Choose your words, for they become actions. Understand your actions, for they become habits. Study your habits, for they will become your character. Develop your character, for it becomes your destiny. – Oliver Wendell Holmes
- Well done is better than well said. – Benjamin Franklin
- Would you do business with you? – Anon
- You have to perform at a consistently higher level than others. That's the mark of a true professional. Professionalism has nothing to do with getting paid for your services. – Joe Paterno
- Your most unhappy customers are your greatest source of learning. – Bill Gates
- Nothing is so contagious as enthusiasm. – Samuel Taylor Coleridge
- Every great business is built on friendship. – J.C. Penney
- Dealing with people is probably the biggest problem you face, especially if you are in business. Yes, and that is also true if you are a housewife, architect or engineer. – Dale Carnegie
- A customer is the most important visitor on our premises; he is not dependent upon us. We are dependent upon him. He is not an interruption to our work. He is the purpose of it. He is not an outsider in our business. He is part of it. We are not doing a favor by serving him. He is doing a favor by giving us an opportunity to do so. – Mahatma Gandhi
- I won't complain. I just won't come back. – Brown and Williamson tobacco ad
- Do what you do so well, that they will want to see it again and bring their friends. –Walt Disney
- Right or wrong, the customer is always right. – Marshal Field
- Under promise and over deliver. – Anon
- The purpose of a business is to create a customer who creates customers. – Shiv Singh
- Customer Service is not a department, it is everyone's job. – Anon
- Rule 1: The customer is always right. Rule 2: If the customer is

ever wrong, re-read Rule 1. – Anon

- Quality is Job One. – Ford ad
- Nobody raves about average. – Anon
- The consumer is not a moron. She is your wife. – David Ogilvy
- Courteous treatment will make a customer a walking advertisement. – J.C. Penney
- Kind words can be short and easy to speak, but their echoes are truly endless. – Mother Theresa
- "We were wrong" may be the three best words for customer service. – Anon
- I think we buy things because we want to create a script – i.e. the script of a loving family sitting around the fire. Or we buy a sports car because we want to create the myth of being young and free (which is why many middle-aged men buy sports car). Think about any catalog, like the LL Bean catalog. They aren't selling clothes – the catalog is about creating a lifestyle, long walks in the woods, front porches, fireplaces that the customer wants as his or her lifestyle. This has nothing to do with logic, everything to do with emotion and selling your customer a lifestyle script they want to write themselves into. That is why I can buy a T-shirt for $2 at Wal-Mart, but will pay $50 for a Polo Shirt with the logo. On a certain level, I have thrown logic out the window, to sell myself a concept of myself as a 'Polo' type person. Think about the products you sell. What lifestyle script are you writing for your customers? – Philip Theibert
- If you work just for money, you will never make it, but if you love what you are doing and you always put the customer first, success will be yours. – Ray Kroc
- Judge me by my actions, not my words. – Anon
- Do unto others as you would have done unto you. – The Golden Rule

234

What? The experts can be wrong? This is a funny list of what experts thought about inventions. Of course, they were wrong. You can pick and choose from this list and say, "Everyone is wrong at one time or another. The problem is that when you are wrong, admit it. When you mess up, admit it. Do not hide the problem from your managers or vice presidents. Hiding problems is how businesses end up in scandals. Do not cover up, 'fess up'."

Quote: He who lives by the crystal ball ends up eating ground glass.
~Anon

Top 25 Bad Predictions

- We don't like their sound, and guitar music is on the way out. – Decca Recording Co. rejecting the Beatles
- The concept is interesting and well-formed, but in order to earn better than a 'C', the idea must be feasible. – A Yale University management professor in response to Fred Smith's paper proposing reliable overnight delivery service. (Smith went on to found Federal Express Corp.)
- Who the h*** wants to hear actors talk? – H.M. Warner, Warner Brothers, 1927
- Everything that can be invented has been invented. – Charles H. Duell, Commissioner, US Office of Patents, 1899
- No flying machine will ever fly from New York to Paris. – Orville Wright
- I'm just glad it'll be Clark Gable who's falling on his face and not Gary Cooper. – Gary Cooper, on his decision to not take the leading role in *Gone With The Wind*
- Louis Pasteur's theory of germs is ridiculous fiction. – Pierre Pachet, Professor of Physiology
- Stocks have reached what looks like a permanently high plateau.

- Irving Fisher, Professor of Economics, Yale University, 1929
- I think there is a world market for maybe five computers. – Thomas Watson, chairman of IBM, 1943
- 640K ought to be enough for anybody. – Bill Gates
- It will be years – not in my time – before a woman will become Prime Minister. – Margaret Thatcher, 1974
- With over 50 foreign cars already on sale here, the Japanese auto industry isn't likely to carve out a big slice of the US market. – *Business Week*, August 2, 1968
- That's an amazing invention, but who would ever want to use one of them? – President Hayes to Alexander Graham Bell, 1876
- It doesn't matter what he does, he will never amount to anything. – Einstein's teacher to Einstein's father
- The problem with television is that the people must sit and keep their eyes glued on a screen; the average American family hasn't time for it. – *The New York Times*, when a prototype television was demonstrated at the 1939 World's Fair
- It will be gone by June. – *Variety*'s opinion on rock 'n' roll in 1955
- A short-lived satirical pulp. – *TIME*, writing off *Mad* magazine in 1956
- This antitrust thing will blow over. – Bill Gates, founder of Microsoft
- You will be home before the leaves have fallen from the trees. – Kaiser Wilhelm, to the German troops, August 1914
- Sensible and responsible women do not want to vote. – Grover Cleveland, US President, 1905
- Everyone acquainted with the subject will recognize it as a conspicuous failure. – Henry Morton, president of the Stevens Institute of Technology, on Edison's light bulb, 1880
- The horse is here to stay but the automobile is only a novelty, a fad. – The president of the Michigan Savings Bank advising Henry Ford's lawyer not to invest in the Ford Motor Co., 1903
- We stand on the threshold of rocket mail. – US Postmaster General Arthur Summerfield, in 1959

- Atomic energy might be as good as our present-day explosives, but it is unlikely to produce anything very much more dangerous. – Winston Churchill
- The cinema is little more than a fad. It's canned drama. What audiences really want to see is flesh and blood on the stage. – Charlie Chaplin

**BUSINESS
BOOKS**

Business Books encapsulates the freshest thinkers and the most
successful practitioners in the areas of marketing, management,
economics, finance and accounting, sustainable and ethical
business, heart business, people management, leadership,
motivation, biographies, business recovery and development
and personal/executive development.